WHITE MAN'S HEAVEN

WHITE MAN'S HEAVEN

The Lynching and Expulsion of Blacks
in the Southern Ozarks, 1894–1909

KIMBERLY HARPER

The University of Arkansas Press
Fayetteville
2010

ISBN-10: 1-55728-941-7
ISBN-13: 978-1-55728-941-4

14   13   12   11   10   5   4   3   2   1

Designed by Liz Lester

♾ The paper used in this publication meets the minimum
requirements of the American National Standard for
Permanence of Paper for Printed Library
Materials Z39.48-1984.

LIBRARY OF CONGRESS
CATALOGING-IN-PUBLICATION DATA

For My Parents

"The past is never dead. It's not even past."
—WILLIAM FAULKNER

CONTENTS

ILLUSTRATIONS

ACKNOWLEDGMENTS

There is an inherent love of the Ozarks within me. I love the deep valleys carved by glimmering rivers; the clear, cold creeks that snake through the bottoms; the tall sycamores in valleys surrounded by fog in late evening; the sight of fresh-cut hay in the afternoon light; green fields rolling in the wind; the limestone bluffs hanging in the distance down many a country road. I love old homesteads, simple framed farmhouses, dusty town squares, and crooked back roads. Wherever I go, the Ozarks go with me, and while I have ventured to the ends of the earth, it is to the Ozarks that I always return.

As a graduate student at the University of Arkansas, I never intended to write about lynchings and race riots in the southern Ozarks. That changed, however, when I took a course on Reconstruction with Patrick Williams. I was enthralled by the story of Redeemers, farmers, Populists, lily-whites, capitalists, Progressives, labor activists, and freedmen. I fell in love with nineteenth-century America, and it was then that I knew I would write about race in my beloved Ozarks.

As the historian Brooks Blevins has observed, the history of the Ozarks has been "unsatisfactorily documented." While much has been written about Ozarks culture, tourism, and stereotype, little has been written about Ozarkers themselves. The works of Brooks Blevins, Katherine Lederer, Milton D. Rafferty, Robert K. Gilmore, Russel L. Gerlach, Carl O. Sauer, Lynn Morrow, and Vance Randolph have been invaluable contributions to the study of the Ozarks. I hope this work sheds more light on a region that remains understudied despite its unique history.

First and foremost, I must thank Dr. Patrick Williams of the University of Arkansas for his unflagging support of my work. He championed my manuscript, gave generously of his time to review the revised draft, and provided me with insightful suggestions. Dr. Williams is an outstanding scholar and an exemplary teacher. I am privileged to call him my mentor.

During my time as a graduate student at the University of Arkansas, Dr. Kathryn Sloan was instrumental in sharpening my writing skills and Dr. David Chappell encouraged me to continue my research. While an undergraduate at Missouri Southern State University I was fortunate to study with Dr. Steven Wagner, Dr. Larry Cebula, Dr. Paul Teverow, Dr. Virginia Laas, and Dr. Charles "Chuck" Fahrer.

I am indebted to numerous individuals for their assistance and expertise including the wonderful staff at the University of Arkansas Interlibrary Loan Services; Geoffery Stark at the University of Arkansas Special Collections; Robert Neumann and volunteers at the Greene County Archives and Records Center; Lynn Morrow, John Korasick, Linda Meyers, and Donna Atkinson of the Missouri State Archives; Gary Daugherty and Judy Reustle of the Lawrence County Historical Society; Steve Weldon and volunteers at the Jasper County Records Center; Randy Roberts at Pittsburg State University Special Collections and Archives; the staff at the Western Historical Manuscript Collection-Columbia; Anne M. Baker, Shannon Western, Tracie Gieselman-Holthaus, and Meghan Walters at the Missouri State University Special Collections and Archives; Danny Walker of the Denver Public Library; the staff at the University of Missouri Interlibrary Loan Services; Sara Przybylski of the State Historical Society of Missouri; University of Virginia Professor Emeritus David L. Rubin, and Mary Dalton Baril of McGuireWoods, LLP. I also want to acknowledge and thank Julie Watkins, Larry Malley, Katy Henriksen, Melissa King, and the rest of the staff at the University of Arkansas Press. Many thanks to Debbie Self, who copy-edited the manuscript with amazing skill. Her attentiveness to detail undoubtedly improved the quality of this work.

I want to thank Barbara Ann Harper-Baldwin for loaning little sister the books she brought home from Robert Gilmore's classes at Southwest Missouri State University. After reading Gilmore's *Ozark Baptizings, Hangings, and Other Diversions,* Vance Randolph's *Ozark Magic and Folklore,* and Miller Williams's *Ozark, Ozark: A Hillside Reader* I fell more in love with my native region.

The two people most responsible for this work are my mother and late father, Kay and Bob Harper, who instilled in me an irrepressible love of learning. My mother made my education her first priority. I thank her for the long, dusty trips from Harper's Farm to the county library and for taking the time to read to me. I thank my father for my love of history, my appreciation of the Ozarks, and an unwavering sense of justice. In 1965 while training to become a Missouri State Highway Patrolman, my Ozarker father welcomed and accepted as his roommate the first African American to be recruited by the patrol.

Ross Brown encouraged me to pursue publication, accompanied me on research trips, patiently listened to me ramble, gave me advice, and provided me with endless encouragement. He is, as the song says, my sunshine.

INTRODUCTION

As midnight approached on April 16, 1903, a train slowly pulled into Pittsburg, Kansas. With a loud hiss from its brakes, the train came to a halt along the station platform, its journey from Joplin, Missouri, finished. Several black passengers disembarked, some carrying small bundles of belongings, others empty-handed. Many seemed shaken as they cautiously surveyed their surroundings, wary of what awaited them in the darkened city. Others appeared to be in shock. As an elderly black couple was helped from the train, a reporter from the *Pittsburg Headlight* approached them for their story.

Just hours earlier, the unnamed couple had been forced to flee from their home in Joplin as a howling mob set fire to it, leaving them destitute. The man, a former slave from Mississippi, had been rescued just before the flames engulfed him. He and his wife, both roughly eighty years old, fled to the outskirts of the city. There, they huddled in a shed until daybreak when they could make their way to safety in Pittsburg. It was not the first time they had been forced to flee.

Over the preceding two years, they had escaped the wrath of an angry mob when a race riot erupted in the Oklahoma town they lived in, and blacks were expelled. The couple then moved to Pierce City, Missouri, to live with their son. But in August 1901, a mob lynched three black men and expelled that town's black residents. In the panic that ensued, the couple lost track of their son. They escaped to Joplin, but their son was less fortunate. Wounded, he traveled to the safety of Springfield, only to die of his injuries. The couple, once again penniless and without relatives nearby, settled at Joplin. The wife worked as a washerwoman to support herself and her husband who was crippled from injuries he received as a teamster for the Union army. But when a Joplin mob of over one thousand whites lynched Thomas Gilyard, a young black migrant, for the alleged murder of a white police officer the couple had once again to run for their lives. When asked where they were headed, the couple said they were bound for Kansas City, as they had relatives there.[1]

In his brief interview, the reporter captured the experience of hundreds of African Americans in the southern Ozarks in the late nineteenth and early twentieth centuries. A series of brutal lynchings and black expulsions erupted in 1894 and ended only in 1909. These lynchings and expulsions were part of a pattern of racial violence repeated across the nation.

At the end of Reconstruction, African Americans were left to fend for themselves, abandoned by their fellow Americans. Blacks gained significant rights under the Thirteenth, Fourteenth, and Fifteenth Amendments to the United States Constitution, but after the end of Reconstruction, these newly acquired rights were quickly eroded by various legal and legislative strategies. Court decisions like *Plessy v. Ferguson,* poll taxes, and grandfather laws sought to segregate and disenfranchise African American citizens. Lynching also served as an effective tool of subordinating blacks.

During a twenty-year period, from 1882 until 1902, a reported 3,080 were lynched across the United States. Of those 3,080 individuals, 1,941 were black men and women. It is unlikely that every lynching was reported and subsequently recorded, so many more probably met their fate at the hands of an angry mob.[2] The motives behind each lynching often varied, ranging from economic, social, political, or criminal factors.

The majority of lynchings occurred in the South, but mob violence was not exclusive to southern states. As the historian Michael Pfeifer has documented, lynchings also occurred in the Midwest and West.[3] As a border state, Missouri stood at the edge of these regions. Missouri entered the Union in 1821 as a slave state. But Missouri's slave population was concentrated in central Missouri along the Missouri River in an area known as Little Dixie. The Ozark region was slowly settled from 1830 until the outbreak of the American Civil War. Those who made their home in the Ozarks primarily came from three southern states: Tennessee, Kentucky, and Virginia but, as the Ozark geographer Milton D. Rafferty has pointed out, because wealthy planters preferred better land, "slaves were not numerous in the interior sections of the Ozarks."[4] By 1860, Greene County was the only county in southwestern Missouri that held a slave population of more than 10 percent of the total population.[5]

Southwest Missouri, with strong Unionist sentiments, was a hotbed of Confederate guerrilla activity during the Civil War, yielding considerable violence between residents. As the historian Matthew Stith contends in his study of Jasper County, Missouri, "warfare in southwest Missouri was as close to total war as any facet of fighting during the Civil War."[6] The historian Lynn Morrow has shown how this left a legacy of bitterness along the Arkansas-Missouri border but also economic hardship. "Loss of land and property destruction radically impacted the landscape and impaired agricultural production— the prospect of recovery amid spiraling debt taxed the resources and imagination of Missourians who looked toward a daunting future of inflation and escalating taxes."[7]

After the war, some who had belonged to the small slave population remained and other freedpeople immigrated into this troubled area. As the era of the New South dawned, Union veterans from northern states such as Indiana, Illinois, and Ohio began to relocate to southwest Missouri. Former Confederates from Virginia, Arkansas, and Kentucky also settled there.[8] A local populace with limited contact with African Americans prior to the war, a small influx of former slaves from the South, "carpetbaggers," and bitter ex-Confederates combined to create a cauldron of racial disharmony. The arrival of the railroad, industrialization, and black suffrage added to the building pressure. It was perhaps only a matter of time before the simmering cauldron boiled over.

Little scholarship exists on the string of lynchings and expulsions that occurred in Monett, Pierce City, Joplin, and Springfield, Missouri, and Harrison, Arkansas, between 1894 and 1909. In 1970, Mary N. Clary was the first to examine the Springfield lynchings in her master's thesis.[9] Her work was expanded upon by Professor Katherine Lederer in *Many Thousands Gone: Springfield's Lost Black History*.[10] In 1987, Burton L. Purrington and Penny L. Harter compared the Joplin and Springfield lynchings in their essay, "The Easter and Tug-of-War Lynchings and the Early Twentieth-Century Black Exodus from Southwest Missouri."[11] In 2006, Jason Navarro published a narrative account of the Pierce City lynching in the *Missouri Historical Review.*[12] The journalist Elliot Jaspin devotes a chapter in his book, *Buried in the Bitter Waters: The Hidden History of Racial Cleansing in America* to the Pierce City lynching.[13] Jacqueline Froelich and David Zimmerman published the first scholarly account of Harrison's race riots.[14] But no study has looked at all five episodes together. This work will examine each episode as part of a larger, interconnected regional experience.

For several reasons, the greatest attention here will be placed on the lynchings in Pierce City, Joplin, and Springfield. First, newspapers from all three cities survived, unlike newspapers from Monett and Harrison. In the case of Joplin and Springfield, newspapers of differing political and ideological beliefs provide insight into the way that African Americans, lynchings, and mob violence were perceived by whites in southwest Missouri.

Second, both Springfield papers and the sole surviving Pierce City newspaper, the *Peirce City Empire,* devoted considerable attention to their respective black communities from the time African Americans first arrived until their expulsion. Black weddings, deaths, minstrel shows, and crimes were reported on a daily basis. Thus it is easier to explore race relations in Pierce City and Springfield prior to the outbreak of mob violence than in Joplin, where newspapers devoted little attention to local African Americans. Third, the Lawrence County Historical Society and the Greene County Archives and Records Center have several dedicated volunteers who devote considerable time researching each county's respective black community. By contrast, Joplin and Harrison lack a strong historical society involved in such work, especially with regard to local African American history.

This study will employ the definition of lynching that W. Fitzhugh Brundage adopted in his work, *Lynching in the New South: Georgia and Virginia, 1880–1930,* and was originally formulated by antilynching advocates in 1940: "there must be legal evidence that a person has been killed, and that he met his death illegally at the hands of a group acting under the pretext of service to justice, race, or tradition."[15]

The events in the southern Ozarks fit within a framework offered by a larger body of scholarship on racial violence. Lynching has been studied since the beginning of the twentieth century, but it was only until the last half of the century that the field began to attract greater attention. The scholarship of lynching came into its own in 1992 with Edward Ayers's *The Promise of the New South: Life after Reconstruction*, which would be followed by the work of Brundage, Michael Pfeifer, and Stewart Tolnay and E. M. Beck. The lynchings and black expulsion that occurred in the southern Ozarks might serve to test their varying models and also shed light on regional difference in racial violence.

Central to Ayers's understanding of racial violence was the economic revitalization of the South that followed the close of Reconstruction. The railroad, according to Ayers, was crucial, bringing economic development, urbanization, and in-migration to many parts of the region. Blacks, one group most affected by the emergence of the New South, experienced the growing pains of a new society in which their role was still unclear. Ayers contends that the primary factor encouraging lynching was black in-migration into areas that had not previously harbored significant black populations. He argues that lynchings often occurred in sparsely populated areas where black transients and strangers lived and worked. These areas had "few towns, weak law enforcement, poor communication with the outside, and high levels of transiency among both races." As a result, whites feared that "black criminals could get away with harming a white person . . . that the lack of retribution would encourage others." Lynching, then, served to provide whites with an answer to "weak governments" and a method with which to "terrorize blacks into acquiescence." [16]

Brundage's *Lynching in the New South*, released to great acclaim in 1993, likewise links racial violence to social change, contending that postwar violence signaled white refusal to accept black strides toward economic and political success. But he sees the roots of lynching as lying in the slavery era. The South's predilection for mob violence stemmed from antebellum disregard for legal authority. Prior to the war, slave owners punished their slaves without regard for the law, rather than have their own autonomy challenged or their own property sequestered. Postbellum southerners continued this tradition of extralegal justice, which manifested itself most commonly in lynch mobs. But what protection their status as valuable property had afforded African Americans disappeared, leaving freedmen all the more vulnerable.[17]

The turbulent transformation of the South, both Brundage and

Ayers contend, often placed young, migrant blacks at the mercy of whites. As Ayers notes, "Lynchings tended to flourish where whites were surrounded by what they called 'strange niggers,' blacks with no white to vouch for them, blacks with no reputation in the neighborhood, blacks without even other blacks to aid them."[18] Brundage, in his examination of lynching, asserts, "Any blacks who led a nomadic life as laborers in a rural industry—railroad workers, miners, lumber and turpentine hands, for example—kindled hostility even without committing a crime."[19] Other blacks, such as those "who failed to maintain good relations" with local whites, were also subject to racial violence.[20] Like Ayers, Brundage found that "lynchings were most likely to occur in sparsely settled rural counties where police protection was inadequate, if present at all, and local officials had neither the means nor the ambition to stop mob violence."[21]

For both Ayers and Brundage, lynching was often used to discipline African American communities. As Ayers notes, "The sporadic violence of lynching was a way . . . to terrorize blacks into acquiescence by brutally killing those who intentionally or accidentally stepped over some invisible and shifting line of permissible behavior."[22] For Brundage, the actions of lynch mobs confronting an influx of black migrants into southwest Virginia "was not an inarticulate, irrational reaction to inchoate fears, but rather a focused effort to control, not stop or reverse, change."[23]

Stewart Tolnay and E. M. Beck's *A Festival of Violence: An Analysis of Southern Lynchings, 1882–1930,* published in 1995, also sees lynching as a means of maintaining social control over the black population through violence. But they give greater emphasis than Ayers or Brundage to lynching as a method by which to eliminate black economic, political, and social competition with whites. For them, lynching perpetuated the existing white class hierarchy and maintained the status of the white elite.[24]

In *A Festival of Violence,* Tolnay and Beck note that after communities experienced an economic downturn, the number of lynchings rose. Whites, they argue, saw any black economic success as a loss for whites. Tolnay and Beck also contend that white elites feared that white and black labor would unite to press for better working conditions. As a result, white elites seized upon opportunities to lynch in order to drive a wedge between the white and black communities to prevent challenges to their status. Whites were not threatened by the act of one black, but by the social, political, and economic progress of local black communities.

Economics does not play as large a role in Michael Pfeifer's *Rough Justice: Lynching and American Society, 1874–1947,* released in 2004. Instead, Pfeifer focuses on what he terms "rough justice." For Pfeifer, rough justice was the product of a struggle between middle-class advocates of due process and the working class over the American legal system as it evolved in the late nineteenth century. Middle-class reformers advocated adherence to the rule of law which clashed with the rural and working-class belief that the criminal justice system was too weak, too slow, or incapable of dispensing justice. Rough justice, to its adherents, preserved social order. Pfeifer contends that postbellum mobs in the West and Midwest drew upon "memories of the history of popular violence in their regions, revived the elastic doctrine of popular sovereignty as an antidote to changing practices of criminal justice in an era of economic and social consolidation."[25] As time passed, however, lynchings slowly faded away. Pfeifer argues that as the working class gained belief in the legal system, due to states' enforcing capital punishment, they felt less motivated to take justice in their own hands.

The work of Ayers, Brundage, Tolnay and Beck, and Pfeifer can all contribute to our understanding of racial violence in the southern Ozarks from 1894 to 1909. The lynchings and race riots that occurred in Monett, Pierce City, Joplin, Springfield, and Harrison, in some ways, resembled southern lynchings. In other respects, however, mob violence in southwest Missouri differed from that in many parts of the South.

Blacks in the southern Ozarks were lynched because, as Pfeifer suggests, whites perceived the local legal system as weak and ineffectual. Mob participants acted to punish black criminal offenders, not black economic or political competitors as Tolnay and Beck would have it. In essence, the local legal system failed to satisfy whites' expectations in the tumultuous and violence-prone Ozark region.

A sparsely populated region with a history of vigilantism and a culture of violence rooted in the southern ancestry of its earliest settlers, the Ozarks were a place where crime, whether perpetrated by blacks or whites, was not tolerated and dealt harshly with little regard for the legal system. The area, which many residents fled from during the war, did not quickly recover from the wounds inflicted by four years of conflict. In his study of the Ozarks Milton D. Rafferty pointed out that after 1865 "a certain class of citizens had grown accustomed to a shiftless way of life and held little regard for laws and the property of their neighbors."[26] As a result, violence continued to plague southwest Missouri. In response, vigilance committees were formed to enforce peace in an area that had been ravaged by bushwhackers and left with little in the ways of law and order.

In 1868, the *Missouri Weekly Patriot* reprinted a vigilance committee notice in Barry County that appeared in the *Cassville Banner*. The notice, addressed to members of the Ku Klux Klan, warned, "The prime movers in this organization are known, as well as the barbarous and hellish purpose for which it is gotten up. We wish to say to such persons, that we deprecate all such movements to disturb the peace and quiet of our county, and the first act of violence will be met with a vengeance both quick and terrible." The group warned Klan members that for every vigilance committee man injured, ten Klan members would be killed in retaliation.[27] A few years later, in 1871, the *Neosho Times* reported that a vigilance committee had killed Aleck King in Barry County.[28] Taney and Christian Counties experienced significant vigilante activity with the rise of the Bald Knobbers. Taney County Bald Knobbers, angered by the conduct of local Democratic officeholders, attempted to wrest power from their political foes. Christian County Bald Knobbers, meanwhile, concerned themselves primarily with enforcing law and order. They quickly became, however, a source of trouble.[29]

Vigilantism also manifested itself in individual mobs that surfaced when the occasion arose and then quickly melted away after imposing extralegal justice. In the winter of 1885, a man named Grubb was lynched by a mob in McDonald County for the murder of Irwin Anderson, a deaf mute.[30] The following year, near the Newton County line in McDonald County, a man known as "Canada Bill," after allegedly assaulting a woman, was lynched by a mob while being escorted to the county seat.[31] J. A. Sturges, an attorney who compiled a history of McDonald County, remarked that at the time of publication in 1897, there "had never been a legal execution in McDonald County."[32] Other counties in southwest Missouri, however, did have legal executions. But many appeared to be the exception in southwest Missouri, not the rule.

But if southwest Missouri, like some midwestern and western regions, had a vigilante tradition visited on both whites and blacks, it also experienced the "southern" conditions that Ayers and Brundage have seen as recipes for racial violence. As in much of the "New South," Missouri underwent a significant economic transformation after Reconstruction. The New South period, characterized by the influx of railroads, industrialization, and modernization, was a time of great social and economic change. Markets expanded because of the intrusion of the railroad into backwater areas. The southern countryside was transformed, as were urban locales, as cities and towns exploded across the South. Many whites and blacks were drawn together in ways that whites were not prepared to accept. African Americans moved to cities in order to pursue employment opportunities, but they also migrated to rural areas that were unaccustomed to members of their race, creating an uneasy tension between whites and African American newcomers.[33]

This tension was often exacerbated by white fears that blacks were reverting back to a state of savagery. White anxiety about predatory African American men sexually assaulting and raping white women strained race relations to the point that "rape could be defined so broadly that an insult, a grimace, an unwanted glance, or an accidental touch might be transformed in white minds into sexual violence."[34] According to scholars such as Joel Williamson and Martha Hodes, the perceived epidemic of black rapists was little more than a myth created by angst-ridden whites to justify racial violence designed to satisfy white fears and anxieties.[35] Anxious whites wary of African American predators also feared the influence of black suffrage.

In *Lynching and Spectacle: Witnessing Racial Violence in America, 1890–1940,* Amy Louise Wood argues, "The figure of the black rapist struck at the heart of the matter—that black autonomy not only diminished white men's authority over African Americans but threatened their dominion over their own households and women."[36] As a result, Wood contends, "Lynching became a predominately southern, racialized phenomenon, as white southerners sought to restore their

dominance in the face of emancipation and the threat of black enfranchisement and social autonomy."[37]

Yet if both the southern conditions cited by Brundage and Ayers
and the broader traditions examined by Pfeifer help explain the lynchings that occurred in southwest Missouri, they are less useful in
accounting for what followed racial killings in Monett, Pierce City,
Joplin, and Springfield—the sometimes permanent expulsion of entire
black communities. Such expulsion by no means inevitably followed
lynching. To the contrary, Brundage finds such expulsions not to have
occurred in southwest Virginia. In Monett, Pierce City, and Harrison,
rather than simply showing a black community how it was expected
to behave, white mobs entirely destroyed African American communities. Unfortunately, the expulsion of African Americans remains an
understudied aspect in the extensive literature of racial violence. At
best, one can argue that expulsion was one of the most extreme forms
of social control as African Americans were forced to leave behind
everything they had worked for and demonstrated their weakness as
they could not prevent their expulsion, and it sent a message to nearby
black communities to remain complacent or else face the same fate.

The first, and so far only major work on the subject, is sociologist
James Loewen's polemical *Sundown Towns: A Hidden Dimension of
American Racism*. Loewen recounts a significant number of expulsions, but fails to adequately explain why entire African American
communities were expelled.[38] Elliot Jaspin's *Buried in the Bitter Waters:
The Hidden History of Racial Cleansing in America* also examines the
expulsion of African Americans in states such as Missouri, Tennessee,
Kentucky, Arkansas, and Georgia.[39] Like Loewen, however, Jaspin fails
to explain why communities chose to expel African Americans en
masse rather than simply punish the individuals who had allegedly
committed the crimes—murder or rape—that precipitated the mob
action.

The circumstances of the southern Ozarks might help us better
understand why some communities lynched and expelled and others
just lynched. Southern communities dependent upon cheap black
labor, whether to service plantations or growing extractive industries,
might use violence to keep African Americans subordinate but could
hardly afford to displace their working class. In the southern Ozarks,

by contrast, blacks were not a critical component of the regional economy, thus their forced departure did not threaten the labor needs of area industries. For whites in such areas, the goal of discipline could give way to disappearance.

If the settings of the lynchings recall places studied by Ayers, some of the lynchings in southwest Missouri defy Ayers's interpretation that transient blacks without ties to the local community were the chief targets of lynching. In Pierce City, the men lynched were part of a black community that had existed for twenty-one years, and they were not transients or seasonal laborers. At least one generation of blacks had grown up in Pierce City. The white community granted "Uncle" Ben Kelly, an elderly black man and resident for thirty years, two days to sell off his chickens. As Kelly said (as rendered by a *St. Louis Post-Dispatch* reporter), "I don' know why dese white folks want to run pore ol Uncle Ben outen dis town. I be'en heah thirty years, an' I ain't nevah done nobody no hahm, sah, nobody at all, sah."[40] This study seeks to answer Kelly's question.

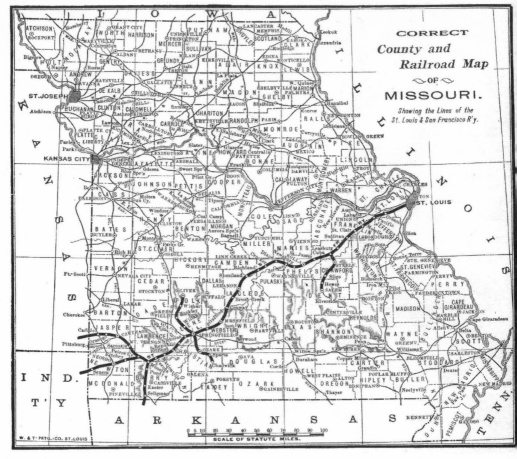

Railroad map of Missouri. *Courtesy of The State Historical Society of Missouri.*

ONE

Pierce City

"We Were Once Slaves"

With the close of the Civil War and the advent of Reconstruction, much of the nation, particularly the South, underwent a revolutionary transformation. From the ashes and cinders of the old antebellum South rose a modernized new South. The arrival of the railroad opened backwater areas to new markets. Previously isolated regions like southwest Virginia underwent extensive industrialization after the war. Coal mines and lumber camps drew young, single black migrants to the region, and it was not long before the black newcomers clashed with local whites.[1] The cotton uplands of Mississippi, Texas, Arkansas, and Louisiana and the mountainous regions of the South also experienced significant rates of black population growth, leading to outbreaks of racial violence.[2]

These regions, all of which experienced rapid economic growth and an influx of large numbers of transient blacks in search of work, were also home to folkways of extralegal violence, honor, and vigilantism.[3] Together, in combination with industrialization, modernization, and the arrival of both new ideas and newcomers, the New South underwent rapid social, political, and economic change. Blacks, once enslaved, found themselves free but facing uncertain futures as anxious whites sought to draw the color line between the races. The South, however, was not the only region that experienced these changes.

Southwest Missouri underwent a similar transformation. Railroads served as the main agent of change. As railroads reached into rural areas markets emerged where before there might have been only a single country store to serve the nearby populace's needs. This economic change brought new towns, new ideas, new in-migrants, and new opportunities to the formerly isolated countryside.[4]

Until 1870, inhabitants of the Missouri Ozarks engaged in subsistence agriculture, with corn and wheat as their main crops. But with the coming of the railroad in the 1870s, farmers in southwest Missouri switched to market farming, which persisted up until the turn of the century. In the 1890s, many farmers turned to the fruit industry, which enabled them to make the most out of marginal land.[5] Apple and peach orchards sprang up across the area. The "Ozark Berry Belt," comprising Newton, McDonald, Jasper, Lawrence, and Barry Counties, became famous for its strawberry production.[6] Agriculture was not the only mainstay of southwest Missouri. The region also held significant lead and zinc deposits. Granby, just west of Pierce City, was, prior to the Civil War, the area's leading producer. Joplin later eclipsed Granby, but miners continued to work throughout the region, part of the Tri-State mining district.[7]

During the early postbellum years, some black southerners moved to other states to pursue jobs in the cotton fields, coal mines, and lumber camps of the region.[8] Southwest Missouri would be a destination for some of these southern blacks seeking new opportunities. These new arrivals sought to establish a better life for themselves far removed from their lives as slaves. They created schools, established fraternal organizations, participated in the political process by voting, and welcomed their white neighbors to celebrate their freedom with them on Emancipation Day. At the same time, the black community of Pierce City had to battle the racial prejudices of the white community. Their struggle to create a new life, in tandem with the rapid, unsettling changes of the New South, combined to ignite the slow-burning fuse of a powder keg.

Pierce City was established in 1870 as the St. Louis–San Francisco Railroad extended westward. It was originally named Peirce City, after Andrew Peirce, president of the Atlantic and Pacific Railroad Company. Peirce donated the land for the town on the condition that the town be named after him. The spelling of the town's name was changed later, however, when the relationship between the railroad and the town's citizens soured. The Atlantic and Pacific eventually merged into what later became the St. Louis–San Francisco Railway Company, commonly known as the "Frisco" railroad, which connected Pierce City to Springfield, Missouri.[9]

Within a year of its founding, Pierce City was a bustling railroad town, with an estimated population of seven hundred residents.[10] The town was home to several hotels, among them the Lawrence Hotel, built in 1872 at a cost of $11,000. The town also boasted the New Windsor Hotel, built in 1884, a three-story structure with seventy rooms and $10,000 worth of furniture. The town had an Anheuser-Busch beer depot, three cigar factories, a wagon factory, two banks, and a booming lime kiln among its many businesses. In addition, it was home to an opera house, the Pierce City Baptist College, and several churches. Pierce City had a small professional class composed of doctors, dentists, and lawyers. The town was particularly proud of its water works system and the electric street lamps that lined the city's gravel avenues.[11]

But its good fortune was not to last. In 1880, the Frisco Railroad decided to add a rail line to Fayetteville, Arkansas, and on to Texas. However, the new line was built four miles southeast of Pierce City where the land was not so hilly. The *Peirce City Weekly Empire* reported, "there are some fears and speculations on account of the line run by the present engineer following the main line to a point four miles southeast of the city." Despite fears of abandonment, the newspaper trumpeted, "That fortune favors Peirce City cannot be doubted." Unfortunately, within a few years, the city's fortunes were far from golden.[12]

Despite boosters' claim that "Peirce City is master of the situation, and will be the railway center of the Southwest," officials from the St. Louis–San Francisco Railway Company had other ideas. A junction was created for a small depot and a telegraph office east of Pierce City that became known as "Plymouth Junction."[13] Soon thereafter, plots of land began to sell at Plymouth Junction. A hotel, a blacksmith shop, and other buildings soon followed.[14] The *Empire* snorted at Plymouth's future, "it is not likely to prove a formidable rival to a town as well established as Peirce City."[15]

By 1886, however, the handwriting was on the wall. The Frisco purchased two hundred acres of land at Plymouth. The *Empire* mournfully declared, "All would feel more confident of the future of Peirce

City if the junction of the Arkansas branch proper was at this city, instead of Plymouth."[16] For a brief moment, it appeared that despite the progress Plymouth had made, it would be abandoned due to a lack of a reliable source of water.[17] Pierce City was home to several large springs, and it was thought that the Frisco management would change their mind in favor of Pierce City's plentiful water supply.[18] Shortly thereafter, Plymouth changed its name to Monett, and fortune soon followed.[19]

An article appeared in the *St. Louis Post-Dispatch* boosting the promise and opportunity that Monett now offered, "It is leaping forward like some phenomenal mining camp. Houses are going up as fast as lumber and building material can be procured."[20] The *Peirce City Weekly Empire* sourly remarked as the end came, "The Frisco boys pulled out Saturday evening with seven engines going to Monett, and the change of divisions was made." The *Empire* cynically speculated the move was a method for the Frisco bosses to line their pockets.[21] Several articles claimed that the railroad chose to create Monett in order to profit from land speculation. Exasperated, Frisco vice president John O'Day sent a letter to the editor of the *Empire* to explain, "the extra cost of running Arkansas and Texas trains from Monett to Peirce City and return, a distance of ten miles, would at least equal twenty-five thousand dollars a year, saying nothing of the loss of time and annoyance to the public caused by this unnecessarily increased mileage. I regret as much as any citizen of Peirce City the inexorable logic of the situation which made it necessary to remove the division headquarters from Peirce City to Monett."[22]

The *St. Louis Daily-Globe Democrat* estimated that "the railroad alone will furnish employment for 300 people, and the transfer of its interests from Peirce City will cause the removal from that place to Monett of not less than 1200 persons."[23] The *Daily-Globe Democrat* was not far off. Before the move to Monett, the population of Pierce City reached 3,500 inhabitants, but fell to roughly 2,000 by 1901. That year the *Empire* bravely declared, "After they left the company said that grass would be growing on our streets in a year, but you can see different, for when a town has enterprising business men like ours, nothing can kill it."[24] Pierce City was never the same.

The intrusion of the railroad into southwest Missouri brought more than just capital, access to new economic markets, and boom and then bust to Pierce City. The railroad also brought the next wave of settlers to the region. From the 1870s through the 1880s, the area in and around Pierce City experienced the in-migration of European families. German settlers, who traveled to Missouri from the eastern United States, settled in Monett, Verona, Pierce City, and Freistatt. In 1875, French and Swiss families settled near the future site of Monett. Finally, in the 1880s, a contingent of forty-five Polish families settled at Pulaskifield.[25] White southerners who had settled in Lawrence County before the Civil War found themselves with foreigners in their midst. In Pierce City, whites also watched as African Americans arrived.

Among those who experienced the rapid boom and bust of Pierce City were black migrants who arrived from Kentucky. While the exact year that blacks began to settle in Pierce City is unknown, an item from the *Lawrence County Chieftain* reprinted in the *Empire* reported in November 1879, "Two colored families with wagons and teams passed through this place last Saturday bound for Peirce City. They were direct from Warren county, Kentucky and had started from home with a view of locating in this county."[26] It seems many came as a group. Census and Civil War pension records reveal that an overwhelming majority migrated to the region from Warren County, Kentucky. Of the seventy-eight blacks enumerated in the 1880 federal census for Pierce City, fifty-seven were born in Kentucky, many belonging to families of black Union army veterans from Warren County. [27] The pension records of George Page, John Farnsworth, John Scott, Alexander Godley, and Washington Robison reveal that the men had been slaves on neighboring plantations in Warren County, Kentucky, until they seized upon the opportunity to escape and sign up with the Union army.[28]

Some of the men joined United States Colored Volunteer Heavy Artillery units, while others served in the United States Colored Volunteer Infantry. After the men were discharged, they returned to Warren County, then headed west with their families in the late 1870s. They probably chose to travel together. Their pension files contain affidavits from one another attesting to their service and their time as slaves in Kentucky, which suggests a tight-knit community.[29]

Among the families who came from Kentucky were the Godley, Kelley, Hampton, Thomas, Robison, White, and Page families.[30] A handful of other blacks came from Tennessee and Arkansas. These new arrivals to southwest Missouri may have been linked with the Exoduster movement in which blacks from former slave states headed west in search of a better future. It is possible that some took jobs on the railroad gangs working on the Frisco and stayed in the area, but no evidence has been found to support this speculation.[31] A few others came from within Missouri. Charles S. Hunter, who served as schoolmaster of Pierce City's black school, came from St. Louis.[32] Others also apparently came from St. Louis, where they had worked as servants. According to one estimate, thirty black families lived in Pierce City by the 1890s.[33]

The presence of black newcomers seems to have stirred trouble early. Little is known about Reuben Thomas, beyond the information provided in the 1880 federal census. Born in Kentucky circa 1832, he worked in the city's limestone quarry. His wife, Mary, was born in St. Louis, Missouri.[34] Apparently Thomas had troubles with his white neighbors late in the summer of 1877 that spurred him to write the following letter to the editor of the *Peirce City Weekly Empire:*

> Ed. Empire: I wish to say that I live one mile west of Peirce City, and that myself and family have on more than one occasion been attacked by some human beings in the shape of men, using the most obscene language that their poor tongues could devise. One of these attacks were made on Friday evening, of last week, about 8 or 9 o'clock p.m. and again at about 11 or 12 that same night. Now, Mr. Editor, I wish to say that I am a black man and have a black family and work for our living, never contract a debt but what we pay, and never get anything but what we get it in an honorable way: we were once slaves, and so far as I know, gave satisfaction to our masters. We have come west and bought land and intend to make a living, but do not intend to be scared away, but intend to live so as to have the respect of all good people, and my just rights I intend to defend at risk of all that I possess. Never were we treated in such a manner before, not even when we were slaves, and I do not think we deserve it now, as we are free, for which we are not responsible, neither are we responsible for being black.[35]

The Thomas family remained in Pierce City.

The economic opportunities that awaited the new arrivals to the city were few. Despite the variety of businesses in Pierce City, blacks were restricted to menial jobs. An examination of the 1880 federal census for Pierce Township shows that most blacks were engaged in a limited number of occupations. Men primarily worked as day laborers, teamsters, and farmhands. A handful held jobs as blacksmiths, shoemakers, and quarrymen. Despite the railroad boom, none of the black men were listed as working for the Frisco, although it is possible that those described as "day laborers" were employed in some capacity by the railroad. Women worked as servants and washerwomen.[36] Little changed over the next two decades.

The 1900 federal census for Pierce Township illuminates the economic and social status of its African American citizens. They still held the least desired jobs, ones that placed them in a subservient role. Out of the forty black men who held jobs, only five men described themselves as farmers. Four men worked as lime burners at the Pierce City lime kiln and fifteen as day laborers. Only four worked as Frisco Railroad porters. The remaining occupations were hotel porter, hotel waiter, plasterer, minister, and teacher. Women either worked as washerwomen or servants. Skilled positions such as railroad brakeman, carpenter, cigar maker, and machinist were off limits as were white-collar jobs.

Whites overwhelmingly held such positions and, in addition, dominated the day labor market. As a result, there appeared to be little, if any economic competition between African Americans and lower-class whites in Pierce City.[37] Newspaper accounts described their homes as rough shanties or cabins, indicating that blacks in Pierce City had not yet achieved a significant foothold in the local economy. This might suggest that the lynching in Pierce City was most likely not motivated by economic factors.

Despite the limited economic horizons African Americans faced, black children in Pierce City did have the opportunity to attend school. Public education, however, was segregated, as mandated by the 1875 state constitution. Educational opportunities beyond the eighth grade were rare.[38] Yet the ability to read and write was an accomplishment that gave young blacks an advantage their parents did not have. It was also an achievement that could not be taken away.

As early as 1879, the *Peirce City Weekly Empire* reported, "A colored school is being taught on the corner of Elm Street south of the railroad."[39] By 1881, "The average attendance at the colored school is about fifty."[40] School programs were held at the Pierce City Opera House, in which the children performed skits and sang songs. The *Empire* applauded their achievement, "The pupils taking part, all performed very credibly indeed, were all well prepared, and manifested enthusiasm in the exercises they rendered."[41] The editor of the *Empire* boasted, "Judging from the words of commendation and praise which constantly comes to us, and the evident enthusiasm manifested by the pupils in all grades . . . certainly some good has been wrought."[42] It was a relief to know that the good will of the white community had not been wasted. A small news item in 1892, however, indicated that blacks were not always satisfied by the educational opportunities offered. "The colored people are so thoroughly displeased with the ward school conducted for their benefit that the Rev. Mr. Jones has opened a subscription school at the colored Baptist church."[43]

African Americans in Pierce City also received a religious education. The town boasted the Second Baptist Church as well as the African Methodist Episcopal Church. Both were founded in 1880 and enjoyed a close relationship.[44] The two held joint revival meetings in which many participants were saved.[45] The Second Baptist also reached out to the white community. Having invited neighboring churches from Neosho, Springfield, Carthage, Granby, Newtonia, and Hopewell to attend a rally the Second Baptist was hosting, an invitation was also extended to "the white citizens as we feel they desire to see our church prosper. We feel assured they will help us. We want to raise on that day $100."[46] The African Methodist Episcopal Church also provided its members an opportunity to engage in educational pursuits with its literary society. Members sang, read papers they had written, and recited poetry.[47]

Churches were not the only social institution that blacks could participate in and manage for themselves. Pierce City also boasted a black Masonic lodge. One of the earliest Lawrence County histories mentioned in passing, "Campbell Lodge, A.F. & A.M. (colored), holds regular meetings and has a good working membership."[48] It was organized in September 1886.[49] Their activities appeared infrequently in the local newspaper, most often when the Masons held benefits to raise money for the organization. One benefit in 1891 was advertised in the *Empire*, "Ice cream and raspberries and other refreshments will be served. An excellent supper for 15 cents . . . Object to pay off indebtedness . . . The public are respectfully invited. Come out and help us."[50]

This vibrant black community with its schools, churches, and fraternal organizations actively engaged in local politics. Black political activism earned the ire of the local white population early on as an article reprinted from the *Cassville Republican* in 1886 indicates, "This is the way the *Peirce City Democrat* describes Matthews the colored appointee for Register of Deeds vice Fred Douglass: 'A black cotton-eyed, thick lipped, wooly headed, knock kneed, cucumber shinned, pigeon toed, gizzard footed nigger."[51] But the *Peirce City Weekly Empire,* the only surviving local source from this period, shows that African Americans persisted in their efforts to maintain a political presence despite such hostility.

Two elections from 1886 and 1891 illustrate the important role blacks in Pierce City played in the political process. Their contribution may have earned them the enmity of white Democrats, who, at the state level, enjoyed overwhelming success but could not tolerate a challenge to their power at the local level. Despite the erosion of black suffrage across the South during the 1890s, blacks in Pierce City remained politically active.[52]

In April 1886 the newspaper crowed, "The Victory Belongs to the People" when Republican mayoral candidate P. O. Snyder was elected as mayor of Pierce City. The *Empire* was edited by Thomas Carlin, a staunch Republican who had been the town's postmaster from 1882 to 1885 when he was removed for being "an offensive partisan."[53] Snyder beat Washington Cloud, the Democratic incumbent and a Confederate veteran, 318 votes to 252 votes. This political victory would have been more difficult without the votes of the black citizens who had supported Snyder. Unfortunately, as with many blacks across the South, their votes became a source of antagonism in the political battle that followed.[54]

On June 7, 1886, Cloud sent a letter to the board of aldermen contesting the election, arguing that vote fraud had taken place. He claimed, "That a great number of persons were permitted to vote for P. O. Snyder at said election who were not legally qualified to vote at said election which is believed . . . to be, in number, two hundred." He alleged that votes had been bought at the ballot box and that several voters had been coerced to vote for his opponent.[55] Cloud then went on to introduce what he termed "Exhibit A" and "Exhibit B." Exhibit A, Cloud stated, was a list of 172 voters who were not lawfully qualified to vote. Of these, 28 were black. Among the 28 listed were 6 members of the Godley family.[56] Other African Americans listed were Anson Farmer, Gentry Bly, Ben Kelly, the Hamptons, the Ropers, and the Brinsons.[57] Of the 131 individuals listed in Exhibit B, only 2 were black, Virgil Godley and Adam White.[58] Cloud had every black Republican voter in town in his sights as he fought to keep his seat as mayor.

The *Empire* reported an incident, in which "Young Ogilvie" proclaimed that "niggers and trash" had voted for Snyder.[59] The role that blacks played in the election, despite their small representation among the voters of Pierce City, did not go unnoticed. Editor Carlin ran a satirical skit in the *Empire* about the "Kurnel And His Klan," which suggested Cloud and his Democratic cronies would go to any length to thwart the will of the voters.[60]

Voters of the First Ward, many black citizens among them, subsequently published a petition in the *Empire* protesting their aldermen's refusal to certify Snyder's election. Voicing their belief that aldermen George Solomon and Joseph Newman had supported Cloud and his dubious efforts, the voters of the First Ward proclaimed, "we do one and all denounce the course of the Aldermen as illegal and corrupt and unworthy of a man or a set of men, and we believe done simply to rob us of the fruits of our election and choice."[61] The petitioners then demanded the resignation of both aldermen and asked that they be replaced with men who "will regard their promises and the wish of their constituency as expressed at the ballot box . . . and who will have the brains enough to know it is not their business to legislate for themselves and the manhood enough not to do it." Among the petitioners who signed the document were nine black voters, including George Page, Tilford Kelley, Sam Brinson, Robert Ewing, and Luke Hampton.[62] At least one of the signers, George Page, was a black Union veteran. That black men signed a petition that challenged the intelligence and character of white Democratic establishment may have garnered them ill will.

As the November elections approached, Democrats attempted to tar Republicans with their association with black voters. The *Empire* recounted, "In its endeavors to be funny, the *Democrat* names colored men for the Republican county ticket. These colored men do not take this as especially complimentary coming from the source it does, but at the same time, they are confident they could carry as much strength as any of the ring outfit."[63] A "Colored Voter," in response to the *Democrat,* expressed their sarcasm to the editor of the *Empire,* "I wish in behalf of the colored ticket recently proposed . . . to recommend the election of J. W. Deaton, to the office of Recorder. The days of the ring in Peirce City are numbered, and he will not be able long to obtain support from the city government, hence Lawrence county should support him for a while."[64]

According to the *Empire,* the Democratic establishment also sought to use black voters to its own advantage. "It is stated on good authority that a gentleman of this city tried to persuade a colored man to work for a few candidates on the Democratic ticket, and finally offered him $10 if he would do it. But the colored man was not even tempted." The small news item that followed noted that on Halloween there were "a lot of ku klux around having lots of fun."[65] Carlin, a Republican and editor who seems to have taken an even-handed approach to race relations in that his paper did not portray blacks in the blatantly racist, stereotypical views of the era, failed to elaborate on the presence of the Ku Klux Klan. Halloween, just days before the November election, certainly gave members of the Klan an excuse to make their presence known to the black voters of Peirce City, one that was meant to intimidate and instill fear.

Ultimately, Snyder and the African American voters who passionately supported him lost their struggle. On March 21, 1887, the Missouri Supreme Court found that Snyder had not lived in Pierce City for the necessary amount of time to be qualified as mayor. Despite their defeat, the black community continued to be a presence in public life.[66] In late August 1888, the *Peirce City Weekly Empire* reported that Greene Campbell, the black postal clerk on the Arkansas branch of the Frisco Railroad, had been dismissed from his patronage post. According to the *Empire,* Campbell "knew that the prejudices against his color could not be overcome except by excellence, and he was a close and hard student." The newspaper claimed that he made such a high score on the exam that no Democrat in the area had exceeded it, although many had tried and failed. The reason for dismissal, the *Empire* reported, was that Campbell had temporarily misplaced a registered pouch. While not lost, the pouch's arrival had been delayed, and thus "it was a chance to decapitate a colored official with a better record than any Democrat upon the line, and he is let out."[67]

The *Empire* also reprinted the *Peirce City Democrat's* take on the matter. Unsurprisingly, the *Democrat* crowed over Campbell's dismissal, "not discharged either because he was a colored man or because he was a Republican, but because of his neglect in attending to his duties." The newspaper claimed that Campbell had also been negligent in earlier postings at Monett and at Fort Smith. The source of the *Democrat's* information, allegedly the Pierce City postmaster, reportedly said, "only his color kept him in this position so long." The defense of Campbell by the *Empire* was just a "flimsy tissue of falsehoods intended to cater to the prejudice of the colored people."[68]

The *Empire,* though, did not let the matter stand. It rebutted the allegation made by the *Democrat* that Campbell held his job solely due to his color. "Democratic politicians howled for his removal, and were informed by a Democratic U.S. Senator that no excuse for his removal could be found in his record; that he stood No. 1 on the records at Washington." Editor Carlin took a bold swipe at Campbell's detractors, "and there are a few Democratic postmasters who have periodical spells when they would not distinguish a striped register pouch from a garter snake."[69] Campbell's dismissal remained in effect and no further mention was made of the matter. A month later, Wash Robison, a leading member of the black community and a Union veteran, was selected as a county delegate at the local Republican convention held in Pierce City.[70] His selection suggests that Pierce City Republicans had not given in to the lily whitism beginning to emerge in some southern Republican parties. The selection of a black delegate is telling of Robison's standing in Pierce City. For every defeat, there was a small victory to be had there.

The next challenge surfaced in April 1891, when Pierce City held an election for city aldermen. Republicans chose not to run for election, save in one race for alderman in the Fourth Ward, home to many black residents, who undoubtedly made up a significant number of Republican voters. Louis Conner, the Republican candidate for alderman, beat the Democratic candidate Elijah D. Deaton by just two votes. The final tally was forty-six votes to forty-four.[71]

The Democrats chose to contest the election because, they argued, Conner had not paid his street taxes. Soon after, an ad appeared in the paper announcing a mass meeting of the Fourth Ward, "without regard to race, color, or previous political affiliation, who are opposed to official discrimination for political reasons." It was held at Pierce City's African Methodist Episcopal Church.[72] The struggle that emerged catapulted one of Pierce City's black citizens into the forefront of the battle for alderman of the Fourth Ward.

On May 28, 1891, the newspaper reported that Henry Colwell, a black citizen of Pierce City, had been nominated in Conner's stead,

> It is sincerely hoped that the citizens of the fourth ward will unite in the support and election of Mr. Colwell. It will then be interesting to see if the present council will make discriminations on account of color. They have refused to seat a white Republican and now should be given an opportunity to either accept or reject a colored alderman.[73]

The *Empire* went on to say that if Colwell was elected by the voters of the Fourth Ward, "it will be an emphasis of their determination to have their votes respected by the council."[74] The newspaper continued, "Voters of the fourth ward elected an anti-ring white man, who was refused a seat, and they should now elect a colored man against the same Democratic candidate, and see if present authorities treat one better than the other." The *Empire* impishly noted that it was rumored if Deaton, who Democrats had renominated, lost once again, "that the whole territory will be declared by ordinance attached to the state of Arkansas."[75] But the Democrats had little to fear, as, according to Republicans, they relied once more upon their chicanery and tricks to ensure victory. The *Cassville Republican* sneered, "Anything to keep a Republican from office seems to be the policy of the Peirce City Democracy."[76]

Deaton defeated Colwell fifty-five votes to forty-four votes. As Carlin, the editor of the *Empire* put it, "Some voters of the fourth ward were persuaded to vote for the Democratic candidate in the belief that if the colored man should be elected that he would not be permitted a seat in the council." Carlin may have expected too much of his fellow Republicans. Some may have simply voted for Deaton because they themselves did not accept a black candidate.[77] Democrats had drawn the color line. Deaton, despite running as a Democrat, placed his name on a ballot titled "White Man's Ticket." It was clear that the Democrats had, as the *Empire* angrily noted, played the "race and color line" to their advantage. One Republican was overheard to say, "We are painted black, very black for our support of Colwell. We heartily wish the subject could be made yet more black if thereby could be made apparent our contempt for the partisan methods adopted by our council in overriding the will of our voters."[78]

James A. Vance, a local attorney and a Union veteran, claimed that "the tickets used by Deaton were unlawful, that no heading with a design of intimidation, nor distinction as to race is a lawful ticket."[79] Carlin, the *Empire's* editor, as well as an attorney, pointed out that Deaton's use of a ballot entitled "White Man's Ticket" violated state law, which only allowed the name of the candidate and the office on the ballot. Any ballot that did not conform to state law "shall be considered fraudulent, and the same shall not be counted."[80]

Vance went before the Democratic-controlled city council to argue against Deaton's methods, but his efforts were in vain. The *Empire* wryly declared, "Mr. Vance may as well present his arguments to the ballot box manipulators in Crittenden county Arkansas, where the colored people were driven before the Winchester rifles, as to attempt to utter a fair or reasonable conclusion before the Democratic board of Aldermen of Pierce City."[81] Deaton retained the seat. Yet the black community continued its struggle to gain a political voice through the years that ensued. Examinations of national and local election returns reveal that African Americans may have been able to serve as a deciding factor in hotly contested political races. In local elections, for example, Democrats lost ground from 1894 through 1900 to their Republican opponents.[82]

Yet in this period the political attitude toward blacks expressed in the Republican *Empire* had changed. By 1900, Thomas Carlin had sold the newspaper to Alex T. Boothe.[83] It is unclear whether or not Boothe accurately represented the majority opinion of Pierce City's white citizens toward their fellow black citizens, but Boothe's attitude may have reflected the wave of lily-white Republicanism that began to sweep across the South.[84] White Republicans in Pierce City seem to have become agitated by the black activism that persisted in Pierce City even as African Americans were disfranchised across the South. Boothe's *Empire* noted, "A few of the colored voters in this city met in the

Methodist Episcopal church recently and organized . . . The object of the meeting was stated to be for the betterment of their condition."[85] Those present elected Wiley Godley as the president of the Independent Colored Voters Club of Pierce City. This independence clearly agitated the editor of the Republican *Empire*. He warned the members of the club that they would do well to "read up on the election held in North Carolina . . . This disenfranchisement of about 80,000 voters in that Democratic State ought to be soothing syrup for those belonging to the 'club' in this city." In the same issue, the newspaper noted that

> Today a number of our colored citizens went to Neosho to cele-
> brate Emancipation day, and we noticed several members of the
> "Independent Colored Voters club" in the crowd, but we couldn't
> hardly understand why they should want to go, as they claim the
> Republican party has never done any thing for them.[86]

Evidently disenchanted with local Republicans, black voters never-theless resisted attempts by Democrats to seduce them. The *Empire* took notice of the violent welcome given to two traveling black sup-porters of the Democratic Party. The men attempted to lobby support for William Jennings Bryan but were met with such fierce resistance by the local black community that they "caught the first train they could and departed for greener fields and newer pastures, and proba-bly concluded that the colored people of Peirce City were not in touch with the party they were paid to represent this year."[87] In early November 1900, the *Empire* refuted the *Peirce City Democrat's* claim that a Republican in town offered to pay black voters four dollars for their allegiance at the ballot box as "absolutely false."[88] Whatever the truth was, the dispute between the two newspapers suggested the piv-otal role black voters played in Pierce City, as well as increasing tension over black political participation.

African Americans remained politically active in Pierce City. Fears of black influence in local affairs may have fed preexisting anxieties that Pierce City whites felt toward their black neighbors who had only arrived in the late 1870s. Such fears prompted southern Democrats to limit black suffrage, and began to devise various methods to disen-franchise blacks. At the same time, southern Republicans began to turn away from black voters, leaving them adrift in a region without a reli-able political ally.[89] By 1900 blacks had formed the "Independent

Colored Voters Club."[90] The black community now posed a potential political threat to Republicans. The support of the Independent Colored Voters Club could have solidified the Democrats' preeminence over the Republicans. Club members ultimately did not throw their lot in with the Democrats. The black community opted to hold out in order to make their vote more valuable and contested. This stubbornness garnered animosity from both of the parties.[91]

This political independence on the part of Pierce City African Americans came at a time of increasingly strained relations between whites and blacks in America. Both former slaves and Confederate soldiers had grown old, replaced by a new generation of whites and blacks who had not grown up in the antebellum South, yet inherited its legacy of racial division. This new generation had grown up in a turbulent period rocked by economic depression, rising fears of black crime, and an uncertain future. Significantly, these younger African Americans often did not abide by the old racial etiquette. In response, many whites feared that only violence would preserve and maintain racial status quo.[92]

In Pierce City, anger at black criminals who seemingly went unpunished likely combined with fear of black influence in local political elections to create an atmosphere of racial tension. The white community's perception of the local black community as expressed in the *Empire* reflected common racial stereotypes of the era. Though Republican in its sympathies, the *Empire* often depicted African Americans as comical and uncivilized. One can only imagine how blacks were portrayed in the *Peirce City Democrat,* which failed to survive for posterity. The day after the town's Emancipation Day celebration the newspaper reported, "The colored folks closed their celebration . . . This has been a rather dull day compared to yesterday, which was equal to an ordinary circus."[93] The *Empire* recounted on another occasion, "A couple of colored women had a lively tussle south of the railroad yesterday afternoon. They went at it in a regular pugilistic style and those who witnessed it say it was quite an amusing scene."[94]

Without the memory of slavery to guide their actions in the midst of white society, the black youth of Pierce City may not have readily accepted the racial hierarchy, in which blacks were inferior to whites. The lack of opportunity, racial prejudice, and boredom of country life may have led some young blacks in Pierce City to act out against the racial boundaries imposed upon them by society by engaging in criminal behavior. Whether or not black crime actually became more prevalent, southern urbanization made it more evident as more people lived in increasingly close quarters.[95]

Black crime was a subject that seized the attention of Americans in the 1880s and 1890s. Accounts of horrific murders, rapes, and theft committed by blacks dominated the front pages of many newspapers across the country, not just the South.[96] Graphic descriptions of brutal crimes carried out by blacks captured the public's imagination. News of lynch mobs across the South also featured prominently on the front page. Editorials supporting mob justice could be found in hundreds of newspapers across the South. As a result, many whites across the South believed that the legal system was slow and ineffective. [97]

In Pierce City reports of black crime were common. Horse thieves, drunkards, and brawlers appeared on a regular basis in the *Empire*. Both black on black and black on white crimes made the paper. In 1889, John Young, a thirty-year-old black resident of Pierce City, was caught "in a very compromising position" with Dell Sullivan, an eleven-year-old white girl by suspicious observers who followed the pair to the Pierce City roundhouse. Young fled, but was quickly captured. The *Peirce City Weekly Empire* reported, "Considerable indignation was expressed in the streets . . . the negro waived examination and requested to be taken to the jail at Mt. Vernon as soon as possible."[98] He was charged with one count of rape as well as one count of assault with intent to rape. Young was acquitted of the rape charge, but was fined one hundred dollars.[99] The fine was not enough for some area residents. The editor of the *Aurora Advertiser* reportedly called for Young to be "hanged by the neck until dead." Young, however, apparently escaped the noose.[100] Andy Boyd, another black man accused of raping a young white girl in nearby Verona, was also acquitted.[101]

In 1899, Phil Bly, the son of the Reverend Gentry Bly, got into an altercation with Roland Reed, a young white man. Bly repeatedly hit Reed's head against the street gutter, injuring him so badly that it appeared Reed would not survive. Bly was jailed.[102] When Reed recovered, however, Bly was released.[103]

Black on black crime was not uncommon in Pierce City. One cold January day, after French Godley expelled his son Joe from the family home for being intoxicated, Joe began throwing rocks at the house. French came outside to stop Joe, but instead, French was hit in the head with a rock. He fell to the ground unconscious with a five-inch gash in his head. Joe was taken to the city jail.[104] Joe was later killed in Mt. Vernon when he and D. J. McKinzee, a white man, got into an altercation while both were drunk.[105]

A cursory search of Lawrence County court records from 1881 to 1894 shows that members of the Godley family appeared in either civil or criminal court at least thirteen times. The majority of allegations against the Godleys consisted of assault and battery but there was at least one accusation of adultery, disturbing the peace, and ejectment. Notably, in 1884, Sarah Godley filed for divorce from her husband, French Godley, citing physical and mental abuse.

Sarah accused French of "cruel and barbarous treatment as to endanger [her] life" and "beating and striking her with his fists and by striking and beating her with a large, heavy club, to wit: a peach tree limb." He made her life intolerable by calling "her vile names and epithets, by attempting to strike and whip her, by threatening to turn her and her children out of doors, declining and refusing to support her." Sarah also accused French of "consorting and openly associating and cohabitating with lewd and abandoned women, particularly one Jane Hayes."[106] The disposition of the case is unknown as no judgment was filed with the court case. Sarah's son from her first marriage also exhibited violent behavior.

In 1891, Robert "Bob" Hampton brutally assaulted a black minister. Hampton was among a group of young black men who disrupted a meeting at the Second Baptist Church. When Reverend McMillan intervened, Hampton "took offense at what was said and left the house." He then waited outside the church with a pick handle and struck Reverend McMillan on the head when he stepped outside after the meeting. Hampton subsequently fled town. By Monday, Reverend McMillan was reportedly "in a serious condition." When Bob Hampton could not be found, his brother Pete was taken into custody instead, but Pete denied any involvement.[107] Life in Pierce City went on, but whites undoubtedly took notice.

TWO

Pierce City

"White Man's Heaven"

By the end of the nineteenth century, African Americans and whites viewed "each other dimly, at a distance." While blacks and whites found themselves drawn together due to new social, economic, and political circumstances, it did little to assuage white anxiety about black crime. In the wake of Reconstruction, black suffrage, and the abolishment of the firm hand of slavery, whites feared blacks were reverting back to a state of savagery. White anxiety about bestial black men sexually assaulting and raping white women strained race relations to the point that "rape could be defined so broadly that an insult, a grimace, an unwanted glance, or an accidental touch might be transformed in white minds into sexual violence."[1]

White hostility toward blacks in southwest Missouri manifested itself with the first major outbreak of racial violence in the summer of 1894. An earlier, minor incident had occurred in 1877 in Pierce City when a young African American named George Gray was strung up for stealing railroad tickets. He survived, but even four days later, "The trace of the rope can be seen encircling his neck."[2] A much more troubling event occurred thirteen years later.

In October 1890, an intoxicated black man reportedly raped sixty-year-old Johanna Filo as she and her son were returning home from church. Will Godley was suspected of the crime as the Godley farm was located between Pierce City and the Filo farm. Small knots of men gathered on the city streets and talked of lynching, but they "insisted that they must know beyond doubt that they had the right man before acting." Godley, arrested at Monett, was brought back to Pierce City. Men continued to linger in the streets and the mayor contacted Governor David Francis to obtain permission to call out the Missouri National Guard. In the meantime, Captain Fred C. Stellhorn ordered Guard members to report to the Guard armory in Pierce City. Thirty men reported for duty and received orders to put four rounds in their belts, but as no attempt to lynch Godley was made, they were later dismissed. Extra police were also sworn in to prevent mob violence.

Still, the threat of a lynching lingered. Peter Filo, who saw his mother's attacker, identified Godley in a lineup. Two or three men reportedly tried to form a mob but no one joined their cause because "the main thing to carry out this purpose was lacking, a leader." Pierce City marshal Reuben Chappell, a former Confederate from Virginia, loaded Godley into a carriage and with the night watchman Wright took Godley to Mt. Vernon "at a brisk trot." Someone called out, "Come on, boys, if there is any good in you!" But no one gave chase.[3]

In August 1891, Godley was sentenced to ten years in the state penitentiary for the rape of Johanna Filo. The penitentiary Dressing Register provides the only known description of Will Godley. He stood five feet, eleven inches tall, weighed 158, and had a bald spot on the crown of his head. It was noted that he could read and write. His signature appears in the register, written in shaky, spidery handwriting. Godley was released early on March 10, 1899, and returned to Lawrence County where his family resided.[4] Godley remained in the public eye, branded as a miscreant.[5]

On June 20, 1894, a group of young white men attempted to chase black residents of Monett, Missouri, from the town. The next evening, Robert Greenwood, a Frisco Railroad brakeman, went out on the town with friends. At some point, the men ran into some of the blacks who had been harassed the previous day.[6] Words were exchanged between the two parties and Hughlett Ulysses Hayden, a black man, was knocked to the ground. His friends reacted by shooting Greenwood in the chest. He died of his injuries a day later on June 22. The *Cassville Republican* reported, "The killing of Greenwood was brought about by the differences between the whites and blacks. The blacks thought they had been run over too much and decided to make a stand. Arming themselves, a number seemed to put themselves in the way for trouble and soon found it."[7]

Hayden was arrested for Greenwood's murder in Neosho, west of Monett, the next day. He was to be taken by train to Cassville with a stopover in Monett. Alerted to his presence in Monett, a crowd gathered, but Hayden was ushered back onto the train. The marshal escorting Hayden placed his prisoner in an empty railroad car for safekeeping. Men boarded the train without tickets as the train began to roll out of town. When confronted a mile and half south of Monett, the men demanded the train stop, and then seized Hayden. He was dragged from the railroad car to a telegraph pole alongside the tracks and promptly hanged. The *Neosho Times* reported "the railroad men have driven every negro out of Monett and won't let a colored man or woman live there."[8]

The absence of blacks in Monett was a point of pride seven years later when the Pierce City lynchings occurred. The *St. Louis Post-Dispatch* reported that "for seven years, whenever a colored man had dared invade Monett, he has heard the warning cry: 'Get a rope!'" The *Chicago Tribune* also emphasized the animosity that remained in the town toward blacks in 1901, "Across the main street of Monett for years there has been a sign reading: 'Nigger, don't let the sun go down.'"[9]

In 1899, Price Hamlin and Witt Cummings, black men, were threatened by an impromptu mob in nearby Stotts City. According to the *Peirce City Weekly Empire,* Hamlin felt "a little bit uneasy when he saw the crowd of fifteen actually coming for him with a rope, and that the rope looked powerful big." Hamlin said he thought it was a bluff, but "he would rather get to some other town if it's all the same."[10] Later that year, in May, an unnamed black man passed through Carthage and told of his experience in Monett. Unaware of Monett's ban on African Americans, he stopped in at a restaurant. "In about ten minutes a crowd of railroad men appeared at the front door and at the same time a lot of them came in the back way. They carried a long rope." The men placed a noose around the black man's neck and led him to the depot. There he was given three minutes to leave town. The black man said he was "plumb skeered to deff" and vowed never to travel through Monett again.[11] In November, Bob Carter, a black man, was strung up for two minutes and beaten by a crowd in Granby on his way to court in Neosho. Carter was allegedly punished for incest.[12]

In April 1901, African American Joe Davis was spirited out of nearby Neosho after he killed Virgil Marrs, a popular young white man.[13]

The lynchings and the subsequent expulsion of blacks from Pierce City began August 18, 1901, with the discovery of Gisele Wild's lifeless body. Gisele's parents, Bernhard and Elizabeth Wild, immigrated in 1873 to the United States from Germany.[14] By 1900, the Wilds had seven children, Gisele being born in 1878. The Wilds settled near Pierce City in the hope that Bernhard's investment in land there would pay large dividends. Unfortunately, Pierce City never became the railroad boomtown that Bernhard Wild anticipated, and the family went into debt.[15]

On the morning of August 18, 1901, Gisele and her brother, Carl, attended Sunday School, then church services. Gisele chose to walk home alone that afternoon. She was within half a mile of the Pierce City business district when she was brutally attacked. Her brother later found her lying in a ditch alongside the road. Gisele's throat had been slit, and there were signs of a struggle. Carl Wild ran to the nearest residence and telephoned Pierce City marshal J. T. Johnson, then returned to the scene with others, only to find his sister had died. As the news of the crime reached Pierce City, the town's fire bell rang frantically, summoning a large crowd.

Eugene Barrett, a young black man, watched as Marshal Johnson rushed out of the Lawrence Hotel, asked a boy for his bicycle, then raced off as fast as he could pedal. Thinking nothing of it, Barrett proceeded to Quinn's Saloon where someone told him that a girl had been killed down on the railroad tracks. Pete Hampton asked Barrett, who was sober, to find out what was going on, and Barrett agreed.[16]

On his way, Barrett ran into John Slaterly and Perry Howard, both young white men. As they reached Vance and Perrott's grain mill, Marshal Johnson raced past them back toward town on his borrowed bicycle. The group called out to him as to what was the matter and Johnson shouted back, "Nothing much but Eugene you better not go down there." Proceeding a little farther, they met Ike Suttles, the night watchman. Suttles informed them that, "Some darn nigger has cut Wild's daughter's throat and Johnson has gone to ring the fire bell and get up a mob to go out and hunt for him." At that, Barrett and the two other young men started back to town. As the fire bell began to ring, the group took off at a run, once again meeting Marshal Johnson who warned them, "You better not go out because the people are so excited they will hang the first nigger they see." The young men heeded his advice and returned to town. Still, other young black men did visit the crime scene, among them Will Young, Charley Price, and George Debow.[17]

Will Roark claimed he had seen a black man sitting on the culvert near where Gisele's body had been found. Search parties were formed and spread out to hunt for the murderer. The *Empire* proclaimed, "No such crime should ever go unpunished, and every citizen should constitute himself an officer for the time being to help [track] down the murderer . . . when discovered no punishment is too bad."[18] Bloodhounds arrived from Barton County, Missouri. The dogs led law enforcement officials to the home of Joe Lark, the black porter for the Frisco Railroad that Barrett would finger. Lark was not at home. In the meantime, Will Godley and Eugene Barrett were arrested by authorities and placed in the city jail.[19]

Lawrence County sheriff John Manlove, for reasons unknown, did not transport Godley and Barrett to the safety of the county seat at Mt. Vernon.[20] Despite threats of violence against the two men, Manlove left Pierce City to return home that afternoon. As a mob gathered, Mayor Cloud and other city officials were able to disperse the crowd, arguing for law and order. Missouri National Guard captain Eugene A. Cuendet of Company E, based in Pierce City, offered his assistance to Mayor Cloud. Cloud, however, insisted he could handle the mob.[21] Unfortunately for Will Godley, Cloud was wrong.

The citizens of Pierce City were clearly growing tired of trouble. Earlier in the summer, the *Empire* reported that Will Godley and Charley Price, another black resident, had been arrested on suspicion of murdering Pierce City night watchman Chappell the previous year. Godley and Price were released after they provided an adequate alibi to authorities.[22] A reporter for the *Carthage Evening Press* noted for his readers, "Pierce City railroad yards are the scene of some of the most dastardly thug crimes in the whole southwest, and what is worse, the criminal so frequently gets away."[23]

Exactly one month before the lynching, some local toughs sought out the Pierce City marshal and night watchman. While shots were exchanged between the night watchman and one of the would-be gunslingers, no one was hurt. The *Peirce City Weekly Empire* growled, "After some one or more of these fellows who have come in to shoot up the town have been killed they will learn that we are going to have peace, if we have to fight for it."[24]

During the chaotic time that followed the murder of Gisele Wild, two young white women stepped forward to accuse Will Godley of attempted rape after he had been taken into custody. According to the women, he had stopped them on their way home from choir practice and attempted to "outrage them." Before he fled at the approach of other whites, their assailant threatened them with death if they revealed his identity, thus their previous failure to identify their assailant. The aborted attack was well known to the town. Interestingly, this incident appears to be the same one reported by the *Empire* in March as a robbery, rather than a rape attempt.[25]

In any event, the women's story was supported by Godley's criminal record. Whether or not the women told the truth, the accusation was enough to seal Will Godley's fate. By evening, a mob of nearly one thousand men converged outside the jail, standing in the glare of electric streetlights. Men stood with shotguns, rifles and pistols as darkness settled over the town. Still, no one attempted to storm the jail until 9:15 P.M. A lone man secured a rope from a nearby hardware store and approached the jail. The mood of the mob immediately went from tense to riotous at the sight of the rope. Sledgehammers were procured and men began to batter down the steel door to the jail. Officers inside the small building attempted to reason with the crowd to no avail. Godley and Barrett were forcibly taken from their cell and nooses placed securely around their necks. The lives of the two black men were now in the hands of the mob.

Godley and Barrett were dragged down the street as gunfire erupted around them in a violent salvo of anticipation. The mob stopped and demanded the identity of Gisele Wild's murderer. Both men remained silent. The two men were pulled further down the street with their hands on their heads before the mob stopped one last time. Eugene Barrett broke down. Professing his innocence, he claimed that the murderer was Joe Lark, a black porter on the St. Louis and St. Francisco Railway who conveniently left town after the murder. Barrett was released and taken to safety. Will Godley, however, kept silent. In a matter of moments, he was strung up over the second-story balcony of the Lawrence Hotel and hanged. Members of the mob fired wildly. Bullets riddled Godley's body as he dangled in the air, but the shots also struck spectators, killing one boy.[26] As the mob lynched his friend, Pete Hampton attempted to shoot at the mob but unnamed men stopped him.[27] For the blacks of southwest Missouri, the lynching of Will Godley confirmed a radical change in race relations, one that forever changed the racial composition of the southern Missouri Ozarks.[28]

A *Carthage Evening Press* reporter arrived in time to watch the lynching and then lingered in the streets. His detailed account provides insight into the events that followed. The reporter looked on as a drunken Polish immigrant hit at Godley's leg, cursing at the corpse. The murder of Wild, the daughter of German immigrants, may have sparked outrage in the nearby Polish and German communities at Pulaskifield, Freistatt, and Sarcoxie.[29] The extent of the participation by members of the nearby immigrant communities remains unknown, but people from other communities did take part in the lynch mob. The *Empire* noted, "The city was full of Monett people today, all intent upon assisting in the search for the man who committed the murder . . . and for the citizens of Peirce City we want to thank them."[30]

A "shirt sleeved businessman" jumped on top of a water trough and yelled, "Boys, the ladies at the hotel want the body cut down. What do you say, boys, in the name of the ladies of Pierce City?" The crowd agreed. After Godley's body was cut down, people gathered around his corpse. Peanut shells were thrown on his face and boys gazed at the bullet wounds their fathers had inflicted.[31] Newspaper accounts do not record any attempts to take a piece of the rope or Godley's clothing as a souvenir of the event.

Another cry went up, "Make way boys, the ladies!" A dozen women were escorted to view the remains, a common practice at southern lynchings.[32] Godley's body was then taken off the street when it became clear that a coroner's inquest would not be held. An observer remarked to the *Press* reporter of the Lawrence County sheriff John Manlove's absence, "'The idea,'" said the onlooker, "'of his leaving this nigger here all day.'"[33]

Even whites were not safe from the mob's frenzy. Jasper County deputy sheriff John Plummer stepped off the train only to be stopped at gunpoint. A member of the mob stationed at the depot, recognizing Plummer as an officer of the law, warned him not to go near the mob. Plummer tried to pass by the guard, but when the barrel of a shotgun was shoved in his face, he meekly complied. Plummer watched as Godley was lynched, and then jumped on the next train as it came into the depot, making his escape to Barry County.[34]

But the mob had not finished its work. When word spread that Pete Hampton had attempted to shoot at the mob during the lynching, the news enraged the lynchers.[35] Someone cried out, "Come on boys, you with guns—out to run the niggers out of town."[36] The crowd quickly moved to the black section of Pierce City. As the *Empire* described it, "the frenzied men thought of some other negroes who needed attention, and the march was taken up to the residence of Pete Hampton."[37]

Hampton, like Godley, had a prior criminal record. As late as 1900, he had been the defendant in a seduction case.[38] Hampton was referred to as a "thoroughly bad man and was feared by all, both white and black."[39] Between 1899 and 1900 alone, Hampton made at least six court appearances. He plead guilty in 1899 to carrying a concealed weapon, disturbing the peace, burglary, and larceny.[40] In 1900, Hampton pled guilty to common assault when he participated in an attack on Roland Reed, a young white man, in Pierce City.[41] Later that year, he pled guilty to carrying a concealed weapon and, in a separate case, was found guilty of seduction by a jury of his black peers. It did not help matters that in 1891, his brother Bob, who also had several run-ins with the law, killed a black preacher after Bob took offense at something the man said.[42]

The mob came to a halt in front of the house of Hampton's stepfather and Will Godley's uncle, French Godley. The crowd demanded that Hampton leave town once and for all. Hampton "assumed the attitude of the desperado he was, reviled the messengers, and, first began hostilities by firing on the people, wounding four white men." The mob returned fire, killing Hampton and French Godley, then set the surrounding houses on fire. Their charred remains were later buried after being viewed the next day by curious spectators. But the mob had undertaken a larger task—expulsion. The *Empire* claimed that "up to this time there was no thought of driving the negroes from the city." The newspaper further asserted that no women or children were shot at, but that contradicts eyewitness accounts.[43]

One eyewitness, First Lieutenant W. C. Gillen, told the *St. Louis Post-Dispatch*,

> It was the wildest mob I ever saw, and I have seen several. I watched the attack on the negro quarters from the veranda of the Windsor Hotel. After the torch was applied, the whole scene was brightly illuminated. The crack of Springfield rifles which the mob had taken from the armory was incessant. Old soldiers said it looked like an attack on a fort at night. The members of the mob were yelling and hooting. The negro women and children were crying and screaming.

Another citizen, whose name went unrecorded, reported that black men, women, and children took shelter in their homes as bullets and flames threatened their lives. One woman took shelter in a cellar after three bullets hit the trunk that she had taken cover behind.[44]

Out of ammunition, men broke into the Missouri National Guard armory in town and took rifles and ammunition. Some intoxicated men hollered, "Here's cartridges—who wants a Springfield!" The *Press* reporter heard one man exclaim, "Our wives and daughters—come on!" He estimated at least fifteen hundred rounds were used in the assault on the black section of Pierce City. The journalist confided in his readers, "It was my first battle—and I felt that it was the real thing."[45] Unfortunately for many blacks in Pierce City, it was a one-sided battle that they lost.

Seventeen-year-old Iola E. LeGrande, a young white woman, sat on the sidewalk in front of her home until three o'clock in the morning, "watching the breaking in of the jail, the hanging, and the burning of the buildings." She remarked in a letter to her pen-pal in Minnesota, "Perhaps it wasn't just the place but I thought of the words, 'Nero fiddled while Rome burned,' as the glare of the burning buildings reminded me of that description." Iola confided, "I couldn't keep from laughing at times at the strange things people did but all in all t'was a serious matter." The next morning she and her family "went to see roast negro, scared negro and a hanged negro."[46]

The Reverend S. S. Pitcher of the African Methodist Church of Carthage and the Reverend L. M. Smith of the Colored Cumberland Presbyterian Church of Lamar left behind their camp meeting tents

Ruins of Emma Carter's house in Pierce City. *Courtesy of The State Historical Society of Missouri.*

in Pierce City and fled to the outskirts of town. There, at the home of James Cobb, a black railroad porter, they came under attack by the mob. Pitcher estimated the house was hit two hundred times before he and Smith made their escape. They made their way to Carthage after walking an estimated twenty five and a half miles to Sarcoxie. A white man armed with a shotgun watched them pass his farm near Sarcoxie. Pitcher and Smith assured him they wanted to leave the area, but the man "seemed so savage that we did not have too much to say to him."[47]

A black resident, Miss Pinky Cobb, told the *Post-Dispatch* her story. Cobb, whom the *Post-Dispatch* reporter described as almost white, said that she and her sister had gathered her sister's children and gone to the family cellar. Afraid that she would burn alive, Cobb fled the cellar and ran outside into the darkness. Members of the mob shot at her continuously but she escaped unscathed, only to return to her family home to take refuge there again. "They made a monkey out of me that night," she told the reporter. Finally the embattled black citizens "chose to risk bullets outside rather than both flames and bullets inside." The refugees ran for their lives as the violence raged on through the night until five

Uncle Ben Kelly's house in Pierce City. *Courtesy of The State Historical Society of Missouri.*

in the morning. A brave few returned only to be told that they must leave Pierce City and never return on pain of death.[48]

At least one African American did not go quietly. Before she left town, America Godley, the wife of Will Godley, boldly walked toward city hall with a revolver wrapped in a handkerchief. Night watchman Murray apprehended her and locked her up in the Pierce City jail.[49] America Godley was later released, but the *Empire* did not comment further on her actions.

For some, the excitement was not over. Iola E. LeGrande, who had watched the riot from the safety of her home on Monday, wrote to a friend about the scare the town experienced a few days later on Thursday: "the cry came through the streets, 'The negros are coming, coming in bunches.'" Reports of a mob of African Americans headed for the town spread quickly and ladies who had been walking on the streets took shelter in the town post office. The lights were extinguished and the door barred to prevent anyone from coming in. Iola remarked of the hysterics that she observed "such screaming, fainting, and crying." She feared that if she opened the door a black man would force his way into the building. Although men from Company E of the Missouri National Guard arrived to patrol the town, she confessed, "every man, woman, and child was frightened." After the chaos subsided, Iola vowed she would "never be found out in the country with a crowd of girls or out after dusk" and admitted she took comfort in the presence of her "sweetest little .38" revolver.[50]

For the black citizens of Pierce City, life would never be the same. In 1900, there were approximately 283 blacks in Lawrence County; it is estimated 166 lived in Pierce City.[51] By 1910, only 91 blacks remained in the entire county.[52] Many of the black residents of Pierce City traveled to Joplin and Springfield. Members of St. Paul's Baptist Church, one of the two black churches in Pierce City, reunited in Joplin and decided that the property be transferred to the Second Baptist Church of Carthage, Missouri, as Carthage was "a haven for the colored race."[53]

Some residents, like Pinky Cobb, fled to Springfield. The Cobb family found refuge in the home of James Abernathy, a black railroad porter. It was in Springfield that the matriarch of the Cobb family, Arminta Cobb, gave an interview to a *St. Louis Post-Dispatch* reporter. Referring to Kentucky, her birthplace, Mrs. Cobb stated, "That's the South too, but give me the South in preference to Peirce City. They are supposed to hate colored people down South, but I was never treated like this. Kentucky is good enough for me, and I want no more of Peirce City."[54]

The *Carthage Evening Press* somberly noted the appearance of a "rattle-trap old wagon drawn by a pitiful recollection of a horse," loaded down with black women, children, and belongings. These refugees from Pierce City were on their way to Joplin in the hope of a new life.[55]

J. V. Taylor traveled to Pittsburg, Kansas, where he met a cool reception. According to an article in the *Pittsburg Headlight*, Taylor had lived in Pierce City for thirty years; he owned his own home and rented farmland. Prior to his arrival, Pittsburg banned refugees from Pierce City, but Taylor told a reporter that "he can show good recommendations as to his character and past life." When he left town the night of the lynching, Taylor left behind five hundred bushels of wheat.[56]

The violence apparently prompted blacks outside Pierce City to flee southwest Missouri. Willis DeHoney, reportedly the only black citizen living in Barry County, sold his farm and moved to Kansas. Several black families who lived to the west of Pierce City in the Jolly area packed their wagons and traveled to Oklahoma to start a new life after they "received a 'request' to vacate, decided that discretion was the better part of valor," and "sold their property at a sacrifice."[57]

For some, the violence continued in the immediate aftermath of their flight. The *Pittsburg Headlight* reported that a small mob in Stroud, Oklahoma, attacked its small black population and expelled them from the town. The reason for the violence, the article noted, was because "insolence on the part of certain negroes toward the whites, and a heavy immigration of negroes within the past few days, believed to come from Pierce City." The *Headlight* reported the same day that law enforcement officials were on their way to Sapulpa, Oklahoma, to prevent a mob spurred on by town officials from running black residents out of that town.[58]

The Reverend Gentry Bly, the former pastor at the Pierce City Colored Baptist Church, returned to Pierce City briefly to check on his home. It is surprising he was not chased out of town, although after living in Pierce City for twenty-one years, he may have been looked upon more kindly than other African Americans. Reportedly, some of Pierce City's citizens had written to him, asking him to return. His nine-room home, Bly discovered, was not damaged during the mob's attack, but he declined to stay.[59] Almost a month after the lynchings the *Peirce City Weekly Empire* reported that a black man stepped off the Oklahoma train and walked around Pierce City until young boys began to yell, "Get a rope." The man quickly left town.[60]

While unwanted in Pierce City, its former African American residents were not unwanted elsewhere. According to the *Carthage Evening Press*, Pierce City mayor Washington Cloud received a letter from F. S. Castering of Vicksburg, Mississippi, saying that he was interested in bringing the black citizens of Pierce City to Vicksburg. He offered to pay for their transportation to Mississippi, hire them to pick cotton and harvest corn, in addition to offering many other employment opportunities. Castering was willing to rent or sell land and promised the land was capable of producing four hundred to seven hundred pounds of cotton per acre. He boasted, "This is the finest country on top side of the globe for the negro. He can earn his money and living with less exertion than anywhere else on earth."[61] Having fled from the horrors of Pierce City, it was unlikely than any of the survivors were willing to take Castering up on his offer, probably fearing the terror of the Deep South.

But the offer is illuminating nonetheless. The loss of African American labor in Pierce City, confined primarily to service and unskilled labor jobs, was inconsequential. But in Mississippi, the African Americans expelled from Pierce City would have been welcomed into the local workforce, where their labor was sorely needed. Mississippi was hardly free from the epidemic of lynching, but in the Deep South where black labor was a valuable commodity, expulsion was rare.

The white press in surrounding communities generally agreed that the lynchings and expulsion were justified. The *Pittsburg Daily Headlight* proclaimed its sympathies with Pierce City's white community. "For years Pierce City has been cursed with a large population of a vicious class of negroes who are continually committing some sort of a depredation or another . . . it is a great wonder that Pierce City withstood their insulting and impudent ways so long as they did."[62] An editorial in the *Joplin Daily Globe* argued,

> The negro who is self-respecting, law abiding and industrious is entitled to all the protection the law can give but a negro that lives in idleness and begs, or steals or exacts by threats of violence, is not so entitled. He is a cancer upon the body politic, a disgrace to our civilization, a menace to virtue and chastity and a living threat to peace and dignity of the community. Something should be done with HIM.

The editorial reminded readers that it was easy to criticize the actions of others when the problem of delinquent blacks could easily be their own.[63] In nearby Aurora, the editor of the *Aurora Argus* pontificated, "Better hang a dozen innocent black brutes than let one guilty one escape."[64] The *Galena Times* sent the following to the *Empire,* "As the Peirce City man oiled his old shotgun, He hummed with ghoulish glee, The strains of his grand old battle hymn, All coons look alike to me."[65]

The *St. Louis Post-Dispatch* reporter in Springfield wrote after the lynchings, "Down here they call it white man's heaven." The reporter chronicled the antiblack sentiment expressed in several southwest Missouri communities, among them Webb City, Monett, and Aurora. White animosity toward African Americans was so severe after the lynchings that a white man with a dark suntan was almost asked to "migrate." The reporter compared the exodus of blacks from the area to the impact of Order No. 11 issued in 1863 that oversaw the depopulation of parts of Missouri. The reporter, however, felt that Order No. 11 was less severe in its punishment than the actions of the mob at Pierce City.[66]

But while whites celebrated expulsions, they did not necessarily want their towns held responsible for them. The *Monett Times,* ever mindful of Monett's image, snorted, "The tendency on the part of certain Peirce City people to lay blame of the lynching on the Monett crowd is far from commendable."[67] Within a few weeks, the *Times* boasted, "Monett is the only city in the state with a population of over 3000 without a resident negro within its borders."[68]

Emmett Newton, quartermaster general of the Missouri National Guard, gave some of the most telling evidence that many white Missourians approved of the lynchings. He admitted to a *St. Louis Post-Dispatch* reporter that he had left Springfield so that he could not receive orders to take back rifles stolen from the National Guard armory in Pierce City by the mob. He told the reporter that officially he did not know there was a lynching, that he did not know that National Guard rifles had been used during the violence, and that he was going to go where there was no mail or telegraph service. Newton stated that the lynching was right, and that the people of southwest Missouri knew how to take care of matters. When asked if he felt the wrong man had been lynched, Newton replied, "No; they burned the right man. They did not burn the man who attempted to assault the young woman ... but they caught a brute who had made two previous attempts to worse than murder white women."[69]

Not every area paper approved of mob violence. The *Neosho Miner and Mechanic* implored Governor Dockery to offer a reward for the prosecution of individuals who participated in the lynching. The *Fayetteville Democrat Weekly* mentioned the plight of one of their own black citizens, Tobitha Taylor, who was visiting Sarah Godley, her sister in Pierce City. It then said simply, "Comment is not necessary on this awful affair."[70]

Nationally, the violence was condemned. The *Nation,* one of the country's leading journals, examined area population statistics and then concluded, "The colored population of the town, as of all that section of the State, is but a trifling percentage of the whole number of people. It is impossible that the whites should live in the dread of the blacks which undoubtedly exists in regions where the blacks outnumber them."[71] In Chicago, where the second annual National Negro Business League convention was being held, S. S. Cooper of Washington remarked to the *Chicago Tribune*, "It is a disgrace to American civilization that such atrocities are committed. Look at the participants as individuals— the black who committed the crime against a woman, and the white men who committed a crime against innocent blacks—do they not belong in the same sentence of condemnation?" Booker T. Washington, president of the league, refused to comment on the events at Pierce City. Washington said it would be too difficult to express his view on the matter without being misunderstood. But other members in attendance at the convention also spoke out against the lynchings when their leader chose not to.[72]

Some area whites also expressed indignation at the lynchings. Dr. H. O. Scott, minister at the First Presbyterian Church of Carthage, decried the mob violence from his pulpit. "We have advocated the death penalty to such an extent that we have been exploited before the community as hard-hearted. But we must utter our protest against mob violence that hangs men . . . and runs people out of town because the Lord who made them gave them black skins. It is simply lawlessness, anarchy, savagery." Dr. Scott declared that mob violence was antithetical to the Declaration of Independence and the Constitution before concluding, "It is a curse to any country in which it takes place."[73]

Local African Americans also voiced their disgust at the mob violence in Pierce City. The Reverend George Abbott of Wesley Chapel in Carthage, a former resident of Lawrence County, sent a letter to the editor of the *Carthage Evening Press* to express the feelings of Carthage's black community. "We are opposed to race colonization, we believe in universal citizenship, that is to say that character should take preeminence over color." He went on, "I have faith in almighty God, if we as a race be true and faithful, at his own time he will interfere and stop the murder lynching and burning of so many helpless victims." Abbott asserted that the phrase "all men are created equal" had lost its meaning over time, but because blacks were not going to leave America, "the sooner each race lays down race prejudice and labors for each others interests the better it will be for all."[74]

The *Joplin Daily Globe* reported that in Springfield the blacks of the city, "want a country of their own." It noted that "the dream of a new black republic somewhere within the later territorial acquisitions of the United States now seems almost a realization to the excited colored men of Springfield." The article concluded, "The negro must seek liberty and the pursuit of happiness in some other land." A meeting to discuss colonization in the Philippines was to meet at a later date.[75] But other Springfield blacks passed a resolution condemning the lynching and announced, "the negro is at home in this country," and resolved to stay.[76]

Residents of Pierce City answered the criticism their town received in the aftermath of the lynchings. When interviewed by Robertus Love, reporter for the *St. Louis Post-Dispatch*, Mayor Washington Cloud seemed weary of the affair. "Print the facts, but don't make this thing worse than it is. It is bad enough, God knows. I do not believe that the sentiment of our people is against the negroes as a race, but this thing has happened because they fear their wives and daughters are not safe." He noted that the town had thirty-five black voters and estimated the black population at roughly two hundred before they were expelled.[77] Cloud, a local attorney, had represented black clients in the past. He served as counsel for Andrew Boyd, accused of raping a young girl, and won an acquittal for his client.[78] Cloud, however, was not typical. During the same interview, a young man told the *Post-Dispatch* reporter that the life of Gisele Wild was worth more than all "the 'niggers' in the United States."[79]

A week after the violence, Mayor Cloud issued a proclamation that appeared in the *Carthage Evening Press*. Cloud stated that law and order had been reestablished in Pierce City and that "there is no danger of any person who is peaceably going about his business without being molested on or interfered with on account of his color." The mayor specifically pointed out that the town held no animosity toward "railroad and Pullman porters on account of their color," and promised that authorities would not allow anyone to be harassed while "discharging their duties."[80]

For its part, the Peirce City Citizens Committee, formed to tell the town's side of the story and defend it from criticism, claimed full responsibility for the lynchings. It also expressed disappointment with the black community, to whom every advantage and opportunity had been granted yet tolerated criminal behavior:

Pierce City mayor
Washington Cloud.
*Courtesy of The State
Historical Society of
Missouri.*

> They were provided with first class educational facilities. They
> had two churches supported by the best white people . . . They
> were given abundant opportunity to be industrious . . . Though
> it was widely suspicion[ed] that nearly all the crimes committed
> in Peirce City, were perpetrated by negroes, it could not be fas-
> tened upon them because of the impossibility to get a negro to
> testify against another negro . . . One of them said, "That under
> the circumstances he could find no fault with the way the people
> had done."[81]

The committee offered its hope that no other town should have to go
through the horror that Pierce City had experienced. Ultimately, it
concluded, "What was done was done by a force that nothing on the
ground could stop."[82]

A Pierce City businessman, Nicholas Perrott, told the *Joplin Daily
Globe,* "The mob that did the work . . . it was a well organized body of
determined men. They were not excited . . . but instead cool and deliberate." Perrott also went on to elaborate that the mob was not composed of ruffians, but of the finest citizens of Pierce City. He concluded

the interview by stating, "I believe that the majority of the Peirce City people are glad that there are no more negroes there, although many did not approve of the lynching." Mr. Perrott spoke of a rational, calculating mob that exacted justice for Miss Wild, not a wild, out-of-control rabble.[83]

Iola E. LeGrande wrote her pen-pal in Minnesota, "We are condemned by some one every day, but as you say should it come to one's own doors many would act differently. Of course I do not exactly endorse mob law neither mob defense but in this case I am glad the mob took things in their own hands."[84] LeGrande shed further light on the character of Pierce City in another letter she later wrote in October 1901. "You asked me if I feel guilty of anything you named—No not a bit. Thats not P.C. Style. We deny every charge and generally end it with a duel or a hanging." She then told her correspondent that since his last letter, the mayor and an attorney had fought in the street, followed by a murder and an additional fight that, if not for the intervention of law officers, would have resulted in death. "Can you beat it?" she asked.[85]

The only official government statement on Pierce City was an investigative report submitted to Governor Dockery, who had remained silent throughout the entire affair, by Adjutant-General W. T. Dameron of the Missouri National Guard. The report assigned blame squarely to one individual. Sheriff John Manlove was condemned for his failure to transport Godley and Barrett to the safety of the county seat at Mt. Vernon. Despite threats of violence against the two men, Manlove left Pierce City to return home that afternoon and failed to intervene when news of the mob raced over the telephone lines. Mayor Cloud was also cited for his failure to accept assistance from Missouri National Guard captain Cuendet.

Adjutant-General Dameron, after investigation, declared that none of the men of Company E "aided or assisted directly or indirectly, the mob." Instead, they stood by and waited for Sheriff Manlove to ask the Guard for assistance, but Manlove remained silent. But Mayor Cloud also refused to ask the Guard to assist in quelling the mob. In 1890, when Will Godley could possibly have been lynched, had it not been for swift action of city officials and Marshal Reuben Chappell, a tragedy was avoided. City officials swore in additional police, called

Missouri governor
Alexander M. Dockery.
*Courtesy of The State
Historical Society of
Missouri.*

upon the Guard, and kept the situation under control until Chappell could take Godley to the safety of Mt. Vernon. Sheriff Manlove and Mayor Cloud, by contrast, failed to act.[86]

As the embers of the firestorm burnt out, the bodies of Will Godley, French Godley, and Pete Hampton were laid to rest in Pierce City. Joe Lark, whom Eugene Barrett implicated in the murder of Gisele Wild, was more fortunate. He would face a jury in the coming months instead of a lynch mob.

While the identity of Gisele Wild's murderer remains a mystery, the causes behind the lynchings and subsequent expulsion of blacks from Pierce City are not. The events of August 19, 1901, provide an opportunity to test the explanations that recent historiography has provided. In the case of southwest Missouri, with its limited black population and traditional culture of violence, it is probable that lynching served two key functions. First, it ensured that suspected criminals were punished, should the legal system fail. Second, it served as the ultimate form of social control, as blacks were reminded of their subservient role in white society through their expulsion from Pierce City. African Americans in Pierce City left with the memory that the white community could and did dictate where they were allowed to live.[87]

Black crime was a reality in Pierce City. With a small African American population in their midst, the white citizens of Pierce City were well aware of the crimes committed within its city limits, and watched to see if criminal offenders were punished. As newspapers across the region, state, and nation published sensationalized accounts of black crime, in addition to accounts of mob violence, Pierce City citizens may well have not been able to separate law-abiding blacks from black criminal offenders. The acquittals of black suspects such as John Young and Andy Boyd may have led some southwest Missourians to believe that local judiciary was too weak and ineffective to uphold the law. The crimes of a handful may have condemned an entire race in the eyes of the southwest Missourians.

An examination of penitentiary records from 1879 to 1906 for individuals sentenced to the Missouri State Penitentiary from Lawrence County reveals much about race and crime. Prisoners were convicted of crimes such as grand larceny, burglary, rape, and murder. A distinct disparity emerges when the percentage of African American prisoners from Lawrence County sent to the penitentiary is compared against the percentage of the total African American population of the county.[88]

In Lawrence County, African Americans represented a small percentage of the population. Over three consecutive decades, 1880, 1890, and 1900, the black population dropped from 1.7 percent to 1.4 percent and finally 0.9 percent. Meanwhile, the percentage of blacks from Lawrence County sentenced to the Missouri State Penitentiary from 1879 to 1890 was 7.6 percent, where in the same time period the percentage of African Americans in Lawrence County dropped from 1.7 percent to 1.4 percent. Over a twenty-eight-year period, African Americans represented 17 percent of the prisoner population being sent to the penitentiary, at a time when the overall black population dropped from 1.7 percent in 1880 to 0.9 percent in 1900.[89]

Interesting trends emerge in the years prior to the lynchings in

Pierce City. In Lawrence County in 1897, the percentage of African Americans sent to the penitentiary was 25 percent, then dropped to 14 percent in 1898, then fell to 8 percent in 1899, but rose to 28.5 percent in 1900. The numbers reveal that the percentage of African American men found guilty and sentenced to the penitentiary was disproportionate to the percentage of blacks in the general population of the county. The high conviction rate, regardless of whether or not the men were guilty, could have led local whites to believe that African American men were generally inclined to commit crime and posed a serious threat to their families and to the community.[90] Will Godley was one of those men.

The lynching of Will Godley, who was later deemed innocent after his death, served two functions: to punish Godley for his transgressions and to send a message to the black community that criminal behavior would not be tolerated. Both Godley and Pete Hampton had previous scrapes with the law. Godley had been convicted of the rape of a sixty-year-old white woman. Hampton was a local criminal with a lengthy criminal record. The Peirce City Citizens Committee, in its public statement, noted that it was a commonly held belief that most crime in town was committed by African Americans, and because blacks refused to testify against one another, black criminals went unpunished.

Not only did the mob want to punish Godley, but the whites of Pierce City wanted to send a message to the local black community. In this most extreme form of social control, blacks were ordered from the town, never to return. The message was received. Blacks caught the last trains out of town or left in wagons loaded with what they could carry.

African Americans "who failed to maintain good relations with 'good local white folk' were extremely vulnerable to mob violence."[91] Both Will Godley and Pete Hampton, because of their criminal histories, were viewed with contempt by the local community. The two men, in addition to French Godley, had the misfortune of living in an area where "rural folkways . . . bred, and in turn, glorified mob violence."[92] In the southern Missouri Ozarks, an area racked by brutal guerrilla warfare, postwar vigilantism and a tradition of extralegal violence, it was almost a certainty that the murder of a young white woman would lead to further violence.

The lynching likely occurred because local law enforcement was weak, ineffective, and lacked the moral fortitude necessary to stop mob violence. Sheriff John Manlove, who was in Pierce City and witnessed the growing crowd, did not transfer Godley to the safety of Mt. Vernon. Marshal J. T. Johnson could have tried to face down the mob, but there is no indication that he did so. Aside from Sheriff Manlove, it appears that Pierce City had only a small number of full-time law enforcement officers, possibly three. City marshal J. T. Johnson worked during the day while two night watchmen tended to the city in the evening. In a town of an estimated two thousand inhabitants, the lawmen were spread thin. The lynching of Hughlett Hayden in nearby Monett in 1894 demonstrated the weakness of local law enforcement when Hayden was seized from the marshal transporting him to jail and lynched alongside the railroad tracks.

The lynching of Hayden set an example for Pierce City of how a community might rid itself of African Americans entirely. An article in the *Neosho Times* stated that the coroner's inquest into Hughlett Hayden's death declared he had died at the hands of unknown men.[93] Thus those who were complicit in Hayden's death were allowed to go free, doubtlessly emboldening the mob at Pierce City. Without Pierce City, Monett would have been an isolated event. Instead, Pierce City served as the turning point for the rest of the southern Missouri Ozarks, confirming the acceptability of lynching and expulsion. The mob had two choices as it crowded the town that August night. It could either let the legal system take its course or it could impose its own justice. After Pierce City's use of Monett's methods, the pattern was repeated over the next decade across southwest Missouri and in an adjacent county in Arkansas.[94]

In Pierce City, like much of the South, the murder of a young white woman was just cause for extralegal justice. Pierce City, perched on the border of the South, Midwest, and West participated in other regional patterns that "postbellum rural and working-class midwesterners and westerners, drawing on memories of the history of popular violence in their regions, revived the elastic doctrine of popular sovereignty as an antidote to changing practices of criminal justice in an era of economic and social consolidation."[95] Adherents of rough justice were often from the countryside as well as the working and middle classes.[96] Among the members of the mob, a later lawsuit revealed, were members of both classes. For example, J. A. LeGrande, one of the more prominent members of the mob, was a lumber and coal dealer in Pierce City. William Abbott, on the other hand, was a young working-class white man.[97]

Rough justice demanded punishment for criminals who engaged in serious criminal behavior. The murder of Gisele Wild, a young white woman at the prime of her youth, could not go unanswered by the citizens of Pierce City. Whites in Pierce City may have felt that the local African American community was culpable because it was unable to control the alleged criminals in its midst, thus the savage turn whites made against the black community as a whole. For many whites, lynching was the most effective response to African American crime. Nor could racist whites trust the legal system to punish criminal offenders.[98]

Will Godley was proof enough for any Pierce City citizen to believe that the law tolerated black rapists by handing out light sentences. With the legal process seemingly unable to prevent black on white crime, the mob lynched Godley and then expelled the black community, acting as a substitute for the law in order to accomplish what the legal system had failed to do.

The *Stotts City Sunbeam* ran an interview with Mr. Fisher of Pierce City, who claimed that because of the lynching, "white women could go their way without being molested and insulted by the black skunks, as heretofore."[99] The *St. Louis Post-Dispatch* reported that several Pierce City citizens claimed that its black residents had committed crimes similar to the murder of Gisele Wild for the last ten years prior to the lynching.[100] A letter to the editor of the *Post-Dispatch* offered an answer as to the cause of the lynchings, "When the negroes let white women alone there will be no 'nigger burning.'"[101]

While explanations for the lynchings may be numerous, explanations for the expulsion of Pierce City's African American community are not. Scholars of lynching have so far failed to provide adequate arguments that explain why the mob decided to expel the town's black population rather than be satisfied that the lynching would cow them into submission. Because Pierce City was not dependent on African American labor, it was far easier to expel the entire community than deal with continual black criminality.

The African Americans who were expelled were not newcomers to Pierce City. The victims of mob violence in southwestern Missouri were not young black transients who traveled from place to place looking for work. The men lynched in Pierce City, Will Godley, French

Godley, and Pete Hampton, were not black migrants or seasonal workers. French Godley was in his seventies and had lived in Pierce City since the late 1870s. Will Godley and Pete Hampton, both young men, were raised in Pierce City after they arrived from Kentucky with their families. In essence, the men lynched in Pierce City were part of an established, vibrant black community that lived in the midst of their white friends and neighbors.

For those who survived, life did not get easier after Pierce City. Many who fled settled in Joplin, which underwent its own struggle with mob violence in April 1903. America Godley and Beedie Hampton, according to census records, lived in the relative safety of Kansas City, Missouri, by 1920. Neither woman had remarried since their husbands had died at the hands of the Pierce City mob. Beedie Hampton died in Kansas City in 1950, forty-eight years after she was forced to leave Pierce City.[102] The fate of America Godley remains unknown. Sarah Godley, the widow of French Godley, remarried in 1909 in Kansas City.[103] She succumbed to heart disease in 1920.[104]

Gentry Bly, the pastor of Pierce City's black Baptist church, moved to Topeka, Kansas. After working as a janitor, he was once again a pastor by 1920.[105] His son Henry, who was eleven when he had to flee Pierce City, died in action as a cook during World War One.[106]

Mary Thomas, whose husband Reuben had written the *Empire* about their ill treatment in 1877, created a stir when she returned in 1902 to take care of property matters. Her arrival came in the wake of lawsuits filed by the widows of the men lynched and the *Empire* reported, "Our people are dead sore over the suits . . . and don't think that the negro should be permitted to stay any longer than to get in and transact her business and get out." If she were to stay long, "then after a while more of them would come and want to do the same, and directly we would have the whole caboodle back on us."[107] She did not stay. Her fate after her departure remains unknown.

As for the people of Pierce City, many of them lived long after the events of 1901. J. A. LeGrande, who figured prominently in the mob violence, died in 1923 at the age of sixty-six.[108] William Abbott died alone at forty-five from excessive drinking in 1916.[109] Sheriff John Manlove died at seventy-seven in 1917.[110] Mayor Washington Cloud died at the State Hospital Number Three for the Insane in Nevada, Missouri, in 1929.[111]

The Godley family faced one final tragedy. On the evening of December 25, 1902, in Pittsburg, Kansas, police officer Milt Hinkle came upon a noisy group of black men who had reportedly been drinking. The group, which included Gus, Mumpford, and Jess Godley, refused to comply with the officer's command to quiet down. Officer Hinkle then attempted to arrest Jess Godley, but Godley resisted. His companions stepped in to stop Officer Hinkle and a struggle ensued. Hinkle blew his whistle for backup and continued to desperately struggle with the group. During the fight, one of the men grabbed the officer's revolver and shot him in the back of the head, and then they fled. Officers coming to Hinkle's aid quickly caught the Godleys, but Hinkle died a short time later. Upon hearing the news of the officer's death, a mob formed. Just as in Joplin, others stepped forward to try and stop the mob, but to no avail. Mumpford Godley, identified by a young boy as the murderer, was dragged outside the city jail and lynched.[112]

The *Pittsburg Daily Headlight* reported, "The Godleys came here from Pierce City at the time the citizens of that place drove the colored people from their population." The Godleys, since coming to Pittsburg, worked at the Pittsburg Vitrified Brick Works.[113] Jess and Gus Godley escaped murder charges as the prosecutor lacked evidence that linked them to the murder of Officer Hinkle. They did, however, plead guilty to public intoxication.[114] Jess Godley was also charged with resisting an officer and fined fifty dollars.[115] Henry Godley, the father of Will Godley, Mumpford Godley, and Jess Godley, sued the city of Pittsburg over his son's death. He asked for ten thousand dollars in damages. The court case dragged on from 1903 until 1905 when the case was settled for four hundred dollars. The money was little consolation to a man who had lost two sons within the last two years. [116]

But in Pierce City, one Hampton reportedly lingered. In March 1902, a ghost was reported by several witnesses near the bridge on Elm Creek. The ghost was allegedly white and devoid of arms and legs. The town buzzed with speculation as to its origin. One of the most popular theories, the *Peirce City Weekly Empire* noted, was that "it is the spirit of the departed Pete Hampton, who left Peirce City so suddenly one night last August." Still, upon further investigation, the *Empire* concluded the source of the ghost was really the electric plant.[117]

THREE

Pierce City

The Lark and Godley Trials

As the embers of the firestorm burnt out, the bodies of Will Godley, French Godley, and Pete Hampton were laid to rest in Pierce City. Controversy over the cause of the lynchings continued to rage. Many residents of Pierce City and area newspapers blamed the outbreak of mob violence on the prevalence of black crime. According to the Pierce City Citizens' Committee, "Though it was widely suspicion[ed] that nearly all the crimes committed in Peirce City were perpetrated by negroes, it could not be fastened upon them because of the impossibility to get a negro to testify against another negro."[1] In this case, the legal system could test this claim of black culpability. Joe Lark would stand trial for the murder that Will Godley had already been lynched for.

The day after the lynchings, Lawrence County justice of the peace E. H. Lambert ordered Pierce City marshal J. T. Johnson to summon "six good and lawful men" to hold an inquest into the murder of Gisele Wild. On the morning of August 19, 1901, the coroner's jury and witnesses made their way to Pierce City's small town hall. The proceedings got off to a slow start and quickly adjourned when it became clear that not all of the witnesses could be examined in one day. The next day the coroner's jury traveled to Mt. Vernon to listen to Eugene Barrett.[2]

Barrett, the young black man seized with Will Godley by the mob only to be spared when he implicated Joe Lark as the murderer, provided the most complete testimony. He was one of two African American witnesses who were questioned in detail. The two statements Barrett provided constitutes the only surviving testimony from Pierce City's black community, but even they are filled with contradictions, further complicating the search for exactly what transpired on August 18.[3] Barrett recounted the day of the murder from the moment he went down to the depot where he joined a craps game in one of the boxcars. Both whites and blacks were present, playing for money. An African American named Will Favors joined the game with his pants rolled up to the knees.

After Favors went on a winning streak some of the players left, while the group that remained decided to go get beer, and proceeded to Hickey's where they bought the last quarter's worth of beer on tap. Barrett could not remember if Favors came with them. It was while the group stood outside Hickey's that Marshal Johnson was informed of the murder and raced off on his bicycle to investigate.

In his testimony, Eugene Barrett fingered not Lark but William Favors. Very little can be found about Favors as early employee records from the Frisco Railroad have not survived.[4] William Favors, sometimes referred to as Flavors, was a porter with the Frisco Railroad. On August 6, 1901, the last land lottery was held in El Reno, Oklahoma, bringing an influx of an estimated forty to fifty thousand people to the small town.[5] To deal with the large number of people traveling to El Reno on the Frisco Railroad, Barrett stated that the Frisco "used all the extra porters they could get." One of the porters on the line was injured and Favors was called upon to replace him on the run from Monett to Oklahoma City for a short period of time. Favors stopped off at Pierce City when "the other fellow went to work, and said that Mr. Quinn was going to give him a job on that end of the road."[6]

According to Barrett, William Favors had been waiting in Pierce City for two weeks when Gisele Wild was murdered. He indicated in his statement to the coroner's jury that Favors lodged with Lark and his wife, Lulu. Barrett stated, "When he [Favors] had money he stayed at Norris' place and slept at Monett. But he generally stayed at Joe Lark's."[7] The bloodhounds that were used in an attempt to track the murderer led officers to Joe Lark's home, which led many to believe Joe Lark was guilty, but the dogs may have well followed Favors's scent. Favors, according to Barrett, left Pierce City the morning after Gisele Wild's body was found. "He came down on a train from Monett and caught that train and I never seen him again until the next morning. He wanted me to loan him my cap and he said he was going to Oklahoma to bring back an excursion train."[8]

When asked what led him to believe that William Favors commit-ted the murder, Barrett responded, "Because he answered the descrip-tion, and the fact that he had his pants rolled up and he was dirty." His pants were "not exactly wet but they were damp," which possibly indicated he had crossed the creek near the scene of the murder. When questioned if anyone ever gave their opinion about Favors, Barrett responded, "Why I heard Pete Hampton and some of those colored people say that he was the colored man that answered that descrip-tion." After the murder was discovered, Favors talked about shaving off his mustache when fellow blacks told him that he matched the description of the man sitting on the railroad trestle near the murder scene. Favors was warned, "Why you are innocent and they will think you guilty if you shave."[9] Aside from Barrett's account, the testimony of additional witnesses offered little insight into the events of that fate-ful day, save that almost everyone recalled seeing a "strange negro" they did not recognize.

On August 22, 1901, three days after the lynchings, the coroner's jury reached its verdict. Having viewed Gisele Wild's body, examined the crime scene and listened to witness testimony, the jury reported, "the deceased came to her death by having her throat cut by a knife or some sharp instrument in the hands of some person or persons unknown to the jury, but from the evidence have reasons to believe that William Favors, Joe Lark and William Godley were implicated in the crime."[10]

The irony in the presumed guilt of William Godley is that the tes-timony given to the coroner's jury mentioned Godley only a few times in regard to his participation in the craps game held on the day of the murder and never in reference to any alleged role in the death of Gisele Wild. Having already been lynched, Will Godley was condemned for a second time, a conviction from which he could not escape.[11]

Joe Lark was also implicated in the murder, and not only because the bloodhounds allegedly tracked someone to his home from the murder scene. J. E. Garrett, along with Marshal J. T. Johnson, former marshal J. H. Vick, Aurora City marshal Connor, and two other indi-viduals searched the Lark premises because Lulu Lark, Joe's wife, had been heard telling individuals that Joe had suffered a nose bleed the day of the murder, leaving blood on his shirt. Suspicious that Lulu was protecting her husband, the party searched the home for evidence on Tuesday, August 20, two days after the murder. The men reportedly found that a shirt had been burned in the stove. In addition, according to Garrett, a knife was found in a bedroom that looked like it had blood on it. Aurora City marshal Connor took it into custody for examination.[12]

A Springfield reporter who visited Lark in jail described Lark as confident that he would be found innocent of Gisele Wild's murder. Lark declared, "I had nothing at all to do with the crime." He admitted he had been in Pierce City the day of the murder. Lark claimed he came in off the train that morning, proceeded to go downtown at eleven to run errands, then returned home at noon. His wife, Lulu, went to church while Lark laid down to rest. After his wife had returned, the couple heard the fire bell ringing but thought little of it.

Lark returned to the depot at nine o'clock that night to catch the train he was scheduled to work on and noticed there was a "great commotion going on." He spoke with several people whom he knew while waiting for the train, but none mentioned that he was suspected of involvement in the crime. Lark boarded the train and left town. On his return trip, another black railroad porter informed him that there was a warrant out for his arrest, and subsequently Lark was taken into custody at Springfield. Of this Lark said, "I am glad I was, for if I had landed in Pierce City, they would have killed me sure."[13]

If Joe Lark was confident he would be set free, his wife was not. Lulu Lark fled east in the ensuing chaos of the lynching and was staying with friends outside Springfield when a Springfield reporter interviewed her. "The woman seems to be uneasy and says but little except to answer direct questions." Still, others appeared to believe in Lark's innocence, including Greene County sheriff W. J. Bradshaw, "who believes the prisoner is innocent and that is the opinion of nearly all the people who have seen Lark."[14]

William Favors was arrested in Oklahoma City. He was released on a writ of habeas corpus, only to be immediately rearrested when a telegram from Missouri governor Dockery was received, stating that requisition papers were on their way to Oklahoma City for Favors.[15] The requisition order was reportedly issued on condition that if honored, Favors would be transferred to Kansas City for safekeeping.[16] Favors insisted that he could prove his innocence with five witnesses who saw him at the Pierce City depot from 10:10 A.M. until the fire bell rang to alert the town to the murder.[17] For the time being, it appeared that Governor Dockery wanted to avoid further bloodshed, despite the failure of the governor's office to publicly condemn the lynchings at Pierce City.

By August 26, witnesses from Pierce City were escorted to Springfield by Lawrence County prosecuting attorney Isaac V. McPherson, a Republican, in an attempt to identify Joe Lark as the man they had seen in the vicinity prior to Gisele Wild's death. On the day of the murder, William Roark and his wife had been traveling along the right of way next to the railroad track in the vicinity of the crime scene when they encountered a "ginger-cake negro going west." Mr. Roark and the man exchanged a few words and then continued on. Sheriff Bradshaw gathered thirteen men from Springfield's black community and placed Lark in among them for the witnesses to identify. William Roark failed to recognize any of them as the man he and his wife encountered.

Mrs. Roark identified two of the Springfield men as similar look-ing to the man she and her husband had met, but did not positively identify either of them. Major Irwin P. Linzee, who had been riding on the train's caboose the day of the murder when it had stopped on the tracks near the murder scene, was called next. Like the Roarks, Lindsey recalled seeing a "ginger-cake negro" pass by and look him directly in the face, but failed to find him in the lineup. Lindsey pointed at Lark and said, "That man I have seen frequently in Peirce City, but I did not see him on the day of Miss Wilds' murder." At that, a roar of elation came from the blacks in the line-up, Joe Lark reportedly "the happiest in the bunch."[18]

Prosecuting Attorney McPherson was not satisfied. He told a reporter that there was other evidence against Joe Lark and that he would hold him until a thorough investigation was completed.[19] To add to the continuing drama, the following day Frisco employees in Springfield reported a rumor that Carl Wild, Gisele's brother, was responsible for the murder of his sister. They insisted he would be arrested in a short matter of time. His alleged motive was to collect on a life insurance policy taken out on Gisele. A source from Pierce City, however, called to inform the paper that there was no truth to the story.[20]

Pierce City resident Nicholas J. Perrott was in Joplin shortly after the lynchings and gave an interview to the *Joplin Daily Globe* in which he weighed in on the culpability of Carl Wild. When asked about the accusations, Perrott replied, "Do I think there is any ground for the statement that Miss Wild's brother killed her? Well, not by a jug full. That report was started by somebody with a view to allure the attention of the people from the negroes." He added, "Why, young Wild is a mere boy, 13 years old, I believe, and the young lady who was killed was about 20. It would have been impossible. That part of the story is fake pure and simple." The citizenry of Pierce City agreed. The accusations against Carl were quickly forgotten and attention remained on Joe Lark and William Favors.[21]

One of the area's most racist newspapers, the *Stotts City Sunbeam*, vented, "We will bet a doughnut to a nickle that Joe Lark, the nigger porter, who has been held at Springfield supposed to be implicated in the murder of Miss Wild at Peirce City will go free as there is being so much 'monkey business' about getting him tried. Lawrence county officers ought to stick to it until they either prove him innocent or guilty."[22] The *Sunbeam* did not have long to wait.

The trial commenced with a successful request for change of venue after his attorney argued Lark could not receive a fair trial before Justice of the Peace E. H. Lambert. Lambert had overseen the inquest into Gisele Wild's death in August. Still, he was unable to escape depositions taken during the coroner's inquest on the day after Gisele Wild's murder.[23]

In mid-November, Lawrence County sheriff John Manlove arrived in Springfield to escort Joe Lark to Mt. Vernon to stand trial for the murder of Gisele Wild. Lark may have been apprehensive about his arrival in Mt. Vernon given Manlove's failure to protect Will Godley. Their trip, however, was uneventful.[24]

Lark's defense attorney, Willis G. Robertson, was eager for the trial to begin. At the age of twenty-six Robertson put down his plow to study law. After three years, the Missouri native was admitted to the Dallas County bar and later served two terms as the county's prosecuting attorney before he moved to Springfield. There he became involved in politics and ran as a Republican candidate for the U.S. House of Representatives in 1898.[25] Although he did not win the election, Robertson's reputation as a skilled attorney kept him busy. Now, almost fifty-one, he found himself up against thirty-three-year-old Lawrence County prosecuting attorney Isaac V. McPherson.

McPherson, a rising star among Republicans in southwest Missouri, attended nearby Marionville College before he was admitted to the Lawrence County bar in 1891. He was in his first year of office when the murder of Gisele Wild occurred. Now as the trial drew near the people of Pierce City looked to McPherson to convict Joe Lark.[26] He was assisted by attorney and former prosecutor Joseph French of Pierce City. Bernhard Wild, father of the slain girl, had hired French to assist McPherson.[27] French, a native of Marion County, Illinois, moved with his parents to Missouri in 1874. He studied law while teaching school and settled in Pierce City after being admitted to the local bar.[28]

As Lark was escorted to the newly built Lawrence County jail, he may have noticed the inscription over the entrance, which read, "The Way of the Transgressor Is Hard." Although Lark professed he was not guilty, there were many who doubted his claim of innocence.[29] The jury responsible for determining Lark's fate was mostly made up of young farmers from the northern section of Lawrence County, rather the southern section where Pierce City was located. Of the twelve men, nine were Republicans and the remaining three were Democrats. The oldest member of the jury was reportedly forty-five and the youngest only twenty-two.[30]

Jefferson Drake, a blacksmith and Indiana native, was forty-two. Robert Knox, born in Ireland, lived outside of Mt. Vernon with his widowed mother and siblings on their family farm. Finis A. Bell, John Seneker, and George R. Fowler were all married farmers in their thirties. Missouri native Wiley Pendleton worked as a zinc miner. James T. Hinkle, only thirty-six, was a widower. L. J. Fortner lived at home with his parents and siblings in Lincoln Township.[31] Lawrence County assessor and carpenter C. F. Porter was also seated on the jury.[32]

Overseeing the trial was Judge Henry C. Pepper, a native of Kentucky, and a graduate of Cumberland University in Lebanon, Tennessee. Pepper traveled westward, first to Kansas, then to Holt County, Missouri, before settling in McDonald County, Missouri, located in the extreme southwest corner of the state. There he practiced law and became involved in the local Democratic Party. Pepper served two terms as prosecuting attorney before moving to neighboring Barry

County. There he was elected circuit judge of the Twenty-fourth District which covered Lawrence, McDonald, Barry, and Newton Counties. When he died, it was noted that Pepper "distinguished himself a scholar and impartial man while on the bench."[33]

As the trial got underway, there were few new revelations. Many of the witnesses repeated the testimony that they gave at the coroner's inquest held in August, although some of the details were far more graphic. The undertaker who prepared Gisele Wild's body for burial, Mr. Seifert, testified that "her head was cut half off, a deep gash on top of her head, the skin broken over her right eye, and blue finger prints on her left arm." Gisele Wild had not just been murdered; she had been brutally attacked by her killer.[34]

A forensic expert, Dr. C. K. Snodgrass from Washington University in St. Louis, testified about the shirt found in Joe Lark's home. After performing both "microscopic and spectroscopic" examinations of the shirt, his tests showed that the alleged blood stains on the shirt were iron stains. He could not be certain, however, because the shirt had been laundered after it was stained and thus could not be properly tested.

The prosecution fought a losing battle. Aside from circumstantial evidence which failed to place Joe Lark at the scene of the crime, McPherson had little else to fall back on. He attempted to sway the jury by arguing that the bloodhounds called in from Barton County had tracked a man to Joe Lark's house. What McPherson did not tell the jury was that the hounds had arrived several hours after the murder and that they were "started from the spot where the [unidentified] negro was seen sitting on the bridge," not at the murder scene. Several witnesses, however, did testify that the hounds were put on the scent at the bridge, not the murder scene, and that they repeatedly lost the trail. If it was not clear to the jury that the state had a weak case, it was clear to others.[35]

According to the *Springfield Leader-Democrat,* "The officers of Mount Vernon have considerable sympathy for Lark since the evidence of the state is in, but they do not express their feelings with much freedom. The prevailing prejudice of the people about Pierce City makes the county officials cautious in their deportment." Not one to rest on his laurels, defense attorney Willis G. Robertson worked hard to establish a credible alibi for Lark, going so far as to put both Lark and his wife, Lulu, on the witness stand.[36] Surprisingly, Pierce City mayor and attorney Washington Cloud took the stand for the defense to "impeach the character of ex-City Marshal Guthrie," who had "sworn for the state that he found tracks around Lark's house where the bloodhounds ran." Guthrie, Cloud proclaimed, "had been mixed up in politics a good deal and his reputation was not good."[37] Cloud's decision to testify for the defense may been prompted by the opportunity to gain revenge against a political foe, not from the desire to help an African American escape the hangman's noose.

If the residents of Mt. Vernon doubted Joe Lark's guilt, the people of Pierce City did not. Groups of Pierce City men gathered outside the courthouse in "small groups" talking about the trial in low voices. Their presence did not go unnoticed. The *Leader-Democrat* warned, "The danger of mob violence has not passed away, and if the negro should be acquitted, Judge Lynch may demand another victim for the murder of Miss Wild." Mt. Vernon's small African American population stayed off of the streets during the trial. It was rumored that if Lark was acquitted, Sheriff John Manlove would help Lark escape into the woods outside of Mt. Vernon as "Lark is a stout, active man, and once outside of the town he will be hard to catch should a mob attempt pursuit."[38]

Lark was not the only African American that drew the ire of local whites. In nearby Monett, African American porters on the Frisco Railroad demanded the company allow them to stay in Springfield, Missouri, and Neodesha, Kansas, after "the bitter hatred of [Monett's] populace for the colored race revived." According to the *Springfield Leader-Democrat*, "The citizens of Monett, especially the lower classes and toughs, have again become ferocious and are terrifying the negroes."

After a group of white men threatened to lynch them in Monett, several porters asked J. A. Quinn, superintendent of the Frisco's Western Division, for help. Quinn, however, did nothing. In response, the porters vowed that if they were not allowed to stay at Springfield or Neodesha, they "will all quit the service."[39] Monett mayor J. H. Farron refuted the claims of the *Leader-Democrat*, "There was no trouble, nor even anticipated trouble, and if you will kindly retract the same you will confer a favor on your many friends here, as we believe you are misinformed and would not knowingly misrepresent us in the premises."[40]

The editor of the *Leader-Democrat,* however, did not back down. He asserted that the porters "not only made the charges stated in the [previous] article, but hold to them." The editor snorted, "The above letter from the mayor is all right, but it does not explain whether the negroes are going to be allowed to lay over in Monett without fearing for their lives, which is really the point in question." Unfortunately issues of the *Springfield Republican* are missing during this time period and cannot shed further light on the situation. It is notable, however, that because Springfield served as regional headquarters for the Frisco Railroad, reporters would have had easy access to Frisco employees, including porters.[41]

The trial ended with a whimper rather than the bang that many anticipated. Several women seated in the packed courtroom listened intently as McPherson, French, and Robertson gave their closing statements to the jury. Joe Lark sat impassively "with a great deal of composure" and showed "no signs of weakness." Carl Wild, brother of the victim, watched the proceedings alone as the rest of his family "went home after giving their testimony."[42] The jury, however, did not return a verdict until the next morning.

There were very few people in the courtroom at 8:25 on the morning of November 26, 1901, when Joe Lark was declared innocent. The jury was divided eight to four in favor of acquittal until early in the morning when the four hold-outs joined the majority. After the verdict was read, Joe Lark "was so overjoyed that he could hardly stand on his feet." Sheriff Manlove promptly escorted him from the courthouse to the depot where Lark was placed on a train bound for Kansas City. Gisele Wild's father and brother followed the two men to the depot, but "made no attempt to do any violence." Some citizens expressed their satisfaction with the jury's decision and felt "that it is the only one that could be rendered according to the law and the facts."[43]

Others, however, were outraged by Lark's acquittal. The *Peirce City Democrat* sneered, "Our citizens are greatly disappointed in the verdict of the jury in the Lark case and are firmly convinced that Joe Lark was one of the parties who murdered Miss Wild." The people of Pierce City "feel there has been some very strange work done and will not forget, but watch." The *Democrat* bitterly observed, "Lark's color saved him. Had a white man stood in his shoes the jury would have hung

Lawrence County
prosecuting attorney
Isaac V. McPherson.
*Courtesy of The State
Historical Society of
Missouri.*

him without a doubt. Strange, isn't it? You can no more tell what kind
of a verdict some juries will return than you can tell where the North
Pole is located."

Citizens joined with the newspapers to express their bewilderment
at the trial's outcome. One woman from Pierce City remarked she
"would like to see the intelligent (?) jury that set Lark at liberty. She is
curious what kind of an animal they look like." The editor of the
Democrat opined that "they resemble the ass." The *Peirce City Weekly
Empire* joined the *Democrat* in denouncing the jury and claimed, "All
of the evidence found in and around this city pointed very strongly in
Lark as the man, and it is going to be mighty hard for our citizens to
believe anything else, and it is just such verdicts as this which causes
mob violence."[44]

The *Stotts City Sunbeam* sneered, "He [Lark] will no doubt go now
for the fields as he well knows the feelings of the people of Pierce City
and Monett toward him and his guilt. He will not likely attempt to

Judge Henry C. Pepper.
*Courtesy of The State
Historical Society of
Missouri.*

take his old run as porter on a train through Pierce City."[45] Will Favors
was released after Lark's acquittal when it became clear that there was
insufficient evidence against him.[46] When informed he would be
released, Favors incredulously asked, "For de Lawd sake, is dat so?" He
then declared upon his release he would be a "good niggah" while
showing off his Bible and hymnal.[47] It is unclear where Joe Lark and
William Favors went after their release. But it is certain they did not
stay in Lawrence County, Missouri.[48]

The *Springfield Leader-Democrat* summed up the Lark trial best:

> The prompt trial of Joe Lark and the evident willingness of the
> negro to go before a jury without any technical dodges did much
> to overcome th[e] prejudices against him. Had the prisoner
> employed a half-dozen lawyers and begun to fight for a delay or a
> change of venue, the sentiment of the people might have been
> greatly exasperated. Lark's course was the best one possible for his
> own safety. His courage in demanding a speedy trial in Lawrence
> County made many people believe the negro was innocent.[49]

The trial of Joe Lark illustrates that despite the flaws of the Missouri judicial system and the prevailing racist attitudes of the day, African Americans were not always automatically at a disadvantage in the courtroom. Court officials sought to ensure that Joe Lark was not legally lynched by selecting potential jurors from the northern half of Lawrence County, not from "the southern district of the county along the railroad, the greatest hostility of feeling being in the towns of Peirce City, Aurora, and Monett."[50]

The small groups of Pierce City men who gathered around the courthouse and whispered of vigilante justice reaffirmed the decision of county officials to obtain a jury from the less-inflamed populace of northern Lawrence County. The threat of violence permeated the tense atmosphere as the citizens of Pierce City had already proven themselves capable of dispensing extralegal justice. Aware that a potential mob waited outside the courtroom doors, it is plausible that the jury reached a unanimous verdict earlier in the night than reported, but withheld their decision until the early morning to avoid a riot.[51]

The men who sat on the jury failed to succumb to racist beliefs of the day. It was notable that the four jurors who first held out for a conviction changed their minds and joined their fellow jurors in a unanimous verdict of not guilty. The decision to change their minds prevented a hung jury and avoided a new trial for Joe Lark. Even more notable is that the men who found Joe Lark innocent were white farmers who likely did not interact often with African Americans on a daily basis. The jurors could have easily accepted the circumstantial evidence and convicted Joseph Lark, but unlike their counterparts at Pierce City they acknowledged the rule of law. Thus both Lawrence County and Joe Lark were spared the emotional upheaval of a retrial.

Ironically, it might have been the thoroughness of the mob's work that saved Lark. The fate of a lone black man paled in comparison to the mass expulsion of Pierce City's African American community. Additionally, because blacks in Pierce City were not a vital segment of the area's labor force, the local economy did not suffer as a result. This perhaps allowed white anger to cool off by the time Lark was acquitted.

Lark's social position might also have helped save him. In *The Promise of the New South* Edward Ayers argues that lynchings often targeted black transients and strangers.[52] Exactly when Lark arrived in Pierce City remains unknown. But as a railroad porter, part of the black economic elite in rural areas, he was a well-known figure in Pierce City. The fact that Lark was not a transient may well have saved his life when he came before a jury. As the *Joplin Daily Globe* put it, "It is not at all reasonable that such a man as the Frisco porter would have any hand in a crime of that atrocious character."[53]

The trial was followed by area newspapers. The *Joplin Daily Globe* was one of the many who reported the latest developments in the case. When Lark was found not guilty, the jury's decision may have struck some of the paper's readers as just another example of a weak, slow, ineffective legal system. The tedious, bureaucratic legal system had allowed passion to subside by the time Lark went to trial and once again a black criminal was permitted to go free.

Racial attitudes, however, may have shifted by 1905. In that year, John Seneker, one of the jurors during Lark's trial, served on the jury that convicted Edward Bateman, an African American hotel porter, of raping a white woman in nearby Aurora. It was later revealed, however, Bateman was involved in a consensual relationship with the woman. Despite a desperate legal battle to save his life, Bateman was legally executed in Mt. Vernon in August 1906.[54]

Another courtroom battle was fought not long after Lark's trial, one that surprised many in Pierce City. Local authorities had taken no action against members of the mob. In some cases, lynch mob members were prosecuted for their participation in Virginia and Georgia.[55] But this was not the case in southwestern Missouri. After the lynching in Pierce City, there was no mention of prosecution against members of the mob. A few newspaper editorials called for prosecution, but they were a vocal minority, and no legal action was taken by local authorities.

After John Rodgers, one of the men who allegedly took part in the Pierce City lynchings, moved to Carthage in nearby Jasper County, the widows of French Godley, Will Godley, and Pete Hampton eagerly seized upon this newly opened avenue for legal recourse. In late 1902, Sarah Godley, America Godley, and Beedie Hampton filed suit in Jasper County, Missouri, against several alleged mob participants. Each widow sought five thousand dollars as compensation for the death of their loved ones.[56]

Sarah Godley's case was selected as the first to go to trial. It was miraculous that the widows were able to bring suit at all. As the *Joplin Daily Globe* speculated, "This case probably would have never been brought had none of the gentlemen who were made defendants not left Lawrence county. Had all of them remained there it would have been necessary to bring suit in that county which would not have been practical on account of the prejudice which existed there against the negro."[57]

At first, the suit was filed against twenty-one individuals, among them four members of the Tate family, two from the Decker family, Harrison Rogers, Edward Greer, and Robert Hamilton. Prior to the trial, the lawyers for both the plaintiff and the defendants met at the law office of Thomas Carlin, former editor of the *Peirce City Weekly Empire*, to take depositions. Attorney John Taylor represented Sarah Godley, while Pierce City attorneys Joseph French and R. H. Davis represented the defendants.[58]

Norman Hudson and Edgar Hayden, young men who admitted that their occupation consisted of loafing, both testified that Harrison Rogers was with them on a camping trip on the Cowskin River in McDonald County, Missouri, the day of the lynching. Herbert Vance, who also went on the camping trip, backed up the testimony of Hudson and Hayden as to the whereabouts of Harrison Rogers. John Taylor, in his cross-examinations of the three young men, repeatedly asked if they had spoken with the defendant's attorneys about what to say during the depositions. All three answered that they had not, but Taylor had his suspicions.

Walter Tate, one of the twenty-one defendants, was the subject of the next depositions taken. Henry Mollering testified that Tate was with him and several other men who set out for Neosho to look for Gisele Wild's murderer. After taking the morning train to Neosho on the day of the murder, some of the men, including Tate and Mollering, walked from Neosho to Granby by wagon road to look for the culprit.

Abe Casey gave similar testimony. He claimed, "Did not exactly anticipate any trouble between the whites and blacks except the man who did the work, did not think the colored people would be run out of town." The town, Casey recalled, was quiet when he returned that night. He watched as one of the bodies was retrieved from the ruins of French Godley's house. He assumed, from its size, that it was French. He remembered, "One side looked like a cannon ball had went through and came out on the other." Both Abe Casey and Ross Cappock also recalled that William Guthrie, another defendant, went with them on their futile search for the murderer.[59]

As the depositions continued, witness testimony did not waver. According to the witnesses, none of the defendants had been in Pierce City during the lynching. Joseph Kuntz, who, along with his wife, testified that defendant William Abbott had been at their home during the violence had this to say, "I know a good many people about Peirce City. I would swear that I did not know a soul in that crowd, did not want to know them, to tell the truth." Kuntz remarked that, "After the thing was over I thought of the matter and was glad that I did not know anybody in the crowd. I do not mean to swear that there were no Peirce City people in the crowd. I did not examine them closely with a view of finding if there was anybody I knew."

According to Carrie Miner, her father, Charles Decker, never left home the night of the lynching. Decker's neighbor, Rady Crawford, backed up her testimony. W. H. Owen's father, Samuel Owen, swore his son was not a member of the mob. He and his son, Owen testified, watched from his porch as three homes in the black section of town burned. They then went to bed. W. H. Owen's brother, however, admitted he and his brother watched as Will Godley was lynched by the mob, but then they returned home.[60]

Defendants Taylor Tate, William Tate, Ed Greer, and Frank Sheets also had relatives and neighbors who testified they were not in the mob that night. William Abbott and William Guthrie were meagerly represented in testimony by friends, family, and neighbors. But none of the depositions helped distance J. A. LeGrande and John Rodgers from the mob. By the time the case reached trial, four men remained defendants from the original twenty-one: William Abbott, J. A. LeGrande, John Rodgers, and William Guthrie.[61]

William Abbott, twenty-six years old at the time of the lynching, worked as a day laborer, presumably for his father, a brick manufacturer. Born in Tennessee, he lived at home in Pierce City with his parents. J. A. LeGrande, a coal dealer, was born in Virginia in 1856. He may have carried childhood memories of the Civil War with him on his westward trek to Missouri. His contemporary, William Guthrie, was born in Illinois in early 1855. Like LeGrande, Guthrie had a respectable job, as he listed his occupation as "engineer, stationary." John Rodgers, the man whose decision to move to Jasper County sparked the lawsuit, was a married thirty-nine-year-old grocer born in Alabama.[62]

Three of the men who went to trial were southerners by birth, while one was a northerner. One, Abbott, was single. The other three were married with children. Three of the men held well-to-do jobs, while Abbott, the youngest of the quartet, was a mere day laborer.

The first stage of the lawsuit got off to a rough start for Sarah Godley. During the deposition process in Pierce City, plaintiff attorney John Taylor called for only one witness to give testimony at a time, as the rule of law directed. Defense attorney Joseph French objected and demanded that all the witnesses remain in the room, contrary to the law. Notary Thomas Carlin sided with French.[63] All of the witnesses were allowed to stay and listen to the testimony given by others. Presumably, the witnesses could alter their own testimony based on the previous accounts. In an earlier failed motion to suppress the pretrial depositions, plaintiff attorney John Taylor alleged that "refusing to have the said witnesses separated was peculiarly unjust and unfair to the plaintiff."[64] His co-counsel, George Grayston, sneered that an attorney who believed in his witnesses would not have objected to the rule.[65]

The trial began on February 18, 1903, in Judge Hugh Dabbs's division of the Jasper County Circuit Court. His appointment to the bench was the result of hard work and perseverance. Born in Madison County, Arkansas, Dabbs and his family moved to Rocky Comfort, Missouri, after the death of his father. His childhood was spent working on his mother's farm, but his aspirations carried him from the fields of McDonald County, Missouri, to the University of Missouri in Columbia. Dabbs graduated with a law degree and returned home where he served one term as the Democratic prosecuting attorney of McDonald County. In 1901, he moved to Joplin where he was appointed to the Jasper County Circuit Court. Upon his death in 1930, Dabbs was remembered as "one of the best legal minds in Southwest Missouri."[66]

Sarah Godley was the first witness to take the stand. The *Joplin Daily Globe* remarked upon her aged appearance and her apparent illiteracy. The *Globe* reporter failed to take into account that despite being only fifty-seven years old, Sarah Godley had lived a hard life. Born into slavery, she was accustomed to hard work with little reward. She helplessly watched as a mob killed her husband and son and then fled into the darkness as all that she knew burned to the ground behind her. It was no wonder Sarah Godley looked old. She applied to sue as a poor person, having little to her name.[67] Unfortunately, the newspaper did not elaborate on her eyewitness account of the mob's actions. The reporter only noted that she stated she had recognized the four defendants in the mob that night and that French Godley had been her only means of financial support.[68]

Another black witness, Shedrack "Dock" Brinson, the neighbor of French and Sarah Godley, testified. He stated that he saw Abbott and LeGrande in the mob, as well as other men who were not defendants, the night of the lynching. Brinson lived, according to the *Globe*, in Joplin at the time of the trial. Charles Hunter, another black survivor, took the stand. Hunter, Pierce City's eloquent schoolmaster, had found a job teaching at a Joplin colored school after he fled Pierce City. He, like Brinson, was near the Godley residence at the time of the attack. Hunter testified he saw LeGrande at the head of crowd and that he was holding either a club or a gun in his hand.[69]

Next, one of French Godley's sons testified, traveling from the relative safety of Kansas City to do so. The son's name was not given, but it may have been Joel Godley. French's other son, Wiley, stayed in the area after the lynching. He stated he saw the mob at Pete Hampton's house and watched as it approached French Godley's home in search of Pete. He then wisely hid in a nearby basement as the mob drew closer, but was able to hear LeGrande say, "Help, Mord, help." He may have been hit by one of his comrade's stray bullets during the fracas.

French's son was then asked if he had attempted to kill John Rodgers in revenge for the lynching. The previous summer, an assailant had fired at Rodgers through the window of Rodgers's home, but failed to hit his target. The gunman fled and was never apprehended. The witness denied he had attempted to kill Rodgers or made threats about traveling to Pierce City to kill members of the mob.[70]

Will Young, a black lime-kiln worker, testified he watched the mob lynch Will Godley. He then went home, which was near Pete Hampton's residence, and watched the mob call for Pete to come out. After Pete failed to appear, Young then bravely followed the mob "at a safe distance" to the home of French Godley. It was there, he said, that he heard

LeGrande's voice above the din of the throng. LeGrande had run into Young earlier after the discovery of Gisele Wild's body and, according to Young, asked Young who murdered the young woman. Young responded he did not know, to which LeGrande reportedly replied, "If you know you had better tell, for if we find out who committed the act it will go as hard with you as any of them." After such a threat, it is surprising that Young was bold enough to follow the mob.[71]

Jessie Hampton, Sarah Godley's sister-in-law, was next on the witness stand. She testified that the morning after the lynching, she was with Sarah Godley at the ruins of the Godley home when LeGrande walked up. He allegedly told the two women, in sight of the charred bodies still in the ashes, "They called for Pete Hampton and as soon as they called shots were fired at the crowd and the crowd returned the fire. They did not intend to kill French Godley; they intended to kill Pete Hampton." Hampton noted that LeGrande's statement led her to believe that LeGrande was a member of the mob. After her testimony, the plaintiff's attorney rested their case.[72]

The defense immediately filed a demurrer. During testimony, it was divulged that both Sarah and French Godley had been previously married to other individuals. The defense pounced upon this. They argued that there was no evidence that Sarah Godley had divorced her first husband, thus she was not legally married to French Godley. As a result, the case did not have a leg to stand on. But Judge Dabbs overruled the defense's demurrer. He pointed out, "in order to sustain their motion it would be necessary to show that one or both had been married before, that the husband of Mrs. Godley was still living and that no divorce had been granted." The court then adjourned for the day.[73]

The next day, when court resumed, the defendants took the stand. LeGrande was the first to take the witness chair. He immediately claimed he was at the Godley home in an attempt to "prevent any harm coming to the old people." LeGrande recounted the day of the lynching. He spent most of the day of the lynching unloading lumber. Later that evening he was sworn in as a deputy marshal to "preserve the peace and quiet of the city."

After LeGrande retrieved his rifle from home, he returned in time to find a mob of people in the city streets. He claimed he did not know there was a black man in the crowd until he saw Will Godley strung up over the balcony of the Lawrence Hotel. LeGrande heard a voice call out, "Let's go get Pete Hampton." The mob surged in the direction of Hampton's home. LeGrande followed. He allegedly pleaded with the leader of the mob to not harm the "old people." The mob leader then pointed a gun in LeGrande's face and retorted, "Who in the hell is running this affair?" LeGrande backed off, and then telephoned the "light plant to turn out the lights to prevent the negroes from killing members of the mob." His phone call did not go unheeded.[74]

The previous day's testimony indicated that the city lights were off at the time of the attack on the Godley home. The *Globe* reported, "All the witnesses testified that there was no moon on the night of the killing and that there were no electric lights close." The oil used to burn the Godley home provided all the light the mob needed to view their ghastly work. [75]

LeGrande had only a few more things to say while on the witness stand. He declared that he had always been on friendly terms with the black citizens of Pierce City. In fact, LeGrande recalled, Sarah Godley had carried his daughter home after she was thrown by a horse. Lastly, he professed, he did not know a single soul in the mob that night. When questioned where he thought the members of mob had come from, he expressed his belief that they came from "the east." LeGrande undoubtedly referred to Monett.[76]

Stonewall Pritchett, one of Sarah Godley's attorneys, cross-examined LeGrande. When asked how he planned to stop a mob with only a handful of recently sworn in deputy marshals, the defendant replied, "Persuasion." LeGrande denied threatening Will Young at the lime kiln. He also insisted he had not spoken with Jessie Hampton or Sarah Godley as they stood near the charred ruins of Mrs. Godley's home. LeGrande repeated that he did not have a gun while at the Godley residence. Nor did he call for Pete Hampton to come out as witnesses for the plaintiff testified.

LeGrande was not the only slippery defendant to take the stand. John Rodgers swore he was at home the night of the lynching. Several witnesses were introduced to support his claim. William Abbott did the same. The plaintiffs produced Robert Hampton, the brother of Pete Hampton, as a rebuttal witness. Hampton stated he was in city hall when Abbott stormed in with gun in hand. Abbott, he said, pointed the weapon at Eugene Barrett. The defendant then allegedly bellowed, "There is the ———, shoot him!"[77]

William Guthrie, who, like LeGrande was sworn in as a deputy marshal the night of the lynching, stated he was only at the Godley residence to protect them from harm. Under cross-examination, Guthrie asserted that intervention "would have been of no use; that there was a crowd of several hundred men there and that it would have been impossible for a few deputy marshals to do anything with them." Just after a shot was fired from the second-story window of the Godley home, Guthrie was hit in the arm by a bullet, and left to find a doctor. He did not see the gun battle and fire that ensued. Lastly, witnesses testified as to the good character of the defendants and the poor reputation of black witnesses Will Young and Robert Hampton. Final arguments followed.

Defense attorney Joseph French stood up from his chair to deliver the first closing argument. Although it was a civil case that the jury was participating in, French said, there were overtones of a criminal case. If any of the four defendants paid even one dollar in damages to Sarah Godley, he mused, they could then be held criminally liable for the death of French Godley and Pete Hampton. Besides, French asked the jury, were they "going to believe the testimony of crap shooting negroes or that of good reputable citizens." He also emphasized that French Godley, at the time of his death, was unable to earn a living. Attorney French then coldly added, "Sarah Godley . . . was better off by reason of his having been killed." Plaintiff attorney John Taylor and defense attorney R. H. Davis followed.[78]

Sarah Godley was represented by Stonewall Pritchett, a Missouri native and graduate of Vanderbilt Law School. His father, Joseph H. Pritchett of Virginia, was a well-known Methodist Episcopal preacher who founded Pritchett College on the banks of the Missouri River in the heart of Missouri's Little Dixie region. After graduating from Vanderbilt, Stonewall Pritchett returned to Fayette, Missouri, and served two terms as city attorney and one term as a Democratic state representative. He was hailed as a "young man of fine ability and more than ordinary eloquence."[79]

As Pritchett delivered the closing argument he stalked the courtroom packed with people from Pierce City. There were also a sizable number of African Americans in the audience who had once called

Joplin attorney Stonewall Pritchett. *Courtesy of The State Historical Society of Missouri.*

the town home. Pritchett turned on defendant LeGrande, seated close to the jury box. They locked eyes. Pritchett thundered, "Why did you not attempt to protect the colored people from the mob by requesting the mob go to their homes?" He then turned on William Abbott and growled, "Abbott, why didn't you remain at home and protect your own family?" It was, the *Globe* remarked, "an excellent address."[80] The jury faced a decision.

The next morning, on February 20, 1903, the all-white jury reached its verdict. It found in favor of the defendants after only "a few ballots." Sarah Godley, the widows of Pete Hampton and Will Godley, and the former black residents of Pierce City had lost. Had she won, the *Globe* speculated, "many other cases of a similar nature would be brought."[81] Despite their loss, Godley's attorneys immediately filed a motion for a new trial. The motion alleged errors in the jury instructions, juror misconduct, and racial prejudice. Jurors Henry Sapp and W. A. Brittain, despite instructions from the court not to do so, spoke about the case outside of the jury room. In regard to racial prejudice, the motion stated "that the verdict against her was the result of passion and prejudice against her because of the fact she is a negro, that her husband was a negro and that her witnesses were all negroes."[82]

But Judge Dabbs ruled that the trial had been fair. No new trial was necessary. The cases filed by America Godley and Beedie Hampton were subsequently dismissed.[83] The not-guilty verdict embodied a particularly extreme mechanism of social control. It was a message to the black community that the senseless killing of blacks was acceptable to certain members of the white community.

Sarah Godley's case, unlike that of Joe Lark, is unique as her lawsuit is one of a few known cases of a black victim pursuing legal action against her attackers.[84] But Sarah Godley had little left to lose when she chose to pursue justice in the courtroom. Her husband and son were dead and her home in Pierce City gone. Her bold effort to seek justice must have disconcerted whites. A victory for Sarah Godley would have opened the floodgate for lawsuits by other blacks who had lost their homes and property in Pierce City. Whites would have then paid a heavy price for lynching and expelling the black community from town. It was a price they did not have to pay.

FOUR

Joplin

"Have Mercy on My Soul"

On the afternoon of April 26, 1903, Deputy Marshal Frank Sowder sat in the Joplin, Missouri, city jail reading his copy of "Correct Dress for Policemen." He was assigned to lock-up duty. A murmur of voices floated in on the early spring breeze. Sowder sat up. The murmurs grew louder. Alarmed, Sowder grabbed his rifle, trying to think of who was in lock-up that "the people wanted to lynch." He was fearful that "Joplin was to be the scene of another necktie party." The sound of voices became more distinct as the crowd drew closer to the jail. Suddenly, a large group of almost one hundred women with parasols in hand marched into the jail, accompanied by a male escort. A lone voice called out, "Mr. Policeman, we want to see the place where the mob broke into the jail."

Relieved, Sowder put away his gun. The women had traveled all the way from Columbus, Kansas. Sowder gave the women a tour of the jail where just eleven days earlier Thomas Gilyard, a young black migrant, had been dragged from his cell and hanged just a short distance away. The visitors insisted on seeing the spot where the mob had broken through the jail wall to seize their victim. The ladies thanked Sowder profusely for his time, then departed, satisfied. Deputy Marshal Sowder returned to his chair and remarked of the visit, "Gee, but it's lucky we had this here shack scrubbed out last week."[1]

It might have been the only peaceful mob in the history of Joplin. The town, founded in 1873, built its fortunes upon the lead and zinc deposits beneath it. Prior to the Civil War, individuals had engaged in pick-and-shovel mining in the area, but it was not until the 1870s that the Joplin mining industry began its journey to modernization.[2] Having emerged after the Civil War, Joplin was one of many cities that sprang up during the New South period, and railroads played a crucial role in its development. They provided Joplin's booming lead and zinc mining industry access to distant markets.

Joplin's early days were rough and tumultuous. The fortunes of the city rose and fell with economic depressions that came and went in the late nineteenth century.[3] In 1875, Joplin reportedly had 225 businesses.[4] In 1880, Joplin was home to 7,038 residents, 246 of whom were African Americans.[5] By 1890, the population swelled to almost 10,000 inhabitants. By the end of that decade, its population had reached 26,023.[6]

Saloons narrowly outnumbered churches in the bustling mining town. Thirty-seven saloons, including the infamous House of Lords where artist Thomas Hart Benton began his career, competed with thirty-three churches in Joplin for the souls of its citizens. Of the thirty-three churches, four were African American.[7] If one would rather join their fellow citizens in fraternal spirit, the Masons, Elks, Knights of Pythias, Eagles, Odd Fellows, Woodmen of the World, Ancient Order of United Workmen, and other organizations boasted multiple chapters throughout Joplin.[8]

Joplin's Main Street was lined with businesses. Billiard halls, furniture stores, mining equipment companies, pharmacies, three newspaper offices, bakeries, architect's offices, and blacksmith shops were among the businesses that beckoned to customers. The Keystone Hotel, with its distinctive Romanesque Revival turret, offered the finest accommodations in town until 1908 when the New Joplin Hotel, later known as the Connor, opened. Among the travelers who crossed the Keystone's threshold were lawyers, mining company representatives, real estate and mining speculators, insurance agents, politicians, and railroad executives. Visitors could patronize one of nineteen barbershops, two of which were owned by African Americans, or stop by clothing stores such as Newman's and The Model to update their wardrobe.[9]

As a booming mining town, Joplin boasted four automobile dealerships, five bicycle shops, and fourteen livery stables.[10] One could purchase a bicycle and have their portrait taken during a visit to T. W.

Osterloh's photography studio and bookstore.[11] The Club Theatre, then Joplin's only entertainment venue, offered live productions of both the classics and the contemporary.[12] Opera, the plays of William Shakespeare, and vaudeville acts were enjoyed by an audience of both upper- and working-class white citizens.

Joplin was home to thousands of individuals from across the United States who came to eke out a better living from the treacherous mines. Among those who flooded into the city were blacks from across the country. An examination of the 1900 federal census shows that many came from southern states such as Kentucky, South Carolina, Mississippi, Alabama, and Louisiana. Others came from Kansas and Texas.[13] Of the 26,023 residents of Joplin, 773 were African Americans.[14]

Unlike whites, however, blacks did not work in the mines. Like the railroad industry, the mining industry was segregated. An examination of the 1900 federal census reveals that only a handful of blacks worked as miners. Those few may have worked their own claims. A visitor to the area in 1910 remarked that he was "surprised to find that there are practically no Negroes at work in the mines of Joplin. What Negroes are there are employed in other occupations than mining. There are scarcely any foreigners."[15]

Mining was not the only industry that was segregated. On April 2, 1903, seventy white workers at the Freeman Foundry in Joplin threatened to strike when J. W. Freeman hired Sidney Martin, a black man. The workers demanded Martin be fired. A worker told a *Joplin Daily Globe* reporter, "while they would not raise such strenuous objections to the one colored man, they believe that if one is allowed to work here it will be but a short time until more are employed, and they want it understood right in the beginning that colored men are not wanted."[16] Freeman promised workers Martin would be gone by the first of May. Instead of industry, blacks worked as cooks, waiters, barbers, porters, servants, hod carriers, and dressmakers. Many were boarders.[17]

If whites held better-paying jobs in the mines, they also stood a better chance of losing their lives to cave-ins, premature explosions, and bad air. As a result, the miners sought the entertainment and pleasure of Joplin's many saloons, drinking away their pay almost as fast as they had received it. Violence, fueled by the alcohol, followed. The town could be as dangerous aboveground as beneath.[18] Thus it was no surprise when news spread that a young black man had been lynched on the streets of Joplin. It was not the first. In 1885, a mob lynched a white criminal, Joe Thornton, who had killed Officer Daniel Sheehan, a popular police officer.[19] Leonard Barnett, an African American accused of raping a young white girl, was almost lynched in 1900 by a white mob before he was spirited out of town.[20]

Thomas Gilyard's ill-fated story began on the evening of April 14, 1903, when Joplin hardware merchant Sam Bullock arrived at the Joplin Police Department. He reported the theft of two pistols and aired his suspicion that two "colored" men were the culprits. The men had visited Bullock's store prior to the theft. A black man had approached Bullock with information as to the whereabouts of the two suspects. According to the informant, the men were hiding in the Kansas City Southern railyards, located in north Joplin. Officer Ben May, Bullock, and the informant set out for the railyards.

Just minutes after the trio left the police station, Officer Theodore Leslie arrived. Leslie, a married father of four children, had earned the reputation as a fearless officer. The thirty-six-year-old worked one of the toughest beats in the city and had been on the police force exactly one year. After he reported to night constable Charles Loughlin, Loughlin told Leslie to join Officer May in searching the railyards. Unable to find Officer May, Leslie began his search in the railyards alone.[21]

As night fell, Leslie noticed an unfamiliar black man standing inside a stock car. The officer cautiously approached the stranger and proceeded to pat him down. Just as the officer finished his search, a single shot rang out from inside the boxcar. Leslie drew his revolver and fired back into the shadows a total of eight times, emptying his revolver at his unseen assailant. After his last shot, however, the officer fell to the ground mortally wounded, struck once in the eye and once in the chest. A black man then jumped down from inside the boxcar and fled north down the railroad tracks into the darkness, away from the lights of Joplin.

The gunfire aroused the attention of bystanders watching roughly one hundred yards away. They saw Leslie crumple to the ground. One of them, seventeen-year-old Ike Clark, ran to the fallen officer's side. After determining there was nothing he could do for Leslie, Clark and the other three men set off in pursuit of the officer's killer. After getting within fifty feet of the assailant, Clark fired two rounds, only to receive return fire. Clark fired again, but his shots failed to hit his target, allowing Officer Leslie's murderer to escape. The men returned to the scene of the shooting to discover the first black man in the custody of Officer Joseph F. Reubart, whose grasp he fell into as he fled the scene. The man was escorted to the city jail as news of the shooting spread quickly through Joplin. Citizens were not going to let Leslie's killer escape.[22]

Within an hour of the murder, hundreds of armed men flooded the streets of Joplin. Many visited the scene of the crime, which was roughly one hundred yards north of Broadway Street. Ripples of excitement and fear ran through the crowds. A request was sent to the marshal of neighboring Webb City to bring his bloodhounds to track the murderer. The hounds arrived by nine o'clock that night and five hundred eager men stood ready to follow them. The dogs were taken to the crime scene and found the scent of the suspected murderer. In the meantime, officers questioned the black man whom Officer Leslie had searched prior to his death, but the black man was of little help. He claimed that he did not know the man who shot Officer Leslie as they had only been acquainted for five minutes before the officer arrived. Nor had he learned the man's name. The officers, it was reported, believed he told them the truth "after all sorts of attempts to get the negro to change his story."[23]

Joplin's police force had faced loss before. Two years earlier, on April 23, 1901, Officers Bert Brannon and Charles Sweeney were shot and killed as they attempted to arrest a gang of white vagrants. Ironically, the officers were killed in the same railyard where Officer Leslie later died, as they shared the same tough North End beat. A temporary vigilance committee was established to rid "Joplin of all suspicious characters, thieves, and thugs." None of the assailants were ever apprehended.[24]

This time, the citizens of Joplin did not intend to allow the alleged murderer to escape. Nor did they act alone. Citizens from neighboring towns came to Joplin in the wake of Officer Leslie's death. For the capture of Leslie's murderer, the *Joplin Daily Globe* enticed many with the promise of a $100 reward, which quickly swelled to $1,650.[25] For others, however, the matter went beyond money. It was a chance to partake in a thrilling manhunt, one in which the mob's quarry was the most vulnerable prey of all, a lone black man.

Webb City marshal Marquiss, his bloodhounds, and a group of twelve armed men followed the man's scent three miles outside the city. Burl Robison, who handled the dogs, slowed their progress. Robison, a rather rotund man, could not ride in a buggy so long as the dogs kept to the railroad tracks. By eleven o'clock the search was called off. Irritated by the delay, Joplin officers telegraphed the Vernon County sheriff in Lamar, Missouri, to bring his dogs to continue the search. In the meantime, men gathered in the city streets, standing in small groups. It was a long night for all.[26]

Rumors ran rampant through the streets of Joplin the next morning. Sightings of a strange black man were reported in Asbury, sixteen miles north. Groups of volunteers from Joplin, Asbury, Carl Junction, and Galena spread out to hunt Leslie's killer. Passions flared when a large black man reportedly said he sided with the actions of Officer Leslie's murderer. Immediately, a handful of men seized him. The men dragged the unnamed black man several blocks before they whipped and severely beat him. At one point, rumors swirled that the killer was surrounded in a brushpile in the railyards. Dozens of armed men rushed to the scene only to be disappointed. The *Joplin Daily News Herald* reported, "Other Joplin men are going to all towns within a radius of fifty miles to stir up enthusiasm in the chase."[27] The mobs of men who lingered at the Joplin police station did not have long to wait.

A black servant girl, Cora Lane, who witnessed the shooting, reported that the individual who fled from the boxcar appeared to be wounded. After he crossed a nearby iron bridge, Lane said she observed that "he was limping as if it pained him to walk."[28] B. C. Drake, who lived just outside Joplin, reported that a black man approached him just an hour after the shooting. The man's trouser legs were bloody and wet. He begged to stay at Drake's barn for the night, but Drake refused to help him. G. W. Smith also reported seeing a "negro" pass near Midway Park that evening. The stranger caught Smith's attention because he forded Turkey Creek instead of taking the more convenient bridge.[29]

Between three and four o'clock on the afternoon of April 16, 1903, just one day after the death of Officer Leslie, his alleged killer was captured. The man was discovered in the Bauer Brothers slaughterhouse by Lee Fullerton and M. R. Bullock. The slaughterhouse, near Midway Park, was just off the St. Louis–San Francisco Railway line. Fullerton, a Bauer Brothers employee, told the *Joplin Daily Globe* that he had just finished feeding the livestock at the slaughterhouse when he encountered a black man walking up the hill toward him. His presence struck Fullerton as unusual as the slaughterhouse was in an out-of-the way location. He admitted to the reporter, "I was just the least frightened at first for the fellow was one of the meanest looking men I ever saw." Fullerton called out to the man who then approached Fullerton to ask if he could stay at the slaughterhouse as he had been in a shootout. He reportedly promised to befriend Fullerton one day and that he would not harm anything at the slaughterhouse. Fullerton, alone and unarmed, agreed. He had noticed that the black man was armed with "a big gun."[30]

The two sat and talked until M. R. Bullock arrived. Bullock, who lived nearby, conferred with Fullerton outside the slaughterhouse. The two agreed that the black man inside fit the description of Officer Leslie's assailant. Fullerton and Bullock went back inside the slaughterhouse. Fullerton began to cut tallow near the man as Bullock stood nearby. Fullerton suddenly lunged out with his knife, bringing it to within an inch of the stranger's throat. As the man tried to pull his Colt .38 revolver, Bullock knocked it from his hand. "After we had the negro's gun we had no trouble with him." The pair loaded the black man into a wagon and took him into Joplin.[31]

As the men made their way to town, the prisoner admitted he was in the boxcar that Officer Leslie approached, but that he was not alone. Two other black men and one white man were also in the car, he claimed. One of the others shot Leslie, he asserted. As the wagon rolled into Joplin, men watched quietly, eyes locked on the prisoner.[32] Shortly after his arrival, at a quarter past four o'clock, "a shout went up, from somewhere, nobody perhaps knew where. But that shout echoed far and wide. 'They have the murderer' was the cry."[33]

After the man was taken into custody at the Joplin Police Depart - ment, Officer Frank Belford sat down to interview him. The young black man stated his name was Thomas Gilyard and that he had just arrived the day before from Mississippi. As Officer Belford conducted the interview, crowds began to form in the streets. Jasper County sheriff James T. Owen and Mayor John C. Trigg, sensing trouble, ordered all saloons closed for two hours. The two men hoped to keep the furious rabble in check, but instead, left angry men without a place to congregate. Large mobs of men gathered near the jail as did women and children. A lone voice called out, "Get a rope!" Another voice cried, "Hang the nigger!" Nervous, Thomas Gilyard continued his interview with Officer Belford. He admitted he was in the rail car when Officer Leslie approached, but that there were three other men present in the car. Gilyard denied he fired on Leslie. Someone outside shouted, "Hang the murderer!"[34]

Within half an hour of Gilyard's arrest, the streets of Joplin were packed with an estimated two thousand people. Tension ran high as men clustered together on street corners, talking to one another in hushed voices, their faces grim and strained. The crowds continued to grow. Officers in the city jail, apprehensive at the size of the mob and the continued calls for violence, moved Gilyard to a separate cell. Fearing the mob might storm the jail, they ensured Gilyard was alone, as they did not want, "the wrong prisoner taken."[35]

Joplin's city attorney, twenty-eight-year-old Perl Decker, pushed his way through the throng of people. Decker, a former oratory champion at Park College, addressed the crowd from the steps of the jail. In a strong, clear voice he called upon the crowd to let "the law run its course." Decker reminded the men and women gathered before him that Gilyard might not be guilty. The tension that had built up over the last few hours appeared to subside. The *Globe* remarked that he "had great influence over the crowd." Two hundred individuals who had cried for blood turned away from Decker and began to leave. Decker's silver tongue still held plenty of charm.[36]

But whatever spell Decker had woven was soon broken. Another group of individuals stepped forward to stir up the mob once more. These men were "as equally determined as the leaders who preceded them." Mayor Trigg and Joplin mayor-elect Tom W. Cunningham took over from Decker and appealed for the crowds to leave. The crowd listened for a few minutes, only to turn a collective deaf ear.[37] Someone barked out, "Break the jail down!"[38] Men, women, and children gathered in front of the jail were shoved out of the way as several men rushed through the crowd with a ten-foot-long battering ram. The men began to pound away at the wall of the city jail. It was five o'clock in the afternoon. Thomas Gilyard had been in police custody for only about an hour when the men began their brutal assault on the jail.[39]

The men ferociously battered at the wall near the police court-room. Their efforts were stymied by an iron door. Not to be denied, the attackers moved to the east side of the jail where they continued to ram the building. When police officers confiscated one battering ram, another soon appeared in the hands of yet another group of determined men. Sweat drenched the shirts of those who heaved the ram over and over again. Within a matter of ten minutes, the wall was breached.[40] Men flooded into the jail, tossing aside police officers who attempted to intervene. Members of the crowd began battering the lock on Thomas Gilyard's cell door with a sledgehammer. In just a few moments, Gilyard had been seized by the mob.[41]

The *Joplin Daily Globe* and the *Joplin Daily News Herald* provided different accounts of Gilyard's last moments in the jail. Both make it clear that all hell broke loose when the wall came down. The *Globe* reported that Gilyard lay as if asleep while members of the mob worked to unlock his cell. As soon as the cell door was opened, Gilyard reportedly sprang to his feet. He lunged at his attackers and "fought like a demon."[42] The *Herald,* however, reported that when the cell door was breached, "Thomas Gilyard, from the floor where he lay, looked at those who came after him with a face from which hope had fled." The reporter described Gilyard's attackers, "like devouring wolves." Despite Gilyard's powerful build "he was tossed about like a feather in the sea of humanity of which he was now the center."[43]

Just before Gilyard was taken from his cell, he told the *Herald* reporter his name and that he was twenty years old. Gilyard managed to gasp that he was on his way from Murphsyburg, Illinois, to Asbury, Missouri, to work on a railroad gang. According to Gilyard, he had worked on railroad section gangs for the entirety of his brief adult life. This is the only substantial information, besides his brief interview with Officer Belford, as to how Gilyard ended up in Joplin.[44]

Gilyard was quickly dragged into an alley east of the jail and onto Second Street. The mob surrounded him from all sides. Arms reached out to hit him, legs kicked at him. Desperately, Gilyard fought to free himself to fight back, but his effort was useless. The mob now num-bered an estimated three thousand participants. Even if he broke free, there was nowhere to go. As the *Globe* described the scene, "Men shouted and women and children screamed."[45] Thomas Gilyard fell to his knees. He asked to be allowed to say something before he was lynched. "Gemmen, I knows I's done wrong, and I knows I got to die, but lemme pray. Yes, for God's sake, lemme pray." The mob ignored his pleas. As he was dragged down the street, the mob paused again. "Did you kill Theodore Leslie?" "Lor' gemmen, I didn't kill him. If you kill me, you's killin' an innocent man."[46] The men holding Gilyard began running with their captive, then suddenly stopped at the corner of Wall Avenue and Second Street, only to find that the man with the rope had been lost in the crowd. Men and children scrambled up onto nearby roofs and climbed trees to obtain a better view. Women with their parasols stood on tiptoe to try to see what was going on.[47] Dr. Francis E. Rohan struggled to stop the mob, but to no avail.[48]

As the man with the rope struggled to reach Gilyard, Perl Decker rode through the screaming mob on horseback, pushing aside those who stood in his way. The young attorney had not given up on saving Gilyard's life. He called to the mob to return Gilyard to jail. Decker again insisted Gilyard might be innocent. He had Ike Clark, the seventeen-year-old carpenter who witnessed Leslie's death, hoisted on the horse. From this vantage point, Clark tried to tell the crowd that Gilyard was not the man he had shot at, and definitely not the man who murdered Leslie. His testimony fell on deaf ears.[49]

Mayor-elect Cunningham stood in a wagon and again asked the mob to stop. He, too, asked that Thomas Gilyard be returned to jail until it could be proven he was the murderer. The mob seemed to pause but then a sudden roar of protest signaled its rejection of Cunningham's efforts.[50]

A rope snaked through the air as someone in the crowd tossed it at Gilyard. It landed on his shoulder. The reporter for the *Herald* recounted, "Those who saw Thomas Gilyard's face at that moment will never forget it." As men attempted to pull on the rope to hoist Gilyard into eternity, Cunningham tried to push them away, but failed. Dr. Jesse May shouted to Tom Cunningham that he had cut the rope. Cunningham ordered May to cut the rope again. Cunningham then recounted that as one of lynchers was pulled from the rope, the man yelled at him, "Cunningham, you must be a negro lover!" The mayor-elect replied, "No, but I want justice."[51] E. D. Nix, a former U.S. marshal and contemporary of the "Three Guardsmen of Oklahoma," argued with the men preparing to hang Gilyard. When reason failed, Nix pulled out his knife, then began to cut the rope. When a man threatened to shoot him, however, Nix backed away.[52] Several voices bellowed, "Kill the next man who does that!" At last, a rope was placed around the condemned man's neck. Gilyard cried out, "Oh, God don't!" He fell to his knees and began to pray an inaudible prayer.[53]

At the same time, two men climbed the nearest telephone pole, their hands stretched out to the mob below. The other end of the rope was thrown up to one of the men and he draped the rope over the arm of the pole. The mob roared, "Up with him!" As reported by the *Globe*, Gilyard pleaded with his captors, "Lor' God knows dat I am innocent. Gemmen, I's got a father an' a mother. Please, foah de luhb o' massey, send foah my poor old mother before you kill me." As members of the mob on the ground began to pull at the rope to lift Gilyard, other men rushed forward. They grabbed on to the rope and hung on in "a tug of war" with those determined to lynch Gilyard. Among the men who fought to save Gilyard's life that day were Perl Decker, Dr. Francis E. Rohan, Raymond Dagley, Lee Yeakee, Bert Luther, and several unnamed others who clung to the rope. But the men were savagely driven off and Gilyard was hoisted skyward. A metal spike on the pole hit Gilyard's head, but he did not respond if he felt any pain. His eyes closed, his jaw fell slack. Thomas Gilyard was dead.[54]

Gilyard, lynched at 5:50 in the afternoon, was taken down thirty minutes later. Judge Potter ordered Gilyard's body taken to the Joplin Undertaking Company to ensure it would not be mutilated.[55] But crowds lingered in the twilight, and a quiet hush fell over Joplin. Saloons, which had remained closed for two hours, reopened. Men began to drink. Just before 8 o'clock a few dozen paraded down Main Street. Many were reportedly from the mining camps just outside Joplin. As they marched, the men yelled out, "Hang the coons!" and "Down with the negroes!" They fired rifles and pistols into the night air. The growing mob demanded that all blacks leave Joplin at once. The *Globe* chillingly reported, "As they swarmed down Main Street, over a hundred boys, ranging in age from seven and eight upward, followed in their wake and yelled like young demons." They pushed bystanders aside and knocked down streetcars. The Joplin police attempted to intervene but to no avail. It was clear that "there was a thirst for blood in that motley crowd that nothing else but rapine could

Joplin city attorney Perl Decker.
Courtesy of The State Historical Society of Missouri.

slake." According to press accounts, city leaders asked businessmen to intervene, as did Mayor-elect Cunningham, but the mob ignored them.[56]

The Imperial Barbershop, which employed only black barbers, was one of the first businesses targeted by the crowd. A few barbers who were in the building made their escape out the back as men broke down the front door. Officer Ben May, who stood just across the street, ran to intervene. He jumped in front of the wild crowd and ordered them to leave. Disappointed to find there were no blacks in the shop, the mob left, only to embark on a new wave of violence.[57]

A white man known as "Hickory Bill" Fields was arrested for disturbing the peace and firing his gun. He was taken to the city jail and locked up. When some members of the mob realized what had transpired, they marched to the jail, where they demanded Hickory Bill be released. The police refused. The mob then threatened to dynamite

AT THE SCENE OF THE LYNCHING.

(Sketched From the East Side of Wall Street Looking to the Northwest.)

Artist's sketch of Thomas Gilyard's lynching as depicted in the *Joplin Daily Globe.*
Courtesy of The State Historical Society of Missouri.

the jail. A brief standoff ensued in which a few individuals tried to reason with the angry crowd. After thirty minutes the police realized that the mob meant business. They reluctantly released Hickory Bill.[58]

The angry throng continued to grow in size as it roamed Joplin's downtown. Between Broadway and A Streets, the mob threw rocks and other objects, "at houses, through windows and at fleeing negroes." The aim of the mob was apparently good, as a reporter observed, "There is scarcely a whole window pane in a window" on either street. The crowd managed to overturn one house before it moved on.[59]

The mob fired pistols into the air as they boldly paraded unchallenged in the night air. The boisterous crowd provided adequate warning

Photograph of man standing next to the telegraph pole where Thomas Gilyard was lynched. The back of the photo reads, "Joplin, Mo. June 17, 1903. This is where Bro. C. H. Button and myself lodged at the home of Mr. Wilson. The telegraph pole is where a negro was mobbed and hung last spring. Taken by Prof. C. H. Button, J. R. Crank. Taken at Bible School Convention." *Courtesy of the Post Memorial Art Reference Library, Joplin, Missouri.*

of their approach as they thundered, "White folks, get in line." They also warned, "White folks keep your lights burning." The crack of rifles and bursts of pistol fire were accompanied by the sound of glass breaking. Curiously, a quartet of young men followed the mob, singing songs that lightened the mood. Their repertoire went unrecorded.[60]

The horde of rioters swept past Fifth and Main Streets, headed for the black section of town located at the north end of Main Street.[61] The area had previously been inhabited by "lewd women" who were driven out by a mob just months earlier. After the prostitutes were chased out, black families moved in, including several from Pierce City. Some of Joplin's black residents had already fled earlier that day. The blacks who were chased from Pierce City undoubtedly knew that they were about to be caught up in another explosion of racial violence. They wisely fled before the mob called on them. Callers from Webb City and Galena phoned to let Joplin officials know that both cities had been inundated

Former U.S. marshal E. D. Nix. *Courtesy Western History Collections, University of Oklahoma.*

by a flood of black refugees, "as soon as possible after the mob began to form to hang the murderer of Theodore Leslie."[62]

Bob Carter was one of the first to leave shortly after the lynching. Carter told a reporter he left because the lynching brought back, "disagreeable memories" of a time when, "owing to a little unpleasantness some citizens of Granby forced him to stretch a new rope for several minutes about two years ago." According to the *Herald,* Carter went on to say, "Ah jes took one look at dat nigger when he went up in de aiah, cause I wanted to see how I looked once an' den I went home. Ah had my turn already."[63]

The mob torched six homes. The Joplin Fire Department raced to the scene to try to prevent the blaze from spreading. As the firemen frantically worked to stop the fire, members of the mob yelled and jeered at them. The mob returned to East Seventh Street, another black area of Joplin, and set more houses on fire.[64] At one of the fires, the firemen were "unable to do much good. As fast as a line of hose was strung the mob stuck knives into it."[65] In contrast to those at the north end of Main

Street, blacks in this section of town, located between Seventh and Tenth Streets, reportedly felt "perfectly safe. They were taken by surprise."[66]

The *Carthage Evening Press* reported that as the mob attacked Joplin's black neighborhoods it was only then that the majority of black residents chose to flee. While the survivors of Pierce City may have left at the first signs of a mob, many blacks stayed, thinking they were safe. As the mob ran rampant, though, Joplin's streets filled with blacks too scared to wait on trains to take them to safety. Instead, many left on foot with what little they could carry. Ike Beechum, a black resident of Carthage, told the *Press* reporter that his nephew was among those who fled Joplin at the last minute. When asked if his nephew arrived in Carthage by train from Joplin, Beechum replied, "Lord, no, he beat the cars—he came over a foot."[67]

Galena, Kansas, took on "somewhat of an emancipation day appearance" the night of the lynching. Others, however, "went far west" in the direction of Columbus and Baxter Springs. Those who remained anxiously inquired for the latest copy of the *Joplin Daily Globe* "to see what was done to the place."[68] Some of the refugees, it was reported, returned to Joplin the next day. Their return was bittersweet. Joplin was no longer home. The *Joplin Daily Globe* gave a "conservative estimate" of blacks who planned to leave and never return at around 200 individuals out of an estimated population of 700.[69] Unlike Pierce City or Monett, though, Joplin's racial cleansing would not be permanent. By 1910, 801 African Americans lived in Joplin, up from 773 in 1900.[70]

The *Globe* noted that the homes burned by the mob belonged to some of Joplin's "best negroes."[71] One such example was that of "Aunt Lou" Barnett, a car cleaner for the Missouri Pacific Railroad, who lived at 315 East Seventh Street. She had purchased the home with her hard-earned salary, only to have it destroyed by the mob.[72] The homes of Joe Cox, Mary Davis, and "Aunt Eliza" also lay in ruins. "Aunt Eliza," a Joplin resident for thirty years, stood on the corner of Third and Main Streets as five hundred volunteers called upon by Mayor John C. Trigg to prevent further mob violence marched past on April 16. Eliza, a red handkerchief on her head, bowed and saluted as they passed. But while Eliza stayed, others caught the train for Galena, Webb City, and other places thought to be safe.[73]

Carthage, the county seat of Jasper County, was on edge the night of the lynching. Sheriff James T. Owen, who stayed in Joplin during the

Jasper County sheriff James T. Owen. *Courtesy of The State Historical Society of Missouri.*

mob's wild frenzy, telephoned his deputies in Carthage to keep a lookout for any sign of mob activity there. Two black prisoners, Dan Bullard and Joseph Clark, were spirited to Carthage after they were arrested in Joplin shortly after Officer Leslie was killed. Both admitted that they were in the railcar with Thomas Gilyard before the shooting but insisted they played no part in the crime. They were fortunate to be taken out of the mob's reach, but Thomas Gilyard was not afforded the same privilege for reasons unknown. Owen ordered his deputies to take the prisoners from the jail and hide them when it became apparent that Thomas Gilyard was to be lynched. A handful of deputies and some hastily deputized citizens spirited the men from jail and hid them in Carthage. Whenever the men suspected their presence was detected, they moved the prisoners to a new location, hiding the men in three separate houses during the night.[74]

The *Press* reporter briefly interviewed Clark and Bullard. Bullard admitted he had patronized Sam Bullock's hardware store shortly before the theft of two pistols, but insisted that he was not involved in the crime. He blamed two other black men for the theft. Clark, allegedly the man Leslie searched just before the officer was shot, stated he did not know Gilyard. According to Clark, Gilyard was a "Mississippi levee negro" who was on his way back to Missouri as a muleskinner somewhere down South. Gilyard told Clark that he was headed to Asbury to work on the Carthage and Western railroad just before Leslie appeared. Clark and Bullard lived to tell their tale. The Carthage mob Sheriff Owen anticipated never materialized.[75]

The *Carthage Evening Press* reported the early reaction of Monett and Pierce City, two of southwest Missouri's most infamous towns, as news of the mob in Joplin spread. Both towns kept abreast of developments by telegram. Carthage resident J. W. Meredith, in Monett when the lynching occurred, reported that "at a drop of the hat a special train could have been organized" to go to Joplin. Several residents of Pierce City reportedly caught the first train to Joplin upon hearing the news. Another Carthage resident, Dr. L. E. Whitney, was on business in Pierce City when news of the mob reached the town. While in a hotel, Whitney overheard Pierce City residents as they discussed "the negro question." He interjected to suggest that blacks should not be treated harshly because of their skin color. At that, "the crowd seemed perfectly dazed for a moment, then the debate began, Dr. Whitney holding out against odds, and a hot time ensued."[76]

As the fires burned out the next day, April 16, Dr. Samuel Grantham conducted an autopsy on Thomas Gilyard's remains. A coroner's jury witnessed the event. Gilyard had sustained a bullet wound to his left leg just above the thigh. The bullet appeared to have shattered his hipbone before it traveled upward into his body and stopped near the base of Gilyard's spine. Dr. Grantham believed that the shot had been fired at Gilyard from below, which gave credence to the mob's belief that Gilyard was the man Leslie shot as he fired upward at his assailant in the boxcar.

Dr. Grantham was fortunate even to have a corpse to examine. During the previous night as the mob prowled the streets, someone raised the idea of burning Gilyard's remains. The body, which was stored at the Joplin Undertaking Company, was spirited away by Warren Armington, the undertaker, to Fairview Cemetery. Once there, he secreted Gilyard's corpse in the sexton's shed. The mob converged on the undertaker's facility, prepared to invade the premises to steal the body, but left when told that Gilyard had been moved. The mob then broke up into small groups to search for the remains, but failed to locate them.[77]

But the coroner's inquest served another purpose beyond conducting an autopsy. During witness testimony, the names of those who led the mob were disclosed. Assistant Prosecutor David E. Blair, present during the proceeding, took detailed notes. He promised, "everybody who had participated in the mobbing of the negro would be prosecuted." At the top of his list were three men: Sam Mitchell, Ellsworth "Hickory Bill" Fields, and Bartimeus H. "B. H." Barnes.

Mitchell, a thirty-year-old lead and zinc miner was living in Galena, just outside of Joplin, with his wife and son.[78] Previously Mitchell worked as a bartender at the John Scruggs' Saloon.[79] Fields, who does not appear in the 1900 census, is listed in a 1900 Joplin City Directory as an engineer. In subsequent years, however, he is listed as a miner.[80]

George E. Wheaton testified that he recognized Sam Mitchell, his former employee, as he climbed the telephone pole. Wheaton said he then watched as Mitchell threw the rope over the arm of the pole prior to Thomas Gilyard's lynching. The other men, he said, he did not recognize. Officer Ben May identified a member of the mob as a teamster named Barnes.[81]

Barnes, originally from Wabash, Indiana, arrived in Joplin in 1895.[82] He lived on East Eighth Street, and when not working as a teamster, had "charge of the Saturday night dances at the hall corner Ninth and Joplin streets." The previous day, Barnes stopped by the police station to inform May that he was in the mob that lynched Gilyard, but did not take part in the mob that ransacked black neighborhoods. The officer stated that Barnes was one of the men who pulled on the rope that lifted Gilyard into eternity. Barnes, however, was not the only man May recognized. The policeman named Sam Mitchell as one of the men who manned the battering ram as well as the man who lifted the rope over the arm of the telephone pole prior to Gilyard's death. Finally, Officer May implicated "Hickory Bill" Fields as another man who played a prominent role in the lynching. Fields assisted the raid on the jail as well as manned the rope. According to May, Fields, Barnes, and Mitchell were the ringleaders of the mob.[83]

The coroner's jury agreed. After thirty minutes of deliberation, the jury found Barnes, Mitchell, and Fields responsible for the death of Thomas Gilyard. Fields was already in jail. After the mob had sprung him on Wednesday night, he sauntered back into the jail on Thursday, at which time Officers May and Loughlin placed him in lock-up. Sheriff Owen and Officer May escorted Fields to Carthage to avoid any further hostilities in Joplin. Ed Smith, arrested for rioting on Wednesday night, was also taken to Carthage. As two hundred spectators watched, the two unruly men were ushered to the corner of Fourth and Virginia Streets to await transportation, handcuffed under heavy guard. Sheriff Owen announced Fields faced charges of arson. Smith, who allegedly stole from many of the black homes that were torched, was charged with petty theft. [84]

A coroner's jury, overseen by Judge Potter and Assistant Prosecutor David E. Blair, also examined the fallen officer's body. Witnesses were called to testify. Ike Clark, the young carpenter who told the mob that Gilyard was not the man who killed Leslie, changed his story. At the coroner's inquest, Clark testified that Gilyard was the man who shot Leslie. Clark recalled that he chased the man up the tracks as he fled the scene. "I shot at him five times. He returned the fire three times. My last shot staggered him." Cy Landis, a black former police officer, also testified. Landis had been in the railyard talking to an acquaintance when the shooting broke out. He stated that he thought the black man who fired on Leslie was shot as he jumped from the railcar. All of the rounds that Leslie managed to fire at his assailant were found in the railcar, except one. The coroner's jury believed the missing bullet was the one found in Thomas Gilyard's body.

A cursory examination of the bullet that exited Leslie's temple led the coroner's jury to believe it was a round from a .38 revolver, the same type of gun that Thomas Gilyard had in his possession when captured. Judge Potter introduced a shiny brass button into evidence that he found when he examined the railcar. The button reportedly matched the buttons of Thomas Gilyard's overalls. Ten minutes after all of the evidence and testimony were presented, the six-member coroner's jury found Thomas Gilyard guilty of the murder of Officer Theodore Leslie. "We, the jury, after hearing the testimony at the inquest held over the body of T. C. Leslie, find that he, T. C. Leslie, came to his death by a pistol shot from a 38-calibre pistol in the hands

Joplin police officer Theodore Leslie. *Courtesy of The State Historical Society of Missouri.*

of a wounded negro, who was afterwards lynched, and whose name is to us unknown."[85]

This did little to calm Joplin down. Rumors circulated of another mob that would not only "destroy the negro quarters but burn and pillage the homes of the white men who oppose the mob." Miners were to receive their pay and were expected to patronize Joplin's many saloons. Once a mob was formed, "thousands of miners with liquor to fire them, would make . . . Wednesday night pale into insignificance."[86]

In response to the fears, Joplin mayor John C. Trigg issued a proclamation that called for five hundred volunteers to put an end to the "violence and mobocracy that have held high carnival in the city to the disgrace and humiliation of all law abiding citizens." Men were asked to step forward so that "the supremacy of the law may be vindicated and upheld, that peace may be preserved and the rights and liberties of all classes of our citizens may be protected." Those who wished to participate were asked to come armed and meet at five o'clock at the courthouse. In addition, Mayor Trigg ordered all saloons closed by six o'clock that evening.[87] Some local miners were angered by an earlier proclamation that required all "minors" to stay home after 8 P.M. The men, who thought the order applied to them, "were making loud protest until it was explained to them."[88]

The *Carthage Evening Press* interviewed a Joplin broker in Carthage on business about the possibility of another mob. The unnamed businessman wearily voiced his belief that a mob was likely. But he added, "Many of the Joplin colored people own their own homes and places of business. They are a quiet, peaceful lot of citizens, but there is going to be some shooting done on both sides tonight if the mob tries to drive the negroes out, and white men will be found lined up with the colored ones in protecting the homes of the latter." The *Press* also reported that "a message came from Aurora, Monett, and Peirce City saying 2,000 men from those towns will visit Joplin this evening to take part in the demonstration."[89]

Fortunately, Trigg's plan worked. At the appointed time, more than three thousand citizens stood on the courthouse lawn, ready to enforce law and order. After he found the courtroom designated for the meeting occupied by a lawsuit, the mayor asked everyone to meet at the Odd Fellows Hall located at Seventh and Main Streets, which turned out to be too small to hold everyone. Instead, Mayor Trigg addressed those who crowded inside, followed by Democratic attorney John W. McAntire. The Kentuckian's denunciation of the mob was met with great applause. Four companies of volunteers were created. The meeting then adjourned and returned to the courthouse where another crowd waited.[90]

As Mayor Trigg climbed onto a wall outside the courthouse, the muffled sound of thousands of men taking off their hats filled the air. A motion for the volunteers to march down Main Street met with hearty approval. The group seemed to be under elite leadership. Joel T. Livingston was appointed commander-in-chief, while W. E. Morgan, Lee Shepherd, and John McManamy served as captains. Livingston, who served as a colonel in the Missouri National Guard, was a local

Democratic leader and attorney.[91] Shepherd, a young assistant prosecuting attorney, was a Republican who had volunteered for service when the Spanish-American War broke out. His regiment did not, however, see active service.[92] W. E. Morgan had been Joplin's chief of police from 1897 to 1898. John McManamy, a Republican, joined the Joplin Police Department in 1890 before serving multiple terms as Joplin's chief of police.[93]

Livingston, at the head of the militia, bellowed, "Gentleman, the mayor has given orders that this mob must disperse. Company, forward march."[94] The group began their march down Main Street in a show of force to dissuade potential rioters. The volunteers were met with cheers and applause from spectators before they disbanded for dinner. The marchers then regrouped after seven o'clock. They were joined by members of the Knights of Pythias as well as graying Union veterans from the John Morton Camp of the Grand Army of the Republic. The crowd of volunteers was armed to the teeth with every type of weapon imaginable. Men draped rifles and shotguns over their arms. Gleaming squirrel guns were clasped tight in the hands of younger participants. Pistols hung from the belts of many. But as fearsome as they appeared, not everyone listened to their order to get off the streets.[95]

Many unnamed men were forcibly removed from the streets after they refused to disperse when ordered to do so. Among the stubborn was John Halliday, the former police court judge at Pittsburg, Kansas. He reportedly was "used to doing just about as he pleased in Pittsburg."[96] When he refused to obey an order from the volunteer force, someone hit him. Halliday spent the rest of the evening "dealing out abuse to Joplin and her citizens." Trigg's volunteers went home at 9:30, but promised to respond if the whistle of the Joplin brewery sounded an alarm. The evening, however, passed uneventfully.[97]

Joplin did not yet relax. The following day, Saturday, April 18, 1903, the *Joplin Daily Globe* published a front-page warning to anyone who still harbored hope for another mob. The paper boldly declared, "Violence Has Had Its Inning—Rioters Warned." The warning mentioned a rumor that "the dangerous element of neighboring cities would flock in here tonight" to create another mob. While the names of the "neighboring cities" were not given, the paper undoubtedly

Joplin courthouse. *Author's Collection.*

referred to Pierce City and Monett, as both cities had engaged in racial expulsion in the wake of lynchings.

Though some had suggested miners might compose the feared mob, the *Globe* seemed anxious to emphasize that miners had not been the ones who had pillaged and destroyed the city's black neighborhoods. "For the most part they are men who spend six days a week in the mines. They are honest toilers between whom and the rioters who blaze a trail for the mob there is a chasm as wide," the paper solemnly proclaimed. Should the mob reemerge in Joplin, the *Globe* warned, "If need be [the volunteer force] will strike and strike hard." In addition, another proclamation from Mayor Trigg was printed, in which he asked the volunteer force to stand ready for any further threat of mob violence.[98] Much to Trigg's relief, no mob emerged.

While Joplin remained quiet, area newspapers did not. Immediately after Thomas Gilyard was lynched, the *Joplin Daily Globe* published a paradoxical editorial. The editorial voiced support for the lynching. After the death of three police officers in two years, it was "a foregone conclusion that Judge Lynch would act swiftly and certainly when the murderer was caught." Yet, the paper continued, "All communities deplore lynchings. But all communities have them sooner than later." The *Globe* continued, "the people of Joplin deplore the unlawful act and give much credit to City Attorney Decker, Mayor-elect Cunningham and many others."[99]

The next day, the *Globe's* editorial page decried the attack on Joplin's black community. "As a matter of fact the colored people of Joplin had no part in the murder of Officer Leslie, and they condemn the act in unmeasured terms. There a number of very disreputable colored people in Joplin, but so are many disreputable white men." But such outrage on the part of the *Globe* may have been based less in any sense of racial justice than solicitude for white property. The paper pointed out that the houses burned belonged to white citizens and that "taxpayers of the city will have to pay for all property destroyed." The mob should be punished, it argued, for this careless disregard for the property of others. The piece ended, "arson is a crime that should always be punished." Lynching, on the other hand, did not appear to be a punishable offense except to the extent that it sullied the city's good name.[100] Both the lynchers and the arsonists had sundered the reputation of Joplin and inflicted great injury upon its citizens. The *Globe* then went on to boldly suggest, "the men who sent lurid, distorted and exaggerated special reports to the various papers throughout the country did Joplin the greatest injury, and they—well, they ought to be lynched."[101]

The *Springfield Republican* carried some of this bad press. An editorial from the *Republican* snarled, "If the reports from Joplin are true that a mob of white men burned the homes of innocent men and women at that place because God made them black, then there was perpetrated a wrong of which it is difficult to characterize." The paper called for justice at the hands of the court, not at the end of a rope. "If men and women and even prattling children are to be hunted like wild beasts by enraged monsters it is time something should be done." Mob participants were savages who were needed to be taught the rules of civilized society as well as prosecuted for their crimes. If they were not, then American society would soon be in "perpetual danger." Men would turn on each other until blood flowed through the streets. The solution was to teach "people to respect the rights of their fellow men." Yet, if that failed, the *Republican* suggested, "There is nothing that cures such marauders so suddenly as cold lead from Gatlin guns and Krag-Jorgensen rifles. Grover Cleveland showed that he knew what to do for them when they organized at Chicago, and that treatment is still good."[102]

Other newspapers condemned the lynching and mob violence. In a reprint published in the *Carthage Evening Press*, the *Kansas City Star* declared, "The most wholesome lesson this country could have would be the shooting down of a dozen mob leaders." The *Saint Louis Globe-Democrat*, referring to the rule of mob law, reasoned, "If that rule were adopted all races would be doomed. The laws of the country are founded on reasonableness. They are the safeguard of the innocent and of stable society. It is best for man, woman and child that the laws be respected." The *Kansas City Journal* applauded the effort made by Joplin's citizens to save Thomas Gilyard.[103]

The *St. Louis Post-Dispatch* proclaimed that, "The violence of the mob was born of the insane spirit of anarchy. Missouri cannot endure the disgrace of such violence." The paper called upon Governor Dockery and other state officials to take note of the violence as "Joplin repeats the orgy of Peirce City almost in detail and enlarges the blot upon the good name of Missouri." The *Post-Dispatch* then concluded, "No community can hold up its head while such vicious terrorism and anarchy go unpunished and unchecked. The stigma must be removed, the stain upon the honor of the state washed out."[104]

Two white Carthage pastors discussed the events at Joplin from the pulpit. At the Cumberland Presbyterian church, the Reverend

A. E. Perry condemned the mob. He argued that the actions of the mob were "brutal, anarchistic and atheistic." As Perry thoughtfully concluded at the first half of his sermon, "Men who believe in God, even though never so closely interested in or related to those who have been wronged, can afford to wait." He urged his congregation to support law and order and refuse to support mob law. At the Carthage Congregational Church, Reverend J. B. Toomay asked his congregation, "Were the officers surprised or did they do their best? Have we not learned yet that the way to quell a mob is not by begging them to subside? A better way is to let them hear the bark of the Winchester which on such occasions speaks eloquently for law and order." Those who had participated in the mob violence, Toomay thundered, should "wear stripes in the penitentiary."[105]

The *Globe* editorials that bemoaned the destruction of property and the injury to Joplin's good name showed that Joplin had learned from Pierce City's experience and did not wish to repeat it. In the wake of the lynching and expulsion of its black residents, Pierce City came under attack from papers across the state of Missouri, and earned a reputation as a belligerent, unrepentant city that did not regret what had happened. A booming mining town, Joplin did not fear a loss of business, but it did not want to attract negative labels that might dull the gleam of its appeal.

Not surprisingly, Pierce City itself endorsed the Joplin mob's action, citing black crime as a menace that threatened white society just as it had after its own lynchings in 1901. The *Peirce City Democrat* snidely noted, "Burglaries, hold-ups and even murders are very frequent where there are many niggers." Joplin, it observed, was full of blacks. The *Democrat* pointed out for its readers that since the lynching and subsequent expulsion of blacks in Pierce City that crime had dropped. "To get rid of them means to get rid of less crime of all kinds, Peirce City never wants another negro and we believe our people will never again allow them to live here."[106] The editor of the *Democrat* newspaper believed that perceived short-term benefits trumped a national reputation for bigotry. A few days later, the *Democrat* crowed that many Joplin blacks met a frosty reception on their eastward trek to Springfield. "They should all go to Africa where they belong. It is impossible to mix white and black and have harmony."[107]

Yet the *Democrat*'s rival, the *Peirce City Weekly Empire*, wanted to absolve its own citizens when it came to the Joplin mob. It lashed out in anger at the state press for having linked Pierce City's name with that of Joplin in the wake of the lynching. The paper claimed that no one from Pierce City played a role in the mob violence at Joplin and that Pierce City citizens were against mob violence. The *Empire* whined, "The Peirce City 'Nigger Chasers' referred to in the dispatches exist only in the imagination of sensational correspondents."[108]

The *Monett Star* echoed these claims. The little newspaper claimed that no one in Monett knew of the excitement in Joplin until it was over. The *Star* admitted, "Monett people don't love a negro very much but they are not inclined to be looking for trouble in that direction."[109]

African Americans in southwest Missouri offered their own response to events. The *Joplin Daily Herald* published an article regarding a former black Joplin resident. The unnamed man declared,

> I, undereducated and ignorant, once a slave and now a freeman, have lived in Joplin for about thirty years. I have been a property owner and taxpayer, and if I refuse to pay my taxes, by the law of my country my property would be taken away from me. I suppose the money I have paid in the way of taxes has gone to the school funds to educate people such as came to my house last Wednesday night and broke out my window panes and routed my wife and children and scared them nearly to death. I found them in a box car near the railroad track, crouched in there for a place of safety, and I sit in my house and hear the howling fiends utter oaths that drove me mad. I appeal to heaven. My country first I call, and if no response, then I guess the last resort of a poor, defenseless, hooted, downtrodden and unfortunate man, who happens to be born with a dark skin, is to at last rid myself of this unfair life, and on the other side of the border lands of eternity there will be equal rights and special privileges to no one. I would say, oh, Lord, if there is any, have mercy on my soul, if a black man, who lives in Joplin, has any.[110]

His was not the only black voice that emerged. Carthage, home to several limestone quarries, mills, and lead and zinc mines, was a prosperous southwest Missouri town. As a result, it had a sizable black population that offered shelter to those who fled Joplin.

The *Carthage Evening Press* published a notice announcing a

"Colored Citizens Meeting" a few days after Thomas Gilyard was lynched. The meeting, to be held at the Second Baptist Church in Carthage, called for black citizens to "imbibe inspiration from the greatest and purest to the humblest of men of our race along industrial, moral and religious lines." The public was invited to attend to see for themselves that the meeting would not serve the desires of any one individual or group. The meeting was organized by the Reverend George B. Abbott of the Sixth Street Methodist Episcopal Church and J. A. W. Young of the Second Baptist Church. Abbott, a former slave who served with the Union army during the Civil War, lived briefly in neighboring Mt. Vernon prior to the lynching and expulsion of blacks from Pierce City.[111] He had had enough of the violence.

At the meeting, which Abbott was elected to preside over, members of the black community stepped forward to speak their mind about recent events. While their words went unrecorded, those in attendance adopted a resolution proposed by R. W. Elmore, which condemned the killing of Officer Leslie as well as general lawlessness. The measure read, "We disclaim responsibility as a race for that atrocity and that we regard as unjust vengeance leveled against us collectively for a crime committed by an individual of our own race." In addition, the resolution applauded the efforts made by Joplin citizens to stop the mob from lynching Thomas Gilyard, and asked "to become good and useful citizens."[112]

But the black community did more than just adopt a resolution. The *Press* announced, "the negroes of Carthage are at work on the organization of a law and order league, and hope later to spread the organization to state-wide proportions." Warren Hansford, a well-known black barber in Carthage, spoke to a *Press* reporter about the proposed league, "We propose to run the bad element out of town, or else help the officers of the law send them to the penitentiary if necessary." In other words, so that black criminality might not become an excuse for lynching and expulsion, the African American community would police itself. Blacks would be expected to observe civil marriage services, abstain from gambling, and send their children to school. Hansford assured the reporter, "Our people are ready and willing to do what is right in society." He proudly pointed out the black Knights of Pythias Lodge as well as the black Odd Fellows Lodge that had been in existence for twenty years. No further mention of the Law and Order League appeared in the *Carthage Evening Press*.[113]

The Joplin lynch mob was distinct from that of Pierce City. Unlike the violence in Pierce City in which longtime black residents of the town were lynched, the victim in Joplin, Thomas Gilyard, was a transient— just the sort of person that southern whites held responsible for the high crime rates of the late nineteenth century.[114] Joplin did not have any vagrancy laws prior to the lynching, but afterward many prominent citizens endorsed the establishment of a workhouse where "the vagrant weary willie . . . might be provided with an 18-pound sledge."[115]

Joplin served as a junction point for the Saint Louis–San Francisco Railway, the Missouri Pacific Railway, the Fort Scott and Gulf Railroad, the Kansas City Southern Railway, and the Girard branch of the Saint Louis–San Francisco.[116] The railroads brought labor to the area as seasonal migrants traveled the rails in search of work. Thomas Gilyard, like many southern blacks, was part of this movement. Originally from Mississippi, he was on his way to work on a railroad gang at Asbury, Missouri. He had the misfortunate to arrive in an area where, due to Joplin's size, "most blacks and whites did not know one another, much less share ties of several generations."[117]

As a young transient black newly arrived in Joplin, Thomas Gilyard was on his own. He lacked crucial ties with both the white and black communities in Joplin that might have saved him from the mob. Many whites "feared that floaters, freed from the supervision of whites, and the traditional controls of the black community, posed a continual threat to white women and children."[118] Suspected of murdering Officer Leslie, Gilyard was condemned by whites because he was an unknown black transient allegedly responsible for the murder of a man who kept white society safe from black criminals.

Brundage observes, "Few crimes were more provocative in the eyes of whites than confrontations between law officers and blacks." Law enforcement officials ensured law and order as well as the stability of the color line. Violent encounters between blacks and white police officers occurred when "law officers attempted to arrest criminals charged with petty crimes as gambling, theft, or vagrancy." Officer Leslie, when he was shot, was in the railyard searching for two black men accused of stealing pistols from a Joplin hardware store. Whites viewed the assault or murder of a police officer as an attack on the white community as a whole; an attack that called for swift retaliatory extralegal action.[119]

Unlike many of their southern counterparts, however, city officials in Joplin attempted to stop the lynching. Mayor Trigg and Mayor-elect Cunningham may have sought to end mob violence because they disagreed with it. The fact that Joplin's white elite did not support the actions of the apparently largely working-class mob was evident with the elite's establishment of a militia to prevent any further unwanted mayhem. Had the elite supported and even assisted the lower class in their violent crusade, there would have been no militia and no post-riot trials. It is also clear that Trigg and Cunningham were well aware of the financial burden that additional mob violence could inflict upon the city. The *Joplin Daily Globe* emphasized that the houses destroyed by the mob belonged to white citizens and that "taxpayers of the city will have to pay for all property destroyed."[120]

Yet others failed to act. There is no indication that the Joplin Police Department and the Jasper County sheriff attempted to stop the lynch mob when it began its raid on the city jail. Law enforcement officials, as crowds gathered in Joplin, could have sensed the trouble that was brewing. Once Gilyard was in custody, he could have been sent to Carthage or Springfield for safekeeping as two other black suspects were. After the lynching, several individuals, including one Carthage minister, suggested that the officers should have dispersed the mob with a show of force. But the police may have been prejudiced against Gilyard as he was the alleged murderer of one of their fellow officers.

Gilyard also had the misfortune to travel through an area of Missouri where an established Ozark culture of violence, despite the modernizing forces of the New South, clung to existence. The inclination to use violence to settle scores may have been exacerbated by Joplin's rough mining industry. In 1949, a poem written by a local miner published in the *Joplin Globe* fondly recalled Joplin's early days,

Way down yonder in Southwest Missouri,
Where the women drink and curse like fury;
Where the barkeepers sell the meanest liquor,

Which makes a white man sicker and sicker,
Where the tinhorns rob you a little quicker,
That's where Joplin is.[121]

This mindset, called rough justice, played a large role in the events at Joplin. Lynching "in postbellum America was an aspect of a larger cultural war over the nature of criminal justice waged between rural and working-class supporters of 'rough justice' and middle-class due-process advocates."[122] In Joplin, the battle for Thomas Gilyard's life literally became a tug of war between working-class lynchers and middle-class advocates of due process—Joplin city attorney Perl Decker, Mayor John C. Trigg, former U.S. marshal E. D. Nix, Dr. Francis E. Rohan, the mayor-elect Tom W. Cunningham, and the assistant prosecutor David E. Blair.[123]

Many of those who fought to stop the lynching were lawyers who saw lynchings as "destructive to the cause of law and order."[124] Their opponents were primarily "rural residents or members of the urban petty mercantile or working class." The three men charged with the murder of Gilyard—Sam Mitchell, B. H. Barnes, and Ellsworth "Hickory Bill" Fields—were all members of the working class. Barnes was a teamster, Mitchell was a paint company employee, and Fields was a miner.[125]

This culture of violence was not new to Missouri, but its focus had shifted. In his article on the history of lynching in Missouri, Pfeifer points out that prior to 1900, "some of Missouri's lynchings reflected the state's frontier heritage: lynch mobs in under populated regions lacking strong legal institutions murdered almost as many whites as blacks." After 1900, however, 89 percent of those lynched were black, reflecting "southern patterns of racial violence."[126]

The lynching, in addition to punishing Thomas Gilyard, was used to enforce white social control over blacks and eliminate black social and economic competition.[127] Statistically, blacks did not appear to pose a social or economic threat to whites. Of Joplin's twenty-six-thousand-plus residents, almost eight hundred were African Ameri-cans.[128] The mining industry was segregated. Blacks were left with menial, lower-class jobs such as waiter, servant, washerwoman, and porter. Yet working-class whites may have nevertheless anxiously viewed blacks as rivals for jobs, as the Freeman Foundry episode illustrates.[129] Thomas Gilyard's death may have been used, then, as an opportunity to reinforce white superiority by working-class whites. Perhaps the working-class character of the lynching left local officials more willing to prosecute members of the mob than their counterparts in Pierce City.

Ironically, the brothers of Gisele Wild may have fired the last shots of the Joplin episode. The *Peirce City Democrat* reported that two black men had the misfortune of passing by the Wild family farm west of Pierce City. As the men approached the yard, Mrs. Wild screamed, "Niggers!" Her cry of alarm prompted her sons to seize their rifles. The boys fired several rounds at the men as they fled but it was not clear if anyone was wounded in the melee. The *Democrat* speculated that the men were among those who had left Joplin days earlier. The ghosts of Pierce City lived on.[130]

FIVE

Joplin

"Hurrah for Hickory Bill"

On the morning of Saturday, April 18, 1903, the courtroom of Judge
Hugh Dabbs buzzed with activity. Saturdays were reserved for motions
and the courthouse was crowded with attorneys who waited to make
their next legal maneuver. Among those present were the attorneys representing Sarah Godley, the widow of French Godley. It was Mrs.
Godley's last chance to win a motion for retrial. But the efforts of her
attorneys were in vain. Dabbs, a thirty-something Missouri lawyer
turned judge, denied their motion. He ruled that Mrs. Godley had
already received a fair trial.[1] With the simple stroke of Judge Dabbs's
gavel, it was made clear that justice would not be served in Jasper
County, Missouri. Just as the legal proceedings stemming from the Pierce
City violence ended, those related to Joplin began—in the same courtroom. Sam Mitchell, the alleged ringleader of the mob that rampaged
through Joplin, and who allegedly played a major role in the death of
Thomas Gilyard, was present in Judge Dabbs's courtroom that day.
Mitchell, along with his accomplices "Hickory Bill" Fields and a teamster
named B. H. Barnes, had been charged with the murder of Gilyard.

Unfortunately, the case files of Sam Mitchell, Ellsworth "Hickory
Bill" Fields, and B. H. Barnes have disappeared, leaving an unclear pic-
ture of the proceedings that followed.[2] The *Joplin Daily Globe* and the
Carthage Evening Press, however, provide a glimpse of the trials. Jasper
County prosecuting attorney Andrew H. Redding made the decision
to press charges.[3]

Mitchell and Fields, when brought before the court, pleaded not guilty. Judge Dabbs refused to grant bond to the two men.[4] At the same time, the *Joplin Daily News Herald* reported, a subscription was being raised for Mitchell's family. Lee Shepherd, Mitchell's attorney, circulated a petition to ensure that Mitchell's wife and children would not be left destitute while he was in jail. A number of Joplin citizens signed the petitions and promised to support Mitchell's family.[5]

"Hickory Bill" Fields, along with Mitchell and Barnes, was among thirteen prisoners transferred from Carthage to Joplin for a court appearance. The deputies who escorted the group, however, did not chain Fields to any of the black prisoners also present. After court, the motley group of prisoners stood outside to await transport back to Carthage, when a crowd of curious spectators approached, a number of whom were African American. Fields, seething with anger, drew himself up straight and bellowed, "Well, this is Hickory Bill, if that's who you're looking for." Then when Fields caught sight of the blacks, he snarled, "All you niggers get away from there. Get you, d—— you. Hit the grit."[6]

Mitchell went on trial in early June. This was not the first time Sam Mitchell had been in trouble. An article on the lynching in Joplin from the *Empire City Journal* wryly remarked he "seems born to trouble." According to the *Journal*, Mitchell was a former Empire City assistant marshal who because of his "scrappy and contentious disposition, had trouble a plenty and to spare." He fought local tough Jim Slatton seven times and repeatedly lost. Mitchell also tangled with one John Norton, who promptly shot Mitchell in the neck.[7] At his trial Joplin police officer Ben May, the head of the Joplin Improvement Association A. V. Boswell, the city councilman Andy Donnan, and mining engineer George Wheaton testified they saw Mitchell climb the telephone and string up the rope used to hang Thomas Gilyard.[8]

A. J. Morgan, proprietor of the Morgan Paint Company and Mitchell's employer, testified that Mitchell had been at work the day of the lynching until six in the evening. One of Mitchell's coworkers also vouched for Mitchell's whereabouts on the stand. The defense called witnesses who swore that Mitchell was not the man who secured the rope used to lynch Gilyard. The *Joplin Daily Globe* reported that many spectators felt as though the state had presented a weak case against Mitchell. In light of the conflicting testimony of the witnesses, the paper went so far as to speculate that Mitchell had a double.[9]

After a series of continuances, Mitchell's fate was placed in the hands of the jury, an overwhelmingly majority of whom were farmers. The *Globe* confidently predicted that Mitchell would be acquitted as the defense had done an excellent job of casting doubt upon his participation in the lynching.[10] The *Carthage Evening Press* reported that at first it appeared the case would end in a hung jury. But once the five holdouts were convinced that Mitchell was the man who secured the rope, a guilty verdict was reached. The jury recommended ten years in the state penitentiary, the minimum sentence for second-degree murder. This decision came as a great shock to some, while others claimed, "I told you so; it couldn't be anything else."[11] Mitchell's attorneys quickly filed a motion for retrial.[12]

In the meantime, Ellsworth "Hickory Bill" Fields and B. H. Barnes went on trial. The two were to go on trial together, but Barnes was eventually granted a severance. Witnesses for the state testified they saw Barnes battering down the door of the Joplin city jail and heard him yell, "Hang the negro!" Several defense witnesses testified that while they saw Barnes in the mob, he did not participate in the lynching of Thomas Gilyard, but was a mere bystander. Barnes's defense attorney, W. N. Andrews, took the stand to testify he saw the owner of the St. James Hotel and "Hickory Bill" Fields break down the jail door. He then asserted a man named Frank Shafer was the leader of the mob. The defense presented many more witnesses than the state, and their testimony may have been enough to sway the all-white jury.[13]

When the not guilty verdict was read that same day, clapping erupted and a cheer went up in the courtroom, "Hurrah for Hickory Bill." The judge ordered those responsible for the noise to step forward, but when no one acknowledged their guilt, the court deputy singled out "Hickory Bill" Fields, Mrs. Sam Mitchell, and G. W. Smith. Mrs. Mitchell and her lady friends were excused from the court. Fields and Smith, however, were not as lucky. Both were sentenced to ten days in jail for their disruption. As he was led out of the courtroom, Fields admitted he meant to cheer for Barnes, but accidentally cheered himself. "I did not mean to toot my own horn," he stated earnestly. Both Smith and Fields were later acquitted of the misdemeanor offense and did not serve jail time.[14]

The trial of "Hickory Bill" Fields appears to be lost to history. There is no mention of it in the *Joplin Daily Globe* or the *Carthage Evening*

Press. Fields may have been acquitted just as Barnes was. Or, perhaps the prosecutor withdrew the charges against Fields after Barnes's acquittal feeling further proceedings would be futile. Interestingly, while witnesses allegedly saw both Barnes and Fields take part in burning down black homes, the Jasper County prosecuting attorney failed to file arson charges, whether due to disillusionment with Jasper County juries or sheer apathy.

Sam Mitchell faced his second trial in November 1903 after his attorneys' motion for a new trial was granted on technical grounds. According to the *Carthage Evening Press,* Mitchell proved to be a model prisoner during his time in jail. One jail official stated Mitchell was "one of the best prisoners." His attorneys argued that Mitchell was not present at the lynching and that Thomas Gilyard was already dead by the time he was lynched. This argument was crafted to counter the state's damning eyewitness testimony from the first trial.[15]

Despite the testimony of several witnesses for the state to the contrary, defense witness J. C. Siegfried swore that he and Mitchell were together at Morgan Paint Company during the lynching. He claimed they arrived at the scene of the lynching to find that Gilyard had already been hanged. The jury was out for an hour before it returned its verdict of not guilty. The *Carthage Evening Press* reported that the jury's first vote returned several ballots in favor of a guilty verdict with a lesser sentence. Someone in the jury room, however, successfully argued that Mitchell should not be punished for the crimes "committed by hundreds of men in his company." Siegfried was charged with perjury and arrested.[16] Yet no further action was taken and Sam Mitchell, "Hickory Bill" Fields, and B. H. Barnes walked free.

The subsequent fate of "Hickory Bill" Fields is unknown. Mitchell, however, remained in Joplin. He died just after Christmas in 1926, nearly sixty years of age, much older than Thomas Gilyard, who had been dead for twenty-three years. At the time of his death, Mitchell worked as a smelterman for the Eagle-Picher Lead Company, which is still in operation today.[17] Barnes died at the height of the Great Depression after working as a concrete contractor in Joplin for several years.[18]

The man who attempted to stop the mob, Perl Decker, enjoyed a successful career as an attorney. In 1912, he was elected to the U.S. House of Representatives as a Democrat and served three terms. Ironically, in his final congressional campaign in 1918, Decker was defeated by Isaac V. McPherson, the former Lawrence County prosecuting attorney who oversaw the trial of Joe Lark for the murder of Gisele Wild.[19] During the 1920s, Decker railed against the Ku Klux Klan. Yet when the Jasper County Bar Association proposed a resolution that would force Klan members to resign their bar membership because the Klan's religious intolerance was "a violation of . . . the Constitution of the United States," Decker disagreed. While he reminded his fellow bar members that he loathed the Klan, he argued that the Klan had the constitutional right to oppose whatever religion it so desired.

Decker went on to say, "I believe in the enforcement of the law, but I do not believe in the taking of human life as a punishment for wrong doing, except after a trial by jury, the sentence of a judge and at the hands of a sheriff." Decker continued, "The fact that murder can be condoned and lightly held by respectable citizens bespeaks a dangerous condition of society." It was as if Decker was arguing with the ghosts of 1903 from the steps of the Joplin city jail. The Jasper County Bar Association promptly passed a resolution that condemned the Klan and asked that any Klan member present resign his membership with the bar.[20]

Decker, eulogized as one of the most gifted orators to grace the House of Representatives as well as a masterful attorney, lost the case of his life when a mob successfully sought extralegal justice at the end of a rope.[21] If Decker could not win their hearts, then no one else could have.

Studies of lynching seldom mention the prosecution of lynch mob participants because local authorities often declined to press charges. In Jasper County, Missouri, though, local prosecutors pressed charges against the three men held responsible for the death of Thomas Gilyard. There is no evidence to suggest that they suffered politically because of their action. It is possible that because it was members of the working class that were accused that prosecutors saw less chance of career suicide by pursuing action. The state of Missouri would not sanction the violence wrought by the Joplin mob by idly standing by. What is even more remarkable than the action of the prosecuting attorney is that Sam Mitchell, thought to be the man who secured the rope used to lynch Thomas Gilyard, was found guilty of second-degree murder and sentenced to ten years by an all-white jury.

Newspaper accounts do not offer a clear picture of why the jury chose to convict Mitchell. It remains unclear if jurors used Mitchell as a sacrificial lamb in order to put the bloody events of April behind them or if they truly believed in the rule of law. Their decision does, however, indicate that whites were not always united in the wake of mob violence.

The second jury flinched, however. One newspaper account indicates that the jury was close to securing a guilty verdict when one juror argued Mitchell could not be held accountable for the actions of hundreds of other men in the mob.[22] If Mitchell were convicted, then collectively, every man, woman, and child in the mob would have been symbolically guilty of lynching Thomas Gilyard, an admission that ultimately the jury did not want to make. It was better that Mitchell go free than admit that an entire community had participated in the lynching and expulsion of blacks from Joplin.

SIX

Springfield

"The Devil Was Just as Good a Friend to God"

In 1878 the editor of the *Springfield Leader* groused, "In many places in the East, Southwest Missouri is looked upon as inhabited by a set of long-haired, ignorant bush-whackers. People there appear never to have heard of any but the very worst class of our people, and one old lady was much surprised when we told her of the seven or eight churches in Springfield."[1]

Springfield, Missouri, in fact was no longer the muddy hamlet of its youth. Founded in 1835 by John P. Campbell, a native of Tennessee, Springfield emerged from a small preexisting settlement that boasted a school, a church, and a racetrack.[2] Campbell and his brother-in-law, Joseph Miller, brought not only their families to the region; they also brought six slaves. When a cholera epidemic swept through the area in mid-1835, two of Campbell's slaves died.[3] They were perhaps among the first African Americans to perish on the vast, rolling Springfield Plain.

During this time, a curious custom emerged. The local historian George S. Escott recalled, "In 1835 and 1836, it became a custom among the youngsters to 'make niggers' of such strangers as they could manage." The perpetrators used burnt cork to blacken the faces of their unsuspecting victims who were then subjected to laughter and ridicule. Escott remembered one episode in which two brothers, passed out from a night of drinking, were subjected to this peculiar prank. The next morning the two men were invited to have a drink together.

When one brother mistook the other for a black man, he snorted that he "was not in the habit of drinking with niggers." The other, oblivious, became enraged and attacked his brother before they discovered they had been tricked.[4]

While some of Springfield's citizens may have felt antagonistic toward blacks, in 1841 permits were granted to free blacks that allowed them to reside in the region, "during good behavior, and no longer." John Rider and Margaret Williams were among the first to receive permits.[5] By 1850, Greene County was the most populous county in southwest Missouri, with a total population of 12,785 residents. The total white population was listed as 11,548 with 1,230 slaves. Only seven free blacks were enumerated in the census.[6] Springfield, which served as both the county seat and the center of regional commerce, prospered. Farmers and merchants found a steady market to the west in Indian Territory. Missouri mules were sold to southern plantations in Louisiana, Arkansas, and Mississippi. Goods from St. Louis were transported west on the Missouri River to Boonville, one of Missouri's bustling river towns, and then hauled overland south to Springfield. Stagecoach service was available to Boonville and Jefferson City and to Fayetteville, Arkansas. Brick buildings began to replace older log structures while churches and schools began to dot the landscape. [7]

Mules were not the only valuable commodity sold in Springfield. One Greene County history reported that in 1857 slaves sold at a "good price." When Daniel Boone's son, Nathan Boone, died at his farm outside Springfield, his eleven slaves were sold at auction.[8]

Despite its economic progress, Springfield still had rough edges. In 1859, Albert D. Richardson, a correspondent for the *New York Tribune,* passed through Springfield on his way to the Pacific Coast. He later published an account of his trip, *Beyond the Mississippi: From the Great River to the Great Ocean* in which he recalled his stay in Springfield:

> After passing some beautiful prairies and enduring another night of uneasy slumber, we woke in Springfield, on the summit of the Ozark Mountains—the leading town of southwestern Missouri . . . Springfield had pleasant, vine-trellised dwellings, and two thousand five hundred people. The low straggling hotel with high belfry was on the rural southern model: dining-room full of flies,

with a long paper-covered frame swinging to and fro over the table to keep them from the food; the bill of fare, bacon corn bread and coffee; the rooms ill-furnished, towels missing, pitchers empty, and the bed and table linen seeming to have been dragged through the nearest pond, and dried upon gridirons.

Springfield, however, was memorable for more than just its lack of modern amenities. During Richardson's stay, a slave named Mart Danforth was arrested for assaulting a white woman. In the excitement that ensued, "some hot-heads proposed collecting all the slaves from the adjacent farms, and burning them on the public square." As Richardson noted, two slaves reportedly had been burned at the stake for a similar crime in nearby Jasper County within the last two years.[9] Springfield, however, "would have no burning declaring it too barbarous." Instead, a mob seized Danforth from authorities and hanged him from a locust tree on the outskirts of town. Richardson lamented, "Leading citizens assured me that for the same offense a white man would have received the same punishment; but how terribly unjust the system which, denying light and education to these poor creatures, still held them to a strict criminal responsibility!"[10]

While slavery vanished from southwest Missouri at the conclusion of the Civil War, Springfield did not emerge unscathed. For four years, conventional and guerrilla warfare ravaged the region with Springfield at its epicenter. Union and Confederate troops alternately occupied the town until 1862, when Union forces finally consolidated control over Springfield. But even Union control of the town brought new challenges. As one Greene County history recalled, "Churches became hospitals and arsenals, private houses barracks and quarters, gardens and parks were converted into camping grounds, and everywhere were soldiers and cannon."[11]

The war left Springfield exhausted. The once-prosperous business community found itself in shambles as much of the town's economic infrastructure was destroyed by the chaos of warfare. Springfield society also experienced significant change. Blacks, once enslaved, were now free to establish their own Baptist and Methodist churches.[12] On January 4, 1866, Emeline Howard and Letitia Townsend of the Iowa Friends Freedmen's Aid Commission founded a school to educate "those so lately freed from bondage, who have heretofore been denied the blessings of instruction." They reported that one hundred and fifty students were currently enrolled.[13] Many of the immediate immigrants to the region were former Union soldiers who, during the war, were posted at Springfield.[14]

When the journalist George Ward Nichols arrived in Springfield in 1867 to profile Wild Bill Hickok, then living in Springfield, he found a "strange, half-civilized people" whose sole characteristic "seemed to be an indisposition to move, and their highest ambition to let their hair and beards grow." When people did move, "they did so slowly and without method. No one seemed in haste."[15] If Springfield was to regain its ambitious spirit, it needed more than just former Union soldiers to revitalize it. Skilled labor, capital, and the railroad were necessary to move Springfield forward.

As Springfield's newspapers advocated progress, the town slowly began to improve as the flow of immigrants and money began to increase. In 1866, the town's first public library opened. The following year, after a fire destroyed most of the town square, Springfield's first fire department was formed. It was at this time that "the town was crowded to overflowing by the large number of newcomers. Hotels, boarding houses, and every room capable of sheltering a human being was occupied." Street lamps appeared for the first time along Springfield's streets and avenues.[16]

At this time, African Americans composed almost 20 percent of Springfield's population and, for the first time, showed the potential influence black voters could have on future elections.[17] In 1870, by a vote of 101 to 54, J. H. Rector, an African American, defeated his white opponent in the race for city council.[18] It was reportedly the first time African Americans were allowed to vote in a Springfield city election.[19] Rector, though, was quickly met with scorn from others in the black community. A letter from the "colored citizens of Springfield" appeared in the *Missouri Weekly Patriot* claiming that Rector "has been attending political meetings, telling everywhere that he was leading the colored people, and that what he said they would do." He "will yet make the Radical party wonder at his dishonesty and regret that they ever trusted him as a representative of colored people." The group alleged Rector had gone to Democrats and stated that, "if the Radical party did not come to a certain proposition that he made in one of his meetings" then he would deliver black voters to the Democrats. Rector's constituents, however, proclaimed, "We are Republicans and are not led by the whims and caprices of Mr. Rector; nor to be transferred to the opposition camp at his will. He has come down here from the East expecting the colored people to support him, but we have no use for him, and hope those who have, will send for him." The letter was signed by eighteen of Springfield's leading black citizens.[20]

Blacks not only exercised their right to vote; they rejoiced in it. On April 21, 1870, Springfield's African American community celebrated the ratification of the Fifteenth Amendment. At ten that morning, a procession marched through Springfield to the city fairgrounds, where the crowd listened to speeches given by J. H. Rector and J. Milton Turner, Missouri's most distinguished black postwar political leader. Local Radical Republican politicians, such as Colonel W. D. Hubbard, also spoke. A second event, held at night, was scheduled at Springfield's city hall. When both blacks and whites arrived, one of the "proprietors" of the hall demanded an admission fee, which meant that "hundreds of the negroes could not go in and many whites would not submit to such an imposition." After a platform was hastily erected outside city hall, more speeches were given before the celebration ended.[21]

After the election of J. H. Rector, blacks continued to exercise a certain political clout. At a mass meeting of black voters in 1874, James Stone was selected as a candidate for the city council, as he was in the words of a Republican newspaper, "a capable, faithful and honest citizen."[22] Stone won the election and was the second African American to be sworn in as a member of the city council. He was appointed to serve on the streets and cemetery committees.[23]

Stone, a former slave, served three terms on the Springfield city council. When Mayor McAdoo could not attend a council meeting, Stone presided in his stead, and was the first African American to act as mayor of Springfield. He often told a story about his first drink as a free man. As a slave, Stone observed white men toasting each other in saloons, which "seemed a glorious prerogative of freedom." Although not fond of whiskey, Stone enjoyed "the high privilege of being allowed to fill his glass and quaff off the beverage at the bar as a free man." When he died, the *Springfield Leader-Democrat* proclaimed, "no negro of the town ever stood higher in the estimation of white men than Jim Stone."[24]

Shortly after taking office, Stone, on behalf of the black citizens of

Springfield, asked that an African American be appointed to the police. Out of six candidates, five of whom were white, Lewis Tutt was selected and sworn in as Springfield's first African American police officer.[25] One Springfield paper remarked, "the action of the council in confirming a colored man and in reject[ing] the son of a rebel will afford a matter for some folks to talk about anyhow."[26]

Tutt, the son of a white slave owner and an enslaved black mother, was born into slavery in Yellville, Arkansas. After Union troops occupied the region, he dutifully escorted his father's widow from Yellville to Springfield. When the war ended, Tutt remained in Springfield and worked for several merchants before entering the grocery business. His venture met with success and Tutt began to invest in real estate. By the 1890s, he was one of the wealthiest African Americans in Springfield. He donated money for the Perkins Opera Building and reportedly assisted in the building of every black church in Springfield. When his white half-brother, Dave Tutt was killed by Wild Bill Hickok on the Springfield square in 1865, Lewis Tutt claimed the body and paid for Dave's burial in Maple Park Cemetery. A biographical sketch of Tutt declared, "Mr. Tutt has always been an honorable man, and is an excellent example of the prosperity that can be attained by the colored man who perseveres in his determination to succeed."[27]

Tutt was not the only black to make headway in the local community. The Greene County bar admitted its first African American attorney in 1870 when J. A. "Judge" Callaway was admitted to the bar. He was followed by T. C. "Bud" Johnston, who was admitted to the bar in 1879.[28] Shadrack "Shade" Coker was the second African American appointed to the Springfield police, although he, like Tutt, served only one term.[29]

Alfred "Alf" Adams, Springfield's most influential African American political leader, served one term as coroner before going on to become the boss of Springfield's Fourth Ward.[30] As the ward's political boss, he wielded considerable power over the black vote. Adams oversaw the "Fishing Scheme" which was an "organization composed of negroes who for years have been trying to force the Republican party to give the negro some recognition for his loyalty to the party."[31] On one occasion, Adams, miffed at fellow members of the Republican Party, was said to have ordered every Fourth Ward black voter to stay at home during an election. As a result, "the Democratic ticket went over with a hurrah."[32]

Adams, a barber by trade, operated one of the finest barbershops in Springfield. There, in his tailored clothes, top hat, and diamond stick pin, he held court over the "rendezvous for the best political brains both locally and statewide." According to one account, Adams served as Chauncey J. Filley's right-hand man in Springfield when Filley was the top Republican boss in Missouri. He remained active in politics until the end of his life. Before his death in 1902, Adams served as a member of the city council.[33]

William Smith, who was elected to serve as coroner for two years, met with controversy, suggesting that area whites were not entirely comfortable with African Americans occupying positions of authority. In 1882, when Smith was up for reelection, the *Springfield Express* snorted, "The nomination for coroner is the only prize the Republican county convention could spare to the colored race, notwithstanding the fact that, without the votes of the blacks the Republicans of Greene County would never have a ghost of a chance to elect a single candidate." Smith, who the *Express* derisively called "as black as the ace of spades" was, according to the newspaper, guilty of "a deed that is still blacker than his face. The details of the affair are too indecent for publication in a newspaper." The *Express* also pointed out that Smith had presided over the "body of Mrs. Randall, the wife of a worthy white mechanic, and by his conduct on that occasion aroused the intense indignation and mortification of the dead lady's friends and others who were present."[34] Smith was not reelected.

Five years later, Springfield Republicans nominated John H. McCracken, an African American barber, for the office of city assessor. Springfield's Democratic newspaper, the *Leader,* labeled McCracken, "the chronic colored kicker." Of the fifty-four delegates at the local Republican convention, only seven were African American, including Alf Adams, William Smith, J. W. Lusk, and John H. McCracken.[35]

When the election rolled around in April, McCracken ran against the Union Labor candidate, John H. Berry. Springfield Democrats, for reasons unknown, had failed to nominate a candidate for city assessor that year. As votes were counted, McCracken was declared the victor by three votes.[36]

The *Republican* prematurely trumpeted, "Mr. McCracken, who went into the office of assessor by a majority of 221, is one of the best known colored men in the city, and he has defeated a very popular man, in Mr. J. Berry, the Union Labor candidate."[37] McCracken's victory was inexplicably short-lived. On April 4, 1888, the *Republican* sheepishly announced, "The counting out of John McCracken last night for the office of assessor was a surprise to his friends and the public generally, but it only illustrates the fallacy of reports of election obtained from other than official sources." Whereas it had first appeared McCracken won by three votes, the final vote count gave Berry a majority of 260 votes.[38] The Democratic *Leader* cackled, "John Berry's election was a surprise to everybody and especially to Deacon McCracken, who thought of the many luxuries he would enjoy this summer. It is said that he will make an effort to contest." Springfield papers, however, did not report any further developments.[39] In the same election, another member of Springfield's African American community was successful, but not without strenuous effort.

City councilman Alf Adams was reelected by voters in Springfield's Fourth Ward by a margin of forty-four votes. The *Republican* sourly reported, "A colored man of that ward assures The Republican that the chief Democratic managers openly displayed handfuls of money there, and that he saw not less than five hundred dollars evidently for the purchase of votes." If true, Adams was fortunate to keep his seat.[40] It appeared that the citizens of Springfield could tolerate an African American as a city councilman when he was limited to serving on the Cemetery Committee, but not one who would be responsible for determining the value of their property.[41]

An event in 1871, however, illustrated that while blacks had made significant gains since emancipation and exercised meaningful political power they were still vulnerable. Bud Isbell, an African American, allegedly assaulted the wife of Peter Christian. Christian, a white laborer, was away from home when Isbell stopped by the Christian household for a drink of water. Isbell reportedly "made an insulting proposition" to Mrs. Christian. When she rebuffed his advances, Isbell attacked her, and then fled. Mr. Christian immediately announced a one-hundred-dollar reward for his arrest. The *Missouri Patriot* growled, "So monstrous an offender against society ought not to be permitted to run at large; and every good citizen should promptly aid in ferreting him out." Citizens were advised that Isbell was about twenty years old, five feet five inches, and poorly clothed.[42]

Within a week, Isbell was captured near Newtonia, in Newton County, Missouri. The *Missouri Patriot* remarked that Isbell was "pursued with much persistency by numerous persons, and was probably concealed somewhere in this city for several days after the commission of the crime, thus evading capture until he ventured to attempt an escape out of the country." Upon his return to Springfield, Mrs. Christian identified him as the man who attacked her. Isbell was then taken to the city square where a small group of men began deliberating his fate. As the men discussed what to do, a crowd began to form.[43]

With the Greene County sheriff, the mayor of Springfield, and the Springfield city marshal present, Isbell was taken to the same tree where, in 1859, Mart Danforth was lynched.[44] There he was put on a horse and a noose was secured around his neck. Major R. B. Chappel pled with the mob to wait until Isbell's guilt had been conclusively proven. He also appealed to the mob to move the lynching outside of town so that Isbell would not be lynched within view of some of Springfield's finest private residences. Pistols were pulled on Chappel and he quietly stepped aside. Someone from the mob led the horse forward until Isbell slid off and was left hanging from a tree branch. A shot was fired into his body as the crowd dispersed. Isbell's corpse was left hanging from the tree until the coroner was summoned to take charge of the remains. The verdict of the coroner's jury was one all too uncommon, "deceased came to his death by the being shot and hung by three parties named, supported by a large number of others."

The jury's verdict and testimony was submitted to local law enforcement officials, but, the *Patriot* mused, "Whether anything will be done in that direction we do not know; though we think the matter will be dropped without further investigation." Isbell was, the newspaper claimed, "ignorant and brutal in his appearance" and had committed a similar assault on a young African American girl just weeks before he attacked Mrs. Christian. This, the *Patriot* claimed, "created considerable feeling on the part of many who had no regrets for the fate of the guilty individual."[45]

Racial violence did not diminish Springfield's hope of continued growth. Despite the economic depression of 1873, business leaders were determined to bring a rail line to town. The project, which was completed over the next few years, was a success. In 1881, the first train rolled into Springfield, bringing with it Springfield's economic resurgence.[46] Outside markets were now connected to the town's industries, which included wagon factories, flour mills, tobacco and cigar factories, a foundry, and pharmaceutical laboratories.[47]

African Americans were among those who benefited from Springfield's economic recovery. The 1880 federal census shows that blacks were employed in a wide variety of jobs, often alongside whites, that they were later excluded from. Many men, like brothers Harry and David Brown, worked in the cotton factory.[48] A fortunate few worked in the railroad shops.[49] Others, including young children, were employed at the tobacco factories.[50] Several women, like Malinda Prater, were employed as seamstresses or as laundresses.[51] Sisters Eliza and Missouri McDaniel listed their occupation as nurse.[52]

Children of African American workers attended public school, but not without difficulty as whites placed a higher priority on the success of the city rather than the future of the black community. When white business leaders backed the expansion of Drury College at the expense of one of the oldest black schools in Springfield, it was clear that black education came at the convenience of the white community.[53]

One of the oldest schools for African Americans in Springfield had become landlocked. The campus of Drury College, founded in 1873 with the intention of becoming the "Yale of the Southwest," now surrounded the school. The college needed the land that the African American school occupied for future improvements to its campus. The school's fate became a city-wide question as a proposal to sell the property went before the citizens of Springfield. The sale was not advocated by Springfield's black citizens; instead, Drury's board of directors and the Springfield Board of Education agreed to the proposal, infuriating Springfield's African American community.

Drury president, the Reverend N. J. Morrison, asserted, "We have no wish to injure the colored school and would not ask for the property if we could not place them in as good condition as we find them; nor have we any objection to their proximity to the College." R. L. McElhany, a banker who served on the city's board of education, stated, "My private views are that the college does not really need the ground," and added that, "from a commercial point of view, that it has no rights superior to those of any other property holder." McElhany observed, "The parties who are directly interested in this proposed removal of the school—the colored people, ought to be allowed to settle this question for themselves."[54]

Other whites were not as open-minded as McElhany. General C. B. Holland, a Union veteran and banker, declared, "I am for Drury. I regard the opposition to this proposed measure as merely fractious, and think ward politics have more to do with it than anything else." Colonel W. D. Crothers argued, "If it were a white school that was to be removed, this opposition would never have been heard of. It is a political measure, no doubt, designed to influence colored voters at the approaching city election." Dr. J. T. Means dismissed black concerns as nothing but "race prejudice and jealousy."[55]

If whites viewed the proposal as agreeable, blacks did not. James Stone, the former Springfield councilman, voiced his opposition to the proposal and noted the "plans of the colored people for using this building as a high school and college." Alf Adams, who helped found the school, was "discovered to be in a state of fiery indignation." Adams viewed the proposed seizure as an "unwarranted attack upon the liberties of the colored people" and angrily remarked, "The devil was just as good a friend to God as Doctor Morrison is to the colored people."[56] Not surprisingly, the proposal to move the school passed.[57] Although members of the white economic elite appeared divided over the issue, the episode demonstrated that Springfield's African Americans were at the mercy of the white community.

Racial tension continued to build throughout the 1880s as daily accounts of black on white crime filled the local newspapers and threatened to spill over with the murder of a Springfield police officer. In August 1888, Springfield police officers Roberts and Palmore prowled the city streets looking for Si Bearden. Bearden, an African American, was wanted for pistol whipping Newton Edmondson.[58] When Officers Palmore and Roberts attempted to arrest Bearden, Bearden shot Palmore. The officer, a Confederate veteran from Virginia, later succumbed of his wounds.[59]

Bearden, in the confusion and darkness, escaped despite being shot through the cheek. Officers were alerted and immediately began searching for him. Bearden's employer, livery owner H. H. Westmoreland, declared, "He is black as the ace of spades and one of the smartest negroes in Springfield. Many darkies around town were afraid of him because he would not hesitate to knock them down if they 'crossed' him."[60]

Anger and outrage rippled through Springfield. The *Daily Herald* cackled, "A great deal of excitement has resulted from the affair and if Bearden recovers it is probable that citizens may take the law into their own hands." The murderer, the *Herald,* suggested, would be "the victim of a 'necktie party.'"[61]

Tempers were already running high in Springfield due to the attempted sexual assault of a young white woman, Nannie Lewis, just days earlier by two African American men. Springfield police officers quickly arrested Sam Turner and Pete Harmon. Lewis identified Harmon as her attacker, but was less certain when she was asked to identify Turner. Nonetheless, both men were jailed.[62] They joined Dick Carr, a black prison escapee from Arkansas, who was arrested for attempting to rape a young white woman near Drury College.[63]

An unnamed white citizen wrote a letter to the *Springfield Daily Leader* and protested the criminal behavior that plagued the city. "Are the whites to be exterminated or not?" the writer asked, "Is the lower class of the nigger element to run Springfield and not to be interrupted for fear of the few votes cast or not?" The anonymous individual declared Good Child's Lane, "a stench to the face of heaven and a disgrace to the fair name of Springfield." For those brave enough to venture there, they would see, "scenes of pandemonium reign supreme in the lane—shooting, yelling, fighting, dancing, gambling, and raising the devil generally." The street was populated with "the hardest lot of the negro element," who kept up "a constant racket that makes night hideous and sleep impossible."

White landlords who rented to these criminals should "be run out of town" because "if the ravishes and murders committed during the past year continue, no decent white man or woman can live here—for they are never convicted, the whites killed and ravished and the negro go free." To stop the hellish carnival that pervaded Good Child's Lane, the writer suggested, "We will be compelled to rise en masse and run them all out of town, as in other places of the South, where they rise up and run the town."

Men like Bearden "should be taken as a wild beast, killed first and taken afterwards." The writer angrily accused Springfield's lawyers of "all joining to clear the devils and let the good man be killed. We warn the lawyers, courts, and officers to do their duty or the blood will not all be shed on one side. The decent men of the community will rise up and assert their rights before they will be entirely exterminated."[64] Passions also ran high among members of the black community.

The night after the shooting, a group of African Americans allegedly cornered Henry Bryant, a black deputy, while Bryant was searching for Bearden. The men notified Bryant that "if Bearden was hung, they would raise a mob and hang him, Bryant, Newt Edmondson, and Taylor Smith."[65] Bearden, however, was shot and captured a few days later by a group of law enforcement officers outside of Springfield.[66]

Mayor Walker and the Springfield city council passed a resolution that kept Officer Palmore on the city payroll for the months of August and September to help his widow and children. Councilman Alf Adams asked for more police officers but was curtly told, "there was no money in the treasury with which to pay them and the subject was dropped."[67]

Si Bearden, despite his wounds, lived. After he attempted to escape from jail, Greene County sheriff Joseph Dodson sent Bearden to St. Louis for safekeeping. Dodson denied that the fear of mob violence motivated him to remove Bearden from Springfield. Bearden was sentenced to ninety-nine years at the Missouri State Penitentiary in Jefferson City, but was pardoned by Governor Lon Stephens in 1899. Judge Charles A. Hubbard, who oversaw the trial, agreed that "Bearden had been sufficiently punished."[68] While some individuals of the black community turned to crime, many more were productive members of Springfield's citizenry, who shared the civic pride of a growing city and proudly stepped forward to serve their country alongside their white brethren.

As the end of the century loomed, the celebratory atmosphere of a unified Springfield dimmed when, in 1898, war broke out between the United States and Spain. Among those who answered the call to arms were members of Springfield's African American community. Many of the men who signed up for service came from the city's black elite, such as Joe Armstrong, Thomas Campbell, and Walter Majors.[69] Captain James J. Mayes, a native Ohioan and graduate of Drury

College, was responsible for recruiting men to serve in Company L of the Seventh Regiment United States Volunteer Infantry. Mayes briefly practiced law in Springfield before working as a reporter for the *St. Louis Globe-Democrat*.[70] Now he found himself responsible for finding enough enlistees to serve in his "Immune" regiment. Black regiments at this time were called "Immunes" because it was widely believed that African Americans, due to their African ancestry, were immune to tropical diseases found in Cuba and the Philippines.[71] The regiment was headed by a white captain, but blacks were permitted to serve as first and second lieutenants.[72] Mayes had little difficulty finding men for his regiment.

Thomas Campbell, a graduate of Howard University's law school and one of city's few African American attorneys, was appointed first lieutenant in the regiment.[73] The *Republican* called Campbell, "one of the most capable and brilliant colored men in Missouri and is well known throughout the state."[74] Campbell, born on July 4, 1869, was among many of men who were "anxious to serve their country and fight under the flag which freed them."[75]

Joe Armstrong, a veteran of the Springfield police force for five years, resigned his police commission to go to war. On July 9, 1898, the *Springfield Republican* announced, "Joe Armstrong will hand in his resignation to Mayor Hall as policeman and go to Cuba, Puerto Rico, or the Philippines as a second lieutenant in the Immune regiment." Armstrong, the *Republican* proclaimed, "will make a first-class military man . . . and has the respect of both white and colored citizens." Mayor Hall and Chief of Police Bishop agreed to reinstate Armstrong to the police force when he returned from military service.[76] After it was announced that Armstrong had joined the regiment, "the recruiting office was overrun with applicants and the captain's mail was loaded down with applications from out of town."[77]

Walter L. Majors, one of Springfield's most mechanically gifted citizens, put down his tools to serve. A skilled inventor, Majors later went on to build the first car in Springfield in 1901.[78] Edward W. Hannah, a teacher, signed up as did Charles Hardrick, whose family ran the largest African American grocery store in Springfield. Other men who served were laborers, blacksmiths, hod carriers, porters, teamsters, and barbers.[79] Altogether, eighty-four men volunteered for military service.

Springfield police officer Joe Armstrong. *Courtesy of the Katherine G. Lederer Ozarks African American History Collection, Special Collections and Archives Department, Missouri State University.*

On the evening of July 16, 1898, the recruits received a rousing send-off from Springfield's white and black communities. As the company marched to the depot, conductor Ben Fay and the Hobart Military Band serenaded the crowd gathered to wish the men well. One journalist reported, "Mothers, sisters, wives, and sweethearts were seeing their loved ones probably for the last time, but it is hoped that the brave boys will return, decked with honors and crowned with victory."[80]

Once at the depot, Captain Mayes and his recruits boarded two special train cars that took them to Camp Edward A. Goodwin at Jefferson Barracks in St. Louis where they received training and instruction before they were sent off to the front. The *Republican* boasted, "Although the company is composed of the best colored boys of city, there are plenty more who are willing to go, and, if necessary, there could be several companies. There was a large number of men rejected on account of the company being filled in so short a time."[81]

After training in St. Louis, the men of Company L were ordered first to Lexington, Kentucky, and then to Macon, Georgia, where they spent the duration of the war until they mustered out February 28, 1899.[82] By March 3, several members of the company arrived in Springfield. Many of the former soldiers expressed disappointment they did not see action in Cuba.[83] On the evening of March 8, the men lined up in formation together for the last time. They marched from their enlistment office, located at Barney Freeman's barbershop on Boonville Street, to the Washington Avenue Cumberland Presbyterian Church where they were recognized for their service. Mayor Hall, local African American politician Aaron White, Lieutenant Tom Campbell, and W. G. Robertson addressed the men and the large crowd that filled the church. Lieutenant Campbell remarked on the honor accorded to the company when it passed in review before President McKinley. The president reportedly remarked that Company L "showed up in as good if not better shape than any other company of the regiment."[84]

But while Springfield's African American community volunteered to fight on behalf of their country, a shift in racial attitudes was beginning to endanger their liberties at home. Area newspapers often carried sensationalized stories of black crime committed in their own community and across the nation. Graphic accounts of African Americans being lynched in the South often made the front page. Some Democratic newspaper editors, such as Daniel Curran Kennedy, an Irish ex-Confederate and founder of the *Springfield Leader,* wrote fiery antiblack editorials on a regular basis.[85] With the coming of a new century, antebellum fears of violent slave uprisings took on a new visage. Whites read detailed accounts of cunning black criminals who committed petty robberies, murdered white men, and, worst of all, sexually assaulted white women. It was into this uncertain racial maelstrom that Springfield's African Americans were cast.

SEVEN

Springfield

"A Slumbering Volcano"

Despite the winter chill outside city hall, the chambers of the Springfield city council were filled with heated debate over a proposed cemetery ordinance on the morning of February 6, 1900. Alf Adams, the longtime black politician, ward boss, and member of the city council, asked that the fence dividing Hazelwood and South Hazelwood Cemeteries be removed. The fence had been erected by order of the city council in 1899 during the city's smallpox scare. While his request seemed simple, it was a delicate issue. Hazelwood Cemetery was solely reserved for whites while South Hazelwood Cemetery was set aside for blacks. What Adams proposed was, in essence, the desegregation of the two cemeteries.

In his report to the city council, Adams noted that due to the fence, blacks were forced to walk through "sloughs of cornstalks and acres of cockle burs to reach the last resting place of our dead loved ones." He pointed out that prior to the erection of the fence, it was "common consent" that allowed "whites and blacks alike [to travel] the same road on performing for their loved dead ones the last sad rites humanity can perform for its kind."

Adams observed that one did not have to travel far to find "the family graveyards of the pioneers of our State, the Campbells, the Berrys, the McElhaneys, the Fulbrights, the Hubbles, and last but no means least, our late distinguished and well beloved Governor Phelps, to find the graves of their onetime slaves touching foot to foot with those of their masters, their wives, and families." He then asked, "And why should we, at this late day, declare that one class of citizens, citizens under the same laws that make you all citizens, should be discriminated against?" Adams solemnly declared, "Call us 'Niggers' if you will, we care not." After a spirited debate at the morning session, the council voted on Adams's request when it reconvened in the afternoon. The proposal passed by a vote of eleven to four.[1]

The *Springfield Leader-Democrat* remarked, "This is the ordinance for which Springfield's famous colored statesman has spent the best part of his life and energy. At last, there is 'no north, no south'—at least so far as the dividing line of Hazelwood cemetery is concerned." Adams, the paper observed, "the champion of the rights of the colored race, has at last met with his long looked for triumph and the opposition are biting the dust in unavailing rage and chagrin."[2]

But the equanimity with which the paper and the city fathers greeted Adams's initiative was deceptive. As the century moved forward, race relations in Springfield did not. The following year, a day after the lynchings in Pierce City, the *Leader-Democrat* glowered, "The emancipation of the negroes did not solve a great race problem as some persons benevolently supposed. The subsequent enfranchisement of the ex-slaves did not abolish the racial strife between the white man and the black man, but rather intensified the spirit of that conflict." The paper blamed "younger negroes" for trouble between whites and blacks. The future looked grim as "the sympathy between the races is dying out. When the old negroes and the white men who owned them are gone, the strongest tie of mutual understanding and friendship between the races will be severed." Once the "honest, respectful, and kindly hearted ex-slaves are all dead and forgotten and the old plantation days have passed out of mind, the negro will have no such defense from racial persecution as now protects him."[3]

But the *Leader-Democrat* was far from done. It declared, "These crimes have increased of late years. There is no denying that fact. Growth of population and the greater publicity of events now occurring must be reckoned in estimating criminal statistics in these days, but the census reports and the newspapers do not account for the prevalence of such outrages as provoked the mob." As for why blacks committed such crimes, the *Leader-Democrat* reasoned, "Liberty came with a sweeping revolution to this race and it was inevitable that the radical change of conditions for the black man should lead to lawlessness and degeneracy among many of the descendants of the old slaves." The editorial ended, "Now the vengeful flame has been kindled in many states of the union and the readers of the daily press are familiar with the shocking headlines that tell of the mob's resistless madness in dealing with the rapist."[4]

Though it embraced common rationales for racial violence, the *Springfield Republican,* however, disapproved of what had occurred in Pierce City, although it did make light of the matter. After a sober editorial that declared, "The murdering of innocent people and the burning of their homes over the heads of women and children is an outrage and crime almost as great as the original one which occasioned the late outbreak at Peirce City," the *Republican* went on to joke, "'Hide and go seek' is the popular game between white and colored citizens at Peirce City." It then added, "That Vandalia minister who preached on the subject, 'Is there a Hell, if so, where is it?' had not heard of the Peirce City incident."[5]

Springfield's African American community, which took in several refugees from Pierce City, met to protest the lynchings. At the meeting, held at the Pitts Chapel Methodist Episcopal Church, a resolution was passed condemning the mob and its actions. The resolution read in part, "While mob violence is of frequent occurrence in nearly all sections of our country, this one at Peirce City savors more of downright barbarism than any that has occurred since the freedom of the slaves."[6] It would not be the last time that Springfield's black citizens would meet to discuss troubling matters.

The following year, on a cold January afternoon, a crowd of two hundred African Americans quietly gathered at Scales Hall on Boonville Street in Springfield to again discuss racial violence. The meeting, called by African American attorney J. A. Callaway, was led by a committee composed of several of Springfield's black elite. Among those on the committee were politician Aaron White, Professor William H. McAdams, grocer B. A. Hardrick, Dr. E. T. Butler, and the Reverend J. S. Dorsey. Together they, along with their fellow citizens, had assembled to address a pressing matter. S. A. G. "Greene" Campbell, a government postal clerk and owner of Campbell's Funeral Home, stood to address those in the hall. "The colored people of Springfield are walking over a slumbering volcano," he warned. "The negroes of Springfield are in peril unless these crimes stop." The crimes to which Campbell referred to were attacks made by black men against both white and black women within the last few months.

The meeting, which appeared to be primarily attended by Springfield's black professional and economic elite, may suggest that there were age and class divisions within the African American community. The Reverend Thomas J. Diemer of the African Methodist church railed against Springfield's "dens of vice," lax law enforcement, and the laziness of young black men. Diemer declared, "Women should quit supporting good-for-nothing men. The washtub ought never to feed a worthless negro buck." His colleague, the Reverend J. C. Nicholson of the Cumberland Presbyterian Church, asked the audience how many men had gone to church earlier in the day. After half the audience raised their hands, Nicholson proposed the black community support its churches as a means of combating crime in Springfield.

Before the meeting concluded, the committee issued a resolution that the black citizens of Springfield "pledge our support, man to man, to aid and assist in running down the criminal or criminals, regardless of color, that justice by the courts of our commonwealth be administered and the moral and social standing of our community retain the high stand it now enjoys." The resolution decried the attacks, but conceded "idleness among the younger and some of the older persons of the race is a source of a great deal of the hellishness which we, as respectable and law abiding citizens, are called upon to endure." Those gathered promised to "aid in ferreting out and running down" the individual or individuals who had committed the assaults and asked that the black community be allowed to select its own candidates for the police force. The committee vowed to meet until the guilty party had been taken into custody before the meeting dismissed.[7]

The attacks that concerned those gathered at Scales Hall had occurred only days before. Within a period of two nights, five women were attacked while on Springfield's city streets. According to the police, the attacker was a lone black male who seized his victims by the throat before threatening to kill them if they screamed for help. Fortunately for all five women, they were either able to fight off the attacker or a passerby came to their aid and frightened the man away.[8]

As word of the attacks spread across southwest Missouri, the *Peirce City Democrat,* never one to conceal its opinion, offered a solution. "It seems to us from the many accounts of assaults and attempted assaults on white ladies in Springfield, by black brutes, that the people would rise up and put an end to such proceedings by hanging a dozen or two of the devils." The citizens of Springfield, the *Democrat* sneered, "seem to take it quietly, and we hear of no punishment being inflicted for the crimes. It has become common to read of assaults on both white men and women in that place by negroes." The newspaper contemptuously ended its harangue, "We don't wonder at the negroes colonizing there, but would not think it an inducement to draw white settlers."[9]

The *Springfield Leader-Democrat,* however, disagreed in its response to the *Democrat,* "Under great excitement and indignation they [the citizens of Springfield] might be as rash and reckless as the people of Peirce City, but there certainly could be no justice in murdering a lot of negroes here because one of the number has been guilty of high crimes." Further, the *Leader-Democrat* retorted, "The negroes here are denouncing the recent outrages and will do all they can to locate the right man." To those in Springfield, it would be "certainly unjust and wrong to take revenge on a helpless and innocent race merely because one of their number has committed a crime."[10]

For two weeks, the attacks stopped as the Springfield police kept a close eye on men they suspected might be the perpetrator. Despite the best efforts of the black community and the police, however, two more women were assaulted on the evening of January 15. The *Republican* noted that "the police have several negroes under suspicion and if there is another similar occurrence, some arrests will be made."[11] The attacks eventually stopped, but it is unclear whether or not the actual culprit was apprehended.

Black criminality may have helped exacerbate racial and political divisions within Springfield. A few months later, in April 1902, Springfield's city council, splitting along party lines, voted eight to seven against appointing Jim Burns, an African American, to the police force. Burns was the only black nominee. In the days prior to the council's vote, Mayor Josiah Mellette wrestled with selecting an African American candidate. Mellette, a Republican and native of Indiana, was faced with several black applicants as well as angry black constituents. Many of

Springfield's African American citizens wanted Mellette to consider character as the primary consideration in selecting a black policeman and demanded he not appoint any African American candidate with ties to the Democratic Party. One group of blacks demanded that Mellette allow the African American community to hold "a popular vote among themselves." This proposal, according to one newspaper, "did not seem at all safe to the white Republican bosses."[12]

According to the *Leader*, "There are not many negroes who would give satisfaction on the police force. That fact all white Republicans admit. It is a serious responsibility for a negro. A bad appointment would cause Mayor Mellette a great deal of trouble." Mellette had over twenty African American applicants to consider, including black politicians Aaron White and Nat Adams, former deputy marshal Ed Wilburn, and saloon porters Bob Cain and Ben Brown. A policeman's salary was sixty dollars a month, but this was not the only incentive for blacks. "The negroes enjoy the honor of the police uniform very much. They are the representatives of their race in these positions and the distinction warms the pride of the colored man more than lugging a heavy load of mail matter over the town."[13] It is not clear why Mellette selected Burns, but once he selected him, Mellette was determined to see Burns in uniform.

Mellette, an attorney by profession, found a way to nullify the council's action by naming Burns a special policeman. An article in the *Springfield Leader-Democrat* trumpeted, "New Officers—Marshal Gideon's Men on Duty—Jim Burns, the Rejected Negro, Is Made a Special Policeman by Mayor Mellette." In a brief ceremony at Springfield's police court, black and white spectators watched as Jim Burns was sworn in as a special officer and given a badge.

The mayor's actions, however, did not please everyone. The *Leader-Democrat* observed, "Some of the colored leaders censured Burns for taking the appointment from the mayor. They said the negro ought to have refused anything but a regular commission from the council. To get on the police force in any other way was considered a discredit to the colored race." Other blacks, however, were not as critical, arguing that Burns "ought to wear any kind of a star he could get."[14] But if Burns caused a stir in Springfield, the case of Jack McCracken created a circus.

On the evening of September 6, 1904, screams were heard coming from the residence of Springfield police officer J. R. "Jesse" Brake at 1122 East Division Street. Several people ran to investigate and found that Brake's wife, Anna Brake, had been physically assaulted. She claimed that an African American named John "Jack" McCracken, who had worked at the Brake home on several occasions, attacked her. Further investigation showed that McCracken allegedly gained entry to the Brake residence by cutting through the screen door on the back side of the house and unlatching the door hook. Members of the Springfield police force quickly located and arrested McCracken, whom Anna Brake identified in a police lineup. Prosecuting attorney Roscoe Patterson filed charges against McCracken for burglary and attempted rape. The *Springfield Republican* coyly noted, "He can be sent to prison for life on the first charge, but only five years on the second."[15]

Some Springfield citizens, though, did not want to wait for a trial. At eleven o'clock the following night, a mob of two hundred men converged on the jail, where several speeches were made urging the mob to act.[16] Sheriff Merwin O. Milliken, who had previously been notified that a mob was forming, had already left Springfield with McCracken. Milliken left two of his deputies, Len Ricketts and John Sheedy, in charge of the jail. Sheedy and Ricketts watched as the mob approached. A man stepped forward to rattle the jail door and demand McCracken. Both deputies testified that Jesse Brake was present in full police uniform and did nothing to stop the mob.[17]

Sheedy and Ricketts informed the man that McCracken had been moved and was not at the jail. They then allowed three members of the mob, their faces covered by handkerchiefs, to enter the jail and see for themselves. Jack McCracken was nowhere to be found. Unsatisfied, the mob then demanded another African American prisoner named Brown who was to be executed for murdering a white man. The deputies refused to hand Brown over. Angered by the deputies' stubbornness, the mob began to smash a hole in the south wall of the jail in order to obtain access to Brown's cell. By two o'clock in the morning, however, the "mob's spirit subsided and it had entirely dispersed."[18]

The *Springfield Republican* was incensed by the mob's actions and ran a scathing editorial that declared, "Those people who formed the mob and wanted to lynch the negro made a very serious mistake." Anyone who would lynch a man "stains his soul with the crime of murder. No private citizen has the right to take life and only the officer of the law can exercise such power without making himself a criminal." The *Republican* also warned "that to take the life of even the guilty may cost several lives of misguided men" and that "the next mob will bring state troops, and, strange to say, we have seen state troops shoot and shoot to kill."[19] Jesse Brake, however, was not satisfied with McCracken's escape from the mob.

A month later, Brake began distributing a pamphlet regarding the race problem around town, which the *Leader-Democrat* published in its entirety. The pamphlet read in part, "The unmentionable crime that has become common in all sections of the country was unheard of during the days of slavery and for several years thereafter. How can this be accounted for?" It then argued that southerners had spent millions of dollars to educate African Americans to ill effect as "they have been forced to pay the expense of the negroes education, they have also been forced to furnish the majority of the victims for his fiendish lust."

The pamphlet snarled, "The greater amount of knowledge that has been forced into his wooly head, the greater the increase in crime that he has been guilty of." Education and freedom had only made blacks more beastly and lustful, which, the pamphlet pointed out, "is just beginning to dawn upon the citizens of some sections." To give an African American an education meant that he "immediately becomes too good to work. He must put on a white collar, derby hat, and wide bottom trousers, and looks wise, and tries to ape the wealthy white man." This sort of African American "was a menace to society, a burden upon the taxpayer, or the vulture upon the reward of honest toil." But, the text argued, ignoring local black leaders' suggestions to the contrary, such a menace would always be protected by the African American community which, it said, "was rapidly hastening the day of their complete deportation or absolute extermination. It is inevitable."[20]

The pamphlet echoed the racist belief that African Americans were savage beasts who, despite the best efforts of whites to educate them, sought to live lazy, unproductive lives and prey upon white women and girls. Jesse Brake believed he could find a receptive audience among citizens of Springfield. It is possible that among those sympathetic to Brake were his fellow police officers.

Little is known about McCracken. The 1904 Springfield City

Directory shows there were two John McCrackens, both of whom were listed as "colored," and one of whom worked for M. H. Allen.[21] Mary Clary, a master's student at Southwest Missouri State College in 1970, interviewed several individuals who remembered the John McCracken charged with the crime. They recalled that he worked as a bill collector for the M. H. Allen Furniture Company and was a "quiet middle-aged man."[22] After he was spirited out of Springfield, McCracken spent the next three weeks at the Christian County jail for safekeeping.

Three weeks, however, was not enough to cool the passions that still ran high in Springfield. After McCracken was returned to Springfield, a mob once again threatened his life, and McCracken was sent back to the Christian County jail. The *Springfield Leader* reported that Anna Brake "is armed ready to take his life when opportunity offers and that she is urged to do this by her husband."[23] To some, it may have seemed unusual that Brake urged his wife to shoot McCracken, especially at a time when Victorian mores dictated that a man protect his wife, family, and honor. Jesse Brake should have been the one to redeem his wife's honor, as well as his own.

But Jesse Brake's actions make sense when the true nature of the relationship between Anna Brake and Jack McCracken is revealed in the letters the two exchanged while Jack was in prison. Anna and Jack had engaged in a consensual relationship that resulted in Anna Brake giving birth to McCracken's mulatto child. McCracken had not attempted to rape Anna Brake; he had simply been trying to visit his child. Thus, Jesse's insistence that Anna kill McCracken seems like a sordid attempt to punish her for taking on a black lover. On December 7, Jack McCracken received a thirty-year sentence to be served at the Missouri State Penitentiary in Jefferson City, Missouri.[24] He pled guilty, but insisted that Anna Brake was lying.[25]

The racially charged atmosphere that developed during McCracken's trial lingered in the region. In nearby Aurora, Missouri, an African American was ordered out of town after he was involved in a verbal altercation with two young white women. The man, a newcomer to Aurora, had been arrested for drunk and disorderly conduct in the weeks before. After working off his fine, he found employment as a porter at the Bank Hotel. The two women reported the incident to an Aurora policeman, Bud Gardner, who told the man to leave town as quickly as possible or else "he would be filled so full of bullets that his hide wouldn't hold mush." Within five minutes the unnamed man "was sailing out of town for the west as fast as his legs could carry him." The local paper remarked that his hasty departure "was a good thing, as there were ominous whisperings, as soon as the affairs became known, and numerous little knots of men were gathered about the avenue, talking the matter over, and all in an ugly mood."[26]

The mood continued to darken as a grand jury convened in Springfield in early 1905. The grand jury's lengthy report suggested that Springfield was a city caught in the grip of alcohol, gambling, and crime. The report includes scores of individuals testifying about the violation of local liquor laws, playing poker and shooting craps, and patronizing brothels and gambling dens. Whites and blacks alike were guilty of engaging in all three.

The entries in the Missouri State Penitentiary Register by Counties for individuals sentenced to the penitentiary from Greene County between 1881 and 1906 help illuminate the relationship between blacks and crime. Individuals sentenced to serve time at the Missouri State Penitentiary were convicted of violent crimes such as murder, rape, and assault. Others were sentenced for lesser offenses such as grand larceny and burglary. The entries reveal a distinct disparity between the percentage of African Americans sent to the penitentiary and the percentage of African Americans in Greene County's population.[27]

Over the course of three decades in Greene County, blacks represented 9.7 percent of the population in 1880, 6.9 percent in 1890, and 6.1 percent in 1900. In 1881, blacks represented 37.5 percent of the prisoners sent off to the penitentiary and on average for the rest of the decade represented 25 percent. In contrast, the black population dropped from 9.7 percent to 6.9 percent in that time. Over a period of twenty-six years, the average number of black prisoners was 27.5 percent. In contrast, the highest number of blacks in the general population of Greene County was only 9.7 percent in 1880. Interestingly, in 1901 in Greene County, the number of African Americans sent to the penitentiary was 46 percent, then fell to 37 percent in 1902, rose slightly to 41 percent in 1903, rose again to 44 percent in 1904, dropped to 36 percent in 1905, and then fell to 31 percent in 1906, the year of the lynching.[28]

As in the case of African Americans in Lawrence County, the numbers reveal that the percentage of African American men found guilty and sentenced to the penitentiary was disproportionate to the percentage of blacks in the general population of Greene County. The high conviction rate, regardless of whether or not the men were guilty, may have led whites to believe that African American men were more inclined to engage in criminal behavior and therefore posed a serious threat. Men like Bud Cochrane, who served multiple sentences at the Missouri State Penitentiary, caught the attention of the grand jury and possibly that of the community at large.[29]

Cochrane, an African American known to abuse cocaine, killed Frank Coleman after a verbal altercation turned violent. Clyde Stanley recalled being caught in the middle of a shoot-out between an African American couple after a lovers' quarrel turned ugly. Charlie Ferguson, a Springfield policeman, testified he was attacked when he attempted to break up a street fight. Ben Porter recalled the murder of Jim Shackelford by a fellow African American named "Fitz." John Farrington, when asked about gambling in Springfield, replied that he had played for money with several prominent Springfield citizens, including a state legislator, C. A. Walterhouse, and Dr. Wilhelm Reinhoff.[30]

There apparently was a degree of official toleration of vice. Police Chief John R. McNutt stated that the mayor ordered him "not to be so strict" on brothels and saloons, and "since that time has not paid much attention to the matter." Jesse Brake told the grand jury that he was forced to resign from the police force "for enforcing the law." Chief McNutt, he stated, ordered him "not to be too diligent about forcing the saloons to close promptly." According to Brake, the mayor also admonished him for enforcing the law, which, to Brake meant, keeping "the saloons closed on Sunday."[31] In the view of the grand jury, Springfield was riddled with crime. The public's perception of a crime wave was exacerbated by continuous local press coverage of African Americans' criminal transgressions and further soured race relations in Springfield.

Such feelings only intensified with the murder of Thomas M. Kinney, an Irish immigrant, on the snowy evening of December 20, 1905. Kinney, a tailor, was shot while entering the front door of his home on St. Louis Street. William E. Crews, a twenty-three-year-old machinist, was arrested. In the past, Crews's mother, Elizabeth Crews, mortgaged some of her belongings to Kinney in order to secure a thirty-dollar loan from him, but had failed to repay it in time. The day prior to his murder, Kinney reportedly filed suit against Mrs. Crews, which the Springfield police suspected had angered William Crews. Crews, however, protested his innocence.[32]

In the days that followed, Crews's alibi proved solid and several witnesses, including two of Kinney's employees, testified that Elizabeth Crews had paid off her debt to Kinney.[33] Further investigation by the police suggested that someone had laid in wait for Kinney, but there was no attempt to rob him, as his watch and pocketbook were found on his person.[34] Crews was released while officers continued their investigation. Jim Burns, the African American who had been denied a police appointment by the Springfield city council in 1902, served as one of the lead investigators.[35]

Stymied by a lack of evidence and eyewitnesses, members of the Greene County court offered a two-hundred-dollar reward for the arrest and conviction of Kinney's murderer in the hopes that someone would come forward with information.[36] Within two days, Willard Caldwell and Elmer Hancock, both African Americans, were arrested for Kinney's murder after Nat Adams, a member of the black community, contacted the police with information. Caldwell, who lived in a boardinghouse, was seen returning home that night with a .41-caliber revolver. When asked why he had a gun, Caldwell replied that "some man had made a gun play on him at the corner of the alley leading from St. Louis Street and that he had shot him."[37]

According to the coroner's inquest, Caldwell had reportedly been detained by police in the wake of the murder, but was soon released. Hancock, a recent arrival in Springfield, was known to be a close associate of Caldwell's.[38] Rumors soon swept across the city that one of the men confessed to killing Kinney, but prosecuting attorney Roscoe Patterson denied that a confession had been made.[39] Their trial was scheduled for May 1, 1906.[40]

If the arrest of Caldwell and Hancock failed to arouse a lynch mob, the theft of a team of mules and a wagon from a farm outside nearby Marionville did. The thief, who gave his name as Ramsey, stole a team of mules, harnesses, and a wagon from the farm of Lon Wiles. Wiles reported the theft to Marionville constable Jim Chamberlin, who, along with two deputies, took off in hot pursuit of the thief. Ramsey, who was headed to Arkansas with the wagon, was quickly caught by Chamberlin and his men. On their way back to Marionville, the men encountered a lynch mob of fifty men at Flat Creek gathered around a large oak with a rope dangling from a tree limb. The men, armed with clubs and shotguns, demanded Ramsey. The mob, however, underestimated Chamberlin's grit.

Constable Chamberlin pulled out a ".44 calibre gun that looked two feet long and pointed it squarely in the faces of the mob." The mob moved forward, ready to call Chamberlin's bluff. The constable announced that he and "his deputies would shoot to kill and that the mob would never get Ramsey as long as any of the officers were alive." Chamberlin's bravado succeeded and he and his men returned to Marionville with Ramsey in one piece.[41]

Accusations involving black on white crime continued with the murder of O. P. Ruark, an elderly, homeless Union veteran. On the cold night of January 11, 1906, Ruark was on his way to the tent he called home on East Webster Street when he said he was stopped by two African American men. The men ordered Ruark to raise his hands, but he resisted. At the old veteran's refusal, one of the men fired at Ruark, but his gun was knocked away by Ruark's cane. The second man, however, did not miss. Ruark fell to the ground with a bullet wound four inches below the heart. The bullet passed through his stomach and lodged in his spine, but despite his injury, Ruark managed to stand up and walk a short distance before he collapsed. A Drury College professor, C. P. Howland, and several Drury students found the elderly victim and carried him to Fairbanks Hall.[42] When Howland asked Ruark who shot him, Ruark replied, "two negroes."[43] Dr. Wilhelm Reinhoff and the police were quickly notified, but it was too late for Ruark. He passed away a few hours later shortly after giving a statement to the police.[44]

In response to the murders of Kinney and Ruark, a large number of African Americans gathered at the Greene County courthouse. A resolution was passed that denounced "crime in any form, either by black or white." Attendees pledged their allegiance to law and order and asked the white community for assistance in "elevating and bettering the condition of the negro by closing all the hellish 'dives' and places that are run by members of our race, or by others, which are harbors for the element which is supposed to commit these crimes."[45]

An editorial in the *Springfield Leader* warned, "Friends of the colored race in Springfield are advising its members to do their utmost to restrain the evil propensities of those among them who are known as 'bad men.' The Kinney and Ruark murders have made a deep impression on the public mind, and another serious crime committed by a negro might lead to lamentable results." The *Leader* did admit that "most of Springfield's colored citizens behave themselves very well and are not in the slightest degree responsible for the evil deeds of a few of their race, but nevertheless they have a great interest in keeping the vicious negroes in bounds." Still, the *Leader* cynically noted, "the negro criminals of this city will do their own race a great service if they will 'swear off' on killing white men for a few months."[46]

Benjamin F. Adams, an African American schoolteacher, responded. He criticized the *Leader* for publishing the editorial as it "does not fairly place the better element of the race in the proper light before a thinking public in these times of agitation and commotion. There is no medium in a community that molds sentiment as does the daily papers." He argued that public schools "will continue to be the best checks upon lawlessness" and appealed to whites to "see to it that the negro and white man alike should be educated each—each educated away from caste prejudice—away from 'previous conditions,' and each educated in the sunlight of perfect freedom and universal liberty." Adams closed by asking that whites give blacks "a man's chance in the race of life." His plea fell upon deaf ears as the *Leader* soon published another editorial that lashed out at Springfield's African American community.

The editorial, entitled "The Negro and Crime," sneered, "The law abiding negroes of Springfield certainly have the right idea when they take a stand against the 'bad nigger.'" It commended the "better element" of blacks who "understand that the way to uplift their race is to make constant warfare on the criminal element." Law-abiding African Americans, the editorial proclaimed, "know that to thousands of whites 'all coons look alike,' although it is a fact that they are not all alike." It urged that African Americans "not to hesitate to offer testimony against them to the proper authorities." The editorial's advice may have been heeded.[47]

The coroner's jury did not return a verdict until the end of the month. When the jury did, however, it named two suspects in the killing of O. P. Ruark. Bus Cain and William Allen were named as Ruark's assailants. Cain and Allen were identified by three African American witnesses. The first, Jake Danforth, testified that Cain told him that he and Allen shot Ruark. Byron Vaughn, a cousin of Cain's, swore he saw Cain and Allen run south down Washington Avenue after he heard gunshots. Vaughn's testimony supported Ruark's dying statement that his assailants ran south down Washington Avenue. The last witness, Rufus Gray, also saw two men run down the avenue the same time as Vaughn, although he did not know either of them.[48]

The *Leader* reported that both Cain and Allen had lengthy criminal records. Cain, the son of Lizzie Cain and an unknown father, had served time at the state reform school in Boonville for grand larceny.[49] According to one account in 1902, he had "spent the greater part of the last five years at the county jail."[50] Will Allen, the son of Granville and Jennie Allen, had a similar criminal history. At age seventeen, he was convicted of grand larceny in Lawrence County and sentenced to two years in the Missouri State Penitentiary.[51] Two years later, in 1903, Allen was found guilty of burglary in the second degree in Greene County and sentenced to three years at the Missouri State Penitentiary.[52] Both men, in the opinion of the *Leader,* were "bad niggers." Despite the best efforts of the police to locate them, both Allen and Cain were nowhere to be found in Springfield.[53]

It did not take long to locate the two men. Bus Cain was arrested February 11, 1906, in St. Louis.[54] Will Allen was picked up a short time later in Neodesha, Kansas, on March 19.[55] He was returned to Springfield within a matter of days. The *Leader* noted that Allen "offered to come back home and did not come without any requisition papers, and no attempt to get any statement from him was successful."[56]

Benjamin F. Adams, the African American schoolteacher, sent a letter to the *Springfield Republican* entitled, "What the Negro Must Do." Adams, troubled by strained race relations in Springfield, offered suggestions as to how African Americans could improve their current condition in American society. He advocated that blacks support education and the African American community, believe in law and order, stand for good society and Christian homes, demand intelligent and competent leadership, and own property.

He expressed his hope that "a new era is just ready to dawn upon the negro." Adams pointed to U.S. senator Blanche K. Bruce as an example of what African Americans had achieved thus far and proclaimed, "We are coming, only give us an equal chance in the race of life and we will prove that the negro is not only susceptible to the highest degree of intelligence, but that he also has the highest ideals of society, good government, the enforcement of the laws, and the protection of the home." Adams then announced, "in the coming spring elections, he will, in common with his good white friends, stand for better government, honesty in administration of the city's finances, improvement in every way that will make Springfield a first class city and the public school system the best in the state." Adams ended by signing, "I am for my race first and the party next."[57]

Adams must have been even more concerned, when, on February 28, it was announced in the *Springfield Republican* that the original theatrical production of *The Clansman* would arrive on March 5.[58] Heralded as the "greatest success story since Uncle Tom's Cabin," the play was an abridgement of Thomas Dixon's novels *The Leopard's Spots* and *The Clansman,* the latter eventually being the basis for the 1915 film *The Birth of a Nation.* Both novels depict African American men as barbarous, unrestrained beasts who lust after white women. Dixon, a native of South Carolina, was a fervent disciple of racist thought.

Dixon, angered by the South's transformation during Reconstruction, was particularly upset by the new freedoms African Americans enjoyed. The antebellum life of Dixon's ancestors was radically upended. Whereas blacks once toiled from dusk until dawn for their white masters, they now worked for themselves. Long kept ignorant, blacks could receive an education. Most troublesome of all, African Americans were politically empowered. Dixon, born in 1864, found himself in a South where African Americans voted, traveled freely, and no longer heeded the commands of their white masters. Without the firm hand of enslavement to keep African Americans in their place, Dixon and other prominent racists believed, blacks began to regress into a primitive state of savagery. In this degenerative state of existence, African American men lusted after white women, challenging Victorian beliefs of chastity, purity, and the role of white men as the protectors of hearth, home, and womanhood.[59]

For Dixon, the solution was simple. African Americans were to be kept in check; however, if they acted upon their animalistic impulses, they were to be destroyed. In *The Leopard's Spots,* Gus, an African American suspected of kidnapping and assaulting the child of an impoverished Confederate veteran, is burned to death at the stake by an enraged mob of whites. Dixon's novels advocated extralegal justice and justified the use of violence to reestablish and reinforce white superiority. As the *Kansas City Journal* exclaimed, "'The Clansman' stirs the hearts and passions of the Southerners against the negro free. In fact, it is an appeal to the white race, North and South, against political and social equality between the white and black races."[60]

The Clansman was immensely popular throughout the South and toured across the nation for the next several years to the delight of enraptured playgoers. Dixon's views of African Americans struck a chord with many white audience members. The play's depiction of violence to keep blacks in check may have made an impression upon the citizens of Springfield who filed into the Baldwin Theater to watch Dixon's spectacle.

For all of the ill-will and hatred that *The Clansman* inspired, the future did not look bleak for Springfield's African Americans as winter melted away. As the spring election loomed, Republican candidates promised to appoint two African Americans to the police force. Josiah E. Mellette, who appointed Jim Burns in 1902, planned to once more run for mayor. At a Republican meeting, when informed that Mellette planned to appoint two African Americans rather than just the usual one, black voters in the audience cheered.[61] Their hopes were not long lived, however, as the Easter of 1906 approached.

EIGHT

Springfield

"The Easter Offering"

At ten o'clock on a cool spring evening, Springfield police officers John Wimberly and E. T. W. Trantham were on duty when a buggy hurriedly pulled up in front of them at the corner of Phelps and Boonville Streets.[1] Charles Cooper, the driver of the buggy, informed Officers Wimberly and Trantham that he and a female companion, Mina Edwards, had been robbed and assaulted by a pair of African Americans. During the attack, Cooper explained, he was knocked unconscious. When he came to, Cooper found Mina Edwards gone, presumably dragged off by their attackers. Together, the three men quickly rushed to find her.[2]

Cooper and the two officers did not have to search very far. Edwards was found sitting on her valise at the intersection of Phelps and Franklin Streets, her throat covered in bruises, and her clothes torn. Officer Wimberly sent her to his home to be looked after while he and Officer Trantham searched for the men who had attacked the couple. It was too late, however, as the officers found no one who matched the description given by Cooper. The robbers reportedly got away with fifteen dollars in cash, a pocket watch, and Edwards's purse.[3]

Both Mina Edwards and Charles Cooper were recent arrivals in Springfield. A week prior to her arrival, Edwards separated from her husband of six years, William Edwards, and left their farm outside of Bolivar, Missouri, to seek employment. She found a job working at the Harvey House in Monett, but quit a few days later because "the work was so hard."[4] Edwards then traveled to Springfield, where she found employment as a house girl in the home of Henry Fox, mechanical superintendent at Springfield's electric plant.[5] She was at the St. James Hotel on the evening of April 13, 1906, picking up the last of her luggage when she ran into Charles Cooper. Cooper, a farmer living outside of Springfield who had served three years with the U.S. Army, offered to give her ride to her new job. The two set off in his buggy and had just reached the corner of Main Street and Phelps Avenue when, they said, two African American men appeared out of the darkness.[6]

One of the men, described as short and heavyset, grabbed the harness of the horse while the other, described as tall, came around to the side of the buggy and pointed a pistol at Cooper and Edwards. Once he had taken Cooper's cash, pocket watch, and Edwards's purse, the robber struck Cooper on the head with his pistol. It was then that the two thieves forced Edwards from the buggy and into a nearby field where they reportedly assaulted her. Notably, neither the *Republican* nor the *Leader* reported that Edwards was raped or sexually assaulted, only that she had been "abused."[7]

The next day, word of the assault spread like wildfire across Springfield and intensified when Charles Cooper thought he spotted one of the men who assaulted him. Horace Duncan, a young African American employed at Pickwick Stables, was arrested on suspicion of assaulting Cooper and Edwards. The men who arrested Duncan, Officers Waddle, Jones, and Kenner, believed that Duncan "was not one of the men wanted" but thought it prudent to question him.[8] Duncan's elderly mother followed closely behind as her son was escorted downtown. At the police station, officers convinced her that Horace would be safe and she returned home.[9]

Duncan was soon joined at the police station by Fred Coker. The two men worked at Pickwick Stables and had left work together the night of the assault. On the orders of Springfield chief of police John R. McNutt, Coker and Duncan were taken to Officer John Wimberly's home. The two men were escorted by the assistant chief of police W. T. Brown and four officers. Once they had arrived, Coker was brought before Mina Edwards, who stated that Coker was not one of the men who attacked her. Duncan, however, was not brought before Edwards because "she described the man that should have corresponded to Duncan as a large, heavyset, not very tall man with a mustache while Duncan was a small man who had never grown a mustache."[10]

After Edwards failed to identify Coker, both men were able to convince the police that it would have been impossible for either of them to have left work at 9:30 P.M. and have made it to the scene of the crime by 10:00 P.M. when the attack occurred. Further, when both men were taken into custody, their pocket watches were examined, but failed to fit the description of Cooper's watch. Coker and Duncan were then released, but Charles Cooper hurriedly swore out a statement that the two men were the guilty parties, and they were immediately rearrested by the police. Duncan and Coker were placed in jail alongside Bus Cain and Will Allen, the two men accused of murdering O. P. Ruark, as well as two young chicken thieves. There they waited while the city around them quickly spun out of control.[11]

As early as ten o'clock the next morning, rumors of a lynch mob began to surface.[12] If Sheriff Everett V. Horner suspected trouble, he made no effort to transport Coker and Duncan to a safe location as Sheriff Merwin O. Milliken did when Jack McCracken was threatened by a lynch mob. Springfield chief of police John R. McNutt did not express any concern, nor did he take any precautionary measures. McNutt, a Democrat, was in his final days of office. Although he ran for reelection in the recent city election, he was defeated by Republican Asa "Acy" Loveless, who was boosted to victory by African American votes.[13] Loveless would take office in just a matter of days. Deputy U.S. marshal Allen Sheldon failed to raise any alarm over the knots of angry men gathered in the streets.

It is not surprising, however, that the men in charge of enforcing the law were slow to act. They were unqualified and unprepared. Horner, formerly employed as an engineer by the Frisco Railroad, was in his first term as Greene County sheriff.[14] Unlike the sheriff, who was an elected official, the police force was appointed. Each time a new administration was elected, the mayor selected his appointees, often from a large number of candidates. While a police officer could expect to work twelve hours a day seven days a week, he received a salary of sixty dollars a month.[15] The continual turnover meant that many of Springfield's police officers were inexperienced, unqualified except for their political allegiances, and were loyal to the current city administration, rather than to the law.

Positions on the Springfield police force were doled out as political patronage. A prospective candidate had to curry political favor in order to be appointed to the police force. Qualifications were few. Appointees had to be at least twenty-one years old; speak English; be a U.S. citizen; have resided in the city for at least two years; have a clean record; be of sound health; stand at least five feet, seven inches tall; weigh more than 150 pounds; and be of good moral character.[16]

Chief McNutt, who worked as a machinist prior to his election, was not a career law enforcement officer.[17] The *Springfield Leader,* however, hailed McNutt as Springfield's best chief of police. It boasted in an editorial that McNutt's officers "arrested one hundred and twenty-four persons charged with felonies. Of this number, more than 90 percent have been convicted, and have done, or are now doing time in the county jail, the state penitentiary, or the state reform school."[18] The men that McNutt oversaw came from a variety of backgrounds.

Officer E. T. Wesley Trantham previously worked as a driver for the Springfield Ice and Refrigerator Company where he may have met Springfield mayor B. E. Meyer. Meyer served as the company's manager and secretary.[19] Martin Keener, a baker in his fifties, was a German immigrant.[20] John Wimberly worked as a grocer.[21] Henry Waddle was both a laborer and a horse dealer.[22]

Mayor B. E. Meyer, a Democrat born in Ohio to German immigrant parents, came to Springfield in 1895 to oversee the Springfield Ice and Refrigerator Company. He quickly became involved in the local business community, serving as the manager and secretary-treasurer of the Ozark Ice and Storage Company and as general manager of Springfield's Anheuser-Busch Brewery Association. Meyer had already served one term on the city council and was about to finish his second term as mayor. He declined, however, to run for a third term. It was Meyer's appointees who filled the ranks of the Springfield police.[23]

Prior to the city election held at the beginning of April, editorials in the *Springfield Leader* harped on the need for a nonpartisan police force. Assistant chief of police W. T. Brown, who was to retire after the election, gave an interview in which he stated, "the best thing that could be done for the good of the police work in a city such as this would be for the political parties to agree to have the force composed of men of both parties." He expressed concern that there were not enough policemen to patrol the city and that the current salary was inadequate.[24]

The *Leader* proclaimed, "It should be Springfield's policy to keep good men on the force as long as they do their duty. There should be civil service rule with the police the same as with firemen." Then, it growled, "Instead of promising to put negroes on the force to catch the negro vote, a candidate for mayor should be offering only to put on good men, regardless of politics, men who will do their duty and who do not rely on political pull for their places."[25] As tension mounted on the streets of Springfield, the responsibility to protect the accused was left to an unprepared and unqualified police force.

The need for strong police presence grew rapidly, as stories of the assault spread from saloons to street corners, undoubtedly becoming more shocking and offensive as the story was embellished and distorted each time it was repeated. Clusters of men congregated in Springfield's streets. Whispers of lynching continued to run rampant late into the afternoon and on into the evening. The attempted lynching of Jack McCracken just two years before seemed all but forgotten by law enforcement officials.

As night fell, Sheriff Horner and Chief McNutt failed to take any precautions to ensure the safety of Horace Duncan and Fred Coker. Passenger trains continued to arrive in Springfield, bringing with them scores of the enraged and the curious from across the area. From Polk County, where Mina Edwards had been raised, reportedly came at least one trainload of men, who immediately demanded of anyone within earshot that Coker and Duncan be lynched. The number of men in the streets grew steadily larger until an estimated three thousand men and boys filled downtown Springfield. They gathered on dusty streets, wooden sidewalks, in hotel lobbies, and under the light of streetlamps. Rising above the rabble in the center of the city square was Gottfried Tower.[26]

The tower, built in 1896, was named for W. H. Gottfried, a member of Springfield's city council who came up with the idea for the structure. Constructed out of steel, the tower stood higher than any of the city's buildings. It, too, cast off a soft glow, as it was draped in electric lights. Near the bottom of the tower were steps that led to a wooden bandstand.[27] But the most striking feature of the tower was the ten-foot-tall replica of the Goddess of Liberty that silently gazed at those in the square below.[28]

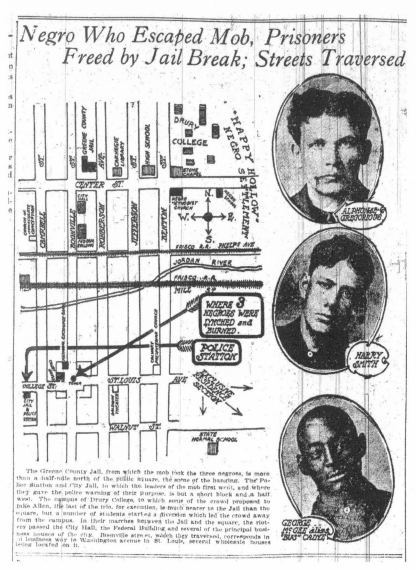

Map of lynching route. *Courtesy of The State Historical Society of Missouri.*

At nine o'clock on Saturday evening, with Easter morning only hours away, a "strip of a boy, not over eighteen years of age, ran out in the northwest corner of the public square and shouted: 'Come on, follow me!'"[29] He was followed by a group of men and boys west down College Street toward the jail, and all hell broke loose. The crowd, now a mob, headed past the square toward the jail. Pistol shots rang out as men yelled for those still standing on the sidewalks to join them.[30]

Passengers on Springfield Streetcar 25, operated by conductor C. M. Box and motorman Highfield, inexplicably found themselves under attack from the mob. As the occupants of the car, mostly women, huddled under their seats, members of the howling throng outside the car shot out the windows and pummeled the car with stones and other street debris. Reportedly on board was William Smith, one of Springfield's few African American mail carriers, who was on his way home from work. Fortunately, motorman Highfield was able to accelerate and escape the full wrath of the mob.[31] But the mob was far from finished.

Turning its attention back to the jail, the mob surged onward. Inside the jail, the sheriff's telephone began to ring furiously. Sheriff Horner, who by now may have suspected the worst, answered the phone. Whoever was on the other end of the line warned Horner that a mob was headed for the jail for Coker and Duncan. Horner then called Chief McNutt to ask for the assistance of Springfield's police force. McNutt promised Horner that he would send every man available, but to Horner's horror, only one policeman, William Bishop, appeared over the course of the evening.[32]

Once off the phone, Horner turned his attention to saving the six African American prisoners in his care. Now Horner not only had to worry about keeping Coker and Duncan safe, but Bus Cain, Will Allen, Elmer Hancock, and Willard Caldwell. Hancock and Caldwell were charged with the murder of Thomas M. Kinney while Allen and Cain were charged with the murder of O. P. Ruark, both white men. Horner hoped he could get the six men out of the city, but discovered it was too late. Horner looked at his deputies and asked, "Boys, what shall we do?"[33]

Shaking off his disbelief at the situation, Horner directed his deputies to close and lock the jail doors. Horner ordered the deputy sheriff and jailer, E. C. King, to lock the keys to the jail cells in the office safe. The keys secured, they turned off the lights in the jail. Together, Sheriff Horner, Deputies E. C. King, C. W. Carr, B. F. Snider, and J. D. Mack, along with U.S. deputy marshal Allen Sheldon waited in the darkness as the mob approached.[34] Prisoners L. F. Barber and Will Allen sat in one of the upper cells playing cards as if it were a typical Saturday night.[35]

The mob came to a halt in front of the jail, which was attached to the sheriff's residence. A rough voice called out, "Give us the niggers!" Sheriff Horner barked in reply, "Boys, if you do not go away, I'll fire into the crowd of you in twenty minutes."[36] A roar of defiance came from the mob. Horner's deputies urged him to let them fire on the mob, observing that it was led by boys who would run if shot at. Horner disagreed and ordered his men not to fire on the mob. According to Sheriff Horner's daughter Mabel, "a lot of his friends were here."[37] Prisoners inside the jail could hear the hellish din outside and hid under their cots. Many of those trapped inside the iron bars began to weep, while others prayed. At least one prisoner yelled out to the sheriff, "Let us out of here, or we'll break out!"[38]

Police officer William Bishop pushed his way through the crowd and stood in the doorway of the jail. He called out, "Men, you are breaking the law. If these are the guilty men, they will be amply punished. You do not know they are guilty. Stop destroying property and listen to reason." Bishop was met with the hoarse bellow, "Damn the law!" Someone else shouted, "We've tried the law and it's too slow. Let us at 'em! Give us the keys or we'll blow the jail up with dynamite!" Bishop fell silent.[39]

As the battle for Horner's prisoners began to unfold, Arthur Noble Sager, the circuit attorney of St. Louis, looked on in horror. A Republican born in Wisconsin and a graduate of De Pauw University, Sager was in Springfield to prosecute a political corruption case.[40] Upon hearing of the mob, he rushed from the home of famed Springfield attorney T. J. Delaney to see what was happening. Sager watched as the mob attacked the jail's steel doors with wooden fence rails, "incited by urchins, yelling as they do, when the cry is 'kill the umpire.'"[41]

Members of the mob quickly realized that wooden fence rails were no match for solid steel doors. Men began throwing rocks, sticks, and firing their pistols at the building out of frustration, which resulted in every window in the building being broken. Those with more feral intelligence procured an enormous wooden pole and began battering the doors while others began using sledgehammers on the steel window frames. One man even tried to set the jail on fire to no avail. It was not long before the doors gave way with a hideous groan and men rushed inside the jail.[42]

Arthur Sager, in the midst of the mob inside the jail, listened in disbelief as two young boys phoned their mothers to say they were playing down at the city square and would be home in thirty minutes. One boy, after he finished speaking to his mother, turned to the other, winked, and said, "We'll get 'em in that time." Sager overheard men boast how they helped lynch African Americans in Mississippi and in Texas while cries of "Kill every nigger in jail!" came from those waiting outside.[43]

Sheriff Horner, alarmed that the sheriff's residence adjoining the jail had been breached, ran to move his wife and children to a neighbor's home. After he returned, Horner begged the mob to let justice take its course, but the men who heard his plea replied, "Yes, and they'll get thirty days in jail." While Horner argued with the mob, men continued to use sledgehammers in an effort to break into the cells. A female prisoner screamed, "For God's sake, take those niggers out!"[44] One man, reportedly Charles Cannefax, threatened a prisoner, "You black son of a bitch, where's those niggers that raped that woman? If you don't show us, we'll hang you."[45] As more and more men pushed their way into the jail, Horner and his men climbed on top of the jail cells.

Members of the mob who could not cram themselves into the jail busied themselves by ransacking the sheriff's residence. Looters smashed the sheriff's furniture, shattered dishes, and ripped holes in paintings. A brand-new rug was destroyed by the hundreds of feet that trampled it in the chaotic atmosphere. Among the items stolen by thieves were Horner's new eighty-five-dollar shotgun, Mrs. Horner's purse, and a brand-new thirty-five-dollar tea set.[46]

Outside, in the throng, some onlookers had no idea what was going on. An older woman pushing an infant in a baby carriage asked a young man, "What is the trouble, young son?" Nonchalantly, the young man replied, "Oh, the circus elephant broke his leg." Others, however, refused to acknowledge the events taking place. A policeman headed east on College Street away from the mob was asked, "What is that mob for?" The officer replied, "I did not ask them."[47] Those trapped inside the jail, however, knew exactly what was going on.

Jail trusties Joe Perry and Manuel Inyard, arrested for stealing chickens, were both younger than sixteen years old. Horner and his men ordered them to hide under their cots, but members of the mob soon noticed them. Terrified at being discovered, Perry and Inyard shouted, "We ain't de men you all is after. We'se chicken thieves, you all don't want to lynch us." Lanterns were brought and it was agreed that Perry and Inyard were not Duncan and Coker. Someone, however, suggested torturing both young men in order to find out where Coker and Duncan were being held. Just when it seemed that Perry and Inyard would be tortured, the mob turned its attention to the lockup doors.[48]

Desperate to stop the mob, Arthur Sager looked for Sheriff Horner in the jail, but in the seething mass of people, he was nowhere to be found. He asked Frank Hull, a Springfield newspaper reporter, if he knew where Horner was. Hull replied that he did not, but offered to help Sager locate him. After ten minutes, the two men gave up. Sager then told Hull he wanted to shut off the gas to the jail. With Hull in the lead, the two men headed to the basement. While Sager guarded the door, Hull used a hatchet to try to bend the gas key, but the noise attracted unwanted attention from the mob. Hull, frightened, dropped his hatchet. Sager, however, used a sausage grinder to break the gas key, pitching the jail into darkness. He and Hull slipped out without being detected.[49] Their plan, however, did not work as the individuals in the mob began lighting matches and lanterns to continue their work.

Deputy Sheriff E. C. King, who also served as the jailer, clambered off the top of the jail cell with U.S. deputy marshal Allen Sheldon and pushed their way into the sheriff's office. King retrieved the jail cell keys from the safe and passed them off to Sheldon, who slipped outside. When members of the mob recognized King as the jailer, they demanded the keys to the cells. King replied that he did not have the keys. Infuriated, men began to punch and kick King, and even pulled his hair before he escaped by giving them a key that did not open the cells. Finding that they had been duped by King when the cell doors would not open, the mob became even more enraged, and attacked the iron jail cells with even greater fury. Men lashed out at the hinges and bars with sledgehammers, wrenches, axes, and chisels.[50]

After two hours of frenzied work, the mob was triumphant. The door to Coker and Duncan's cell was wrenched off and dozens of hands reached for them. The two men were dragged out through the wrecked windows of the jail into the waiting fury of the mob. According to a *Republican* reporter, "The negroes struggled desperately. They cried piteously, screaming that they were innocent, and not the men wanted. After they had struggled in vain for some time, both of them lost strength and almost fainted." Upon seeing the two men being pulled from the jail, someone cried out, "How do you know they are the right men?" The reply came, "We know them, besides, the sheriff pointed them out. He showed them to us and said that they were the men and that we could have them if we could get them."[51] A man bellowed, "To the square!" With that, the mob headed toward the city square and Gottfried Tower with Duncan and Coker.

In the midst of the writhing mass of whites was a lone African American man who, for unknown reasons, had ventured into the mob. He gripped a revolver in one hand and kept a wary eye on those around him. A farmer cried out, "There's a nigger, hang him!" The man waved his revolver at the whites who turned toward him and then fled. He was pursued by several dozen men who fired at least twenty shots before he managed to escape down an alley.[52]

Arthur Sager, thinking the worst was over, was almost to his hotel when a pack of small boys ran past yelling, "They've got 'em and are going to bring 'em down to the square to hang 'em!"[53] In disbelief, he turned and watched as the mob charged toward him, Coker and Duncan in tow. According to Sager, "Lanterns were held at their heads, and their faces showed a ghastly green in the dim light."[54] The two men gasped, "Oh, oh, oh" as they were dragged down the street.

Upon arriving at the square, boys draped ropes from the tower, just below the Goddess of Liberty. By this time, Duncan and Coker were reportedly unconscious, most likely the result of having their air supply cut off when the mob dragged them downtown with ropes around their necks. Now new ropes dangling from Gottfried Tower were secured around their throats. The two men, who had grown up and worked side by side, found themselves dying together. Coker remained unconscious, but Duncan revived and fought until the end. He struggled violently against his captors until his clothes were almost completely torn off.[55]

A man stepped forward, reportedly Mina Edwards's brother John Reeves, and yelled, "I want to be the one to hang the ——— fiends!" The other men around him stepped aside. Reeves grabbed onto the end of the rope around Coker's neck and pulled with all his might. The limp man was drawn upward into the air. Together with others, Reeves then grasped the rope that encircled Duncan's neck and strained to lift him.[56] Arthur Sager, who looked on as Duncan was lifted up into the air hand over hand, observed, "He died hard."[57]

Together the two men dangled in the cool April air, the soft light of the electric lights shining upon their expressionless faces. A cheer went up, "Hurrah for Bolivar!" One reporter at the scene wrote, "With a wild shout, the two negroes were strung up to the tower beneath the Goddess of Liberty. Both bodies hung limp and when fires were started under them and bullets pierced their bodies there was not a single muscle in their bodies that moved. Both had probably been scared to death."[58]

But even in death, Horace Duncan and Fred Coker could not rest. The mob immediately doused their corpses in oil. Boys shoved their way through the crowd to find wooden boxes to serve as kindling. Dozens of hands fumbled for matches, eager to light the fire that would desecrate and destroy the final remains of the two men. Within minutes, the corpses of Coker and Duncan were ablaze, and members of the mob found "their nostrils filled with the fumes of the burning victims."[59]

James J. Mayes, the Springfield native who recruited and led men from Springfield's African American community during the Spanish-American War, was in the crowd. Mayes, now a newspaper reporter for the *St. Louis Globe-Democrat,* watched in disgust as a group of young boys, ranging in age from ten to fourteen, stood watch over the bonfire. Using barrel staves, the boys made sure that none of the remains fell outside of the fire. Two of them threw rocks at Duncan's charred skull and then rolled it back into the flames so that it would "get cooked done." According to Mayes, "Not a man in the crowd reproved. In fact, these boys seemed to be there by consent of their parents who were possibly members of the mob. They seemed to have no doubt they were doing the proper thing."[60]

Over the din of the crowd, the faint sound of music could be heard, but as the smell of burning flesh permeated the air, it stopped. Participants at an Easter dance, held in a building overlooking the square, found their festivities interrupted by the noise and the stench. Dancers in their best Easter finery poked their heads out of the windows to look at the chaotic scene below in shock. Men and women alike numbly watched as the flames consumed the bodies of Coker and Duncan.[61] Other women in the mob below, however, cheered with glee at the ghoulish spectacle.

A reporter for the *Springfield Republican* observed of the crowd, "A noticeable thing about the crowd was that there were many women

Horace Duncan. *Courtesy of the Katherine G. Lederer Ozarks African American History Collection, Special Collections and Archives Department, Missouri State University.*

in it standing all about the square, and many of them audibly urged the lynchers to get in their work. Many women were seen interestedly watching the spectacle as the negroes went up into the air at the ends of the ropes, and hurrahed with the men when the lynching was accomplished."[62]

James J. Mayes observed, "In the crowd that came from Bolivar were several women, all of whom went with the mob to the county jail and marched with it back to the public square where the negroes were hanged. When the ropes were being adjusted on the electric tower, the women cried 'Hang them! Hang them!'"[63]

Mayes, who had served in the Philippines with the U.S. Army, lamented, "I have seen a Filipino woman stand with tearless eyes and watch her husband hanged, but last night I saw four nicely dressed American women walk to within fifty feet of the light tower and look at the dangling, naked forms of these negroes and smile when a man ran a burning brand up and down the back of Coker's corpse. The stench of human flesh did not appear to annoy them when men retired before it."[64] If the women of Springfield thought the spectacle was over, they were mistaken.

The mob, momentarily enthralled with the ghastly spectacle before it, watched as Coker's charred body fell into the fire. Duncan's body tumbled outside of the fire, only to be kicked back onto the burn pile by onlookers. Men and boys carried wooden boxes and other debris to the fire and dumped it on top of the smoldering corpses. The stench of burnt flesh permeated the night air as the oily light of dark flames flickered across the faces of the mob. A man, perched on a balcony that overlooked the crowd, cried out, "Ladies and gentlemen, there is another man up in that jail who killed old man Ruark; shall we get him?" Shrieks, roars, and yells came from the men, women, and children below. The mob began to surge toward to the jail once more.[65]

Two bystanders, Hollet H. and Ernest Snow, recognized one face in the mob. It belonged to their neighbor, Springfield blacksmith Doss Galbraith, who marched determinedly toward the jail with a large coil of rope wrapped around his arm. Ernest Snow called out to Galbraith and asked what he was doing with the rope. Galbraith replied he "had run out of niggers and that [he] was going after more niggers."[66] Another bystander, Harry Williamson, attempted to protest the lynching of Coker and Duncan, but was immediately shouted down by Galbraith that "every goddamn negro ought to be done the same way and that [Williamson] was no better than a damn negro."[67]

Despite the thousands of people who occupied downtown Springfield, police officers failed to act, as a reporter for the *Leader* observed, "The only interest the officers of the city manifested in the proceedings was that of curiosity and they seemed to satisfy that without exhaustion." Any officer on duty could not have avoided the teeming mass of humanity that populated the city streets. Nor could any officer have not heard the cries of, "Hang every negro in jail!" that pierced the night air as the mob converged on the jail.[68]

Resistance was nonexistent at the jail. Sheriff Horner and his men, absent since Duncan and Coker were seized, were nowhere to be found. Members of the mob strolled through the door of the jail unopposed. Men, armed with hammers, chisels, and other tools, walked through holding cells looking for Bus Cain and Will Allen. Bus Cain, however, was nowhere to be found. Apparently his cell was damaged during the first assault on the jail and Cain was able to slip away without being noticed. Cain, in his eagerness to escape, left Will Allen behind. When Cain's absence was discovered by the mob, a litany of curses filled the air. Infuriated by his escape, men began to shout, "Take any negro and hang him!"[69]

Allen, trapped in his cell, watched from his cot as a rough assortment of men began to coolly and methodically remove the lock from the cell door. Despite the cool night air, the men were drenched in sweat from their exertion. As men tired, they were relieved by fresh replacements. After almost two hours, sledgehammers were brought forth, and men began to steadily pound at the cell door with as much force as they could muster in the middle of the night. Just before two o'clock in the morning, the door to the cell was torn open, leaving nothing between Allen and his attackers. The emptiness between the men was momentary, as the mob rushed forward and seized the man who had been tortured by hours of violent screams and the prospect of the inevitable fate that awaited him.[70]

Allen was blinded as a lantern was shoved in his face, as the mob, with a skewed sense of justice, sought to ensure they had the right man. Unwilling to meekly accept his fate, the 5'5" tall Allen wrested himself free from the hands of his attackers, and seized a nearby wooden club. He ferociously lashed out at the men around him, but "blows rained on his face and body like hail from a score of arms, and he was quickly subdued." Allen's bold attempt to defend himself enraged the mob. While curses and clubs flew freely at Allen's obstinance, his hands were jerked forward and tightly bound together before he was dragged out of the jail. Once outside the jail's battered brick walls, Allen insisted on walking, rather than be carried by the mob.[71]

Screams and yells eerily echoed through the air as men fired their pistols in anticipation of a third lynching. In the midst of the chaos, Will Allen walked steadily forward with his head held high, determined not to show fear. The mob guided Allen toward the campus of Drury College where only months before he, together with Bus Cain, allegedly murdered O. P. Ruark. Hoarse voices cried out, "Hang him where he killed old man Ruark!"[72]

Several Drury students who were in the crowd, fearful that a lynching on Drury's campus would sully the college's reputation, hurriedly held an impromptu meeting. It was decided that they would try to head off the mob and quickly spread out through the crowd yelling, "Take him to the square! Hang him with the other two! Take him back so the others can see!" The plan worked as the mob suddenly shifted direction and with one voice bellowed, "To the square!"[73]

As the mob streamed toward the scene of Coker's and Duncan's grisly end, "Men talked to themselves and each other, swore fluently at nothing at all, and shouted all sorts of bloodcurdling things into the air without regard of their significance. Grown men shrieked and howled like demons, shouting to the leaders to hang the negro, to burn him." It was on the corner of the square, as the howling processional began to arrive that Hollet H. Snow spotted Chief John McNutt and Officers John Wimberly, Henry Waddle, A. R. Sampey, E. T. W. Trantham, and Martin Keener, "laughing and talking and making no effort to stop the mob."[74] As Allen and the mob approached the square, it was shrouded in darkness, save for the harsh light that came from the bonfire built over the bodies of Fred Coker and Horace Duncan.[75]

As Gottfried Tower loomed before him, Allen trembled almost imperceptibly, but regained his composure. He walked unaided up the steps that led to the tower's bandstand. In front of Allen was a sea of faces, dimly illuminated by the flames of the bonfire, tense with anticipation. Those who stood on the fringes of the mob were shrouded in darkness. Allen, as he stood on the tower's bandstand, may have recognized familiar faces. If he did, he did not cry out for help. Instead, he stood silently as an unknown man shoved a lantern into his face for those below, which caused the mob to call out, "Hang him!"

The man motioned for silence and then spoke, "Ladies and gentle - men, here before you is Will Allen, the man who cruelly murdered old man Ruark on the corner of Benton Avenue and Center Street. What will you do with him?" Over a thousand voices thundered in unison, "HANG HIM!" The man turned to Allen and asked, "Are you Will Allen?" Allen replied, "I am." The unknown man then asked Allen if he had anything to say. Allen looked out at the crowd, straightened, and said, "Only that I did not kill Ruark." Several men from the crowd howled, "Make him tell who did!" Allen, his hands still bound, declared, "Bus Cain killed Ruark. I had nothing to do with it." The mob, unsatisfied with his answer, roared, "HANG HIM!"[76]

Postcard of South Street in Springfield, Missouri. The inscription on the postcard reads, "Hello, The X marks the place of the lynching of 3 nigros two weeks ago which took three of Uncle Sam's troops to cool them down." *Author's Collection.*

Allen's composure in the face of death was remarkable. From the moment he was dragged from the jail, Allen knew he would die at the hands of his fellow men. Surrounded by a mob of thousands that cried out for his blood, Allen stood below the strained visage of the Goddess of Liberty, and looked upward as a noose was tightened around his neck. The sickening smell of charred flesh, the ragged corpses of his fellow prisoners in the fire below, and the screams of men subjected Allen to Hell without having yet died and faced the judgment of Heaven. In the last minutes of his life, Allen knew that he would not awaken with the coming Easter sunrise, nor would he survive the next hour. Forced to look into the face of death, Allen refused to flinch.

As Will Allen attempted to pray, George Queen, a laborer at the United Iron Works Company, struck him in the face.[77] Yet he continued to pray and to profess his innocence in "a firm voice, a little husky but not trembling to the least." The end of the rope was thrown over the end of a yardarm that extended from the tower. As Allen continued to

Postcard of the Springfield, Missouri, square. The postcard reads, "This is where they hung and burned the niggers." It was sent to a sixteen-year-old white girl in Bevier, Missouri. *Author's Collection.*

stand, someone called out, "Jump off and show your gameness!" It was then that Allen either jumped to his death or was shoved off of the platform. A sharp crack filled the air as Allen's neck snapped. His body tumbled to the ground, but was quickly retrieved and strung up again.[78]

Satisfied that Will Allen was dead, his body was cut down and thrown on the bonfire on top of the remains of Horace Duncan and Fred Coker. Harry Williamson watched in disgust as J. Hill Gooch took a board from the fire "and hammered on the privates of one of the negroes."[79] Mayor-elect James L. Blain made his way to the front of the mob and wearily declared, "Men, you have done enough. You have had your revenge. You would better go home." The mob, exhausted, complied and slowly dispersed over the next few hours.[80] Before he left, Doss Galbraith collected a few souvenirs, including a piece of the rope used to hang Duncan and a scrap of Duncan's pants. After eight hours of mob violence, Springfield was quiet.[81]

NINE

Springfield

"They Certainly Had Not the Bearing of Deacons"

Save for a foul odor that lingered in the air, it was a beautiful Easter morning as the sun rose over Springfield on Sunday, April 15, 1906. Absent a visit to the square or county jail, the morning was like any other, with few signs of mob violence. Dogs barked, church bells solemnly tolled, and gradually, news of the events of the night before began to spread.

Jonathan Fairbanks, superintendent of the Springfield school system, recorded in his diary, "Sunday, Temperature 36, 5 a.m. Wind N. Fair, Fair and cool all day. Great mob gathered at the gaol burst it open and took out three colored prisoners, hanged them on the tower in the center of the square and burned them. One of the most brutal affairs I ever knew. Two of the men supposed to be innocent."[1]

Reuben T. Peak, the sixteen-year-old son of a prominent Springfield dentist, was on his way to Sunday School at the First Congregational Church when he "noticed that the Negroes were hurrying down the streets with wheel barrows of clothing and other household goods, some had loaded wagons and carts. All were headed toward the city limits." It was not until he arrived at church that Peak found out that a triple lynching had occurred the night before.[2]

Peak was not the only one to rise early. A few hours earlier just before dawn, a knock came at Ely Paxson's door. Paxson, the white owner of Paxson's Undertaking Company, opened the door to find the mother of Fred Coker standing on his doorstep. She quietly asked Paxson to

Crowd gathered around base of Gottfried Tower on the Springfield square the morning after the lynchings. *Courtesy of the Katherine G. Lederer Ozarks African American History Collection, Special Collections and Archives Department, Missouri State University.*

bury her son. Paxson dispatched men to the square, but when they arrived there was only a pile of ash and bones. Unable to discern the ashes of Coker from those of Will Allen and Horace Duncan, the men collected what was left. The ashes and bits of bone were stored in a small box that was then placed inside a pine coffin. The remains were then transported to the undertaking company where they would stay until Mrs. Coker arrived to claim them.[3]

Mrs. Coker was joined on the streets by her fellow African Americans, but they were bound for a far different destination. An unknown number of men, women, and children headed for the train depot and bought tickets to Joplin, Carthage, Kansas City, and St. Louis. It is probable that among those that left Springfield were survivors of the race riots in Monett and Pierce City. For many of Springfield's black community, southwest Missouri was no longer home.[4]

As the sun climbed higher in the sky, a constant stream of people began to venture toward the square. Dressed in their best Easter finery,

Crowd gathered at base of Gottfried Tower on the Springfield square with the bodies of Horace Duncan and Will Allen inked in by an enterprising entrepreneur who sold the image as a postcard. *Courtesy of the Katherine G. Lederer Ozarks African American History Collection, Special Collections and Archives Department, Missouri State University.*

some walked gingerly, others hurriedly, to see the remnants of the mob's handiwork. They were joined by visitors from out of town who arrived by train to see the square for themselves. The significance of the religious holiday, a reporter for the *Springfield Leader* observed, "was lost sight of and the race question was the paramount subject discussed." The unpaved portion of the city's streets around the square "was packed as solidly as if a steam roller had been used and on the surface the prints of thousands of feet were clearly visible."[5]

Many went to the edge of Gottfried Tower to peer at the blackened, still smoldering spot of earth where Horace Duncan, Fred Coker, and Will Allen were cremated. But there was little to look at. The few bits of rope and pieces of charred wood left were quickly seized by souvenir hunters. One woman at the square, who the reporter wryly called a 'predestinarian,' tried to rationalize the mob's action, "Well, it had to happen, anyway, or it wouldn't have happened; so, I suppose, it was all right; but it must have been terrible to kill them and burn them."[6]

As the crowds milled around Gottfried Tower, a dozen black men stood near the courthouse just off the square. "All of a sudden," an eyewitness recounted, "a rough looking fellow with tears in his voice and excitement in his neck began to howl that the negroes had been talking against the whites." The man "warned the negroes of the wrath to come." One of the younger black men present "made matters worse by telling a special duty sheriff, when asked to move on, that he could stand where he wanted to." The deputy, however, persuaded both men to move on. Yet the festive, almost carnival-like atmosphere, continued to pervade Springfield.[7]

Curious citizens in new suits and stylish hats congregated at the county jail. Thick ropes stretched around the facility to prevent bold onlookers from entering the building, which looked like it had "passed through the ravages of a Kansas cyclone." Windows were broken, their steel frames torn out with crowbars. The jail doors, bent and dented like they had "undergone an artillery barrage," were now useless. Inside the jail, cell doors laid to one side, their hinges battered. The *Republican* estimated that it would cost at least one thousand dollars to repair the jail.[8]

The ruined jail was not the only concern for Sheriff Everett Horner, who like his counterparts in Pierce City and Joplin, had all but stepped aside to let the mob run rampant the night before. In the midst of the chaos, fourteen prisoners had escaped, many of whom had been awaiting transfer to the Missouri State Penitentiary in Jefferson City. The prisoners who remained behind were transferred to a more secure location by Horner and his deputies, who were eager to avoid any further embarrassment.[9]

Sheriff Horner not only had to contend with a wrecked jail and escaped prisoners; he was also preoccupied by rumors that Springfield's African American community had seized dynamite from a local lime kiln to defend themselves from further attack. As he watched the crowds of men, women, and children stroll past his office during the day and on into evening, Horner continued to hear wild rumors that three hundred African Americans from Springfield's Westport neighborhood planned on lynching Mina Edwards.[10]

In response, Springfield's lame-duck mayor Benjamin E. Meyer, like Mayor Trigg of Joplin, issued a proclamation which read in part,

Men standing at entrance to Greene County Jail. *Courtesy of the Katherine G.
Lederer Ozarks African American History Collection, Special Collections and Archives
Department, Missouri State University.*

"To the People of Springfield: Excitement incident to the deplorable
event which transpired in our city last Saturday night is subsiding and
quiet has been restored. As Mayor of your city, I call upon every citizen
to assist in promoting peace an good order by refraining from inflammatory remarks or reckless criticism, whether in public or in private."
He then asked citizens to remain off the streets and away from the
square unless assigned to special police duties. Mayor Meyer also coun-
seled against gathering in crowds and asked, "Let us keep cool and be
law abiding, and counsel each with the other against further agitation
or discussion."[11]

Meyer ended his proclamation with a final plea, "The reputation
of this city is at stake, and every good citizen is interested in maintaining and upholding the law. There is absolutely no further danger to
life or property if citizens regardless of color will go about their own
business in a quiet way and refuse to be led into heated arguments or
useless discussions of that which has already passed."[12]

Mayor Meyer and Sheriff Horner deputized one hundred fifty

Crowd gathered at the Greene County Jail and sheriff's residence. *Courtesy of the Katherine G. Lederer Ozarks African American History Collection, Special Collections and Archives Department, Missouri State University.*

volunteers to police the city streets in an effort to keep the city calm.[13] The volunteer police force roamed the streets in squads overseen by a regular commissioned police officer. The men focused their patrols on the Jordan Valley section of Springfield where the majority of the city's African American community lived. Guards stood watch outside hardware stores and other businesses that sold firearms. Sentries were posted at the South Side Fire Station because officials feared that a resurgent mob would set fire to the black section of town and, like the mob in Joplin in 1903, try to "capture and disable the fire fighting apparatus so that the city firemen could not combat the flames."[14]

Horner and Meyer both knew, however, that they needed additional assistance. Sheriff Horner approached Lieutenant James J. Mayes, military instructor and head of Drury College's Corps of Cadets, and asked for his help. Lieutenant Mayes, however, declined Horner's request. Mayes "explained that the cadets were not subject to military duty, being mere boys studying the science of war." He advised Sheriff Horner to contact the governor if he wanted military aid.[15]

Sheriff Horner, running out of options, telegraphed Missouri governor Joseph Folk late in the afternoon, "Send me all available state troops at once. Town is in immediate danger of mob violence." Governor Folk, informed of the tense situation, immediately ordered companies A, B, C, E, G, and H of the Second Regiment of the Missouri National Guard to assist in maintaining order in Springfield.[16] Within an hour of Folk's order, men from each company had assembled at their respective armories.[17]

News of the governor's response to Horner's telegram created excitement throughout Springfield. Men began to gather at the Mill Street depot and, according to one reporter, "at least a dozen men a minute asked the patient ticket clerk when the train would come and if the troops were on board."[18] The wait, however, had just begun.

The troops were slow to arrive. Company E of Pierce City and Company G of Aurora were the first to arrive by train at 10:30 P.M. on Sunday evening. A vast crowd of onlookers waited on the platform as the train pulled into the station. As the engine rolled slowly by before coming to a halt, soldiers in khaki uniforms could be seen standing inside the passenger cars. The curious horde of men, women, and children swarmed around the cars, but were quickly pushed back as soldiers began to disembark and line up in formation. Captain Norman B. Pearman of Company G from Aurora and Captain Stephen L. Plummer of Company E from Pierce City began barking orders at the sixty-six men on the platform, much to the entertainment of the crowd.

Captains Pearman and Plummer, however, meant business. Sheriff Everett Horner and Police Chief John McNutt, who had waited for the men to arrive, stepped forward to introduce themselves. After introductions, Sheriff Horner handed Captain Pearman a telegram from Adjutant General James A. DeArmond, ordering him to "Report to the sheriff for duty in preventing rioting and disorder, and will act with sheriff to that end." DeArmond also cautioned, "See that the men preserve their tempers, and under no circumstances do any unnecessary shooting."[19]

After the orders were read, Horner and McNutt provided the two officers with a brief account of what occurred the night before and expressed their concerns about another outbreak of mob violence. As Plummer and Pearman listened, the crowd began to grow restless and

Missouri governor
Joseph W. Folk.
*Courtesy of The
State Historical
Society of
Missouri.*

unruly. At Sheriff Horner's urging, Captain Pearman ordered, "Forward march" and together with their men, headed for the square.[20]

As the troops marched toward Gottfried Tower, the hostile crowd mobbed them. In his report, Pearman later recalled, "Upon detraining we were immediately surrounded by a crowd, a part of it cat-calling and deriding the troops whose conduct can only be commended." Men and boys yelled and jeered at the soldiers, calling out, "Blow your horn to show 'em that you're coming!" and "Right about face!" The men of companies E and G, however, ignored the insults. When the soldiers turned onto Main Street, they were confronted by an additional one hundred and fifty men and boys, who joined in mocking and taunting the guardsmen.[21]

A journalist for the *Republican* reported, "Some of the men appeared so menacing that both companies were halted and Captains Pearman and Plummer ordered their men to fix bayonets. This was done, and the soldiers continued their march with shining bayonets fixed to their Krag-Jorgensens." Pearman later recounted the moment the troops arrived at the square, "We were confronted on the city square by several hundred people, whom we found not so inflamed and aggressive as those encountered enroute. Many were there no doubt, because of curiosity rather than riotous impulse." Ironically, the troops from Pierce City may have carried the same Krag-Jorgensen rifles that were stolen from the Pierce City National Guard armory by the mob in 1901, but were later recovered.[22]

As the men came to a halt at the square, "several prominent businessmen" approached Captain Pearman and Sheriff Horner. After a brief discussion, the men decided to clear the square and order people to go home. Sheriff Horner stepped forward to address the scattered crowd. In a clear voice he called out, "Men, the town is in charge of the soldiers. You must go away. All men not sworn in as deputies and not connected with the troops are requested to leave the square at once. This is made as a request, but if you do not obey, the request will be reinforced with arms."[23]

In his report to officials, Captain Pearman stated, "This proved effective, except for some of the tougher element, however, and by midnight the city was quiet." Pearman did not elaborate on the resistance he and his men met with from the local toughs. He established neighborhood patrols and set up a command center at the sheriff's office. Troops who were not assigned to patrol duty bivouacked on the square.[24]

Former Greene County sheriff Joseph Dodson, along with a group of private citizens, walked the streets of Springfield to alert African Americans that troops had arrived. He assured the blacks he encountered that "the soldiers had come and that no further trouble need be feared." The actions of Dodson and the men who accompanied him helped to calm the tense and uncertain atmosphere that enveloped the black community.[25] The tension was further eased by the arrival of the top National Guard officer in the state.

Brigadier General Harvey C. Clark, ordered to take command of the six companies, arrived after midnight. Clark was accompanied by

Colonel Harry Mitchell, commander of the Second Regiment, to which the six companies belonged. Clark and Company B left Butler on a special train for Springfield, stopping only to pick up Mitchell and Company H from Nevada and Company C at Lamar before they transferred to a Frisco express mail train. Clark, a graduate of Wentworth Military Academy, veteran of the Spanish-American War, and two-time prosecuting attorney of Bates County, had risen through the ranks of the Missouri National Guard from the time he was elected captain of Company B in 1888.[26]

When Clark took command, however, only five companies had arrived. Company A, the Carthage Light Guard, was the last to reach Springfield at two o'clock in the morning. Upon their arrival, Captain Allen McReynolds and the men of Company A were directed to the county courthouse where they spent the night sleeping on the floor. The company was minus their cook, Shell Mitchell, because "of his color." By Tuesday, however, Mitchell had joined his fellow troops and "took up his usual duties."[27] But before the troops even arrived, Springfield's Christian community had already acted.

Local religious leaders, outraged by the lynchings and mob violence, echoed the righteous indignation of their brethren in Jasper County after the lynching of Thomas Gilyard. Reverend Curtis V. Criss of the Benton Avenue Methodist Episcopal Church declared, "Let it be understood that while the best citizens of Springfield deprecate this crime so frequently bringing trouble to and hatred for the colored people, they sympathize heartily with the law abiding negroes and stand ready to defend them in their rights." If Criss was ready to help defend the rights of African Americans, other local religious leaders were ready to denounce the mob.[28]

As the crowd slowly filed into the pews at the First Christian Church of Springfield, Pastor W. E. Harlow studied the sermon he was to give, which he titled, "Weighed in the Balances and Found Wanting." When the time came to approach the pulpit, Harlow was ready to cast his judgment on Springfield, "Only about four weeks ago while in a revival at the First Christian Church and on the same evening the Clansman was pulled off at the opera house, I said in a sermon, 'This show will do more to inflame the prejudices and incite the lawlessness element of the city than anything since the Civil War and all it will need to burn the negro in some Southern cities is a leader.'"

Harlow thundered, "It was just such a crowd as controlled Springfield last night that put the blessed Christ on the cross and led the great Apostle Paul out of a Roman prison to his death. I am utterly ashamed of the mayor and police force of our city for offering no resistance whatever to the mob." He continued, "It is a blot on our civilization and shows that we are not far removed from savagery, barbarism, and anarchy. The leaders of the mob ought to be hunted out and made to pay the penalty, and, if the courts or proper authorities do not do their duty, we may look for a repetition of the horrible affair at any time."

Harlow paused and looked at his audience. He studied their faces, and then ended his sermon, "A divine command, 'Go not after the multitude to do evil' was disobeyed by hundreds last night and before Him who said it all must stand and accounted for their ungodly acts."[29] Harlow would soon have his chance to render judgment.

If Harlow blamed Thomas Dixon's The Clansman for the lynchings, Reverend J.W. Stewart of the Grace Methodist Episcopal Church saw alcohol as the cause of Springfield's mob violence. Stewart informed his congregation, "Mob violence is never justifiable in a land of civil government. We must deal with crime, however cruel, according to civilized plans for seeking justice. It is my deliberate judgment that the saloon was the foundation head of the awful tragedy Saturday night."[30]

Pastor Harlow and Reverend Stewart were joined in their denunciations of the mob by the Reverend W. T. McClure of Saint Paul Methodist Episcopal Church, although McClure did not try to analyze the catalyst for the lynchings. He urged his flock, "It is your duty and mine as Christian citizens, publicly and privately, to express our disapproval of that sort of thing in the very strongest terms."[31]

Springfield's ministerial alliance joined together to condemn the lynchings and mob violence. While the organization was to hold a mass meeting, members canceled it after civil and military authorities asked them to forego their original plan due to fears the meeting might spark another wave of violence. Religious leaders, however, met in private and passed a resolution denouncing the events of Saturday night. The Reverend H. Paul Douglas of the First Congregational Church, when asked his opinion of the local law enforcement officials, snorted derisively, "We might as well have a jelly fish for a sheriff and a set of rag dolls for police."[32]

African American members of the ministerial alliance promised "there would be no effort on the part of the colored people to secure revenge for the work of the mob." They also emphasized that there would not be "a general exodus of negroes from the city if law and order are restored and the negroes can be sure of protection."[33] Reverend Williams of the African Methodist Church informed a reporter, "All that the better class of colored people ask is that their lives and homes be protected." Williams wryly added, "In case the negroes should be driven out, the meanest class would be the hardest to get out of the city."[34]

Williams also voiced his disappointment in the local white community, "I know of one prominent white family who refused to give a negro girl servant shelter in their house when she was frightened almost to death." He continued, "I condemn that and want to say that I would have given shelter to as many women and men, white or black, as asked my protection in that hour of terror." While the pastors of Springfield came together to denounce the lynchings, it was not enough to prevent others of accusing some among their ranks of consenting to the mob violence.[35]

Dr. William M. Smith wrote to the *Springfield Leader* in response to the paper's claim that the mob was sanctioned by local Christian leaders. Smith declared, "In this I think you are mistaken. I mingled freely with the crowd and with the mob around and in the jail and at the square from 9 o'clock until 2 a.m. and while I heard some expressions of approval, I do not believe any of the speakers were Christians—they certainly had not the bearing of deacons."[36] Springfield's Christian community was not alone in standing against the mob.

On Monday morning, Governor Joseph W. Folk, a Democrat and former prosecutor, reacted quickly with a vigorous response to the mob violence. Unlike his predecessor, Governor Alexander Dockery, who failed to act when mobs ran rampant through Pierce City and Joplin, Folk instructed Missouri adjutant general James A. DeArmond to order Brigadier General Clark to arrest members of the mob. DeArmond, like Clark, was a graduate of Wentworth Military Academy, served in the Spanish-American War, and then returned to Missouri to study law in the same Butler, Missouri, law office as Clark. He served as city attorney of Butler until his appointment as adjutant general in 1905 by Governor Folk.[37] The governor also announced a three-hundred-dollar reward for the arrest and conviction of those complicit in the deaths of Will Allen, Horace Duncan, and Fred Coker.[38]

Clark and his men wasted no time in carrying out the governor's orders. Sheriff Horner and Deputy Dyer were accompanied by troops as they searched the streets of Springfield for members of Saturday night's mob. In his hand Horner carried bench warrants sworn out by prosecuting attorney Roscoe C. Patterson and issued by Judge Azariah W. Lincoln of Springfield's criminal court for the arrest of five men identified as having participated in the mob.

Charles Cannefax, found standing in the Baker Arcade, was the first man Sheriff Horner arrested. Cannefax, the youthful proprietor of Cannefax and Rozell Billiards, seemed surprised when he was taken into custody. He was soon joined by Oney Calvey, who was discovered leaning against a telephone pole at the corner of Boonville and Olive Streets, laughing and talking with acquaintances. Horner approached Calvey and growled, "Consider yourself under arrest." Calvey, a laborer, laughed as he was transferred, along with Cannefax, into the custody of troops from Aurora's Company G. The two men were then marched to the county jail where they were formally charged with first-degree murder.[39]

Cannefax and Calvey were soon joined by Dan Crane, Jesse R. Brake, and Oat Hall.[40] Although the men were charged with first-degree murder, Patterson and Lincoln agreed to allow the five men to give bond, although under normal conditions they would not have been able to do so. Prosecuting attorney Patterson and Judge Lincoln based their decision on the fact that the five men were "not under indictment and their cases had not been acted upon by a grand jury." Judge Lincoln set bail at ten thousand dollars. If he expected that the five men would not be able to give bond, Judge Lincoln was wrong. Dan Crane immediately bonded out and was quickly followed by Calvey and Cannefax.[41] What Lincoln did not anticipate was who stepped forward to provide bail.

As Mary Newland Clary observed, "the quality of the men who stepped forward to provide bonds for those arrested was an indication that Springfield's solid citizens would resist any serious attempt to punish the lynchers." Among the men who provided bond were Judge Frank B. Williams; city treasurer C. H. Dalrymple; mayor-elect James Blain; prominent attorney Oscar Hamlin, brother of future Democratic

U.S. congressman Courtney Hamlin; and William J. McDaniel, vice president of the Union National Bank.[42]

Willis G. Crane, the father of Dan Crane, issued a statement regarding his son's arrest. The elder Crane claimed his son had arrived home at 6 o'clock, had supper, and went to bed by 8 o'clock. He claimed, "I was awake till the lynching was over, and during all that time Dan was at home. He slept in a room next to me and we were both awake listening to the mob and talking about it. In this way I know Dan was home during the whole proceedings." A friend of Crane's, R. H. Walker of Nathan Clothing Company, alleged that Dan Crane called him at the store around 9 o'clock and asked what the noises were coming from the square. Walker reportedly replied that "a mob was forming for the purpose of going to the jail, but that the crowd seemed to be composed mostly of boys and that the indications were that no violence would be done." Satisfied, Crane said he would go back to bed.[43] Alibis, it appeared, were already in the works.

Judge Lincoln and prosecuting attorney Patterson, however, were not finished. At Patterson's request, Lincoln instructed the clerk of criminal court to order Sheriff Horner to call a special grand jury to investigate the mob's actions and indict those who participated. Governor Folk, who spoke by telephone with Patterson, warned the young prosecutor against any mass meetings. He promised, "I will do everything possible to help stop the riots in Springfield and will assist the local authorities in any way that I can. Keep the troops there as long as you think it is necessary. I will send one of [Attorney General] Hadley's assistants tonight to assist you in your investigation."[44]

Patterson's zealousness may have been borne of out of indignation and a sense of justice, but he was also ambitious. After graduating from Washington University at the age of twenty-one, the young Republican launched his political career. In 1903 he was elected prosecuting attorney of Greene County and now, three years later, found himself embroiled in one of the biggest cases of his life.[45] He may have been eager to prosecute the alleged mob participants, who were overwhelmingly Democratic, in an effort to appease blacks and other Republican voters. Patterson, however, appears to have been a man of principle.

Judge Azariah W. Lincoln, a native of Wisconsin raised in Ohio, was far more experienced than the young prosecutor. Admitted to the

Ohio bar in 1881, Lincoln relocated to Springfield a few years later, but did not stay in private practice for long. Like Patterson, he quickly became involved in the local Republican Party. Prior to his election as judge of Greene County's criminal court, Lincoln served as judge of the county probate court.[46] Together, the two men sought to bring the mob to justice.

As soldiers continued to patrol the streets, members of the Springfield police force, all Democratic appointees, scowled in contempt. According to the *Leader,* the police were "greatly incensed at the appearance of the militia and the pride of many a member is sorely wounded." One unnamed police officer growled, "As long as those things are here, I'm doing nothing. I'd go and get fifty of our own men and work with them, but I intend to stay right here as long as they're in town." He was not the only policeman upset. A fellow officer declared, "Why, I wouldn't take them fellers to a drink of water."[47]

Assistant chief of police William Brown was "terribly hurt" by the presence of the National Guard and informed prosecuting attorney Patterson that "it wasn't necessary to have aid brought in here; that the local force was strong enough to handle the situation." Patterson glared at Brown and snapped, "You haven't been taking care of the situation." Brown's protests were ignored.[48]

Brown may have been jealous and humiliated because of the attention the National Guard received. Streetcars brought crowds of people downtown to watch the troops as they lounged in camp, stood watch at the jail, and conducted street patrols. People gawked at the neat rows of canvas tents pitched in a quadrangle formed by Center Street, Robberson Avenue, and the county jail. Men, women, and children scrutinized the soldiers' khaki uniforms, noted the gleam of their bayonets, and inhaled the strong smell of camp coffee. Not everyone, however, quietly watched as the soldiers kept the peace. There were "frequent gatherings of irresponsible men and boys who jeered at the soldiers, but they were easily dispersed."[49] One incident, however, required force. When two inebriated men tried to take the rifle of a young private in Carthage's Company A, they were met with fierce resistance. "When the affair was over," the historian of Company A recalled, "one of the drunks had a bayonet wound in his hip and the other a smashed nose and loosened teeth from the violent impact of the gun butt, whereas the soldier was still in good

Missouri National Guard encamped at Greene County Jail and sheriff's residence. *Courtesy of the Katherine G. Lederer Ozarks African American History Collection, Special Collections and Archives Department, Missouri State University.*

condition and in possession of his rifle and the field."[50] The fragility of the imposed peace was threatened not only by occasional conflict between state troops and the citizens of Springfield, but by bold criminal opportunists.

Despite the presence of the Missouri National Guard, tensions flared when two African American men allegedly attempted to rob a young white couple on Monday evening. Just after eleven o'clock, Leslie Peters and Ollie Fielder were on their way home from the theater when a pair of African American men stepped out from the shadows. Startled, Peters demanded, "What do you want?" One of the robbers growled, "We'll show you, you—. Damn you, we've got you now." Both men pulled revolvers and fired at Peters and his date, but their shots went wild. Peters drew his pistol and returned fire. One of the men slumped to the ground while the other fled into the darkness.[51]

Peters escorted Fielder home and then left to look for a police officer. On his way back, he tripped over the body of Ralph Burns, whom he had shot. Peters, realizing the severity of what had happened, proceeded straight for police headquarters. He walked in and announced, "I've killed a nigger and want to give myself up. Here is my gun."[52] Upon the young man's confession, "every available policeman and such of the citizens' posse as could be notified hastened to the scene in carriages, in buggies, and on foot."[53]

At the scene of the shooting, officers found a man lying in the street with a new .44-caliber Colt revolver with two empty chambers clutched in his right hand. Two shell casings found next to him were "new and shining." Police identified the wounded man as Ralph Burns, a petty criminal. Burns, despite gunshot wounds to the head and shoulder, stubbornly clung to life. He was transported to Paxson's Undertaking Company where he received medical attention, but died within a few hours.[54] A thorough search of the area did not turn up Burns's accomplice.

Leslie Peters and Ollie Fielder were not the only individuals targeted by criminals. R. W. Catlett, a stenographer, reported being held up by an African American robber while on his way home earlier in the evening. Catlett managed to scare off his assailant by throwing rocks at him. The man fled and was not apprehended. In response, military patrols in the area were increased, but they could not prevent the stoning of Street Car 65 operated by motorman Miles and conductor Williams.[55]

As the car idled on the rail switch between Mill Street and Phelps Avenue in Jordan Valley, which was a predominately black area of town, the men began to hear stones hitting the car. According to Miles and Williams, "a gang of six negroes, secreted partly behind the billboards and box cars, hurled a shower of stones at the car." Their aim, however, was poor as "most of the rocks fell too low to injure any of the passengers." The torrent of rocks and stones dissipated when passengers began to disembark from the car. The rest of the night passed uneventfully.[56]

The next day, Tuesday, was just as eventful yet more peaceful. Coroner Matthews convened an inquest regarding the death of Ralph Burns. The coroner's jury was composed of six men: John Coombs, T. E. Whitlock, William Doty, Samuel Herrick, H. T. Moyers, and J. W. Cato. The jury intently listened as nine witnesses testified over the course of the afternoon, including assistant chief of police William

Brown; temporary police officers Crown, Flory, Dillard, Hazen, and Hollingsworth; businessman J. T. White; African American laborer Woody Bird; Ollie Fielder; and Leslie Peters.[57]

J. T. White testified he overheard Burns boast to another African American man that he had purchased a new gun "and would 'show them something.'" White also stated he heard Burns say he had assaulted a white woman in the past and "intended to do so again." Woody Bird, an African American employed at the Kirby Saloon, testified that he lived in the vicinity of the shooting and counted six or seven shots, but had little else to say. Ollie Fielder, when called to the stand, recalled that one of the men grabbed her before she fainted and lost consciousness.[58]

The coroner's jury did not take long to return a verdict. The jury declared, "We find that the deceased came to his death at the hand of Leslie Peters in defense of himself and for the purpose of defending the person of Miss Ollie Fielder from felonious assault about to be made upon her person by said Ralph Burns and one other negro to the jury unknown, and in our opinion the said Leslie Peters was justified in doing so."[59] Several of Springfield's citizens enthusiastically agreed.

Peters, accompanied by a reporter from the *St. Louis Republic,* was on his way to have his photograph taken when hundreds of people surrounded him to shake his hand. According to the reporter, it took Peters three hours to cross the Springfield square because of the large number of people who wanted to meet him. An unnamed individual reportedly sent a telegram to industrialist Andrew Carnegie asking the robber baron to "award Peters a medal." It was reported that Springfield's citizens were raising money to purchase Peters and Fielder a home for when they married. The reporter, however, noted that "there is a clause in the contract which provides that the couple must wed. The girl will get a diamond engagement ring when the wedding date is set."[60]

At the same time the inquest was held, Democratic mayor James Blain and the newly elected members of the Springfield City Council were sworn into office. In his first speech as mayor, Blain briefly mentioned the lynching before he declared street improvements as the city's most critical issue. Notably, Blain called for an increase in the size of the Springfield police force, as "our population has increased probably 60 per cent in the last ten years, our police force has not been increased in that time and is now inadequate to the demands upon it."

He recommended the police force be increased to twenty-two positions from the current ten, so that there would be "one officer to 1500 inhabitants."[61] Blain was not the only one who thought Springfield's police force was inadequate.

An editorial in the *Springfield Republican* snorted, "If the police could get it out of their heads that they are for political and ornamental purpose only and would vigorously busy themselves to ridding this city of the idlers and toughs who have made Springfield their refuge and loafing place these many, many months, no more effective service could they render the city at this time." The editorial huffed, "It ought to be and is an easy matter for the police to spot the professional loafer and the tough. The policeman who cannot do this has missed his calling and should either resign his commission or have it taken from him by the appointing power."[62] The *Republican* viewed Springfield police officers as less than effective, but Mayor Blain thought otherwise.

Despite their lack of action during the mob's reign of terror, Mayor Blain reappointed Officers Frank Jones, A. R. Sampey, James Walsh, Henry Waddle, and John Wimberly. As for his own appointments to the force, he selected Benjamin Lamb, John Crass, W. C. Dillard, Lee Harman, and A. M. Franklin. All of the appointees were Democrats save for Lamb and Dillard, who were Republicans. The ten men would serve under the newly elected Republican chief of police Asa "Acy" Loveless.[63] While the mayor's new police force was sworn in, Sheriff Horner and his deputies were busy arresting three more men alleged to have been in the lynch mob.

Horner and his deputies arrested Harry Carson, Fred Stracke, William "Tobe" Wimberly, and Emmett Kinney on a "charge of complicity" in the lynchings. Kinney was the son of the Irish tailor allegedly murdered by Elmer Hancock and Willard Caldwell the previous year. Tobe Wimberly was the brother of Police Officer John Wimberly. After the four men were taken into custody, prosecuting attorney Patterson ordered Sheriff Horner to refrain from making further arrests until a grand jury could be convened to investigate the lynchings and possibly issue indictments. Carson, Wimberly, Stracke, and Kinney posted bond within a matter of hours and were released.[64]

While arrests for participation in the lynchings were halted, it did not stop the police from arresting others for inappropriate behavior in the post-lynching atmosphere that pervaded Springfield. Isaac Stephens was brought before Judge Lincoln on a charge of disturbing the peace of Clara Brown. Brown, a young African American woman, complained to authorities when Stephens, a white man, "made some remark about the lynching Saturday night." Lincoln fined Stephens one dollar and court costs, then sent him to the county jail.[65] But whites were not the only ones who acted out.

One Tuesday evening, a group of blacks allegedly attacked the crew of Engine Number 3683, showering the cab with rocks. The cab's windows were smashed and a switchman's lantern was broken, but no one was injured. By the time the train crew reported the attack to the National Guard, the men were gone.[66] African Americans had reason to be upset.

According to a correspondent from the *Kansas City Star* sent to Springfield, "Everywhere this threat is heard: 'This town is too small for negroes and whites to live in. One or the other must go.'" The same reporter was on the scene when a young African American man reportedly boasted, "Give the colored men the guns and we'll show you." Several white men standing nearby heard the remark and began to move toward the man when "officers hustled the man away to jail. In another minute he would have been trampled to death." On reflection, the journalist observed, "These are the things feared by the conservative citizens. They know how deep seated is the hatred here toward the whole negro race and how trivial an incident may start a riot."[67]

Springfield officials were not the only ones who had to contend with fallout from the lynchings. Governor Joseph W. Folk, in attendance at the Southwest Commercial Clubs Convention in St. Louis, found himself deluged with questions from newspaper reporters. After the governor was informed of the shooting of Ralph Burns, Folk was swarmed by reporters. When asked if he anticipated a mob storming the jail, Folk replied, "If anything like that occurs, it will mean trouble of a grave sort." Throughout the day the governor received updates by telegram and telephone of the situation in Springfield. In an interview with the *St. Louis Globe-Democrat,* Folk stated in part, "Lynching is murder. No one against whom evidence can be obtained will be allowed to go unwhipped of justice." He noted that arrests had already been made, then added, "The guilty will be punished. Missouri will, I believe, furnish a salutary lesson to the rest of the country of lynchers convicted and punished by due process of law."[68]

Not everyone, however, agreed with Folk. As the first session of the conference came to a close, George Russell Brown of Little Rock proposed a resolution supporting Governor Folk's actions. The resolution read in part, "Resolved, That this convention view with approval the efforts of Governor Folk to suppress crime in general and the apprehension and punishment of the perpetrators of the recent violations of the laws at Springfield, which resulted in loss of life and destruction of property."[69]

Buckley B. Paddock, a Confederate veteran and former Democratic mayor of Fort Worth, Texas, jumped to his feet in outrage. He yelled, "Mr. Chairman, move to table that resolution. The people of Springfield did just exactly right. They ought to do more like it! Whenever a brute lays his hands on a woman, whether he be white or black, they can't make the fire too hot to suit him." For Paddock, the answer was simple, "I do not ordinarily favor mob law, but I tell you that whenever they lay a hand on a woman, burn them!" In the heat of the moment, Paddock, unlike Governor Folk, must have forgotten the right to due process.[70]

Delegates from Texas, Arkansas, Missouri, and Indian Territory leaped to their feet to second Paddock's motion. The resolution was overwhelmingly defeated. Later that evening, Governor Folk, when asked by a reporter if he authorized the statement "that every member of the mob that took part in the disgraceful proceedings at Springfield deserved to be hanged," the governor declined to answer.[71]

Other governors readily shared their opinions with journalists. Arizona governor Joseph H. Kibbey told a reporter that members of the lynch mob should be punished. He hastily added, "This statement is general. I do not wish to express an opinion on a purely local affair which might be construed as a criticism of Governor Folk or the officials in Springfield."[72]

New Mexico territorial governor Herbert J. Hagerman, a Republican, boasted, "No such affair could occur in New Mexico. There is not a sheriff in my territory who would surrender a prisoner as long as one shot was left in his gun." He paused and then added, "The lynching took place under the very Statue of Liberty. That is somewhat ironic, is it not?" Edward W. Hoch, the Republican governor of Kansas, remarked, "That was a most terrible affair and Governor Folk has my hearty commendation for his prompt steps to suppress it."[73]

Reporters approached the author of the resolution, George Russell Brown, in the lobby of the Southern Hotel to ask if he regretted his action. Brown, the secretary of the Arkansas State Board of Trade, shook his head. "I have no apologies to make," he said, "I do not consider that I made any mistake, but, on the other hand, believe that grave error has been made in voting down my resolution." Brown continued, "When the businessmen of a country approve mob law, then human life is bereft of protection, property loses its value, and chaos has come again."[74]

Buckley Paddock's fiery defense of the Springfield lynch mob won him many admirers. Members of an unnamed women's club in St. Louis sent the crusty Confederate veteran a bouquet of one hundred American Beauty roses with a card that read, "Thank God for such a father, husband, and brother, who can and will protect us if the law and politicians cannot." Paddock, pleased with his bouquet, declared, "I appreciate more than I can find words to express the kindly feelings which prompted the beautiful gift. Thanks, dear women; thanks. My heart is always with you."[75] But if Paddock and Folk may have disagreed about punishing the mob, they found common ground in Leslie Peters.

At the convention's evening banquet, Governor Folk took the stage. In his speech, he defended Leslie Peters, who "shot to save his life and the honor of the lady he was escorting. His act was courageous and entirely blameless in the eyes of the law." He proclaimed that Peters's "prompt release was commendable." The audience leapt to its collective feet and "applauded his sentiments enthusiastically, shouting to him to continue speaking after he had taken his seat."[76]

Kansas governor Hoch, who followed Folk on stage, dutifully denounced mob violence. He somberly advised, "A mob has about as much sense as a herd of Texas cattle in a stampede. This is a republic of law and the laws must be enforced." Hoch was not applauded.[77] Governor Hoch did not stand alone in his criticism of the mob.

Presbyterian ministers in St. Louis gathered to condemn the lynchings. The Reverend Dr. S. J. Niccolis of the Second Presbyterian Church, speaking on behalf of his colleagues, asserted, "It is barbarism equal and in many respects surpassing the horrible deeds that excited

The *St. Louis Post-Dispatch*'s depiction of Springfield's "Easter Offering." *Courtesy of The State Historical Society of Missouri.*

our feeling against the Chinese in their dealings with our missionaries. The Springfield occurrence, indeed, exceeded those deeds in barbarity."[78] The Presbyterians were joined in their outrage by their Christian brethren.

After three hours of debate at the Monday meeting of the African American Baptist Ministerial Alliance of St. Louis, ministers passed a resolution that called upon the best citizens of Springfield to stop "cruel negro hating, bloodthirsty mobs" and applauded Governor Folk and Brigadier General Clark for their swift action. Notably, the resolution commended Lieutenant James J. Mayes "for the manly position he took, and for his courage in giving the public a graphic account through the *Globe-Democrat,* of the real situation in the mob's hatred to the negro race, rather than any desire on their part to avenge the alleged crime."[79] Sheriff Horner, however, was not lauded.

The Methodist Ministerial Alliance, like the Presbyterians and Baptists, met. A committee was formed to write a resolution to express their indignation at the mob. One of their members, Deputy Grand Master George E. Temple of the Grand United Order of Odd Fellows, sought to "enlist the active cooperation of the various benevolent and fraternal organizations of the state in making an united protest against the increasing spirit of mob violence against members of the race, whenever members of the race, whenever charged or even suspected of a crime."[80] St. Louis was joined by Kansas City in its criticism of Springfield.

The *Kansas City Journal* thundered, "It was grotesque irony that the mob conceived the idea of hanging and burning these negroes at the feet of the statue of the Goddess of Liberty. It is hard to believe that this mob could not have been dispersed had men of brains and bravery taken the initiative when only a gang of boys and hoodlums were inciting themselves and the rabble of the town in violence. This is not just Springfield's shame. The whole state must suffer the stigma of outlawery that the mob has brought upon it. The only thing that can be done now is to hunt down the leaders of the mob and help them to summary punishment."[81]

The *Kansas City Star* remarked incredulously, "Three negroes suspected of crime, but two of whom were declared by their white employers to be absolutely innocent, were hanged and burned without trial, without even a casual investigation, by a mob in Springfield, Mo., early Easter morning—Easter morning, remember!"

The *Star* blamed the lynching on Thomas Dixon's *The Clansman*, "But the feeling against the negro race in Springfield has been strong for some time. And it was because of this feeling that the negroes of that place made a plea that '*The Clansman,*' a fierce propaganda of race hatred, should not be presented in that city." Still, the *Star* concluded, "The plea was in vain, and while this play did not create race hatred in Springfield, it intensified it and gave eloquent encouragement to the passions that resulted in this tragedy."

The editor of the *Star* lamented, "It is a terrible crime to be born black, especially in this 'land of the free.' Thomas Dixon, author of '*The Clansman,*' used to be a minister of the gospel. What does he think of the Easter services in Springfield, Mo.?"[82] As the editors of Kansas City denounced the Springfield mob, reporters were busy gathering stories from those who fled to the safety of the midwestern metropolis.

One African American who fled to Kansas City recounted his experience, "Before 9 o'clock crowds of men and boys were going up and down the streets abusing every negro they met and occasionally striking and kicking them if the negroes said anything. Before the crowd got large nearly every negro had gone home. Race prejudice in Springfield has been strong for a number of years."[83]

One Kansas City reporter who met the train from Springfield complained, "It was impossible to find a member of the Frisco train crew who came in with the local train from Springfield, Missouri, yesterday afternoon at 5:30 who would admit that he had seen the work of the mob there the night before in stringing up three negroes." When the reporter asked the conductor if he saw the lynching, the man replied, "No. I didn't get up when I heard the noise. The brakeman, however, knows all about it. He was there." The brakeman, however, denied any knowledge of the lynching. The frustrated journalist then approached the African American porter, but he refused to talk. Other employees told the reporter that the porter "did not come down to the train yesterday morning until just a minute or two before it left, evidently fearing abuse himself."[84] Ministers from Kansas City's black community, enraged at the mob's actions, gathered to discuss the lynchings.

At the meeting of the Kansas City Ministers Alliance, Reverend Samuel W. Bacote, pastor of the Second Baptist Church, expressed his outrage at the lynchings. "Some poor colored men were arrested for an attack on a 5 cent woman—maybe a 2 ½ cent woman, or a 12 ½ cent woman—and the rabble of the town gathered up those men who were supposed to be innocent."

Bacote, like the Reverend W. E. Harlow in Springfield, found fault with the recent theatrical production of *The Clansman* that had recently played in Springfield. He declared, "The Clansman, Tom Dixon's story, had been dramatized and had inflamed their minds." Bacote, when confronted about his comments about the character of Mina Edwards, backpedaled, "I did not know a reporter was present. I did not expect to be quoted. I had no intention of reflecting on the standing of the woman."[85]

George Creel, editor of the *Independent* in Kansas City, jeered, "Such talk as that from a pulpit, and yet the negroes wonder why there is feeling against them. And the negro ministers of Springfield cry aloud in wonderment, even while two other negroes attempt an assault the very night after the burning, and later fire into a house where white women and children are sleeping." He added, "These things are worthy of consideration as well as the burning, and may perhaps explain why the white citizens of Springfield are not so frantic in their desire to punish the mob."[86]

Creel, unlike Reverend Harlow, was unable to see the influence of Thomas Dixon's *The Clansman*. The claim that Dixon's work was responsible for the mob, Creel snorted, "is a newspaper idea advanced for its dramatic effect, and eagerly seized upon by cheap sensationalists without brains enough to think for themselves." Creel was the pot calling the kettle black.[87] But his argument that black crime was to blame may have made sense to many Springfield citizens, especially after a brief outbreak of racial violence.

The African American community in Springfield came under further scrutiny following the incident that Creel remarked upon in his editorial when "unidentified negroes" fired two shots at the home of S. P. Fielder, the father of Ollie Fielder, in the early morning hours of April 17.[88] One bullet passed through the wall of the house and fell to the floor. The other "passed over the foot of the bed about a foot above the three sleeping occupants." No one, however, was harmed.[89]

The unknown individuals who fired at the Fielder house were the ones that Robert Kennedy, editor of the *Springfield Leader,* railed about in his editorials. The first, entitled, "The Bad Negroes," scolded, "Let it be hoped that the bad negroes, the defiant, insolent sort will not mis-understand the situation here. The best they can do is to keep quiet and reform. All this militia and general condemnation of mobs must not be construed as in any way upholding the bad negro." Kennedy warned, "The bad negro must reform or suffer the consequences. The people are in no temper for defiance now. The best thing that all negroes can do is to remain quiet and not hang around on the corners and discuss mat-ters." He grimly concluded, "To do so is to play with fire."[90]

Kennedy, the son of a Confederate veteran, was not done ranting. In an editorial on race supremacy, he thundered, "The white race is now and always has been an aggressive, uncompromising advocate and fighter for this principle. Nothing but a complete overthrow of the white race can ever bring about a compromise of this belief." He advo-cated that the rest of America could learn from the example of the South, where "it handles the race problem in a cool, scientific way. It believes there are good negroes and bad ones. All 'coons' do not look alike to the Southerner. He can see a difference. He corrects the bad negro and the good one knows his place. This should be learned by both whites and blacks."[91]

But not everyone from Springfield agreed with Kennedy's views. State senator F. M. McDavid told a *St. Louis Post-Dispatch* reporter, "There is no denying the fact, however hard and embarrassing it may be for a resident to admit it, that the lynching was utterly unprovoked." He then confessed, "Springfield has a population of 35,000. The negroes number from 4,000 to 5,000. We have had considerable trouble with them lately, but it has not been enough such as to justify mob violence." When asked about Sheriff Horner, McDavid conceded that the sheriff was most likely unprepared for the mob, but added in Horner's defense, "It is difficult to say just what one would do when placed in such a critical position. It is very easy to figure out afterwards what would have been the best course to pursue."[92]

Missouri attorney general Herbert S. Hadley, however, disagreed. He sent a telegram to Assistant Attorney General John Kennish, who was in Springfield to aid prosecuting attorney Patterson, which read, "Published reports would seem to justify proceedings to remove the sheriff. Advise such a course if investigation warrants." Despite Hadley's misgivings about Horner, the sheriff remained in office.[93]

Horner, Police Chief Loveless, and the National Guard were kept busy as Mike Phillips, an engineer, reported being accosted by two African American men while on his way home. The two men beat Phillips before he managed to break away and flee. His attackers pursued him for several blocks until he arrived at the Owl Drug Store. Phillips suffered a broken nose and busted lip, but escaped further injury. At roughly the same time, two white traveling salesmen were approached by three armed black men. One of the armed men growled, "If you white ———— want anything you can get it and get ———— quick, too." The salesmen managed to escape before the situation escalated.[94]

Only hours earlier Governor Folk had made a surprise visit to Springfield to observe the situation firsthand. In an impromptu speech at the Springfield Club, Folk reiterated his interest in seeing justice served. "I understand that there is a disposition on the part of some citizens to hush the matter up," he admonished, "This would be the greatest disaster possible. Such a course would place Springfield and the entire state of Missouri back a quarter of a century." Displeased at the negative publicity Missouri received in the wake of the lynchings, Folk chastised the actions of the mob, "If these negroes had not been lynched they would have been placed on trial for their alleged crimes. Now that they have been lynched, Springfield and the state of Missouri are on trial."[95] Not everyone in the audience agreed with the governor, not even his fellow Democrats.

The editor of the *Springfield Republican,* E. E. E. McJimsey, lamented, "Ever since the lynching, persistent and frequent warnings have been served on the negroes to the effect that they must get out of Springfield. These warnings have been served secretly, of course, and therefore cowardly." These efforts, the editor alleged, were backed by Springfield's Democratic politicians in order to make significant political gains among voters.[96]

McJimsey pointed out that the police "at that time Democratic and under Democratic control" failed to act and that there was "virulent and widespread criticism of Governor Folk on the part of his party associates for his sending of the troops." Most important of all, McJimsey crowed, was "the frigid attitude of the great majority of his erstwhile followers toward the Governor what time he appealed to them in his Springfield Club address to stand for law enforcement and the punishment of every man who participated in the lynching and the burning of the negroes."[97]

The fiery editor lambasted the "almost total lack of disapproval from the lips of local Democratic politicians of the systematic persecution through intimidation of the better element of Springfield's negro citizens." Those politicians who failed to denounce the lynchings, McJimsey argued, should be labeled as "bad men at heart and therefore not to be trusted."[98] In response, the *Springfield Leader* growled, "As we have pointed out, the principle trouble with the race question are the ideas put into the heads of the negroes by Republican politicians." The *Leader* admitted, "We must say again that the Democracy does not believe in the negro in office and the Republican party in this section does."[99] Despite the impassioned editorials that appeared in the Springfield newspapers, many of Springfield's residents were ready to move on.

Life began to return to normal for the white citizens of Springfield. The *Republican* reported that "business has resumed, the work of construction is going busily forward on the many buildings under process of erection," and "merchants are getting busy and their trade is showing an increase each day."[100] The Springfield Public Library saw an increase in the number of its patrons as "the scare growing out of the recent mob and negro lynchings has temporarily demoralized the attendance at the library. Perhaps less than half as many books as formerly have been issued in the past two weeks."[101] But life was not the same for the African Americans who called Springfield home.

The *Republican* estimated that three hundred African Americans had left Springfield as of April 24 after receiving "notice to leave town by a certain time and those notified have lost no time in making their get away." Among those who left were twenty-five families who gathered their belongings and left for Memphis and Kansas City. As E. E. E. McJimsey, editor of the *Republican,* alluded to in his editorial, "these notices have been in circulation is known by authorities, but they are unable to find out where they originate or who had been sending them." Blacks remained "frightened and in many cases whole families carry their bedding out in the woods and sleep there for the night, afraid to remain at home for fear the mob will burn their home and injure them."[102] Rumors of black vengeance continued to swirl around the city, but the police and the National Guard found that hysterical reports of black mobs was the result of "negroes gathering together for protection, afraid to go home, and get separated from each other." According to the *Republican,* the police and National Guard troops would "assure the negroes that there is no danger and that the best thing to do is to disperse."[103]

Grant Brown and Tom Kimbrough, members of Springfield's African American community, thought it best to leave on their own accord. Brown, Kimbrough, and Kimbrough's wife were charged with stealing forty-nine pounds of lard. Brown, who "moved here from Kansas, where he married a white woman," thought it best to leave Springfield. When Brown and the Kimbroughs agreed to leave Springfield, Patterson asked Judge Lincoln to dismiss the charges against them.[104]

While some Springfield residents left for good, others returned to the city, but not of their own volition. Two prisoners, Alphonse Grigorious and Harry Smith, were captured in Pittsburg, Kansas, after they were caught burglarizing a hardware store. The two men told officers that after escaping from their cells, they stayed in the mob for several blocks, and then walked to Nichols Junction where they hopped a westbound train. They were promptly escorted back to Missouri in chains.[105] The two men were joined a few days later by escapees Fred Depres and John McMartin who were apprehended in Lamar, Missouri.[106] Emmett Vaughn, another escapee, was killed during a crap game in St. Louis.[107]

Springfield grew weary of the uniformed troops who patroled its streets. Adjutant General James DeArmond told a reporter from the *Republican* that the soldiers would probably leave on Monday, April 23, having been in Springfield for only a week. Even until the end of their stay, the troops were kept busy. A few nights earlier, a group of African Americans allegedly surrounded the Springfield Lighting Company's power plant and "threatened the fireman." The next night, a different fireman was on duty when "three negroes appeared at the plant and fired four shots in the door, but no one was hit." By the time the police and the National Guard arrived, the men were gone.[108]

Soldiers were once again on alert when it was reported that Bus Cain, one of the escapees, was seen hiding in the barn of Henry Fox, superintendent of the Springfield Gas and Electric Company. Cain, who was arrested with Will Allen for the murder of O. P. Ruark, had slipped out after the mob seized Duncan and Coker. Coincidentally, Fox's wife was the woman who hired Mina Edwards as domestic help prior to Edwards's alleged assault. When troops arrived to search the barn, there was no sign of Cain, except for an opening that had been forced open by someone from the inside.[109]

On Wednesday, the *Republican* announced that the National Guard would be ordered home in the afternoon. Governor Folk, after consulting with Assistant Attorney General John Kennish and Adjutant General James DeArmond, decided the troops were no longer needed in Springfield. Folk's decision may have been influenced by published reports that the soldiers were restless and wished to return home. As one reporter noted, "Many of the militiamen are in business in their home towns and they are getting anxious to get back to their private affairs."[110] The *Carthage Evening Press,* the hometown newspaper of Company A, reported that the privates were paid forty-three cents a day.[111] Service in the Missouri National Guard was not a profitable venture.

The men of Company A were so disgruntled that they boldly held a meeting and "all signed a paper denouncing the action of Gov. Folk in needlessly keeping the troops at Springfield and, at the same time, endorsed the action of their captain, Allen McReynolds, who was doing all in his power to get permission for the return of the company." Fortunately, the next day the men were ordered home with a new mascot, a bulldog named "Riot," in tow.[112]

Carthage's Company A and Aurora's Company G were the first to leave. They were soon followed by Company E from Pierce City. The last to depart Springfield were the companies from Lamar, Butler, and Nevada. Each company was accompanied to the train depot by a large crowd of Springfield citizens. When the last company left, the only sign that the troops had been in town was the five barrels of lime that they spread on their former campsite. Sheriff Horner expressed his appreciation for their service, stating that the citizens of Springfield slept much easier due to their presence. Taxpayers, however, may not have been amused when it was announced that the estimated cost of keeping the troops in Springfield for a week was eight thousand dollars.[113] As the dying embers of Springfield's Easter offering cooled and the soldiers were borne away by trains, it was now up to a jury of twelve men to serve as the conscience of a city.

TEN

Springfield

"Murder in the Air"

As the special grand jury convened at the Greene County courthouse
to investigate Springfield's triple lynching, few African Americans were
to be found. The *Springfield Leader* reported that while the number of
customers patronizing businesses on the square had increased, "on the
streets the negroes were scarce." The section of Olive Street that ran
between Boonville and Patton Alley, once "the old haunt of the black
man," was now deserted. African Americans who ventured out "are
on business bent, and when that 'bent' is finished, they move on." In
an interview with the *Leader* the deputy sheriff and county jailer, E. C.
King, remarked, "In the past two weeks, we've only had one negro sent
to jail for petty thefts. Before the mob broke loose, we had from two
to six a week regularly."[1]

As the black citizens of Springfield disappeared from public view,
white citizens came together to serve as jurors for the grand jury. The
twelve men selected to serve were: G. W. Miller, Joseph C. Dodson,
August A. Mehl, Charles A. Walterhouse, Albert B. Appleby,
W. T. Chandler, B. F. Dennis, Charles A. Hubbard, George O'Bryant,
William E. Harlow, C. G. Noblette, and Fred Marshall. Once the men
were seated, Judge Lincoln addressed them. In a lengthy speech,
Lincoln implored the jury, "You are expected to do your duty without
fear or favor. Let the lash fall where it may." He urged, "You should
indict every man proved in your reasonable satisfaction to be guilty.
Whether friend or foe, rich or poor, high or low, wherever you find

guilt, let that guilt be punished. The path of safety lies in the direction of the most vigorous, rigid, and exhaustive investigation."

Judge Lincoln also asked the jury to investigate "any attempted holdups of our citizens by any of the colored race." He advised that should the jury find that "any colored man or men have molested or interfered with any man, woman, or child, or in any way threatened, disturbed, or abused them, do not hesitate to indict any offender." The men that Lincoln addressed came from a variety of backgrounds and experience. All were prepared to accept the duty to redeem the honor of Springfield.

Charles A. Walterhouse, foreman of the jury, was president of the Springfield Guaranty Abstract Company.[2] Reverend William E. Harlow, who strongly denounced the lynchings on Sunday morning, served as secretary.[3] Former Greene County sheriff and Maple Park Cemetery sexton Joseph C. Dodson, who walked the dark streets of Springfield on Monday night to tell African Americans that the National Guard had arrived, was also seated on the grand jury.[4] He was joined by former county judge and farmer Albert B. Appleby.[5] G. W. Miller and Charles A. Hubbard dealt in real estate.[6] August A. Mehl, the son of German immigrants, was a dry-goods merchant from Republic.[7] W. T. Chandler hailed from Ash Grove, B. F. Dennis from Palmetto, farmer George O'Bryant from Republic, C. G. Noblette from Campbell Township, and Fred Marshall from North Campbell Township.[8] Of the men, only three were Democrats: Noblette, Marshall, and Dennis. Together the twelve men began the arduous work of determining who was responsible for the deaths of Horace Duncan, Will Allen, and Fred Coker.

As the grand jury convened, Mina Reeves Edwards, the woman whose accusations sparked the lynchings, granted an interview to a reporter from the *Springfield Republican*. In the interview, Edwards calmly asserted, "I am now certain that he [Coker] was one of the men who attacked me and I feel that he got his just deserts at the hands of the mob." The reporter remarked that "she showed not the least interest or emotion" during the interview.[9] But Edwards did not stay long enough in Springfield for the grand jury to question her.

The *Republican* reported that her father, Robert W. Reeves of Polk County, arrived in Springfield to escort his daughter to safety in light of threats against her life. The two "declined to tell where they are going, saying that they do not want their whereabouts known because of the many threats that have been against the woman." The majority of the letters were anonymous and were "insulting and defamatory, and most of them declare vengeance upon her for Saturday's troubles." Edwards called one letter, postmarked St. Louis, "a highly indecent attack." While Edwards may have truly feared for her life, once she left Springfield she would be out of the grand jury's grasp, and thus would not have to testify.[10]

The work of the grand jury moved at a glacial pace due to the sheer number of witnesses that were called to testify before it. The jury was also stymied by changes in its composition as when the *Republican* reported, "A. A. Mehl, one of the grand jurors, upon application, was released from duty, and John B. Glass was summoned as a substitute."[11] There was no doubt, however, that the grand jury sought to redeem Springfield's reputation.

The first witness to appear before the special grand jury was Greene County sheriff Everett V. Horner. He, as well as other witnesses, testified to the lack of action on the part of the local law enforcement officials. Horner testified he "saw but one policeman during the entire evening."[12] Frank Jones, a Springfield police officer, testified, "He [Chief McNutt] gave me no orders to assist in quelling the mob. I know of no efforts being made by the Chief of Police to quell the mob."[13] Police officer Martin Keener stated of the mob, "I did nothing to stop them. [Officer] Henry Waddle and I walked around on Center Street till they got the negroes out. We walked the square while the first two were hung. Did not see the hanging. Did not want to see it."[14] When Officer Waddle testified, he admitted, "I did nothing to stop the mob, nor do I know of no one who did."[15] Springfield attorney T. J. Delaney, when brought before the jury, snorted, "I don't think the marshal or the police made the least attempt to do their duty in suppressing the mob. From my information I believed Coker and Duncan to be innocent."[16]

Delaney was not the only Springfield citizen who thought Coker and Duncan were innocent. James Johnson, who worked with both men at the Pickwick Livery and Transfer Company, did not think they were guilty. Johnson saw "Coker and Duncan at about 9:40 p.m. Coker went to 1003 Benton Avenue and Duncan went to the [livery] barn."

He asserted, "In my opinion they were innocent of the alleged assault." Johnson was joined by fellow Pickwick employee W. T. Morrow, who declared, "I am of the opinion that these boys were innocent of the alleged assault on the Edwards woman."[17] Another Pickwick employee, Frank Ferguson, advised the jury, "The Coker negro was as good a man as [you] would want to work with. I considered both are average good darkies. The night clerk phoned me that they left the barn at 10:00 p.m. My opinion is that they were not guilty."[18]

If many members of Springfield's white community voiced their belief that Duncan and Coker were innocent, there were others who expressed doubt about the character of Mina Edwards. Polk County resident M. T. Easley testified, "I have known her husband and her father for several years. I don't think her reputation is good."[19] H. T. Hull, a reporter for the *Leader*, interviewed Edwards after the alleged assault. He claimed, "She did not impress me as one who had been ravished so recently by two negroes."[20] Dr. W. L. Purselly and Springfield city physician J. S. Tillery both examined Mina Edwards the night she was reportedly assaulted. Both men testified there that while her face was a "puffed a little," there were no marks on her body, and that they "found no evidence at all of any assault or rape."[21]

As for the testimony of Mina Edwards, she was nowhere to be found. A subpoena was issued, but authorities could not find her in Springfield. The subpoena was then sent to Polk County where her family resided, but it was returned after Polk County authorities failed to locate her. Assistant Attorney General John Kennish was informed that upon her return to Bolivar, Mina Edwards reconciled with her husband, packed up their belongings, and "left for parts unknown."[22] The special grand jury proceeded without her testimony.

Witness after witness took the stand to divulge what they knew about the lynchings. As each individual recounted what they saw and heard on the night of the lynchings, two names continually kept coming up: Daniel D. "Doss" Galbraith and J. Hill Gooch. Galbraith, a blacksmith, testified before the special grand jury. He conceded that he was in the crowd, but that Duncan and Coker were already dead by the time he reached the square. Galbraith admitted, "[I] cut and got a piece of the rope that was used to hang Duncan. Also a piece of the pants that burned off his legs."[23] Hollet H. Snow, a retired law enforcement official, remembered seeing Galbraith at the square. When Snow asked Galbraith about the rope he had coiled on his arm, Galbraith reportedly laughed, "He [Galbraith] had the rope, but had run out of niggers and that they [the mob] were going after more niggers."[24]

Everett Harris, who attended school with Hill Gooch and had known him for twelve years, saw Gooch standing on Gottfried Tower's wooden bandstand as the mob prepared to lynch Will Allen. Harris adamantly declared, "[I] know his voice and I thought it sounded like his voice on the tower and my best judgment is that Gooch was on the tower when Allen was hung [sic]." Hill, he claimed, was "the man on the tower who made the speech and asked if [Allen] was guilty."[25]

Harris was not the only man brave enough to identify Gooch. Dick Anderson and Harry Williamson were also certain that Hill Gooch was the man responsible for Will Allen's death. Williamson also recounted how Gooch took a wooden board and "hammered on the privates of one of the negroes."[26] W. F. Noe, an acquaintance, recognized Gooch on the tower and recognized his voice when "someone said on the tower, 'My name is Hill Gooch and I want the public to know it.'"[27]

On May 24, the special grand jury issued a scathing report that dismissed the credibility of Mina Edwards based on the lack of physical evidence and because "she was at the time a married woman riding at night with an unmarried man in a dark, remote and unfrequented portion of town on a journey to no particular place so far as we can learn." The grand jury questioned Edwards's character, dismissing her as "a woman whose reputation for virtue and chastity is not good," with the result that it made "it at least doubtful whether her story is worthy of belief."[28]

As a result of Edwards's questionable character and the testimony of their coworkers at Pickwick Transfer and Livery Company, Fred Coker and Horace Duncan were declared innocent. But the man charged with keeping Coker and Duncan safe, Sheriff Everett Horner, was absolved of his failure to protect them from the mob. The jury found that Horner, a Republican, undertook every precaution possible to safeguard his prisoners. Politics may have been at play. Horner's colleague, Democrat and Springfield police chief John McNutt, was not so fortunate.[29]

McNutt and his men, with the exception of Officer William Bishop, were found negligent in their failure to stop the mob. The report commended, "Policeman William Bishop as the single exception among all the city officials as one whose conduct evinced a proper realization of his duties and responsibilities as a sworn officer of the law."[30]

The most important development that resulted from the special grand jury was the indictment of twenty-two individuals for their involvement in the destruction of county property and the lynching of Horace Duncan, Fred Coker, and Will Allen. The indictment of a white man, much less twenty-two white men, was extraordinary. Rarely were white men indicted, let alone prosecuted, for the murder of African Americans. It may have been that the local Republican Party and the political influence of Springfield's African American community led to the indictments. The names of those indicted were not published, however, which sparked public speculation on who might face criminal charges.[31] The same day, Dan Crane, who had been detained by officials for his involvement in the lynchings, was released after the court learned he was mistakenly arrested.[32]

Just as the special grand jury finished its investigation, the coroner's jury was called upon to begin its own investigation. On May 29, six weeks after the lynchings, the coroner's jury finally convened.[33] It would be weeks before the coroner's jury concluded that Horace Duncan, Fred Coker, and Will Allen came to their deaths "at the hands of a mob composed of persons to the Jury unknown."[34] In the meantime, on June 5, Doss Galbraith and J. Hill Gooch were arrested by Deputies John Mack, Lafayette Dyer, and Charles W. Carr after being charged with the murder of Horace Duncan in the first degree. Harry Hacker was arrested the next day for committing perjury when he appeared before the grand jury.[35] Hacker, it was alleged, lied when he stated that he did not see Hill Gooch on Gottfried Tower's bandstand, but had later made statements to the contrary.[36]

Daniel "Doss" Galbraith, a thirty-three-year-old blacksmith and married father of two young sons, was arrested just after six in the evening. He and his wife ran a boardinghouse located on South Campbell Street. Hill Gooch, who was twenty-three and unmarried, was apprehended at M. T. Mayfield's blacksmith shop where he worked. Both Gooch and Galbraith appeared surprised and shaken when they were arrested by officers, but went quietly. Judge A. W.

Lincoln set bail at $7,000 for Gooch and Galbraith. Both men posted bond after several citizens stepped forward to help.[37]

Among those who signed their names to Gooch's bond were his father, Thomas T. Gooch, a night watchman at the Eisenmayer Mill Company; uncle and former Springfield city councilman Jerome "Bone" Gooch; lumber dealer W. T. Bruer; and Hill Gooch's Democratic attorneys, Oscar T. Hamlin and M. C. Smith.[38] Galbraith was bonded out by farmer Thomas L. Adams; prominent banker George D. McDaniel; former Springfield chief of police and grocer Brice C. Howell; former Springfield city councilman and livery owner William Waugh; businessman William A. Sherrow; and bookkeeper J. H. Flora.[39] Hacker was bailed out by his father, J. R. Hacker; attorney Elmer Wadlow; Charles W. Starks; and real estate dealer Henry Trevathan.[40]

It appeared that the local Democratic establishment was determined to support Galbraith and Gooch. Many of the men who came to the aid of Galbraith, Gooch, and Hacker were present at the Greene County Democratic Convention that convened four days after the arrests. Attorneys A. Hunter Wear, Val Mason, and Oscar T. Hamlin, who along with fellow lawyer and Democrat Mitchell C. Smith, were Doss Galbraith's defense attorneys, attended. Three of the men who provided money for Harry Hacker's bond were present. Lawyer Elmer Wadlow served as a clerk, Charles W. Starks lost the contest for criminal court clerk, and Henry Trevathan failed to secure his party's nomination as county collector. Brice Howell, who helped bail Galbraith out, lost out on the Democratic nomination for Greene County sheriff.[41]

William Bishop, the only Springfield police officer who attempted to stop the mob and who had not been reappointed to the police force, was nominated for justice of the peace. The *Republican* cheekily remarked, "Bishop met with a better fate at the hands of the convention than he did at the hands of Mayor Blain when he asked for reappointment to the police force."[42]

Springfield's Democrats, however, were a fractious lot. The convention was deemed "not unlike a Kilkenny cat fight." A fistfight broke out on the convention floor over the nomination for probate judge. Owen "Oney" Calvey, one of the men originally arrested on a bench warrant for participating in the lynch mob, dove into the middle of the fray. He was prevented from throwing any punches when the

Springfield police burst in to stop the melee. Once everyone regained their composure, Springfield's Democrats dedicated considerable time to passing resolutions that condemned the grand jury's report regarding the recent lynch mob.[43]

One such resolution passed by what remained the party of white supremacy read in part, "The Democratic party declares for the enforcement of all the laws of our land without fear or favor," and demanded "speedy and full enforcement of the laws protecting the honor of the home and the purity of women." The resolution condemned Springfield's Republican politicians "who have for political advantage so pandered in recent years to the lawless negro element of the city" of whom a "large number [are responsible] for the late acts of lawlessness which have been so numerous in our community for years and culminating in the recent deplorable acts in the city." Despite endorsing William Jennings Bryan for president and Courtney W. Hamlin for U.S. senator, Springfield's Democrats remained silent on Missouri's Democratic governor, Joseph W. Folk. [44]

While the Democrats begrudged the Republicans for reportedly supporting lawless citizens, one Republican, Sheriff Everett Horner, was busy trying to process hundreds of subpoenas. Horner and his deputies attempted to deliver over five hundred subpoenas, the majority of which were reportedly the result of the lynching, but had difficulty in doing so. Deputies reported that individuals resorted to hiding under their beds, in cellars, and even in their outhouses to avoid being served. The *Republican* advised citizens, "there is no use in a witness trying to beat the process server unless he packs up and leaves the country."[45] Witnesses had reason to hide.

Missouri attorney general and future governor Herbert Hadley reportedly notified prosecuting attorney Roscoe Patterson that he would assist Patterson if circumstances permitted. If he could not help, Hadley would send assistant attorney John Kennish in his place.[46] Kennish, together with Greene County prosecuting attorney Patterson and assistant prosecuting attorney Alfred Page, would represent the state. Page, the son of a Confederate veteran who served under Nathan Bedford Forrest, was a staunch Republican. A graduate of Drury College, he was known for his "thorough preparation." Together, with Patterson and Kennish, the three men posed a formidable challenge in the courtroom.

Greene County prosecuting attorney Roscoe C. Patterson. *Courtesy of The State Historical Society of Missouri.*

But the attorney general and the Greene County prosecuting attorney were not the only ones making plans and outlining strategies.[47]

Doss Galbraith was represented by one of the craftiest, if not the most skilled and formidable, defense teams in the history of Greene County. Springfield native Valentine Nicholas Adolphus "Val" Mason, like many of his colleagues in Greene County, was an ambitious, self-made man. In 1893, while working as a baggage and express agent for the Frisco Railroad and serving as a justice of the peace, Mason read law, and was admitted to the bar. He carved out a reputation as a clever, witty opponent skilled at defense. After his death, one local columnist recalled, "The courtroom would always be crowded to hear him, because his mere appearance always promised fine entertainment."[48]

Mason was joined by Oscar T. Hamlin, a native of South Carolina, and the son of a Baptist preacher who moved his family to Missouri after the end of the Civil War. Hamlin studied at Southwest Baptist College in Bolivar before going to work as a clerk and commercial traveler. Life on the road must not have appealed to Hamlin as he began to read law under the careful eye of his brother, future U.S. congressman Courtney W. Hamlin, and was admitted to the bar. He, like the other men on the defense team, was a devoted Democrat.[49]

A. Hunter Wear, born and raised in neighboring Barry County, Missouri, served three terms as the Barry County prosecuting attorney before he moved to Springfield. In 1888, due to his allegiance to the Democratic Party, President Grover Cleveland appointed Wear to the United States Land Office in Springfield. He then served two terms as the Greene County prosecuting attorney before taking up private practice.[50]

Rounding out Galbraith's defense team was Mitchell C. "MC" Smith. Born in Mississippi, Smith grew up in eastern Kansas, the son of a Confederate veteran. He was admitted to the Kansas bar in 1882, but moved to Springfield in 1893.[51] Smith, although he never sought political office, served as the secretary of the Greene County Democratic Committee.[52] It was to these distinguished and experienced lawyers that Gooch and Galbraith left the formulation of their defense.

Rumors swirled around Springfield that Hill Gooch would enter an insanity plea. One of his lawyers, Oscar T. Hamlin, informed the *Republican* that the rumor was false. Val Mason boasted, "You might just add that we feel reasonably certain of an acquittal in these cases. We are ready to put up a hard fight, and feel that the state will have no easy job to convict our clients."[53]

Sheriff Horner, anticipating that crowds of spectators would descend upon the Greene County courthouse to watch the trial, began making preparations. Plans were made for extra guards and for permitting only the maximum number of occupants in the courtroom. Once a spectator left the courtroom, their seat would be given to the first person waiting in line.[54]

As the trial drew near, at least one of the accused men began to show signs of anxiety. The men who signed Harry Hacker's bond appeared before Sheriff Horner and notified him that "they would no longer be held responsible for his appearance before the criminal court." Hacker, much to the dismay of one of the men who signed his bond, had "not comported himself as a man should who is being watched as closely as are the three men who are indicted in connection with the mob. He has made almost no preparations for his defense that we can learn, and we do not want to get caught." Attorney Elmer Wadlow, one of the men who helped arrange for Hacker's bond, stated that he was not representing Hacker and had not seen him since he had helped bail Hacker out in June.[55]

The arrival of John Kennish, assistant attorney general, may have added to Hacker's anxiety. Kennish, a former Republican state senator, was born on the Isle of Man and raised in Holt County in northwest Missouri. After graduating from the University of Missouri in 1884, Kennish practiced law, and was elected prosecuting attorney of Holt County before he joined the attorney general's office.[56] Kennish reportedly was Attorney General Hadley's chief assistant, thus his presence signaled that both Hadley and Governor Joseph Folk considered the case a priority.[57]

As one attorney arrived to take up the case, another one said goodbye. From the outset, Governor Folk, a Democrat, and Attorney General Hadley, a Republican, insisted that a Democratic lawyer be present on the prosecutorial team to counter any claims of political shenanigans or partisanship. Folk, with the approval of Hadley, asked T. J. Delaney, a Democrat and one of Springfield's most prominent attorneys, to assist the prosecution.[58] But a few weeks before the trial of Doss Galbraith commenced, Delaney and prosecuting attorney Roscoe Patterson clashed over the trial of one of Delaney's clients, Bruce Campbell. As a result, Delaney withdrew from the prosecutorial team. While he would not comment on his departure, his son, J. B. Delaney, told a reporter, "his father had openly declared that he would have nothing to do with the prosecutions." Patterson, when asked, stated that he had not spoken to Delaney, but admitted, "I understand from other sources he is dissatisfied. He did not like some of the things in the Bruce Campbell case."[59] Patterson may have later regretted Delaney's departure.

Val Mason, attorney for Hill Gooch and Doss Galbraith, was anxious to locate Mina Edwards. Since reportedly leaving Polk County with her husband, Edwards's whereabouts was unknown. One rumor stated she was in Wyoming; another suggested she was in Colorado. Edwards's cousin reportedly told a Springfield police officer that Mina Edwards died in Colorado and was brought back to Missouri for burial, but her parents, the station agent, and the minister who allegedly gave the funeral sermon denied she had died. Her parents, however, insisted they did not know where she was.[60]

The legal process continued without the presence of Mina Edwards. During pretrial proceedings the court decided to try Doss Galbraith first when the requisite witnesses failed to appear when the case of Hill Gooch was called.[61] Val Mason, attorney for Galbraith, presented Judge Lincoln with an affidavit from his client that stated Galbraith believed Sheriff Horner and Coroner Matthews were "prejudiced against him." He asked that an elisor be appointed in their stead to select the jury. Judge Lincoln, the prosecution, and the defense agreed upon the appointment of former Greene County sheriff T. A. H. Grantham to serve as elisor.[62]

In the meantime, the trial of Harry Hacker, charged with perjury, would have to wait until Hill Gooch received his day in court. As the *Republican* observed, "for unless the jury returns a verdict of guilty against Gooch, it cannot be legally known that he [Gooch] was upon the platform. If he was not there, then Hacker cannot be tried for perjury."[63] Harry Hacker, after his bondsmen withdrew from his original bond, languished in jail until August 9, when his father J. R. Hacker, attorneys Val Mason and Oscar Hamlin, and Democratic politician Harry Durst signed a new one-thousand-dollar bond.[64]

As Grantham busied himself with securing a jury, prosecuting attorney Roscoe Patterson found himself facing more distractions. Charles Cannefax, a key witness and one of the first men arrested on a bench warrant after the lynchings, had left Springfield for the Indian Territory. When he would return was unknown. Cannefax was undoubtedly not the only witness who quietly left town to avoid testifying in court.[65]

Patterson was further distracted when he began receiving letters from across the country regarding the upcoming trial. One anonymous letter from St. Louis declared that, "the negro is a beast, and it is not a crime to hang a black man, anymore than to take the life of a beast." The letter writer allegedly professed to be "a strong believer in the Bible, and quotes from the Holy Writ to maintain his point."[66]

Rumors spread that threats were made against potential jurors, witnesses, and even Governor Folk. It was also believed that Springfield's business community had offered to pay for Galbraith's defense, but both stories were denied in the *Springfield Republican* by prosecuting attorney Patterson, Chief of Police Acy Loveless, Sheriff Horner, and J. H. Rathbone of the Springfield Commercial Club. Patterson asserted, "Rumors of threats are sometimes heard, but these threats come from irresponsible parties and disturb no one connected with the mob cases."[67]

While Patterson had to contend with distractions as he prepared for the case of a lifetime, elisor Grantham was faced with the difficulty of seating an impartial jury. With five hundred witnesses subpoenaed, constant local press coverage of the lynching and court proceedings, and the prevailing racial prejudice of the day working against Grantham, the former sheriff found he was faced with a formidable task. As Grantham told the *Springfield Republican,* "he worked harder than he ever did before in his life."[68]

This task was made no less easy as jurors disqualified themselves or were disqualified by others. Real estate dealer Simon B. Phifer, when examined, replied, "If my wife or daughter were raped by a negro, I should let the law take its course." Boos and hisses erupted from the spectators gathered in the courtroom. One of Galbraith's defense attorneys asked if Phifer believed in mob violence. He said that he did not. Then the attorney went one step further and asked what Phifer would do if the attorney's wife or daughter were raped. Phifer stood his ground and replied, "I would let the law take its course. I do not approve of mob violence." Phifer was disqualified after three men swore out affidavits claiming Phifer had told them he "wanted to get on the jury in order to find guilty and hang the indicted men."[69]

Others were more candid with the court. When farmer W. E. Hood was asked if he had discussed the case, he responded, "Well, as I was coming to town this morning to attend court, I passed Uncle Tommy Yeakley. He asked me where I was going. I told him I was a-coming up to Springfield to hang them there fellers that hung them there niggers."[70] Hood was disqualified. When questioned why he did not know about the case, S. L. Peck declared, "I am a farmer and can plow better than I can do anything else."[71]

When Assistant Attorney General North Todd Gentry, sent at the last minute to assist the prosecution, asked potential jurors if they were related to Doss Galbraith or the late Horace Duncan, "they did not appreciate the humor of the situation one little bit."[72] Despite difficulties, both the prosecution and the defense were able to agree on the men who would hold Galbraith's fate in their hands.

On August 20, the jury was secured. The twelve men who qualified were forty-eight-year-old farmer J. P. Sneed; fifty-one-year-old farmer George Smith; forty-seven-year-old farmer C. J. Diemer; fifty-six-year-old retired farmer M. P. Rogers; sixty-five year-old capitalist P. C. Freeman; fifty-six-year-old preacher W. M. Justice; forty-year-old carpenter P. C. Johnson; forty-five-year-old carpenter E. E. Hussey; seventy-one-year-old farmer George Van Zandt; twenty-five-year-old farmer, clerk, and musician Fred Peck; forty-year-old farmer George Flannery; and seventy-year-old farmer E. F. Wilson. Of the twelve jurors, eight were Republicans and four were Democrats. Three jurors were from Fair Grove in the far northeastern corner of Greene County; three others hailed from Springfield, Ash Grove, and Republic, respectively; and the rest came from either northern or western Greene County.[73]

Unlike the special grand jury, which counted businessmen, a retired judge, and a former sheriff among its members, the trial jury was overwhelmingly made up of rural farmers. Many of the jurors most likely had a rudimentary education and may not have had daily interaction with Greene County's overwhelmingly urban African American population, unlike the men who sat on the special grand jury. Because the men were selected to try Doss Galbraith for first-degree murder, it came as a surprise when the prosecution changed the original charge of murder in the first degree against Doss Galbraith to murder in the second degree without explanation.[74] It was not the only unexpected surprise that day in the courtroom.

As prosecuting attorney Roscoe Patterson prepared to give the opening speech, Attorney General Herbert Hadley walked into the courtroom and took a seat at the prosecution's table. Hadley had not informed Kennish or Patterson that he would be in attendance that morning. He quietly listened as Patterson declared the state would prove that Doss Galbraith was responsible for the death of Horace Duncan, and then proceeded to recount the events that led to the triple lynching on the square. Patterson claimed that Doss Galbraith helped break down the walls of the jail with a hammer from his blacksmith shop and then used the hammer to strike Fred Coker in the back of the head before he helped the mob lynch Coker and Horace Duncan.[75]

A reporter observed that there were "perhaps twenty or twenty five women in the courtroom." Onlookers included Doss Galbraith's wife, described as a "frail looking woman, dressed in black, whose face showed her anxiety for her husband's safety." Seated next to her were her two children, Virgil and Vollie Galbraith.[76] The Galbraith family listened as Val Mason, lead attorney for the defense, rose to speak.

Mason professed his belief in the innocence of his client and asserted the defense would show that Galbraith not only did not help lynch Duncan, but that Galbraith had tried to stop the mob as it stormed the jail. According to Mason, his client begged the mob, "For God's sake, men, get out of here. You cannot afford to destroy county property this way." He also alleged that a stranger had stolen Galbraith's hammer.[77]

Before he ended his opening statement, Mason thundered, "We will show that this woman was assaulted brutally and that the negroes were identified by her in such a way that you all can understand it." He was interrupted by Kennish's objections. Mason had hinted at the trial to come, one that would not try Doss Galbraith, but Horace Duncan and Fred Coker.[78]

As the trial resumed the next day, journalists noticed a new face in the courtroom. Mary Duncan, mother of Horace Duncan, was seated in the courtroom where the jury could see her. She was dressed in black and appeared "old and care worn" with a "sorrowful look."[79] Whenever her son's name was mentioned, she "shook her head violently."[80]

Attorney General Hadley once again sat passively behind the pros-ecution's table, offering advice from time to time to Patterson and Kennish. He listened as the defense called witness after witness, includ-ing Doss Galbraith's thirteen-year-old son Virgil, to testify that while they had seen Galbraith in the mob with a rope, he was not on the platform of Gottfried Tower when Coker and Duncan were lynched.[81] The trial proceeded smoothly, although there were a few moments when the atmosphere turned tense, such as when Patterson questioned defense witness and former police officer E. T. Wesley Trantham.

Patterson asked Trantham a series of questions regarding the mob and what actions, if any, he undertook to stop the lynchers. When asked if he had tried to "do anything at all to control the mob," Trantham testily replied he had not. Patterson then asked Trantham if he was standing in front of Peter's Saloon as the mob passed. Trantham, irritated, replied, "Yes, sir. I met you there." Patterson growled, "You met me there?" Trantham smirked, "Yes, sir. I met you there, you and Mr. Delaney and Mr. Page and Mr. Sager." Patterson, growing angry, asked, "Did you do anything that night at all to stop the mob?" Trantham coolly responded, "No, sir. You asked me why I did not do something and I asked you in return why you did not do something." Spectators in the courtroom laughed and applauded Trantham's response before being abruptly silenced by Judge Lincoln.[82]

The defense, sensing an opportunity to humiliate Patterson, took a swipe at the prosecutor as he questioned the next witness. W. P. Johnson, a watchman for the Springfield Traction Company, testified he, too, was at Peter's Saloon but did not see Galbraith. Defense attorney Val Mason leapt to his feet and yelled, "Did you see Mr. Patterson pass?" Patterson bristled and retorted, "What's the inference? You are trying to create a false impression." Mason, smiling, fired back, "I simply wanted to see if the witness was good at recognizing faces. You passed there." Patterson, his voice low, snarled, "You're trying to create a false impression," before Oscar Hamlin interrupted the exchange with a question.[83]

Another tense moment came when the defense began to question defense witness and Springfield police officer Henry Waddle about statements Mina Edwards had made regarding the alleged guilt of Fred Coker and Horace Duncan. The defense wanted to paint Coker and Duncan as rapists and attempted to do so at every opportunity. Patterson and Kennish immediately objected, but defense attorneys Hamlin and A. Hunter Wear quickly routed them by arguing that the state had introduced the issue in its opening statement.[84]

This prompted Attorney General Hadley to stand and address the court. The defense's argument, Hadley argued, was "absolutely inconsistent." The attorney general illustrated his point, "The defense they have made for the defendant is this: 'I did not take any part in the mob. I in no way helped it. I offered my distinguished services to the state for the total space of two hours. That service consisted of carrying a rope around and offering to hang a man.'" Hadley concluded, "They say, 'I did all I could to preserve the peace, and to prevent the mob in its work, but the mob was justified, because the negroes were guilty of assault.'" Hadley then returned to his seat.[85]

No cheers or applause followed his precise dissection of the defense. Instead, the courtroom remained uncomfortably silent until Judge Lincoln, swayed by Hadley's argument, ruled that the defense could not introduce testimony or allude to the assault on Mina Edwards. Thus, the defense was prevented, at least temporarily, from turning Galbriath's trial into an indictment of Coker and Duncan.

Assistant Attorney General North Todd Gentry, absent on the first day of the trial, arrived in Springfield on the second day. He was not alone. Gentry, upon the orders of Governor Folk, traveled to the Missouri State Penitentiary in Jefferson City to escort three state witnesses to Springfield. The men, all African Americans, had been in the Greene County jail the night of the lynchings. As the men entered the courtroom, a murmur of disapproval rippled through the crowd. Robert Culp testified he shared a cell with Fred Coker and saw Doss Galbraith pound on the cell with a sledgehammer. Culp, when questioned, admitted he had "been twice sentenced to the penitentiary, had been arrested so many times he could not remember, and had once been arrested and convicted of stealing a ten dollar guitar from Galbraith." Fellow prisoners Marshall Cox and Manuel Inyard offered similar testimony.[86]

After they finished testifying, the three prisoners were immediately returned to the Missouri State Penitentiary. State penitentiary captain Finley told a reporter from the *St. Louis Republic,* "I am not afraid of actual trouble, but the people are talking so much that I think it best to get out. It is probable that nothing would happen, but I will feel better with the men out of town."[87] Assistant attorney Gentry accompanied Captain Finley and the prisoners back to Jefferson City.

At the noon recess, Patterson told a *Springfield Leader* reporter, "We have proved a lot. We have made a strong case. We do not have to prove that Galbraith hanged Duncan or even touched him, or a rope or a hammer." Patterson paused, then continued, "If he was at the jail or in the square aiding, abetting, approving or encouraging the mob, he is guilty. The court will so instruct. We are satisfied."[88] Despite Patterson's optimism, the trial was far from over.

The high point of the trial came when Doss Galbraith took the stand in his own defense. As he nervously strode to the witness stand, the jury could see Galbraith was a powerfully built man dressed in "a black suit, with spotless white shirt and collar and white cravat. His coal black hair was brushed until it shone." He clutched a small fan in one of his hands to keep the oppressive August heat at bay.[89] Once he was sworn in, Galbraith testified his full name was Daniel D. "Doss" Galbraith; that he was married and the father of two young sons; and that he and his wife ran a rooming house on Campbell Street. Oscar Hamlin, one of his attorneys, carefully questioned Galbraith regarding his whereabouts the night of lynchings.[90]

According to Galbraith, he went downtown to purchase a mirror for a client, talked to friends, then returned home for supper. He then left to deliver the mirror and subsequently heard noise coming from the direction of the county jail on his way home. Galbraith claimed he went to the jail to see what was going on and found the mob inside trying to remove Fred Coker and Horace Duncan from their cells. He claimed that he tried to intervene and stop the mob, telling a group of men tearing up the sheriff's carpet, "You cannot find them under the carpet."[91]

When the mob seized Coker and Duncan, Galbraith testified he followed the crowd to the square, but left to check on his blacksmith shop before the first victim was lynched. Upon returning to the square, he had a heated exchange with Harry Williamson when Williamson said, "These negroes are as good as the men who hanged them." Galbraith, whose son Virgil was at his side, retorted, "If you say that again before my little boy, I'll bust you in the mouth." Galbraith admitted that at this time he had a rope coiled over his shoulder, but that he taken it as a souvenir. After Duncan was lynched, Galbraith stated, he returned home just after midnight and went to bed.[92]

When prosecutor Roscoe Patterson questioned Galbraith, the exchanges between the two men were often sharp. When Patterson asked Galbraith why he allegedly tried to escape the mob at one point, Galbraith grunted, "For the same reason that you did. I saw you going past toward the square." The courtroom was filled with laughter and applause from the spectators. Judge Lincoln banged his gavel and yelled, "You deputies scatter out through the audience and arrest everyone who makes a noise. If another outbreak occurs, the room will be cleared."[93]

If the prosecution could not establish that Doss Galbraith had actively participated in the lynching of Horace Duncan, it could prove that he engaged in ghoulish behavior not uncommon to lynchings. Jim Rhodes testified that the day after the lynching Galbraith showed him a piece of rope, a skull fragment, and a bit of pants leg he retrieved from the ashes that came from either Fred Coker or Horace Duncan.[94]

One final witness was called before the state rested its case. Sheriff Everett V. Horner took the stand. He testified that on the night of the lynching he saw Doss Galbraith standing in the dining room of the sheriff's residence. He also stated that he had appealed to Galbraith for assistance in stopping the mob to no avail. Horner's testimony contradicted Galbraith's account that he never entered the sheriff's residence. Clearly, someone was not telling the truth, but it was up to the jury to decide.[95]

As attorneys for both sides prepared to make their final arguments, the courtroom was packed with onlookers. Men and women sat elbow to elbow on benches, stood awkwardly in the aisles, and peered in through the doors to listen.[96] Deputies stood ready to intervene should anyone in the audience test the limits of Judge Lincoln's patience. The closing arguments in the Galbraith trial were not recorded for posterity by a court reporter. The *Springfield Leader* and the *Springfield Republican*, however, published accounts of the closing arguments made by both sides.

Assistant prosecuting attorney Alfred Page delivered the first closing argument. Speaking in a strong, clear voice he addressed the jury, "These men who were lynched had the misfortune to be born with black faces, but they were not to blame. The God Almighty painted them black and they could no more help having black skins than I can help having blue eyes."[97] Page paused, his voice rising, "But they were born under the starry banner of freedom." Horace Duncan and Fred Coker "were put in jail because they could not furnish a five hundred dollar bond for robbery. They had no arms and could not fight. They could not run because they were in a cage. They were defenseless."[98]

He turned, looked at the audience that crowded the courtroom, and then continued, "If this city is to be ruled by mobs, then Springfield,

Greene County, Missouri, will, in my opinion, be a very poor place in which to live." Page appealed to white masculinity, arguing, "This mob not only took the negroes, but attacked the sheriff's private home and family. The most sacred thing under heaven is a man's home and family."[99]

After Page concluded his closing argument, defense attorney Val Mason jumped to his feet and began to give what one reporter deemed "a vigorous and pyrotechnic speech." While Page relied upon rational thought and logic to sway the jury, Mason relied upon pure, unadulterated racism. Mason looked at the jury and rhetorically asked, "What have you got to prove that Galbraith is guilty?" He smiled. "The testimony of that big, black, fat, slick, buckle-headed nigger from the penitentiary, Bob Culp, and that other buckle-headed nigger, Marshall Cox." Mason again rhetorically asked the jury why Culp stated he saw Galbraith in jail before he answered his own question, "Because he [Culp] admits he was convicted for stealing a guitar from him."[100]

Mason had just begun to warm up. Glancing at the packed courtroom, then back at the jury, he thundered, "We would be ashamed to put on nigger convicts in this case and you would be insulted if we did." He shook his head. "Our prosecuting attorneys are not to blame. We have all the respect for Mr. Patterson. We believe him honest. Had he been left alone, he would never have brought these niggers here." Mason shook his head again and gestured at the prosecution table where Assistant Attorney General Kennish sat. "But he did not. It was those attorneys from Cole County who brought those big, black, slick, buckle-headed niggers here to testify." Cheers and wild applause burst forth in the courtroom.[101]

Mason, knowing he had the courtroom under his spell, continued. He blamed the State of Missouri and Assistant Attorney General North Todd Gentry for bringing the three prisoners to testify. He snorted, "It was our friend Gentry who brought those infernal black scoundrels here to testify and the night they returned, that gentleman lost his sight. He stuck his head under his wing like a turkey gobbler, folded his tent, and sneaked back his buckle-headed skunks to his skunk farm up there on the Missouri River." Mason ended his closing argument in a more rational, rather than emotional, manner by reviewing the testimony of witnesses and reiterating Galbraith's alibi.[102] As Mason returned to his seat, jurors E. F. Wilson and George Van Zandt openly wept.[103]

He was followed by fellow defense attorney Mitchell C. Smith. He, too, reviewed the evidence against his client for the jury. Like Mason, Smith pointed out that the prosecution failed to produce eyewitness testimony to support the state's argument that Doss Galbraith struck Horace Duncan in the back of the head with one of his blacksmith's hammers.

He then unleashed a virulent racist diatribe, "Mr. Page must have had a nightmare last night," Smith scoffed, "thinking about his speech and some evil spirit brought him a vision of Doss Galbraith running like the devil with a hammer in his hand." Smith rolled his eyes and snorted, "I do not blame the prosecution, I would have nightmares every night and my shoes would be filled with snakes and niggers, if I were trying as hard to bolster up a case as is the prosecution." The *Leader,* Springfield's Democratic newspaper, cackled, "Smith devoted a great deal of time to 'roasting' the negro convicts."[104] After Smith finished, the court took a recess for an hour.

Despite the passionate and emotional appeals that the defense had made thus far, the prosecution doggedly stuck to logical, legal arguments. When the court resumed after one o'clock, Assistant Attorney General John Kennish took center stage. He explained to the jury that if Doss Galbraith, "whether he was present or not, if he was a party to it, he is equally as guilty as if he had hanged Horace Duncan with his own hands. It was not necessary for him to touch the rope to adjust the noose."[105]

Kennish then drew attention to the men who had lost their lives at the hands of the lynch mob. He acknowledged Galbraith's right to testify on his own behalf, but somberly noted, "the poor negro whose fragments he [Galbraith] had was denied every one of these rights." He continued, "We have one law for the right and poor alike. We have one law for the white and black alike. I am not defending the negroes as a race. I am not eulogizing them, nor am I calling them black, slick, and buckle-headed," Kennish urged the jury, "You are to treat them as citizens who have rights."[106]

Galbraith, Kennish claimed, was not telling the truth. His testimony was unclear and contradictory. Despite the defendant's claims he was acting as a "special officer" on behalf of the sheriff, Kennish asserted, "Doss Galbraith was none other than the 'master of ceremonies that night.'" The young lawyer was not finished. He reiterated the testimony of witnesses, including that of Galbraith himself, who claimed he had threatened to punch Harry Williamson after Williamson spoke ill of the mob. "They [the mob] wanted to shoot. Galbraith said, 'Do not shoot.' Why? Galbraith was the leader of that mob. His orders were respected."[107]

Kennish was followed by defense attorneys A. Hunter Wear and Oscar T. Hamlin. Hamlin, although prohibited from mentioning the alleged assault upon Mina Edwards, slyly asked the jury, "What brought this about? I'll tell you what brought it about. When those men went into that jail, they asked for 'those niggers, the rapists.'" Hamlin declared, "There's the keynote of the whole affair. I want my argument and my prayers to go up for the ten thousand virtuous women in Greene County."[108] A man stood up in the audience and yelled, "Give it to 'em, Oscar!" before deputies arrested him.[109] Tears once again streamed down the faces of jurors E. F. Wilson and George Van Zandt.[110]

According to a reporter from the *St. Louis Republic,* whenever the defense "scored a point or referred to the action of the mob as being in defense of a woman's honor, it seemed no power could stay the tumult." The reporter observed, "Arrests by deputies seemed only to aggravate the crowd, which frequently broke through the ropes to congratulate the attorneys for the defense or to shake hands with the defendant himself."[111]

Prosecuting attorney Roscoe Patterson was the last to speak. As he began to speak, Patterson admitted he had not prepared written remarks, but the *Leader* remarked it was a "most telling and effective speech." He rebutted Val Mason's claims that the State of Missouri, notably Governor Folk and Attorney General Hadley, had sent the three African American prisoners to testify without Patterson's approval. Patterson wryly remarked, "It seems to me that the counsel for the defendant are very easily displeased because I have had associate counsel here to assist me with the number of cases that have been before the court at this term," Patterson glanced at Galbraith, "especially when innocence is represented by four such able attorneys."[112]

Patterson then vividly recounted the mob's actions for the jury and scolded the defense, "They have attempted to go into the question of the guilt or innocence of these negroes. How revolting, how monstrous it is to hang a man and then try him! Try him three months after his death!"[113]

Patterson looked briefly at the floor, then back at the jury. "I have been seeking something with which to compare a mob," he said. "Science teaches us that certain sea dragons and monsters live at the bottom of the sea. They never show themselves above the surface except when a storm is raging, or a ship is wrecked, or a body tossed overboard." Patterson's face grew stern. "So with the mob. It starts secretly, with only a few men. Then they join it from the saloons, they join it from the gambling dens, they join it from the disreputable houses. They join it from every class of criminal."[114]

He narrowed his eyes as he looked intently at the jury. "Tell me that these men cared anything for property, law, the purity of woman, or the sanctity of the home. They wantonly fired into a street car and showered it with rocks." Patterson thundered, "They demolished the sheriff's home and dragged his wife and children from bed. Does that look like they cared for the purity of woman and the sanctity of the home? Your wife might have been on that car. Murder was in the air."[115] Patterson shook his head. "These same men turned loose fourteen felons and told them to go. They set them free to prey upon this community. Does that look like they cared for law and order?"[116]

Patterson castigated the police force for not intervening to stop the mob. He stomped one of his feet and contemptuously declared, "I say it will be an everlasting shame on the police power that this thing happened. It was the duty of the police officers to organize and save the day if possible. But they did nothing." Patterson praised Officer William Bishop, "He was the only man who had sense of duty and bravery enough to go to the jail or near it, and he tried to dissuade the mob. He is entitled to the everlasting praise of the people of Springfield."[117]

Prosecuting attorney Patterson concluded his closing argument by observing there were two classes of people at the jail on the night of April 14, 1906, "the one in jail and the other class that ought to have been in the jail." He looked solemnly at the jury and made one last appeal to reason, "This contest is not between a white man and a negro," he said, "but between the state of Missouri on the one hand and the mob rule and lawlessness of the other." At 5:45 P.M., Patterson finished one of the toughest legal battles of his career.[118]

The jury deliberated on the third floor of the Greene County courthouse. Throughout the day, "heated discussions among the members of the jury" could be heard in the room below. As the jury argued, Doss

Galbraith and his family stood outside the courthouse on the square. Despite periodic rain showers, Galbraith, his wife, and two sons waited, "hoping to gain some intimation of what was going on behind those doors." After twenty-four hours, foreman P. C. Freeman emerged to announce that the jury could not agree upon a verdict. When Judge Lincoln asked Freeman if he was certain, Freeman replied, "It would be impossible to arrive at a verdict." With a bang of his gavel, Judge Lincoln dismissed the jury with the thanks of the court. As the jurors filed out of the courtroom, ten of them went "by the defendant's table to shake hands with Galbraith and his attorneys."[119]

As he left, P. C. Freeman wasted no time in telling a reporter from the *Springfield Republican* that fellow jurors J. P. Sneed and E. E. Hussey, both Republicans, were the two men who argued for Galbraith's conviction. Both men, according to Freeman, "contended that while the state had not proved that the defendant was a leader, it had shown that he aided and abetted by his presence and his actions." When asked what he thought about the jury's decision, Doss Galbraith replied, "The ten men did what they could for me, but I don't think the other two did."[120]

Val Mason, ready to engage in legal combat once more, boldly declared he was ready for a new trial. The cocky attorney crowed, "I am ready for a second trial. Our evidence is ready, I tell you, truth will prevail, and our story is true." Galbraith, when asked what he thought about a second trial, declared to a reporter, "Yes, my lawyers announced that they were ready for a new trial, and I am not afraid of the result." Prosecuting Attorney Roscoe Patterson refused to discuss the case.[121]

Perhaps Patterson suspected, as the *St. Louis Post-Dispatch* asserted, "No one believes that Galbraith will ever be brought to trial again, and no one believes either that the Gooch case, which was set for September 3rd, will ever be tried." The newspaper continued, "It is taken for granted that the State, after the experience of its attorneys in this case, realizes the improbability of getting witnesses who will make a case against any of the men under indictment," and, the *Post-Dispatch* concluded, "most of the people who have followed the trial go further and declare that they do not believe it would be possible to obtain a qualified jury." A Springfield businessman told the *Post-Dispatch* reporter covering the trial, "This case was tried by a jury of public opinion a long time ago before it ever got into a courtroom."[122]

Although the local newspapers did not interview members of Springfield's black community, the *Post-Dispatch* correspondent did. According to the reporter, "The negroes are avowedly thankful that it was not an acquittal. They say that if it had been, it would have created a panic among their race. It was in anticipation of such a possibility that the negroes have been arming themselves. They insist that they never have had any intention of starting any trouble but that they really believed they would have been in danger if Doss Galbraith had been cleared and his friends had started the demonstration they had planned."[123]

When the *Post-Dispatch* correspondent spoke to African Americans in Springfield, they refused to speak publicly out of fear they would be "putting a rope around their necks." In private conversation, blacks told him, "they see nothing but trouble for them ahead in Springfield." Other "more educated" African Americans expressed their contempt for the lynchings, but "realize that a certain lawless element among their people has had a bad influence on the politics of the city, and that general conditions before the killing" had "made the white population very angry." Because of the lynchings, one black confided to the reporter, Springfield's black community was making an effort to "get the negro vote out for local option and a dry town." This, it was hoped, would prove to Springfield's white community that "the negro population of Springfield as a whole is opposed to lawlessness."[124]

African Americans, however, may have had another motive for voting local option in the hopes Springfield would become a dry town. The *St. Louis Globe-Democrat* reported, "A poll of the electors of the city indicates that the negro voters will ally themselves with the temperance element here in a spirit of revenge than to secure the adoption of local option." Whites, though, were quick to enact their own unofficial local option against blacks, "Soon after the triple lynching last April, many of the saloonkeepers refused to sell drinks over the bar to negroes for fear if the black man's temper should become ruffled a race riot might result."[125]

As dusk settled over Springfield, a large crowd gathered outside the Missouri Rooming House, the boardinghouse that Doss Galbraith and his wife owned, to celebrate the mistrial. It was hard not to notice a large sign with the state seal of Missouri and emblazoned with the state motto, "Let the Welfare of the People be the Supreme Law" hanging over the front door. Galbraith shook hands with the men, women, and children who came to wish him well.[126]

He also received hundreds of letters, some of which congratulated him, while others castigated him. One letter reportedly declared, "If the court was correct, every man on the square was equally guilty and the State would have to build a new penitentiary to hold the crowd." Another letter urged, "Stay with them, old boy. We are the people and must be respected. They had to prosecute somebody and they picked you as a sacrifice. There was not enough evidence to convict you of a disturbance of the peace. You have been made a 'fall guy,' a scapegoat, by the State."[127]

The lynching in Springfield, unlike those that preceded it in neighboring towns, contained elements of a classic southern lynching. Faced with the allegation that a young white woman had been assaulted by two African American men, white men rushed to assert their superiority and impose extralegal justice to preserve social and racial order. Ineffective local law enforcement failed to protect the prisoners in its custody. Once Horace Duncan, Fred Coker, and Will Allen were dragged from the jail, they were as good as dead. After they were given a mock trial, their bodies were mutilated and burned in an orgy of violence. Spectators came to ghoulishly view the men's remains and picked through the ashes for a souvenir. Commemorative metal discs were forged to celebrate Springfield's "Easter Offering."[128]

Springfield, however, differed from the typical southern lynching because the white community indicted several white men and prosecuted one of them. The power of the local Republican Party and the political influence of Springfield's African American community may have led to the indictments and prosecution. It is notable that the Democratic governor of Missouri, Joseph W. Folk, reacted swiftly in response to the lynchings and went so far as to denounce the actions of the Springfield mob unlike his predecessor, Governor Alexander M. Dockery, who turned a blind eye to the mob violence at Pierce City and Joplin. At this time in history, the Democratic Party was the self-proclaimed party of white supremacy, so Folk may not have been spurred to act by moral indignation, but rather by a desire to limit damage to the state's national reputation. The partisan struggle

Daniel D. "Doss" Galbraith. *Courtesy of The State Historical Society of Missouri.*

between Republicans like prosecuting attorney Roscoe C. Patterson and Democratic attorneys Oscar Hamlin and A. Hunter Wear illustrate that local Democrats were determined to uphold the banner of white supremacy at the expense of the lives of three African Americans.

Mary Newland Clary, in her analysis of the Springfield mob, argues that Doss Galbraith served as a "whipping boy" because "his boasting and his connections with the Democratic newspaper, the police and other Democratic officials had made him a natural target for the Republican dominated courthouse."[129] Clary's assertion is valid. The charges against Dan Crane, one of the first young men to be arrested, were quickly dismissed without explanation, other than a mistake had been made. Crane, unlike blacksmith Galbraith, was from a prominent and well-connected Springfield family.

From the beginning, prosecuting attorney Roscoe C. Patterson must have suspected that it was improbable Doss Galbraith would be found guilty, especially with a jury made up of middle-aged farmers. All ages, political and social classes, and genders were represented in the lynch mob the night Will Allen, Horace Duncan, and Fred Coker were murdered. Republicans, Democrats, mechanics, businessmen, women, and railroad workers all joined in the fray. Together they imposed their own concept of justice upon three hapless victims.[130]

The prosecution was hindered by a lack of witnesses who conveniently left town the moment it became apparent they would have to testify in court. Patterson's hope that the testimony of three African American prisoners would sway the jury backfired as the defense cleverly used their appearance to vilify the state and the attorney general's office in one fell swoop, despite Patterson's protestations that the prisoners testified at his request. The people of Greene County, the defense implied, knew how to handle African American criminals and did not appreciate the assistant attorney generals who had brought black convicts to testify against a local white man.

In the end, if the jurors had not already made up their minds the first day of the trial, then they were most likely swayed by the passionate and emotional arguments made by the defense. Patterson and the rest of the prosecution's team delivered logical, rational, and well-reasoned arguments to the jury as to why Galbraith should be convicted. But Val Mason, Oscar Hamlin, and Mitchell Smith relied upon racially charged arguments that hinted that Horace Duncan, along with Fred Coker, were guilty. Using arguments that any proponent of racism would have recognized, the defense referred to the three black witnesses in racially inflammatory terms. They appealed to the jury as defenders of hearth and home and the guardians of the virtuous and chaste women of Greene County. The defense almost swayed the jury, but not quite. Two of the twelve jurors, both Republicans, sided with the prosecution's assertion that Galbraith aided and abetted the mob, and therefore should be held accountable.

The other ten jurors, however, disagreed. They must have believed that the life of one white man was worth more than the lives of three

African American men. But it was not only the life of Doss Galbraith that hung in the balance. If the jury were to convict Galbraith, they would implicate Springfield as a whole. Galbraith's conviction would open the floodgates for additional trials that could drag on for years and implicate dozens of individuals. It is not remarkable that Galbraith escaped a prison sentence. What is notable, however, is that the case ended in a mistrial. It is probable that Springfield could have erupted in violence if a conviction was obtained. Conversely, an acquittal of Galbraith might have resulted in an excessive celebration that easily could have spun out of control with negative consequences. After Galbraith's acquittal, Springfield moved on.

At the same time, opportunists such as E. D. Sherrick, a representative of the Kansas Portland Cement Company, took advantage of black flight. Sherrick acted out of economic opportunism when he arrived in Springfield to recruit fifty African American families. Sherrick told a reporter he was "after a bunch of married coons to go to LeHunte, Kansas" to work for the company. New employees were told they would live in new houses with gas heat and running water.[131]

After one day Sherrick had signed up half a dozen families and anticipated that he would get more recruits as "the negroes seem to like the prospect immensely." He boasted, "Many of them are now dissatisfied here, and several hundreds have sought new homes since April. Now they have an opportunity to leave free of charge with good wages and comfortable homes are guaranteed in Kansas where they [are] accorded more recognition and privileges than in Missouri."[132] The majority of Springfield's African Americans, however, remained.

In the aftermath of the Doss Galbraith trial, the Democratic *Springfield Leader* waged political war against the African Americans who remained behind in Springfield. Likely angered by Republican prosecuting attorney Roscoe Patterson's failed attempt to prosecute Galbraith as well as his decision to pursue charges against local Democrats suspected of participating in the lynchings, the *Leader* launched a vicious campaign against both Republicans and their African American political allies. Beginning in September, the *Leader* ran editorials denouncing politically active African Americans and the Republican Party. One editorial penned by Val Mason, one of Doss Galbraith's defense attorneys, warned that if former Republican mayor and state senate candidate Josiah E. Mellette, who appointed African American

Jim Burns as a special police officer after the city council failed to approve his nomination to the police force in 1902, had not "lost his love for the colored politician, and that after the election he will wield his influence for offices for his friends."

Mason mused, "It was thought that the hanging of three negro wretches by the mob in April last would put an end to this miserable practice of white men who set themselves up as leaders in their party, hobnobbing, co-horting, and pandering to the criminal class of negroes for political purposes." Instead, the local Republicans "packed their convention with negro delegates, among whom were the worst and most dangerous characters in the community." As a result, "the criminal negro element" controlled both Springfield and Greene County.

He then declared, "Every white man knows that the negro is not his equal. The negro is not made to hold office." To give an African American political power, Mason asserted, "is the same as endangering the safety of our women, our homes, and our children." Mason closed by asking his audience, "Is it not time to administer such a rebuke to the negro-lover as will forever silence him so far as Greene County is concerned?"[133]

In a later editorial the *Leader* proclaimed, "The Republican party, which two years ago polled a majority of two thousand in the county, today stands on the brink of utter defeat for their county ticket." The question to be decided at the polls, according to the editorial staff of the *Leader,* was "Shall the criminal negro run the politics of Greene County?" Democrats, it declared, were "for the elimination of the negro from politics, and against the corruption of the ballot by buying the negro vote." Republicans, however, "stand for the negro in politics and as a corrupting influence in conventions at elections."[134]

As the election drew closer, the *Leader* published a list of the twenty-two African American delegates who attended the Greene County Republican County Convention. Among those listed were George Allen, the brother of Will Allen, and Robert "Bob" Cain, the brother of Bus Cain. The *Leader* made sure to remind readers that Will Allen was "the murderer who was hung on the public square in April" and that Bob Cain was a "runner for a gambling joint." Should the Republicans win the election, the *Leader* warned, "the criminal negro is in politics in this city and county to stay."

But if Democrats were elected, "the gang who packed the Republican convention with negroes is down and out and hereafter criminal negroes will not be sent as delegates to city and county conventions." The *Leader* pointed to the local Republican Party's refusal to sign an agreement local Democrats created and endorsed pledging not to buy black votes on election day as proof that "the Republican ticket is dominated by the corrupt negro vote."[135]

Despite its boast that Republicans were finished in Greene County, the *Leader* and its Democratic candidates may have realized that the election was far from won. As the election drew nearer, the Greene County Democratic Committee began to sound desperate. In a message published in the *Springfield Leader,* the committee appealed to Republicans to vote Democratic in an effort to rid both the Republican Party and Greene County of "the offensive domination and pernicious activity of lawless negroes in the political affairs of our county." The unsatisfactory conditions in Springfield were the result of "short-sighted, self-seeking Republican politicians who have controlled and used the negro vote to advance their own personal interests without regard to the welfare of the county or your party."[136]

On November 5, the *Leader* ran two cartoons on the front page entitled "Negro Domination in Republican Politics." One cartoon showed an African American man dressed in a top-hat and tuxedo driving a buggy pulled by an exhausted elephant. The second featured a similarly dressed African American man smoking a cigar and holding a riding quirt in his hand looming over a tiny elephant labeled "G.O.P." at his feet. Next to the cartoons an article entitled "Buying the Negro Vote" detailed alleged efforts on the part of white Republicans to buy black votes prior to the election. Among those active, the *Leader* noted, were Bob and Will Cain, the brothers of escaped prisoner Bus Cain.

The *Springfield Republican* remained silent on the issue of race in spite of the *Leader*'s attempts to sling mud at any Republican that moved. Its silence may have helped its candidates as Republicans swept the election and, according to the *Republican,* made significant gains.[137] According to the *Republican,* the increase in Republican votes was the result of the "clean, honest, upright ticket" as well as the dirty campaign waged by Democrats. "Abuse, vituperation, invective, billingsgate, and the indiscriminate slinging of mud might have won at one time in the

"The Negro Domination in Republican Politics" political cartoon from the *Springfield Leader*. In the wake of the lynchings, the *Springfield Leader* waged a brutal political campaign against Republicans and their African American allies, but Democrats failed to win at the ballot box. *Courtesy of The State Historical Society of Missouri.*

history of the county," the *Republican* observed, "but that time is past and gone, never to return." Instead, "people are demanding something better," and "to yell 'negro domination' in double-headed editorials and picture in two-column cartoons—that is not any more the way to win elections." The *Republican* concluded, "The Democrats may thank themselves and their organ for the stunning defeat."[138] Further disappointment followed for local Democrats when prosecuting attorney Patterson chose not to prosecute two African Americans who were charged with the murder of a white man.

The case of Willard Caldwell, one of the two young black men charged with the murder of tailor T. M. Kinney, went to trial. According to the *Republican,* the evidence against Caldwell and his alleged accomplice was entirely circumstantial. Prosecuting attorney Patterson dropped the charges against Caldwell the day after Galbraith's trial ended in a mistrial. Caldwell, however, did not live long. In 1912, after he assumed an "alleged threatening attitude" toward coworker Charles Reynolds at the Swift Packing Company, Reynolds struck Caldwell in the head with a hatchet. Caldwell died the next day from massive head injuries. His alleged accomplice, Elmer Hancock, died from pneumonia in 1923.[139] Caldwell's case was not the only one to end quietly.

One year later, on August 25, 1907, it was announced that Greene County's new prosecuting attorney, William R. Self, dismissed the charges against Doss Galbraith and Hill Gooch. Self cited his inability to "obtain material evidence" as the reason behind his decision. The Republican prosecuting attorney also dropped the perjury charges against Harry Hacker due to a lack of evidence and the absence of key witnesses. Self explained he thought it was "a useless expense for the state to go into the trials again."[140]

On December 24, 1909, in the courtroom of Judge Alfred Page, prosecuting attorney J. C. West dismissed the charges against the sixteen men indicted by the special grand jury three years earlier. Like his predecessor, West believed "it would be impossible to convict the men as charged." Judge Page, who helped prosecute Doss Galbraith, dismissed the cases. The *Springfield Republican* somberly declared, "all legal history of the celebrated lynching here is now closed, and all that remains of the lynching now is what is in the memory of the people who witnessed the execution of the negroes and read the accounts published in the newspapers."[141]

As the most dramatic episode in Springfield's history came to a close, so too did the lives of many of the men who were involved. In 1914, at the age of forty-one, Doss Galbraith died of cirrhosis of the liver. Mary Newland Clary, while researching the lynchings, interviewed Grace Stroud Ince about growing up in the same area of Webster County, Missouri, as Galbraith. Ince recalled that she "repeatedly heard the tale of 'Old Man' Galbraith who had died begging that the 'niggers' be kept away from him."[142] Perhaps the ghosts of Horace Duncan, Will Allen, and Fred Coker stayed with Galbraith until his last breath.

J. Hill Gooch, however, lived to be an old man, as did Harry Hacker. Gooch remained in Springfield, but Hacker lived out the rest of his days in St. Louis as an ironworker.[143] Charles Cannefax, one of the first men arrested but later released, also moved to St. Louis where he worked as a car salesman.[144] Jesse R. Brake, the former Springfield police officer who tried to lynch John McCracken and reportedly aided in the lynching of Horace Duncan, Fred Coker, and Will Allen, died in 1935. He left only one survivor, his second wife, Ida Brake, to mourn his passing.[145]

Other alleged lynch mob participants met grisly ends. Oat Hall, one of the sixteen men indicted by the special grand jury, was killed on the streets of Springfield. Hall, well known for his tendency to fight at the drop of a hat, was knifed to death by Walter Hodge in self-defense.[146] Intoxicated after a night of drinking, Owen "Oney" Calvey was struck and killed while stumbling along the railroad tracks through Springfield.[147]

Sheriff Everett V. Horner was not selected by the Greene County Republican committee for reelection. He founded the E. V. Horner Realty and Insurance Company and had a successful career before he died in 1918.[148] Policeman Henry Waddle continued to work in law enforcement; prior to his death in 1933, he was working the desk at Springfield police headquarters for his son, Chief of Police Ed Waddle.[149] Waddle's colleague, William Bishop, worked in the Detective Bureau as late as 1932.[150] Bishop was the only police officer who reportedly tried to stop the mob.

According to one apocryphal account, a mob participant named Geisler, who had screamed "Hang 'em! Hang 'em! Hang 'em!" underwent a religious transformation after hearing a Pentecostal street preacher in Joplin proclaim, "Everybody that gave their consent for the killing of these Negroes was a murderer and has committed murder. Geisler, overcome with guilt, questioned his role in the lynchings. He joined a Pentecostal church, got baptized, and "never ceased talking in tongues."[151]

Assistant prosecuting attorney Alfred Page went on to become a judge and assistant U.S. attorney general. At his funeral it was said, "The world needs many things today. It needs wisdom and food and shelter and clothing and work and play—but perhaps most of all, it needs kindness and good will, such qualities as were displayed in Mr. Page's life."[152] One of his legal adversaries, Mitchell C. Smith, died quietly after a long career.[153] Just four years after the trial, Smith's colleague A. Hunter Wear unexpectedly died after a sudden illness.[154] When Oscar T. Hamlin, another member of the defense team, passed away, both former prosecuting attorney Roscoe C. Patterson and Alfred Page served as pallbearers.[155]

Lead defense attorney Val Mason went on to found a law office with Alfred Page. When he died in 1941, the *Leader-Press* recalled Mason was "a picturesque figure in the Springfield bar, striking in appearance, with snow-white hair, extremely witty, and famous for his repartee both in and out of court." Both Alfred Page and Roscoe Patterson served as pallbearers at his funeral. Although Mason was renowned in Greene County, his success was eclipsed by that of his courtroom foe, Roscoe Patterson.[156]

After serving as Greene County prosecuting attorney from 1903 to 1907, Patterson returned to private practice. In 1920, he successfully ran for the United States House of Representatives and served one term. Patterson attracted enough attention as a congressman that President Calvin Coolidge appointed him U.S. attorney for the Western District of Missouri. The Springfield native remained politically ambitious and returned to Washington, D.C., in 1928 as a U.S. senator. In 1934, Patterson lost his Senate seat to Harry S. Truman. After his defeat, Patterson returned to the practice of law before his death in 1954.[157]

Missouri attorney general Herbert S. Hadley went on to become Missouri's thirty-second governor. Ironically, while serving as governor, Hadley oversaw the conclusion of one of Springfield's more infamous scandals. Anna Brake, the wife of former police officer Jesse Brake and the woman who accused Jack McCracken of assaulting her in 1904, lobbied Governor Hadley to pardon McCracken. Her efforts did not go unnoticed. In early July 1908, the front page of the *Springfield Leader* announced, "White Woman Assaulted By Negro Wants Him Pardoned." The article reported that Mrs. Brake perjured herself on the witness stand because "she feared for her life if she told the truth." She now asked "for her sake and 'the little one' a pardon be secured for the negro." McCracken, she said, "has been a good friend."[158]

Anna Brake's letters to Jack McCracken while he was in prison have survived over time, contained in McCracken's commutation file at the Missouri State Archives. His replies to her, however, have not. But what remains reveals a complicated portrait of tangled relationships. Despite apparently being threatened by Jesse Brake if she refused to testify against McCracken, Anna Brake continued to live with Brake, along with her two young children, one of whom was the child of Anna and Jesse; the other, Clarence, the mulatto son of Anna and Jack McCracken.

In her rambling, often illiterate letters to McCracken, Anna called him "pet" and often referred to herself as McCracken's wife. She repeatedly asked McCracken for money and often inquired if he would take care of her children. In one letter, dated April 1908, Anna wrote, "say Pet would you be willing to take care of me and my two little ones if the Governor will turn you loose and you could take care of little Clarence I could take care of the other little one." Later on in the same letter Anna told McCracken of her desire to leave her husband, but "Brake says I shant have a penny and he is going to take the children from me he shant have neither of the little ones I may leave little Clarence with him until I can get me a place." For some unknown reason, Anna repeatedly told McCracken that she was going to take her child by Brake with her when she left Springfield and that she would leave Clarence behind, hoping that McCracken's mother would look after him.

Life with Brake, according to Anna's letters, was unpleasant. "I am not a worrying over my old man as I fairly Hate the ground he walks on it is my too little babes that I am aggrieving over I don't want him to have them and I could not make aliven for them if I am turned out penniless. If I did not have my little ones I could make a living for myself but I hope I may raise them." Apparently McCracken asked Anna to send him photographs of her and Clarence, but she replied, "say Kid I can't have them pictures taken because I haven't the money." At some point, however, Anna sent McCracken a photograph, but it was of her and her child by Jesse Brake, not of their son, Clarence.

If Jesse Brake mistreated Anna, he was kind to the children. In one of her letters to McCracken, Anna noted that Brake "goes with the children to the branch to catch crawdads." In her next letter, she announced her intent to leave Brake, but she was distraught at leaving Clarence behind "to think I have got to leave him for someone to mistreat. The little darling, of course, Brake will be good to him but when he is working the woman that keeps house for him may mistreat him, poor little dear." She continued "to think I have to leave poor little Clarence it just seems as though [I] cant stand it, of course Brake is awful good to him if he wasn't I wouldn't go at all. My old man bought Clarence a toy pistol and 5 cents of caps, he was so pleased." Jesse Brake, however, reportedly wanted McCracken to take care of Clarence as Anna reported that "B said he wanted you to help support little Clarence and I told him to turn you loose and then you would, but couldn't do anything in that place." McCracken did not have to wait long.

Anna Brake's letters professing McCracken's innocence were not in vain. Judge James T. Neville, the trial judge, and Roscoe C. Patterson, the prosecuting attorney, wrote to Governor Herbert S. Hadley and asked that McCracken be pardoned. Patterson, in his letter to Governor Hadley, stated, "It was my understanding at the time McCracken claimed that he had been intimate with Mrs. Brake for a long time prior to the alleged offense, however, I placed no credence in his story then, but subsequent developments indicate that it was true." Patterson went on to say, "I have been reliably informed that the Brake woman gave birth to a negro baby near this time. I also understand that it was common talk in the neighborhood where the Brake woman lived that she was intimate with McCracken." Anna Brake committed perjury because "she had been forced by her husband to make the affidavit."[159]

Governor Hadley, in his commutation letter, remarked, "The woman in question has written many letters to the convict, couched in affectionate terms, and she seems to be sorry that he was sent to the penitentiary. The prisoner has always protested his innocence and says that on account of the nature of the charge made against him and the bitter feeling in Greene County against negroes at the time he was arrested, he pleaded guilty upon the advice of his counsel." After four years and five months in the Missouri State Penitentiary, McCracken's sentence was commuted with the condition that he "obey the laws of the State, conduct himself in all respects as a law-abiding citizen and refrain from associating with white women; failing in this, or upon the order of the Governor at any time, he is to be returned to the penitentiary, there to serve the remainder of his sentence."[160]

Jack McCracken was released on May 26, 1909, and disappeared without a trace, as did Anna Brake.[161] She had been divorced by her husband the previous year, leaving her free to pursue Jack McCracken.[162] They could not, however, be lawfully married in the state of Missouri because interracial marriages were illegal.[163] One story reports that he and Anna lived together in Chicago, while another states that they lived with McCracken's daughter in Kansas City. Neither McCracken nor Brake appears in the census or city directories in either city.[164]

Perhaps the most interesting story of all is that of Bus Cain. Cain, accused of murdering Civil War veteran O. P. Ruark, escaped the night of the lynching. His alleged accomplice, Will Allen, was not so fortunate. As the mob prepared to hang Allen, someone asked if he killed Ruark. Allen, in a clear voice, replied, "Bus Cain killed Ruark. I had nothing to do with it." Although the mob cried out for his death, it is probable that Allen was telling the truth.

Years after his escape, it was reported Cain traveled to San Francisco "where he got a job on a ship and went around the world," ending up in New York.[165] A more detailed account indicates he joined the U.S. Army under the name Frank J. Kelley and served in the Philippines where he once again ran into trouble and served time in a military prison. In 1909, he was allegedly imprisoned at Fort Leavenworth, Kansas, after being convicted of desertion. By 1912, however, Cain surfaced in New York where he served time at Sing Sing Prison for burglary under the alias Frank J. Kelley. After his release, he was later convicted of larceny and served time at New York County Prison.[166] Cain eventually ended up in Brooklyn, New York, where he married and had two children.[167] While in Brooklyn, he killed Catherine Dunn, a white maid, when she surprised Cain burglarizing her employer's home.[168]

He was quickly captured and charged with Dunn's murder. While in police custody, Cain confessed to killing Emma McDonald, a white railroad ticket agent, in Flatbush, New York. He contended his pistol accidentally discharged while the two were walking together and McDonald had been wounded. According to Cain, Mrs. McDonald "begged him to shoot her as she feared the disgrace that might come when her friends learned she had met Kelley and had been wounded while alone with him." He could not explain why, if he had killed her out of mercy, he had dumped her body in a sandpit in Brooklyn.[169]

Cain, it was soon revealed, had conspired with a black maid, Emma Robinson, to rob the house, but their plans had gone awry when Catherine Dunn surprised him in the act. Cain's defense attorney, Edward J. Reilly, claimed his client suffered from "elliptic psychomania" because Robinson "dominated" Cain in a "hypnotic manner." Cain told detectives he had planned to go straight "after I got out of the penitentiary until I met this woman."[170] Reilly, however, was wasting his time. During his trial, Cain did not endear himself to the jury as he sometimes slept during proceedings.[171]

The *New York Times* reported, "He [Cain] grinned when the foreman of the jury announced the verdict and jested with the deputy sheriffs when he was led away to the Raymond Street jail."[172] In a letter to his attorney, Cain asked that he be sentenced on any day except Friday, which he believed "is a hoodoo day, bad luck to try anything." According to the superstitious Cain, "I believe that if I am sentenced on Friday I will have bad luck in my appeal and would rather try to kill myself than be sentenced on that day."[173] The smile may have been wiped off his face when, on Friday, he was sentenced to be executed.[174]

Shortly before midnight on August 26, 1920, Bus Cain, alias George McGee, alias Frank J. Kelley, was taken from his cell and escorted to Sing Sing's execution chamber. Just hours before he was scheduled to die, Cain enjoyed a dinner of steak, fried potatoes, biscuits, watermelon, cake, and coffee. According to a *Times* reporter, he "maintained his bravado to the last. He was smoking a cigar when he entered the death chamber and did not toss it away until he was about to sit in the death chair." As he was strapped into the electric chair, Cain looked at those around him and said, "Goodbye, boys. I hope I'm the last man." At 11:31 P.M., Cain was pronounced dead.[175]

Cain's fate may have remained a mystery because he never divulged his real identity to New York authorities. News of his death, however, appeared in the Springfield papers. The *Republican* reported Cain's execution at Sing Sing and announced that his body was shipped back to Springfield for burial. His mother, Lizzie Cain, and his brother, Marcellus Cain, still lived in Springfield. A private funeral service was held for Bus Cain before he was interred in Lincoln

Bus Cain.
Courtesy of The State Historical Society of Missouri.

Memorial Cemetery.[176] In the years that had passed since Cain fled Springfield, Springfield's African American community suffered setbacks due to fallout from the lynchings.

Without the political leadership of men such as Joe Armstrong, Alfred Adams, and James Stone who forged successful relationships with the white community, Springfield's African Americans were left adrift. In September 1906, one of the city's last black Republican powerbrokers, Bud Anderson, met his political downfall. Anderson was charged by Democratic authorities with shooting craps along with fellow black Republicans Floyd Burns, Kern Neece, Tom Burns, and Wallis Ransom. The men were hauled before Justice W. W. Wilkerson, but they were unable to pay the ten-dollar fine.

The *Springfield Leader* crowed about Anderson's arrest and demanded that "the Republican leader in the Fourth Ward who brings down the party lash with resounding thwacks on such respected men as McLain Jones and C. A. Walterhouse, must go to jail." Black Republicans who were not in jail were busy "fixing their slates, picking out the men who are to hold Greene County offices next term, and making up a schedule of prices for votes."[177]

The *Springfield Republican,* however, disavowed Anderson. According to the *Republican,* Anderson had "devoted his energies to the election of the Democratic mayor two years ago" and was "saved from the penitentiary by the efforts of Democratic counsel" for buying votes with Democratic slush funds. Further, the *Republican* opined, a "Democratic negro is at best a poor specimen, and it is therefore not surprising that he is occasionally found turned up in the courts."[178]

With both sides disavowing Anderson, African Americans in Springfield were left politically adrift.[179] "Colonel" Richard Hockett would later try to lead his Republican brethren, but unlike Adams and Stone, who held city council seats, Hockett was relegated to the position of "superintendent of brooms and mops at the court house." The patronage position of courthouse janitor was a tenuous one. "With changing administrations," a newspaper columnist reminisced, "he lost out and dropped off the map."[180]

The decline of African Americans from the political scene in Springfield was not due to lack of interest or ambition. Instead, it appears that the local Republican Party no longer needed their support to win elections, and without political patronage as an incentive, the black vote in Springfield became marginalized. As one local writer astutely observed in 1932, "Campaigning now does not take the negro vote into consideration as once was done. In the '80s and '90s attention was directed largely at the negro vote. The lines were so closely drawn between the whites that the belief seemed to prevail that the only independent voting was among the negroes." In a recent election, it was observed, "not a single negro voted. The negro is not as active in politics as he was in earlier days. The younger generation of negroes is not as loyal to the Republican party as the older generation. Negro political leaders are absent."

Although the writer could not have anticipated the historic shift of African American voters to the Democratic Party or the coming rise of Democratic African American politicians such as U.S. congressman Arthur Mitchell of Illinois, he remarked, "In present times [Alfred] Adams would no doubt be heard from. He would be a factor in this campaign if now on earth." The battles Adams waged during the 1890s, such as the desegregation of Hazelwood Cemetery, were short lived when the political gains he had made were tossed aside when white Republicans turned their backs on their former African American allies.[181]

After Bud Anderson was abandoned, the next political loss for Springfield's black community came when, on March 11, 1907, the city's Republican committee met to discuss candidates for city council and the school board. In years prior, Republicans had given a token school board seat to an African American. B. A. Hardrick, of the famed Hardrick Brothers Grocery Store, had held the seat for the past few years. He anticipated that he would continue to hold the seat, but white Republicans believed otherwise.

The *Republican* ominously reported, "Hardrick is a candidate to succeed himself, but considerable color sentiment has been worked up in the committee, and he may be defeated." It was rumored that a "white lawyer" wanted Hardrick's seat. The meeting was expected to be tense as Chairman James Yarbrough had resigned earlier in the day when he was informed that Hardrick was not to be nominated. The new chairman, George Culler, was expected to "carry out the will of the faction" because "some lily white leaders put their heads together and declared that in view of the disturbances of a year ago, a white man must be put on the ballot this time."[182]

Hardrick's fears were confirmed the next day when he was "turned out bag and baggage and Ed Merritt was chosen." He did not find solace in the assertion that "the city committeemen were not so much for Merritt or any other individual, as they were for a white man." Members of the committee argued that there were plenty of "negroes who opposed Hardrick and that they named a white man for the sake of harmony." Whether or not there were blacks who opposed Hardrick, he and "scores of other negroes say that the colored Republicans were unanimous for Hardrick," but were met with "the marble heart and the icy stare." Springfield's African Americans declared they "went there for a share of the spoils, and got nothing but a lemon." Some black Republicans vowed to avoid the polls, while others declared they would run "an independent negro candidate." Their hope was short lived. While blacks were not expelled from Springfield after the lynchings, local politics and government were cleansed of African Americans. After 1907, African Americans would not hold office again in Springfield until the end of the twentieth century.[183]

ELEVEN

Harrison

"Their Voices Filled the Air"

"It was in an era of defiance, discord, and bitter hatred that Boone County and Harrison were born," observed local historian and attorney Ralph R. Rea in his history of Boone County, Arkansas.[1] Political struggles among former Confederates, carpetbaggers, Republicans, and Democrats after the close of the Civil War rocked even the most isolated corner of the Arkansas Ozarks. Northwest Arkansas was no exception. On April 9, 1869, Boone County was formed from the eastern portion of Carroll County after state representative James T. Hopper "introduced a bill for the division of Carroll County."[2] Six years later, Boone County grew even larger when land was taken from the western edge of neighboring Marion County.[3]

A temporary county seat was established at the "store-house of H. W. Fick, in Jackson Township" until an election could be held to elect county officers, who would then determine the location of the county seat as "near the center of said county" as possible.[4] Marcus LaRue Harrison, chief engineer for the Pacific and Great Eastern Railroad, was in the vicinity with a survey crew when Fick asked Harrison to survey a town on the banks of nearby Crooked Creek.[5]

Harrison, a former brevet brigadier general in the Union army, may have already known the area. He had led the First Arkansas Cavalry Volunteers, heralded as "the finest of the Union counterguerrilla units raised in the state," across northwest Arkansas on a "brutal and effective counterinsurgency campaign against the Confederate guerrillas from 1863 to 1865."[6] Harrison agreed to survey a town site.

Fick, subsequently appointed postmaster at Crooked Creek, changed the name of the post office from Fick's Store to Harrison on February 7, 1870. The town was incorporated six years later on March 1, 1876.[7]

Henry W. Fick, an attorney and Union officer from New York, was a staunch Republican. His efforts to establish Harrison as the county seat were met with resistance from the residents of nearby Bellefonte, heavily populated by former Confederates, who wanted their town named county seat. According to Rea, "Most of the former Confederates were pulling for Bellefonte, because it was definitely a community that had favored the southern cause. On the other hand, Harrison had been fathered by former Union soldiers and carpetbaggers, and it was openly called, 'a Carpetbagger's town.'" Fick persuaded several former Confederates who lived in and around Harrison that the value of their property would rise with the fortunes of the town. When the election was held to determine whether Harrison or Bellefonte would serve as the county seat, Fick's town emerged victorious.[8]

Fick, who allegedly served as carpetbagger Arkansas governor Powell Clayton's right-hand man in Boone County, was a clever backwoods politician.[9] He counted many former Confederates among his friends, including his brother-in-law James O. Nicholson.[10] It was said that Fick "bore no ill will toward the former rebels."[11] Together with a small group of likeminded Republicans and Union veterans that included D. B. Jernigan, W. W. Jernigan, James T. Hopper, Gillum Hopper, and Fick's son-in-law Isaac Moore, they established a powerful political clique.[12]

Fick, reportedly in an effort to bolster Republicanism and consolidate his considerable influence over Harrison, invited newspaper publisher Thomas Newman to move to the Arkansas Ozarks. Newman, a native of England, arrived in Philadelphia as a boy, but he soon moved westward. While he first worked as a railroad engineer, Newman quickly became involved in the abolitionist movement, and moved to Kansas where he published an abolitionist newspaper. While in Kansas, "the publication of his paper came to a speedy termination, for the party that he was opposing threw his machinery and type into the Missouri River." During the war, Newman moved to St. Louis. He did not stay long, however, as he quickly signed up for service with the Ninth Regiment of the Enrolled Missouri Militia. After the war, he returned to St. Louis, but did not stay long as he quickly accepted Fick's invitation to move to Harrison.[13]

Once in Harrison, Newman began publishing the *Boone County Advocate,* which was published until 1876 when the *Harrison Times* replaced the *Advocate.* A biographical sketch of Newman noted, "Although he was a strong Abolitionist and Union man, he was a man of Democratic principles and became the first mayor of Harrison."[14]

According to one account, politics in the Arkansas Ozarks could be tenuous. During one election when "Negroes were being permitted to vote when former Confederate soldiers were not," three ex-Confederates, Dan Johnson, Bill Rowland, and Joe Bailey, gathered one hundred of their former Confederate brethren to "march on Harrison." A small group of Federal troops were in Harrison to supervise the election and were no doubt surprised when the motley rabble converged on the town. Johnson and Rowland approached the Federal troops and demanded to vote. When informed that they were not registered to vote, Dan Johnson retorted, "they would register or their 'navies' would register." Apparently the officer in charge, in an effort to avoid bloodshed, allowed the disgruntled men to register and vote.[15]

Former Confederates were not the only ones who were disappointed. After Reconstruction faltered, Arkansas joined the ranks of redeemed southern states in which Democrats had regained control of the state government. After the demise of Reconstruction in Arkansas, African Americans struggled to find their place in the state, unable to obtain land. This, in conjunction with tenant farming and abysmal crop prices, "kept them in a position of economic and social inferiority, and the advent of Jim Crow segregation in the 1890s closed the brief window of political, social, and economic opportunity that many had enjoyed." For African Americans in Arkansas, as well as the rest of the nation, it was a monumental struggle to escape from poverty.[16]

There was no exception for African Americans in Boone County. Although blacks had been in Arkansas since it was first settled, their numbers remained small, and grew smaller still in northern Arkansas after the failure of Reconstruction. The only northern county to see an increase in the number of blacks from 1860 to 1870 was Boone County, which was already home to a small population of African Americans. In the 1870 federal census, there were 74 blacks living in Boone County and by 1880, there were 88. In 1890, only 91 African Americans called Boone County home, but by 1900 the population had increased to 142, the largest number of blacks to live in the county at any one time before or since.[17]

According to one native, "Harrison in the 80's and 90's was far different from today. Both the town and the county looked and acted like a chapter from a story of the wild and wooly west. There were dirt streets then—streets that stood in powdery whiteness and sent up great billows of dust in the dry summertime, or became quagmires when it rained."[18] The county courthouse dominated the town square that was intermittently lined with businesses as well as hitching racks. Perhaps the largest business in town was a brickyard.[19] Whites and blacks alike walked the dusty streets of Harrison, but they lived apart.

Harrison's African American community lived in an area "from Rush Avenue and Sycamore, east to Chestnut, and north up Dry Jordan; also that section lying southeast of Rose Hill Cemetery was inhabited by Negro families." Many of Harrison's African American residents were said to be former slaves who, after the close of the Civil War, remained in the region and started their own families.[20]

In 1885, the *Harrison Times* exclaimed, "Our negro population is perhaps the smallest of any county in the State, and in this particular differs widely from most sections of the south. We have not a hundred blacks, all told in the county, and those we have are industrious, peaceable, and fast civilizing themselves up to the standard of their white brethren."[21] According to Clyde R. Newman, blacks in Harrison "were very religious" and attended A.M.E. church services in an unpainted, wooden building in "their own settlement—up Dry Jordan." Newman remembered, "When they had a singing, their voices filled the air in that part of town."[22]

When the local historian and journalist Jesse Lewis Russell arrived in Harrison to attend school in 1889, he recalled that "the few hundred inhabitants were liberally divided in color. There were enough negroes to form something of a society of their own." African Americans in Harrison attended school and church services in a single wooden building and "almost every home where servants were employed had its negro."[23]

If there was one thing that the people of Harrison lacked, however, it was the railroad. Rail service arrived only after the decline of the lumber industry and the subsequent discovery of zinc deposits outside of Harrison.[24] Until the arrival of the St. Louis and North Arkansas Railroad, Harrison was linked to the outside world by a daily stage that "operated with three relays of horses connecting with the railroad at Eureka Springs" in nearby Carroll County.[25] Despite Harrison's short-comings, Jesse Lewis Russell observed, "it was putting on that brag-gadocio spirit, boasting something like a town bully." Russell believed that "there has always been something about the people here that has maintained optimism and push that has given the community prestige above every other of like size in the Ozark area."[26]

The construction of the rail line to Harrison was not without inci-dent. W. A. Spalding, a civil engineer, recalled, "While laying track up the hill east of Long Creek, we had a small race riot. Snow was on the ground and the tracklayers had built a fire and were huddled around it, when a negro tie bucker pushed into a white man who pushed him away and the negro shot him in the leg and fled. He was easily tracked in the snow, captured, and sent to jail in Harrison."[27]

It was not until March 22, 1901, that the St. Louis and North Arkansas Railroad reached Harrison.[28] As the first train rolled into town, "people swarmed" along the track to watch, strains of music from the town band faint amidst the shrieks and murmurs of excitement and astonishment. Farmers and their families, having traveled in from the surrounding countryside, watched in awe as the first vestige of the new century arrived in Harrison. The *Harrison Daily Times* reported, "When the locomotive whistled for the corporate limits and the triumphant march of 200 spikers and others progressed toward the depot grounds, our people could hold their delight no longer, and the demonstration began which included everybody and lasted throughout the day."[29] It was hailed as "one of Harrison's greatest days."[30]

The railroad was not the only dynamic force to arrive that year. On January 18, 1901, almost two months prior to the arrival of the rail-road in Harrison, a new governor was sworn in at Little Rock. Jeff Davis, former Arkansas attorney general and son of a Baptist preacher, was an avowed Democrat and populist demagogue. Despite coming from a privileged background, Davis relied on fiery populism and inflammatory racist rhetoric to establish his political power. During his first race for governor, he declared, "The war is on, knife to knife, hilt to hilt, foot to foot, knee to knee, between the corporations of Arkansas and the people."[31]

He used racism to appeal to thousands of poor whites across

Arkansas in the same manner as U.S. senators James K. Vardaman of Mississippi, Tom Watson of Georgia, and "Pitchfork" Ben Tillman of South Carolina.[32] After Davis inspected a state prison camp, he told a horrified crowd at Hot Springs, Arkansas, that "the first sight that greeted my eyes was a great, big, black negro with a pump gun guarding the white men and driving them down the row and saying: 'Hoe that cotton, damn you, or I will kill you.'"[33]

Davis was not afraid to challenge even President Theodore Roosevelt. In 1901, Roosevelt earned the ire of southerners for daring to entertain Booker T. Washington at the White House. When Roosevelt visited Little Rock in 1905, Davis seized upon the opportunity to cement his reputation as a "defender of the 'Southern way of life,'" and delivered a speech that was "a curious mixture of racial moderation and undisguised Negrophobia." Davis argued that lynching was an appropriate and justified response to African American men preying upon white women. Roosevelt, never one to back down, especially in the face of ignorance, rebuked Davis, "And you, as governor, and all other exponents of the law, owe it to our people, owe it to the cause of civilization to do everything in our power, officially and unofficially, to drive the menace and reproach of lynch law out of the United States."[34] Davis's popularity remained intact, allowing him to continue to effectively use fear as political capital.

Far from the racially charged atmosphere of Little Rock, African Americans in Harrison eked out an existence as servants, day laborers, porters, and washerwomen. Efforts to reconstruct what happened to the black community in Harrison are hampered by missing court records and gaps in surviving newspapers that coincide with the dates of racial unrest in 1905 and 1909. Further, only one handwritten note by the grand jury foreman, Max Dampf, has survived.[35] What little can be gleaned about the racial upheaval in Harrison comes from the newspapers of neighboring towns, but the newspapers are limited in their coverage of events that began in the autumn of 1905.

On the evening of September 30, 1905, an African American named Dan broke into the home of Dr. John J. Johnson to escape the cold night air. Dan was promptly arrested and joined another black prisoner, known only as Rabbit, in the Boone County jail. Earlier that day, a deadly confrontation had taken place between an African

American and a white posse outside of Harrison. An article in the *Springfield Leader* reported, "George Richards, a negro cocaine fiend at the Omaha railroad camp, ran amuck last Saturday [September 30], and, armed with a Winchester, proceeded to terrorize the camp." After a warrant was obtained for Richards's arrest, a posse led by Constable Davis set out to apprehend him. When the men located Richards, he reportedly declared he would shoot Constable Davis on sight. Davis, fearful for his life, asked posse member J. E. Hibdon to disarm and arrest Richards. A brief struggle ensued between the two men before Hibdon emptied his .44-caliber revolver into Richards, killing him.[36]

Two days later, as darkness settled over Harrison on the night of October 2, 1905, a small mob of white men approached the county jail. The mob "took these two Negroes [Dan and Rabbit] from jail, along with several others, to the country, where they were whipped and ordered to leave." As a result, it was anticipated, "a movement has begun here which it is believed will result in the driving out of most of the negroes from this city."[37]

One Harrison resident, Loren Watkins, remembered, "Some eight to ten [African Americans were] tied to trees, and whipped with five foot bull whips [while] several men and women [were] tied together and thrown in a 3 to 4 foot deep hole in Crooked Creek. Twenty or thirty well-armed men with guns, clubs, etc., burned three or four of the Negroes' homes, shot out windows and doors of all the other Negroes' homes they could find and warned all Negroes to leave town that night, which most of them did without taking any of their belongings."[38]

The morning after the riot, Watkins and his father were working near a road when an African American man named Clark stopped to talk to them. Clark was "bare headed and bare footed, face scratched and legs below the knees bleeding." He explained that "he had been whipped, beaten, and ordered out of town by a mob the night before, along with all the other Negroes in town." As flames devoured the homes of Harrison's African American community, Clark had escaped into the woods with a group of blacks, but got lost and became separated from them. Clark expressed his intent to go to Oklahoma before he hurriedly went on his way.[39]

Ralph Rea, like Watkins, recalled the events of 1905, "From house to house in the colored section they went—sometimes threatening,

Harrison, Arkansas: West side of Harrison (Boone County) town square; circa 1905.
Courtesy of the Butler Center for Arkansas Studies, Central Arkansas Library System.

sometimes using the lash, always issuing the order that hereafter, 'no Nigger had better let the sun go down on 'em.' Many Negroes left that very night and made their way on foot to Eureka Springs, Springfield, or Fayetteville." But not all blacks left right away as "some of the older ones remained for a few days, hurt and dejected. They knew no other home. They and their parents had been brought here by their white people, and now they had no place to turn."

Harrison, however, was no longer home. According to Rea, "The poor whites had found someone upon whom they could vent their suppressed hatreds. In a few days most of the older Negroes had moved on too, but a few families remained here as late as 1909." One of those who chose to stay was Aunt Vine, who remained with the James A. Wilson family. She reportedly often remarked she was "the best nigger ever born 'cause all the rest were run off."[40]

Some African Americans who did not immediately leave were subjected to physical violence by local whites. The *Marshall Mountain Wave* reprinted an article from the *Harrison Times* that reported, "A party of five unknown men attacked Thos. Armstrong, colored, as he was on his way home from his work. After beating him severely with a leather strap, they notified him that he must leave town immediately or he would be killed." The *Times* sympathetically noted, "We have been unable to learn of any conduct on Armstrong's part which would justify such treatment, and are inclined to think that the matter calls for an investigation by the federal grand jury next week."[41]

Although the citizens of Harrison professed ignorance of the riot and "no effort" was made to identify members of the mob "which drove the Negroes away," not everyone condoned the violence.[42] Judge John Henry Rogers and United States district attorney James Kent Barnes of the Western District of Arkansas, in town for federal court, sought to bring mob participants to justice.[43]

At first glance, Judge John Henry Rogers appeared to be an unlikely individual to come to the aid of Harrison's African American community. Rogers, a native of North Carolina, served in the Ninth Mississippi Infantry during the Civil War. After the end of the war, he attended the University of Mississippi, and upon the completion of his studies, Rogers moved to Fort Smith, Arkansas. There he was admitted to the bar, served as a U.S. congressman, and was elected to the Arkansas Circuit Court. In 1896, after the death of Judge Isaac Parker, President Cleveland appointed Rogers U.S. district judge of the U.S. District Court for the Western District of Arkansas.[44]

United States district attorney James Kent Barnes, unlike Rogers, was a Republican. Barnes, the son of a prominent attorney from Kentucky, arrived in Arkansas in 1871. After being admitted to the bar, his career quickly took off. He was appointed postmaster by Presidents Arthur, Harrison, and McKinley before he accepted appointment as the United States district attorney of the Western District of Arkansas. After his death, he was remembered as a man who "never sought conviction when he doubted the justness of a conviction."[45]

Because they were federal officials, both Barnes and Rogers were immune to the pressures of reelection and local politics. On October 11, 1905, U.S. district attorney Barnes presented evidence to the federal grand jury in the matter of "the United States versus certain persons unknown for a conspiracy to deprive of civil rights persons of African descent." The only surviving note from the grand jury foreman, Max Dampf, regarding the Harrison riot remarked, "Investigation begun October 11, 1905 and concluded October 12, 1905 and this cause was referred for further investigation to the next grand jury." The efforts of Barnes and Rogers, however, were futile. Although the case was referred to the next federal grand jury, nothing came of the matter.[46]

The whipping and expulsion of African Americans from Harrison may have been the result of years of simmering tensions between whites and blacks. Ralph Rea recalled the construction of the railroad "brought in additional white laborers, and soon friction began to build up between them and the colored population." Race relations may have been strained even further when a local white woman allegedly gave birth to mulatto twins. Further, Rea claimed that sometime prior to 1905, "a mob had hung a Negro to a large oak tree on the bank of Crooked Creek."[47]

In his history of Boone County, the local historian Roger B. Logan Jr. quotes a 1939 interview with a former Harrison resident, Guy B. Freeling. Freeling recalled that some of the "well to do" African Americans in Harrison worked in the saloons. According to Freeling, the city of Harrison voted to close the saloons, which left many African Americans out of work. As a result, Freeling stated, many blacks left Harrison.[48] One of those who left was Charley Stinnett.

As twilight fell across the Ozarks on January 17, 1909, Emma Lovett, an elderly white spinster, was outside her home chopping wood when she was approached by twenty-three-year-old Charley Stinnett. Both were natives of Harrison, although it is unknown if the two knew each other prior to this night. Stinnett, who recently lost his job as a bellboy at the Colonial Hotel in Springfield, Missouri, had returned home to Harrison. Save for a handful of brief newspaper accounts, what transpired between Emma Lovett and Charley Stinnett that evening is unknown.

According to Lovett, Stinnett offered to chop the wood for her. She accepted and watched as he split up the rest of the wood. Stinnett then carried a "backstick" into Lovett's house and sat down by the fireplace to ward off the winter chill. After resting for a short period of time, he told Lovett that if she would open the door he would leave. When Lovett opened the door, however, Stinnett reportedly "grabbed her," threw her onto a nearby bed, and sexually assaulted her. She stated that he then "drew a knife and told her that if she did not promise to never tell it he would kill her." Lovett quickly promised before Stinnett left.[49]

After she was certain Stinnett was gone, Lovett hid in her barn, afraid that he would return. When the sun began to rise over the hills, she crept out of the barn "nearly frozen" and crawled to her neighbor's house for help. Stinnett was quickly taken into custody. When questioned, he allegedly admitted he had been at Lovett's home, but denied harming her.[50]

Judge Hudgins immediately "called upon the people to refrain from unlawful acts and assured them that a fair and speedy trial would be had." Hudgins called a special grand jury to investigate the assault on the morning of January 18. The special grand jury wasted no time in returning an indictment against Charley Stinnett the same day.[51] "Feeling is running high," a reporter observed, "but as court is in session and a speedy trial is assured, it is thought that the law will be allowed to take its course. There are not more than a dozen negroes in this county and the few that are here are usually well behaved."[52]

Little is known about Stinnett. Newspaper accounts name him as the stepson of Tom Stinnett, an African American farmer, and his wife, Lettie Coker Stinnett. In the 1900 U.S. federal census, the Stinnett family lived in Yellville, Marion County, Arkansas. According to the census, Charley was born in November 1890. At the age of nine, he was listed as being unable to read or write, and was the eldest of six children.[53] After 1900, the Stinnett family moved to Harrison where Tom Stinnett had a "good reputation."[54]

Even less is known about Emarintha "Emma" Lovett. The 1900 U.S. federal census states that she was born in November 1851, but her obituary listed her birth date as March 30, 1847. She lived with her spinster sister Adeline, nephew Walter, and elderly father John. John Lovett, a native of Alabama, had brought his family to Boone County, Arkansas, from Hickman County, Tennessee, in 1852. While her sister Adeline was listed as a farmer, no occupation was given for Emma.[55] One newspaper account remarked, "Her life, according to rumor, has been a romantic one, as she has chosen a single existence because of a love affair years ago."[56]

On the morning of January 21, 1909, Charley Stinnett went on trial. He pled guilty and, unable to secure a lawyer, Judge B. B. Hudgins appointed attorney Guy L. Trimble to defend Stinnett. It took all afternoon to secure a jury as "most every one had formed and expressed an opinion and was disqualified." In the brief trial that ensued, Emma Lovett testified that Stinnett had assaulted her, but he took to the stand and swore he did not. Stinnett did, however, admit that he went to her home to rob her. As court proceedings unfolded, "Sentiment is very strong against him, but the citizens are going to await the action of the jury in this case."[57] Perhaps the prosecution of Doss Galbraith in Springfield made the citizens of Harrison hesitant to lynch Stinnett.

Trimble provided an "able defense" as his client sat "silent and sullen" in the courtroom. Newspaper accounts do not provide any details of Trimble's arguments, but he must have been somewhat persuasive because the jury deliberated for four hours before it returned a verdict. When Judge Hudgins asked for the jury's decision, the foreman announced that the jury found Stinnett guilty of assaulting Emma Lovett. Stinnett did not show emotion as the verdict was read. It was observed that although it was Prosecuting Attorney W. F. Reaves's first term, he had only lost two cases thus far. He came close, however, to a hung jury as one juror "held for a lower offense but at the end of four hours agreed with the other eleven."[58] The next day Judge Hudgins sentenced Stinnett to hang.[59]

As soon as word spread of Charley Stinnett's conviction, "all negroes in Boone County and Harrison" swiftly left and Stinnett was "spirited away, fearing mob violence." It was rumored that Emma Lovett was "seriously ill" and that if Stinnett remained in Boone County, "he would be lynched." One African American, "Uncle" Dick Fancher, stayed behind to sell his property. A journalist described "Uncle" Dick as "well behaved and has no fears of violence," but he wanted to go "where there are more negroes, as they have no church or school here." So many blacks had already left Harrison that there were not enough to fill the church pews or school desks. "If Fancher leaves," the journalist somberly noted, "there will not be a negro in Boone County."[60]

Lettie Stinnett launched a desperate campaign to save her son. Although she and the rest of the Stinnett family now lived in Muskogee, Oklahoma, Lettie Stinnett returned to Harrison to save her son's life. She implored local citizens to sign her petition that asked Arkansas governor George W. Donaghey to commute her son's sentence to life in prison. Guy L. Trimble, Charley Stinnett's court-appointed attorney, helped her gather signatures. The two must have been persuasive as seven of the twelve jurors that convicted Charley Stinnett signed her petition. Lettie Stinnett reportedly collected almost one thousand signatures on her son's behalf.[61]

Her effort was in vain. Governor Donaghey refused to commute Charley Stinnett's sentence. Donaghey sent a telegraph that stated, "Petition for commutation received and denied. Reprieve granted for 30 days expires March 24, which will be the date of execution."[62] She helplessly watched as workmen began to build a scaffold outside of the jail in Harrison.

The day before his execution, Lettie Stinnett arrived at the jail to visit her son. What ensued was "a scene in the jail corridor which brought tears to the eyes of the rough criminals behind the bars with Stinnett."[63] After seeing her son for the last time, Lettie Stinnett reportedly returned to Muskogee, unwilling to watch her son's execution. She had "exhausted every effort to secure a commutation of the sentence."[64]

On March 24, 1909, Charley Stinnett was escorted from his cell outside to the jail yard. He could not help but notice the scaffold was draped with canvas to ensure he met a dignified end. Although an estimated three to four hundred curious spectators hoped to watch Stinnett hang, Sheriff Keef permitted only twenty-five onlookers. Stinnett, originally scheduled to hang at one in the afternoon, delayed his execution by drinking a bottle of whiskey that someone slipped him earlier that morning. Sheriff Keef decided "not to execute him until he had sobered." At some point prior to his execution, Stinnett signed a statement that declared in part, "This is the truth so help me God, and on the eve of my execution I ask all who hope for the sinner's return to pray for me. If I had told the truth at my trial I would have come clear of death."[65]

By four o'clock, Stinnett had sobered up and announced he was ready. As he stood on the scaffold, he was asked if he had any last words. Stinnett replied that he "was guilty of having attempted to assault the aged woman, but that he had not accomplished his purpose." He admitted he planned to rob Emma Lovett and when he failed to do so, he threatened to kill her, but he did not intend to harm her. After he finished speaking, a black cloth bag was pulled down over his head and a one-inch-thick sea grass rope was secured around his neck. Sheriff Joe Keef, satisfied the noose was secure, pulled the lever. Stinnett plunged toward the earth, but his neck did not snap. The final cause of death was strangulation. Funds were reportedly raised among the people of Harrison to ship Stinnett's body to Muskogee for burial.[66]

After his death, the Stinnett family remained in Muskogee. Notably, when asked in 1910 how many children she had, Lettie told the census enumerator that she had eight children, but only seven were living.[67] By 1930, Tom and Lettie Stinnett lived in Joplin, Missouri. Lettie passed away seven years later.[68] Tom worked as a street sweeper for the city of Joplin until his death in 1942.[69]

Boone County remained quiet until the spring of 1922 when the Ku Klux Klan surfaced in the wake of "a declining moral atmosphere, a plethora of moonshiners and bootleggers, and a debilitating railroad strike."[70] After it was announced they would receive a pay cut, Missouri and North Arkansas Railroad workers went on strike. A wave of violence spread across the region as striker and anti-striker factions squared off.[71] The unrest and violence culminated in the lynching of a white man, Ed C. Gregor, believed to be sympathetic to the strikers. After the late 1920s, "the Klans which sprouted in the communities of the hidden hills along the Ozark section of the Missouri and North Arkansas Railroad withered and died as the urgency for resistance and reaction faded with the passing of time."[72]

In 1947, Jesse Lewis Russell reminisced, "The whole colored population disappeared practically overnight after a hanging of one of them took place, around the turn of the century, for an alleged outrage of which he was found legally guilty. For many years negroes were so afraid of the place that none of them spent a night here. None have attempted to locate here since."[73] The decrease of the African Americans in northwest Arkansas was dramatic in the wake of racial unrest in Harrison. From 1900 to 1910, the black population in Boone, Madison, and Carroll Counties substantially decreased.[74]

Other factors contributed to the decline of blacks in northwest Arkansas. Upcountry farms in the rugged Ozark Mountains overwhelmingly consisted of small tracts of marginal farmland and could not compete with the rich, fertile farms of the Arkansas Delta and southern Arkansas. Further, the region lacked reliable transportation networks and the financial capital necessary for economic growth. Blacks who ventured to the region worked in the timber industry or in quarries, but "after the decline of these employment possibilities they left to seek work elsewhere."[75]

In 1950, Rea received a letter from S. P. Porter, an African American who once lived in Harrison. In his letter, Porter inquired if African Americans still lived in Harrison, as he had heard blacks had been expelled. Porter, who left Harrison in 1892 at the age of seventeen, recalled that he attended school in "a little log schoolhouse." Since that time, he had done well for himself. Porter declared he owned "two business locations and eleven residential houses in Watonga [Oklahoma] and one quarter section of farm land northwest of Watonga." Now he wanted to help others. "If there are any colored people and they have a colored school," he proclaimed, "I would give at least $25,000.00."

Unfortunately, Porter's offer was in vain. According to federal census statistics for 1950, Boone County did not have a single African American resident.[76] Boone County, Arkansas, like southwest Missouri, was truly a "white man's heaven."

TWELVE

Conclusion

The August 1952 issue of the *Ozarks Mountaineer* announced, "A few negroes—tourists and fishermen—are beginning to show up in the taboo sections of the Ozarks. A large number may create a problem."[1] These two simple sentences sparked a flood of letters asking if there was a "law" against African Americans in the Ozarks. In response, the *Mountaineer* sought to find the answer for its curious readers, but acknowledged the "task [was] far from easy because there are no 'history books' or other written material dealing with them. Information has had to be sought word-of-mouth." The explanations the *Mountaineer* obtained illustrate how Ozarkers chose to remember their collective past, or, their failure to do so.[2]

The *Mountaineer* explained that "local folk in the taboo communities assert that there is a 'law' prohibiting a negro from residing there or even 'to let the sun set on him.'" These individuals "admit that this is not 'legal' law, backed up by official state and local authority, but assert that it has been in force for so long that no one, negro or otherwise, questions it." But when pressed to explain why the "law" existed in the first place, Ozarkers were divided in opinion.[3]

According to "old-timers," the "law" forbidding African Americans "grew up during Civil War days when the negro throughout the nation constituted a serious racial problem. Ozark communities were afraid of possible disturbance of their peace and tranquility, and having no negroes, decided that in the future [they] did not want any."

Judge Tom Moore, a native of Ozark, Missouri, and then presiding judge of the 31st Circuit Court which included Springfield, disagreed. Moore asserted that the "law" was a myth. Instead, he argued, the reason the Ozarks lacked a significant African American population was because "they never had any." Moore erroneously insisted, "The early settlers before the Civil War did not bring slaves with them (except to three small areas in Christian, Greene, and Wright counties, where the descendants of those slaves still reside)." At the same time, he claimed, "We do not have any today simply because negroes do not like the hills any more than the hills apparently like them. They are not true farmers. They simply work garden patches and do not want rocky soil. And, furthermore, they like to live close together in groups, and they shun the isolation of Ozarks rural life."[4] Had the *Mountaineer* asked an African American resident in Springfield about the "law," however, the magazine may have told a different, more accurate, story.

Instead, the *Mountaineer* opined that "there is much to Judge Moore's opinion" and agreed "that the idea of a 'law' is fairly widespread, and that the relationship of the two races may be a matter of concern should the law be violated." Still, the magazine observed, African American outdoor enthusiasts "have been received without friction, and have not sought facilities, such as overnight lodging, that may be denied to them." Still, "The answer, if the negro seeks to buy land and become a permanent resident, has yet to be found. Today there is no racial problem. Let us hope that there will be none tomorrow."[5]

As late as 1932, local history columns in Springfield newspapers reflected upon the lynchings in Springfield and Pierce City. One such column, published in the *Springfield Daily News,* asserted that the lynchings and expulsion of African Americans in Pierce City "had an influence on Springfield" and blamed "attacks made by Negroes on spooning parties" and the "Clansman" as catalysts that sparked the 1906 Easter lynchings. It is hard to believe that such brutal, transformative events could be collectively forgotten.[6] Having expelled African Americans from their midst, whites later chose to exclude black Ozarkers from their collective memory, denying African Americans their rightful place in the region's history.

Arkansan Charles Morrow Wilson, writing in the late 1950s, lamented, "The loss of the Negro was unquestionably the gravest sociological loss suffered by the Ozarks region. More than any other one component of frontier population the Negro had added depths and richness to the folk culture of the region and to its potential scientific and economic development." Wilson pointed to George Washington Carver, America's most famous African American scientist who was born a slave in Newton County, Missouri, as an example of the loss of black talent due to "avoidable mass prejudice and degeneracy" in the Ozarks.[7]

After the deaths of eight African Americans and the expulsion of blacks from communities in the southern Ozarks from 1894 until 1909, the message was clear that blacks were not welcome in the region. African Americans left southwest Missouri and Boone County, Arkansas, in significant numbers. Left behind in their wake, with the exception of Springfield, Carthage, and Joplin, were the vibrant black communities that once populated the Ozark region.

In 1900, Jasper County, Missouri, had a total population of 84,018 with 1,428 black residents. By 1910, the total population of Jasper County was 89,673, which included 1,368 African Americans.[8] In 1920, the total population had decreased slightly to 75,941 with 1,227 African Americans living in Jasper County.[9] In 1930, Jasper County's total population had fallen to 73,810 with 1,094 black residents present.[10]

The trend was more significant in neighboring counties. In 1890, 364 African Americans called Lawrence County home, but by 1900, only 283 blacks remained. In 1910, after the Pierce City lynching in 1901, there were only 91 African Americans left in the entire county.[11] Their numbers only continued to decline. In 1920, the total population of Lawrence County was 24,211 with 81 African Americans.[12] By 1930, only 74 blacks remained.[13] Neighboring counties experienced the same decline, despite having escaped the ravages of mob violence.

Barry County, to the immediate south of Lawrence County, was home to 97 African Americans in 1890. After the expulsion of blacks from Monett in 1894, only 9 lived in Barry County in 1900. By 1910, only 6 remained.[14] In 1920, only one African American lived there. McDonald County never had a large black population, but it steadily fell in the postbellum decades, from 37 in 1870 to 2 by 1900 and 0 by 1920.[15] The only other counties in southwest Missouri that retained a significant black minority, besides Jasper County, were Newton and Greene. In 1920, Newton County had 318 African Americans and Greene County had 2,261 African American residents.[16] The region was a "white man's heaven."[17]

For the blacks who were driven from the region, life would never be the same. A resilient number returned to Joplin and Springfield. African Americans would not move back to the rural countryside of southwest Missouri and Boone County, Arkansas, until the end of the twentieth century as the region's isolation began to break down with the advance of a new wave of economic growth. Black people might have felt more secure in the region's larger cities, but even there their safety was not ensured. In 1921, Tulsa, Oklahoma, witnessed a brutal episode of racial violence as blacks were attacked and chased from town.[18]

As W. Fitzhugh Brundage has observed, "Of the various forms of lawlessness prevalent in the United States during the past two centuries, lynching remains one of the most disturbing and least understood."[19] Economic and social explanations for mob violence fail to explain why whites turned on their black neighbors in Pierce City and why some tried to save Thomas Gilyard, while others fought to lynch him.

Instead, economic, social, and political factors must be considered in combination with a culture of violence. This culture of violence scorned the law as well as the criminal justice system. The men who adhered to its harsh code favored swift, brutal punishment in reaction to perceived criminal behavior. These factors, combined with a historically small number of blacks in the region, came together to create unique conditions for a tempest of mob violence in the Ozarks during the late nineteenth and early twentieth centuries.

Southwest Missouri, like its southern counterparts in the state's Little Dixie region on the Missouri River and the Bootheel on the Mississippi River at the crossroads of the South, was entrenched in a southern mindset. The swift, firm reaction of Missouri governor Joseph Folk in response to Springfield's triple lynching, in conjunction with significant numbers of blacks leaving the region, led southwest Missourians to gradually cast mob violence aside. For the blacks that chose to remain behind, their behavior was dictated by the fear of memories of the past and unspoken rules of racial etiquette. [20]

The region's southern heritage of violence, in tandem with a vigilante view of justice in a postbellum nation, led to mob violence when blacks began to settle the area in substantial numbers for the first time. While blacks may not have been true economic, social, or even political competitors in the region, whites viewed blacks as a threat to their wives, daughters, and police officers. But whites were able to go beyond the traditional method of disciplining African Americans through the use of mob violence to the actual expulsion of blacks from the area. African Americans in the Ozarks had the misfortune of residing on the region's economic margins, which left them vulnerable to the disposable nature of mob violence.

The failure of whites to integrate black labor into the regional economy kept African Americans economically insignificant. Their failure to do so may have been due to the fact that most Ozarkers engaged in subsistence farming, which did not require additional labor. This was in contrast to black-majority regions of the South, where inexpensive and readily available black labor composed a significant segment of the local economy, making African Americans indispensable to local white employers. In towns like Pierce City, Joplin, and Harrison, however, cheap white labor was prevalent, and as a result, respective black communities could be driven out with little to no impact on the regional economy.

In the case of Pierce City and Springfield, African American participation in the political process may have earned them the ire of their Democratic foes. Blacks in both cities ran for office and were an invaluable voting bloc for the local Republican Party. Fears of black influence in local affairs may have fed preexisting white anxieties. As recent scholarship has pointed out, "White Southerners explicitly conflated black men's alleged sexual misconduct toward white women with the exercise of their newly won political rights." Antilynching crusader Ida B. Wells observed that lynching was "wholly political, its purpose being to suppress the colored vote by intimidation and murder." Thus lynching served as a systematic method for whites, cloaked in claims of punishing black sexual transgressions, as a way to stifle and control black suffrage.[21] The political involvement on the part of African Americans came at a time of ever increasingly strained relations between whites and blacks in America due in part to a perceived rise in black criminality.

The rising visibility of black crime in the late nineteenth century fueled by the rapid growth of southern cities and the transience of laborers helped create a fear of blacks that exacerbated preexisting white anxieties. It was widely believed that women were not safe in the country or the city, so long as African American men roamed free.[22] Transient African Americans played a significant role in the racial unrest that erupted in Joplin, Missouri, and Harrison, Arkansas. In Pierce City and Springfield, citizens, in response to a perceived rise in black crime, acted to prevent further black criminal behavior at the expense of three African Americans. In addition, the late nineteenth century was an era in which any attack on a white individual by an African American was perceived as an attack on all whites. Thus in Monett, Joplin, and Springfield, the white community responded by lynching the individual thought to be guilty in order to punish the offender as well as send a message to the local African American population that blacks were at their mercy. But while a few men were held responsible, an entire race was condemned.[23]

"And so Missouri has fallen," lamented Mark Twain upon hearing of the Pierce City lynching, "that great state! Certain of her children have joined the lynchers, and the smirch is upon the rest of us!"[24] Missouri's most famous son overlooked the fact that mob violence had long been a part of the state's history. For all of the fury and angst the aging novelist exhibited in the essay that ensued, he chose not to publish it in his lifetime. In his own way, Twain captured the nature of the Ozarks at the turn of the century. It was a land and people not quite southern, but definitely children of the Confederacy, still locked in the traditions and customs of their rebellious forefathers. In this unusual childhood, introduced to their long-neglected brothers, violence ensued, leaving a dark mark upon the land yet to be removed.

NOTES

INTRODUCTION

1. *Joplin Daily News,* April 20, 1903, 1. The unnamed couple may have been the parents of St. Louis–San Francisco Railway porter George Brady. Brady, who, along with his wife and son, appears in the 1900 federal census, was the only black resident of Pierce City, Missouri, who listed Mississippi as his birthplace. *Twelfth Census of the United States, 1900, Population Schedule,* "Lawrence County" (National Archives Microfilm Publication T623, roll 870).

2. Tuskegee Institute, *Lynchings by States and Race 1882–1959* (Tuskegee, AL: Tuskegee Institute Department of Records and Research, 1959), 1–2. The historian Christopher Waldrep has raised questions about the reliability of these figures in his article, "War of Words: The Controversy over the Definition of Lynching, 1899–1940," *Journal of Southern History* 56 (February 2000): 75–100.

3. Michael J. Pfeifer, *Rough Justice: Lynching and American Society, 1874–1947* (Chicago: University of Illinois Press, 2006).

4. Russell L. Gerlach, *Immigrants in the Ozarks: A Study in Ethnic Geography* (Columbia: University of Missouri Press, 1976), 29. In this study, southwest Missouri comprises the following counties: Jasper, Newton, McDonald, Lawrence, Barry, Greene, Christian, Stone, and Taney; Milton D. Rafferty, *The Ozarks: Land and Life,* 2nd rev. ed. (Fayetteville: University of Arkansas Press, 2001), 58.

5. Milton D. Rafferty, *Historical Atlas of Missouri* (Norman: University of Oklahoma Press, 1982), 42.

6. Matthew Stith, "At the Heart of Total War: Guerrillas, Civilians, and the Union Response in Jasper County, Missouri, 1861–1865" (M.A. thesis, University of Arkansas, 2004), 1.

7. Lynn Morrow, "Where Did All the Money Go? War and the Economics of Vigilantism in Southern Missouri," *White River Valley Historical Quarterly* 34 (Fall 1994): 1–2.

8. *History of Newton, Lawrence, Barry and McDonald Counties, Missouri* (Chicago: Goodspeed Publishing Co., 1888), 909–10.

9. Mary N. Clary, "The Easter Offering: A Missouri Lynching, 1906" (M.A. thesis, Southwest Missouri State University, 1970).

10. Katherine Lederer, *Many Thousand Gone: Springfield's Lost Black History.* [S.l: s.n.], 1986.

11. Burton L. Purrington and Penny L. Harter, "The Easter and Tug-of-War Lynchings and the Early Twentieth-Century Black Exodus from Southwest

Missouri," *Visions and Revisions: Ethnohistoric Perspectives on Southern Cultures,* ed. George Sabo (Athens: University of Georgia Press, 1987), 59.

12. Jason Navarro, "Under Penalty of Death: Pierce City's Night of Racial Terror," *Missouri Historical Review* 100, no. 2 (2006): 87–102.

13. Elliot Jaspin, *Buried in the Bitter Waters: The Hidden History of Racial Cleansing in America* (New York: Basic Books, 2007).

14. Jacqueline Froelich and David Zimmerman, "Total Eclipse: The Destruction of the African American Community of Harrison, Arkansas, in 1905 and 1909," *Arkansas Historical Quarterly* 58 (Summer 1999): 131–59.

15. W. Fitzhugh Brundage, *Lynching in the New South Georgia and Virginia, 1880–1930* (Chicago: University of Illinois Press, 1993), 291. The historian Christopher Waldrep has raised questions about the definition of lynching in his article, "War of Words: The Controversy over the Definition of Lynching, 1899–1940," *Journal of Southern History* 56 (February 2000): 75–100.

16. Edward L. Ayers, *The Promise of the New South: Life after Reconstruction* (New York: Oxford University Press, 1992), 156–57.

17. Brundage, *Lynching in the New South,* 4–14.

18. Brundage, *Lynching in the New South,* 157.

19. Brundage, *Lynching in the New South,* 81.

20. Brundage, *Lynching in the New South,* 84.

21. Brundage, *Lynching in the New South,* 104.

22. Ayers, *Promise of the New South,* 157.

23. Brundage, *Lynching in the New South,* 144.

24. Stewart E. Tolnay and E. M. Beck, *A Festival of Violence: An Analysis of Southern Lynchings, 1882–1930* (Chicago: University of Illinois Press, 1995), 50.

25. Pfeifer, *Rough Justice,* 14.

26. Rafferty, *The Ozarks,* 93.

27. *Missouri Weekly Patriot* (Springfield), June 18, 1868.

28. *Neosho Times,* October 12, 1871.

29. Thomas M. Spencer, ed., *The Other Missouri History: Populists, Prostitutes, and Regular Folk* (Columbia: University of Missouri Press, 2004), 32–45.

30. J. A. Sturges, *Illustrated History of McDonald County, Missouri, From the Earliest Settlement To the Present Time* (Pineville, MO: J. A. Sturges, 1897), 119–20.

31. Sturges, *Illustrated History of McDonald County,* 111–13.

32. Sturges, *Illustrated History of McDonald County,* 120.

33. Ayers, *Promise of the New South,* 1–33.

34. Martha Hodes, *White Women, Black Men: Illicit Sex in the Nineteenth-Century South* (New Haven, CT: Yale University Press, 1997), 203.

35. Joel Williamson, *The Crucible of Race: Black-White Relations in the American South Since Emancipation* (New York: Oxford University Press, 1984); Hodes, *White Women, Black Men.*

36. Amy Louise Wood, *Lynching and Spectacle: Witnessing Racial Violence in America, 1890–1940* (Chapel Hill: University of North Carolina Press, 2009), 7.

37. Woods, *Lynching and Spectacle,* 3.

38. James W. Loewen, *Sundown Towns: A Hidden Dimension of American Racism* (New York: Touchstone, 2006).

39. Jaspin, *Buried in the Bitter Waters,* 11.

40. *St. Louis Post-Dispatch,* August 25, 1901, 1.

ONE • PIERCE CITY: "WE WERE ONCE SLAVES"

1. Brundage, *Lynching in the New South,* 146.
2. Ayers, *Promise of the New South,* 156.
3. Pfifer, *Rough Justice,* 24, 83.
4. Ayers, *Promise of the New South,* 7.
5. Rafferty, *The Ozarks,* 153–56.
6. G. K. Renner, "Strawberry Culture in Southwest Missouri," *Missouri Historical Review* 1 (October 1969): 18–19.
7. Rafferty, *The Ozarks,* 132–34.
8. Ayers, *Promise of the New South,* 22–24.
9. *Peirce City Weekly Empire,* May 17, 1900.
10. *Peirce City Weekly Empire,* April 15, 1901, 3.
11. *Peirce City Weekly Empire,* 3.
12. *Peirce City Weekly Empire,* April 8, 1880.
13. *Peirce City Weekly Empire,* October 7, 1880.
14. *Peirce City Weekly Empire,* October 20, 1880.
15. *Peirce City Weekly Empire,* October 27, 1881.
16. *Peirce City Weekly Empire,* October 21, 1886.
17. *Neosho Miner and Mechanic,* April 23, 1887.
18. Goodspeed Publishing Company, *History of Newton, Lawrence, Barry and McDonald Counties, Missouri,* 525–26.
19. *Peirce City Weekly Empire,* May 5, 1887.
20. *St. Louis Post-Dispatch,* September 20, 1887.
21. *Peirce City Weekly Empire,* October 6, 1887.
22. *Peirce City Weekly Empire,* November 10, 1887.
23. *St. Louis Globe-Democrat,* October 22, 1887.
24. *Peirce City Weekly Empire,* April 15, 1901, 3.
25. Gerlach, *Immigrants in the Ozarks,* 47.
26. *Peirce City Weekly Empire,* November 20, 1879.
27. Lem Compton, *1880 Federal Census: Lawrence County, Missouri* (Mt. Vernon, MO: Lawrence County Historical Society). Of the remainder, ten were born in Arkansas, six born in Missouri, two in Tennessee, and four from Texas, Virginia, Georgia, and Indian Territory, respectively.
28. Pension file, Washington Robison, 109th U.S. Colored Volunteer Infantry; Pension file, John Farnsworth, Fourth Regiment U.S. Colored Volunteer Heavy Artillery; Pension file, George Page, Thirteenth Regiment U.S. Colored Volunteer Heavy Artillery; Pension file, John Scott, 108 U.S. Colored Volunteer Infantry; Pension file, Alexander Kelly, 115th Regiment U.S. Colored Volunteer Infantry, United States Army, NARA Record Group 15: Records of the Department of Veterans Affairs, 1773–2001.
29. Pension file, Washington Robison, 109th U.S. Colored Volunteer Infantry; Pension file, John Farnsworth, Fourth Regiment U.S. Colored Volunteer Heavy Artillery; Pension file, George Page, Thirteenth Regiment U.S. Colored Volunteer Heavy Artillery; Pension file, John Scott, 108 U.S. Colored Volunteer Infantry; Pension file, Alexander Kelly, 115th Regiment U.S. Colored Volunteer Infantry, United States Army, NARA Record Group 15: Records of the Department of Veterans Affairs, 1773–2001.

30. Compton, *1880 Federal Census,* 194–95.

31. *Peirce City Weekly Empire,* July 15, 1880.

32. *Tenth Census of the United States, 1880, Population Schedule,* "St. Louis County, Missouri" (Washington, D.C.: National Archives and Records Administration, Roll T9–727).

33. Miriam Keast Brown, *The Story of Pierce City, Missouri, 1870–1970* (Cassville, MO: Litho Printers, 1970), 47.

34. Death Certificate for Mary Thomas, December 13, 1910, File No. 38993, Missouri State Archives.

35. *Peirce City Weekly Empire,* August 11, 1877.

36. *Tenth Census of the United States, 1880, Population Schedule,* "Lawrence County, Missouri" (Washington, D.C.: National Archives and Records Administration, Roll T9–698).

37. *Twelfth Census of the United States, 1900, Population Schedule,* "Lawrence County" (Washington, D.C.: National Archives Microfilm Publication T623, roll 870).

38. Lorenzo Greene, Gary R. Kremer, and Antonio F. Holland, *Missouri's Black Heritage,* rev. ed. (Columbia: University of Missouri Press, 1993), 107.

39. *Peirce City Weekly Empire,* April 24, 1879.

40. *Peirce City Weekly Empire,* November 10, 1881.

41. *Peirce City Weekly Empire,* June 2, 1887.

42. *Peirce City Weekly Empire,* November 16, 1899.

43. *Peirce City Weekly Empire,* September 22, 1892.

44. *Peirce City Weekly Empire,* July 8, 1880; June 30, 1881.

45. *Peirce City Weekly Empire,* February 9, 1888.

46. *Peirce City Weekly Empire,* July 25, 1899.

47. *Peirce City Weekly Empire,* January 4, 1893.

48. Goodspeed Publishing Company, *History of Newton, Lawrence, Barry and McDonald Counties, Missouri,* 538.

49. *Peirce City Weekly Empire,* September 30, 1886.

50. *Peirce City Weekly Empire,* June 25, 1891.

51. *Peirce City Weekly Empire,* November 4, 1886.

52. It does not appear that Missouri enacted legislation to prevent African Americans from voting. The standard history of African Americans in Missouri, *Missouri's Black Heritage,* does not indicate that blacks were disenfranchised. Blacks, however, could still be intimidated at the ballot box with dogs, guns, and lawyers. Greene, Kremer, and Holland, *Missouri's Black Heritage.* Alexander Kessyar does note that the 1865 Constitution of Missouri required voters to be able to read and write after January 1, 1876. See Alexander Kessyar, *The Right To Vote: The Contested History of Democracy in the United States* (USA: Basic Books, 2000), Table A13.

53. *Peirce City Weekly Empire,* June 10, 1886, 4; *History of Newton, Lawrence, Barry and McDonald Counties, Missouri* (Chicago: Goodspeed Publishing Co., 1888), 907.

54. *Peirce City Weekly Empire,* May 27, 1886, 2.

55. *Peirce City Weekly Empire,* June 10, 1886, 2.

56. *Peirce City Weekly Empire,* June 10, 1886, 2.

57. *Twelfth Census of the United States, 1900, Population Schedule,* "Lawrence County" (National Archives Microfilm Publication T623, roll 870).

58. *Peirce City Weekly Empire,* June 10, 1886, 2. Virgil Godley was Will Godley's older brother.

59. *Peirce City Weekly Empire,* June 17, 1886, 5.

60. *Peirce City Weekly Empire,* June 24, 1886, 2.

61. *Peirce City Weekly Empire,* July 1, 1886, 2.

62. *Peirce City Weekly Empire,* July 1, 1886, 2.

63. *Peirce City Weekly Empire,* August 19, 1886, 3.

64. *Peirce City Weekly Empire,* August 26, 1886, 5. J. W. Deaton refers to John W. Deaton, the son of a Kentucky plantation overseer who moved to Pierce City in 1874. He drove a stage between Pierce City and Fayetteville, Arkansas, before he served as the Pierce City marshal for ten years. His brother, Elijah Deaton, ran for alderman in 1891. Jonathan Fairbanks and Clyde Edwin Tuck, *Past and Present of Greene County, Missouri* (Indianapolis: A. W. Bowen & Co., 1915), 856.

65. *Peirce City Weekly Empire,* November 4, 1886, 3.

66. *State ex rel. Snyder v. Aldermen of Pierce City,* 3 S.W. 849 (1887).

67. *Peirce City Weekly Empire,* August 23, 1888.

68. *Peirce City Weekly Empire,* August 23, 1888.

69. *Peirce City Weekly Empire,* August 23, 1888.

70. *Peirce City Weekly Empire,* September 13, 1888.

71. *Peirce City Weekly Empire,* May 20, 1891, 4. Elijah D. Deaton, brother of John W. "J. W." Deaton was the son of a Kentucky slave plantation overseer who moved to Pierce City in 1874. Fairbanks and Tuck, *Past and Present of Greene County,* 856.

72. *Peirce City Weekly Empire,* May 20, 1891, 4.

73. *Peirce City Weekly Empire,* May 28, 1891, 4.

74. *Peirce City Weekly Empire,* May 28, 1891, 6.

75. *Peirce City Weekly Empire,* May 28, 1891, 6.

76. *Peirce City Weekly Empire,* June 18, 1891, 2.

77. *Peirce City Weekly Empire,* June 4, 1891, 5.

78. *Peirce City Weekly Empire,* June 4, 1891, 5.

79. *Peirce City Weekly Empire,* June 4, 1891, 5.

80. *Peirce City Weekly Empire,* June 4, 1891, 5. James A. Vance was born in 1841 in Paris, Illinois. He spent one semester at the University of Michigan School of Law before leaving to help his father. When the Civil War erupted, Vance signed up with the Twelfth Illinois Volunteer Infantry but did not see combat. After he was discharged, Vance studied law and was admitted to the Illinois bar. Shortly thereafter he moved to Barry County, Missouri, and became involved in local politics before finally settling down in neighboring Pierce City. *History of Lawrence County, Missouri* (Springfield, MO: Interstate Historical Society, 1917), 174–75.

81. *Peirce City Weekly Empire,* June 4, 1891, 5.

82. Missouri, *Official Manual of the State of Missouri, 1897–1898* (Jefferson City, MO: Office of the Secretary of State, 1898), 153; *Official State Manual of the State of Missouri, 1901–1902* (Jefferson City, MO: Office of the Secretary of State, 1902), 204.

83. *Peirce City Leader-Journal,* January 23, 1925.

84. C. Vann Woodward, *Origins of the New South, 1877–1913*, rev. ed. (Baton Rouge: Louisiana State University Press, 1971), 219.

85. *Peirce City Weekly Empire,* May 17, 1900.

86. *Peirce City Weekly Empire,* August 9, 1900. Wiley Godley was the cousin of Will Godley.

87. *Peirce City Weekly Empire,* October 25, 1900.

88. *Peirce City Weekly Empire,* November 7, 1900.

89. Tolnay and Beck, *Festival of Violence,* 173–74.

90. *Peirce City Weekly Empire,* August 9, 1900.

91. Significantly, French Godley, Will Godley, and Pete Hampton were among the politically active African American community in Pierce City.

92. Ayers, *Promise of the New South,* 427. Iola E. LeGrande, a seventeen-year-old resident of Pierce City, observed in a letter to her penpal in Minnesota in 1901, "We have decoration day on the 30th. Also on the 6th of June. This town [is] divided—the north and the south—the Federals and the Confederates. They celebrate at different times and the band and soldiers form part of the procession each time. They are divided in the Churches too—the north and the south church but not to such an extent as in politics." Fred Mieswinkel, ed., "The Strawberry Letters," *Lawrence County Historical Society Bulletin,* July (Mount Vernon, MO: Lawrence County Historical Society, 1985), 30.

93. *Peirce City Weekly Empire,* August 11, 1881, 4.

94. *Peirce City Weekly Empire,* September 25, 1884.

95. Ayers, *Promise of the New South,* 68. Ayers points out that "towns and cities contained those blacks in the early stages of family formation and of working lives, those most likely to move often, look out for new opportunities, resist indignities and join new organizations, adopt new forms of music and dress, commit crimes or be accused of crimes."

96. Ayers, *Promise of the New South,* 155.

97. Ayers, *Promise of the New South,* 154–55. Stewart Tolnay and E. M. Beck echo Ayers's assertion that "many whites believed that there was an increasing wave of black crime against the white community—that blacks were out of control, especially those who, recently born, had not known the 'domesticating' influences of slavery." In addition, "Many whites found little to separate law-abiding from law-breaking blacks." Tolnay and Beck, *Festival of Violence,* 17–18.

98. *Peirce City Weekly Empire,* February 7, 1889.

99. *Mt. Vernon Fountain and Journal,* September 12, 1889.

100. *Mt. Vernon Fountain and Journal,* September 5, 1889.

101. *Lawrence County Chieftain,* September 6, 1894, 3.

102. *Peirce City Weekly Empire,* July 6, 1899.

103. *Lawrence County Chieftain,* July 13, 1899.

104. *Peirce City Weekly Empire,* January 17, 1889.

105. *Mt. Vernon Fountain and Journal,* September 3, 1891. The two men reportedly quarreled over Joe's brother, Will Godley, who was convicted of raping an elderly white woman. He would later be lynched by the Pierce City mob in 1901.

106. *Sarah Godley v. French Godley,* 1884, Lawrence County Circuit Court, Mt. Vernon, Missouri.

107. *Peirce City Weekly Empire,* March 19, 1891. Robert "Bob" Hampton was the brother of Pete Hampton.

TWO · PIERCE CITY: "WHITE MAN'S HEAVEN"

1. Hodes, *White Women, Black Men*, 203.

2. *Peirce City Weekly Empire*, May 30, 1877.

3. *Peirce City Weekly Empire*, October 23, 1890.

4. Missouri State Penitentiary, *Record of Inmates, Volume R, 1891–1893* (Jefferson City: Missouri State Archives).

5. Chappell, who saved Will Godley from a possible lynching in 1890, was a popular figure in Pierce City. He was killed in 1900 as he investigated the report of a shot fired on a miserable November night marked by snow and rain. Pete Hampton, Will Godley's cousin, joined Chappell to see what was going on and was with the officer when they encountered three men coming into town. As Chappell questioned one of them, the man fidgeted with his pocket, and when Chappell grabbed his hand, a shot discharged. Chappell was struck in the left eye. Pete Hampton returned fire but missed. One man was later captured; the other two remained at large. Marshal Chappell later died of his injuries. *Peirce City Weekly Empire*, November 19, 1900, 3. Pete Hampton was one of the three men lynched in Pierce City.

6. Barbara P. Easley and Verla P. McAnelly, eds., *Obituaries of Benton County, Arkansas, Volume I, 1884–1898* (Bowie, MD: Heritage Books, 1994), 164–65.

7. *Cassville Republican*, July 5, 1894. What exactly transpired in Monett remains murky. There are no extant Monett newspapers that can shed light on matter and the coroner's inquest seems to have been lost, misplaced, or destroyed. Area newspapers briefly mentioned the lynching, but do not provide detailed accounts.

8. *Neosho Times*, July 5, 1894, 4.

9. *Chicago Tribune*, August 21, 1901.

10. *Peirce City Weekly Empire*, February 2, 1899.

11. *Peirce City Weekly Empire*, May 11, 1899.

12. *Peirce City Weekly Empire*, November 30, 1899.

13. *Joplin Daily Globe*, April 16, 1901, 1.

14. *Twelfth Census of the United States, 1900, Population Schedule*, "Lawrence County" (National Archives Microfilm Publication T623, roll 870).

15. Brown, *The Story of Pierce City*, 21.

16. *State v. Lark*, 1901, Lawrence County Circuit Court, Lawrence County Courthouse, Mt. Vernon, Missouri. A New York native, Johnson traveled west in his youth where he worked as a stagecoach driver in Arizona, buffalo hunter, and teamster. He moved back east after marriage and was in charge the day that Gisele Wild was murdered. Unlike Reuben Chappell, who knew when the situation called for prudence, Johnson's background may have made him unwilling to yield ground to the mob. Lawrence County sheriff John Manlove, a Union veteran from Indiana, also failed to act. *Peirce City Leader-Journal*, October 4, 1934; June 15, 1917.

17. *State v. Lark*, 1901, Lawrence County Circuit Court, Lawrence County Courthouse, Mt. Vernon, Missouri.

18. *Peirce City Weekly Empire*, August 22, 1901, 3.

19. *Peirce City Weekly Empire*, September 5, 1901, 3.

20. Sheriff John Manlove was a native of Henry County, Indiana. During the Civil War, he joined the Thirty-sixth Indiana Infantry and reportedly fought in several major battles. After the war he married and moved to Jasper County, Missouri,

but later returned to Indiana. In 1887, however, he returned to the Ozarks and settled in Lawrence County, Missouri, where he served two terms as sheriff. He died in 1917. Lawrence County Historical Society, *Lawrence County, Missouri History* (Mt. Vernon, MO: Lawrence County Historical Society, 1974), 100–101.

21. *Report of the Adjutant-General of the State of Missouri for the Year 1901* (Jefferson City, MO: Tribune Printing Company, 1901), 16–19. Captain Eugene A. Cuendet, the son of a wealthy Swiss widow who immigrated to southwest Missouri because of its small Waldensian population, may have known some of the African American families that fled. In a history of the Waldensians, Mrs. J. Fred Mermoud recalled, "In 1880 a wealthy widow, Mme. Eugene Cuendet, came from St. Croix, Switzerland and settled one mile east of Pierce City. She obtained Negro maids from Pierce City to care for her large home. Her sons, Louis, Eugene, Gaston, and daughters, Eliza and Henrietta, came with her." *Monett Times*, January 16, 1951, 1–2.

22. *Peirce City Weekly Empire*, July 4, 1901.

23. *Carthage Evening Press*, August 20, 1901, 1.

24. *Peirce City Weekly Empire*, July 26, 1901.

25. *Peirce City Weekly Empire*, March 21, 1901, 3.

26. Harold Bell Wright, the future author of *The Shepherd of the Hills,* may have been in the crowd that night. He had arrived the day prior to the murder to visit friends in Pierce City where he once served as pastor. Wright had moved on to Pittsburg, Kansas, but the area and the people of Pierce City must have held its charms for him. If Wright left an eyewitness account of the lynchings, it did not appear in any area newspapers or any of his papers. Perhaps he could have quelled the mob, but there is no indication he tried to do so or that he was in the mob that night. *Peirce City Weekly Empire*, August 22, 1901, 3; *Fayetteville Democrat Weekly,* August 22, 1901.

27. *Joplin Daily Globe*, February 21, 1903, 8.

28. *Fayetteville Democrat Weekly*, August 22, 1901.

29. *Carthage Evening Press*, August 20, 1901, 1; Gerlach, *Immigrants in the Ozarks,* 48–50.

30. *Peirce City Weekly Empire*, August 22, 1901, 3. According to the *Empire*, attorney Joseph French cut Godley's body down.

31. *Carthage Evening Press*, August 20, 1901, 1.

32. Michael J. Pfeifer, "The Ritual of Lynching: Extralegal Justice in Missouri, 1890–1942," *Gateway Heritage* 13, no. 3 (Winter 1993): 22–33.

33. *Carthage Evening Press*, August 20, 1901, 1.

34. *Carthage Evening Press*, August 23, 1901, 5.

35. *Joplin Daily Globe*, February 21, 1903, 8.

36. *Carthage Evening Press*, August 20, 1901, 1.

37. *Peirce City Weekly Empire*, August 20, 1901.

38. *Peirce City Weekly Empire*, August 30, 1900.

39. *Peirce City Weekly Empire*, September 5, 1901, 3.

40. "Record of Bills of Cost on Information 1898–1901," Lawrence County Historical Society, Mt. Vernon, Missouri.

41. *Peirce City Weekly Empire*, July 6, 1899.

42. *Peirce City Weekly Empire*, March 19, 1891.

43. *Peirce City Weekly Empire*, September 5, 1901, 3.

44. *St. Louis Post-Dispatch,* August 25, 1901, 1.

45. *Carthage Evening Press,* August 20, 1901, 5.

46. Mieswinkel, "The Strawberry Letters," 43–44.

47. *Carthage Evening Press,* August 21, 1901, 2.

48. *St. Louis Post-Dispatch,* August 25, 1901, 1.

49. *Peirce City Weekly Empire,* August 22, 1901, 3.

50. Mieswinkel, "The Strawberry Letters," 43–44.

51. *Twelfth Census of the United States, 1900, Population Schedule,* "Lawrence County" (National Archives Microfilm Publication T623, roll 870).

52. Department of the Census, *Negro Population 1790–1915* (Washington, D.C.: Government Printing Office, 1918), 818.

53. *Cassville Republican,* October 24, 1901.

54. *St. Louis Post-Dispatch,* August 25, 1901, 1.

55. *Carthage Evening Press,* August 31, 1901, 4.

56. *Pittsburg Daily Headlight,* August 27, 1901, 2.

57. *Peirce City Weekly Empire,* September 19, 1901, 3. In 1886, Willis DeHoney served as the key witness in the murder trial of Ed Clum, a white man, in neighboring Barry County. It was on DeHoney's testimony that Clum was convicted of murdering J. J. White and Ella Bowe. Clum was later executed. *Peirce City Weekly Empire,* July 22, 1886, 4.

58. *Pittsburg Daily Headlight,* August 23, 1901, 3.

59. *Carthage Evening Press,* August 30, 1901, 5.

60. *Peirce City Weekly Empire,* September 26, 1901, 3.

61. *Carthage Evening Press,* September 12, 1901, 2.

62. *Pittsburg Daily Headlight,* August 23, 1901, 3.

63. *Joplin Daily Globe,* August 21, 1901.

64. *St. Louis Post-Dispatch,* August 25, 1901, 1.

65. *Peirce City Weekly Empire,* September 9, 1901, 3.

66. *St. Louis Post-Dispatch,* August 25, 1901, 1.

67. *Monett Times,* August 22, 1901, 2.

68. *Monett Times,* September 2, 1901, 2.

69. *St. Louis Post-Dispatch,* August 22, 1901.

70. *Fayetteville Democrat Weekly,* August 22, 1901.

71. "The Lynching Horror," *Nation,* vol. 73, August 29, 1901, 162.

72. *Chicago Tribune,* August 22, 1901.

73. *Carthage Evening Press,* August 24, 1901, 2.

74. *Carthage Evening Press,* August 27, 1901, 5. Sadly, Abbott would again write a similar letter to the *Press* in 1903 after the lynching of Thomas Gilyard in Joplin.

75. *Joplin Daily Globe,* August 24, 1901.

76. *Carthage Evening Press,* August 28, 1901, 4.

77. *St. Louis Post-Dispatch,* August 25, 1901, 1. Robertus Love, a native of Irondale, Missouri, was a career newspaperman. At the age of nineteen, he was appointed editor of the *Louisiana Press* in Louisiana, Missouri, and in 1900, became a staff reporter for the *St. Louis Post-Dispatch.* He later worked for the *St. Louis Republic* and the *St. Louis Globe-Democrat* before his death in 1930. Today he is remembered for his book, *The Rise and Fall of Jesse James. St. Louis Globe-Democrat,* May 8, 1930, 4.

78. *Lawrence County Chieftain,* August 23, 1894, 3; September 6, 1894, 3.

79. *St. Louis Post-Dispatch,* August 25, 1901, 1.

80. *Carthage Evening Press,* August 31, 1901, 5.

81. *Peirce City Weekly Empire,* September 26, 1901, 3.

82. *Peirce City Weekly Empire,* September 5, 1901, 3.

83. *Joplin Daily Globe,* August 29, 1901. Although identified as "Noel Perrott" it is highly likely that it was actually Nicholas J. Perrott, the owner of a mill at Pierce City, who gave the interview.

84. Mieswinkel, "The Strawberry Letters," 44.

85. Mieswinkel, "The Strawberry Letters."

86. *Report of the Adjutant-General of the State of Missouri for the Year 1901,* 16–19.

87. Tolnay and Beck, *Festival of Violence,* 18.

88. Missouri State Penitentiary Register by Counties, Lawrence County, 1879–1896, Missouri State Archives, Jefferson City, Missouri.

89. Missouri State Penitentiary Register by Counties, Lawrence County, 1879–1896, Missouri State Archives, Jefferson City, Missouri.

90. Missouri State Penitentiary Register by Counties, Lawrence County, 1879–1896, Missouri State Archives, Jefferson City, Missouri.

91. Brundage, *Lynching in the New South,* 84.

92. Brundage, *Lynching in the New South,* 104.

93. *Neosho Times,* July 5, 1894, 4.

94. Froelich and Zimmerman, "Total Eclipse," 131–59.

95. Pfeifer, *Rough Justice,* 14.

96. Pfeifer, *Rough Justice,* 3–4.

97. *Twelfth Census of the United States, 1900, Population Schedule,* "Lawrence County" (National Archives Microfilm Publication T623, roll 870).

98. Pfeifer, *Rough Justice,* 67.

99. *Stotts City Sunbeam,* August 30, 1901.

100. *St. Louis Post-Dispatch,* August 21, 1901.

101. *St. Louis Post-Dispatch,* August 26, 1901.

102. Death Certificate for Beedie Hampton, June 8, 1950, File No. 20232, Missouri State Archives.

103. Marriage Record for Nathaniel Woods and Sarah Godley, Jackson County, Missouri.

104. Death Certificate for Sarah Woods, January 3, 1920, File No. 951, Missouri State Archives.

105. *Thirteenth Census of the United States,* 1910, Population Schedule, "Lawrence County" (National Archives Microfilm Publication T624, roll 795), *Fourteenth Census of the United States,* 1920, Population Schedule, "Lawrence County" (National Archives Microfilm Publication T625, roll 932).

106. *Twelfth Census of the United States, 1900, Population Schedule,* "Lawrence County" (National Archives Microfilm Publication T623, roll 870); *Shawnee County, Kansas; World War One Honor Roll,* Topeka Genealogical Society, Topeka, Kansas.

107. *Pierce City Weekly Empire,* September 11, 1902.

108. *Pierce City Leader-Journal,* February 9, 1923.

109. Death Certificate for William Abbott, July 9, 1916, File No. 27024, Missouri State Archives.

110. *Pierce City Leader-Journal,* June 15, 1917.

111. *Lawrence Chieftain,* September 12, 1929.

112. *Pittsburg Daily Headlight,* December 26, 1902, 3. Although identified as "Mumpford" his name was most likely "Mumford" or "Montgomery."

113. *Pittsburg Daily Headlight,* December 26, 1902, 3.

114. *Pittsburg Daily Headlight,* January 8, 1903, 6.

115. *Pittsburg Daily Headlight,* January 9, 1903, 5.

116. *Henry Godley v. The City of Pittsburg,* 1903, Crawford County District Court, Crawford County Courthouse, Girard, Kansas.

117. *Peirce City Weekly Empire,* March 6, 1902.

THREE • PIERCE CITY: THE LARK AND GODLEY TRIALS

1. *Peirce City Weekly Empire,* September 26, 1901, 3.

2. *Joplin Daily Globe,* August 21, 1901. In some newspaper accounts Eugene Barrett is referred to as Eugene Carter. *State v. Lark,* 1901, Lawrence County Circuit Court, Lawrence County Courthouse, Mt. Vernon, Missouri. The coroner's jury was made up of Spruce Woodruff, Harry Parr, Wes Rice, George Howard, George Donlavy, and Ed Kane. *Peirce City Weekly Empire,* August 22, 1901, 3.

3. *State v. Lark,* 1901.

4. *State v. Lark,* 1901.

5. E. H. Linzee, "Registration and Drawing For Opening of Kiowa and Comanche Country, 1901," *Chronicles of Oklahoma* 25, no. 3: 289.

6. *State v. Lark,* 1901. Quinn was Superintendent of the Frisco Railroad's Western Division.

7. *State v. Lark,* 1901.

8. *State v. Lark,* 1901.

9. *State v. Lark,* 1901.

10. *State v. Lark,* 1901.

11. *State v. Lark,* 1901.

12. *State v. Lark,* 1901.

13. *Joplin Daily Globe,* August 21, 1901.

14. *Joplin Daily Globe,* August 23, 1901.

15. *Joplin Daily Globe,* August 24, 1901.

16. *Joplin Daily Globe,* August 25, 1901.

17. *Carthage Evening Press,* August 21, 1901, 1.

18. *Joplin Daily Globe,* August 27, 1901.

19. *Joplin Daily Globe,* August 27, 1901.

20. *Joplin Daily Globe,* August 28, 1901.

21. *Joplin Daily Globe,* August 29, 1901. According to the 1900 federal census, Carl Wild was seventeen years old when his sister was murdered.

22. *Stotts City Sunbeam,* September 6, 1901, 3.

23. *State v. Lark,* 1901.

24. *Lawrence Chieftain,* November 21, 1901, 8.

25. *History of Laclede, Camden, Dallas, Webster, Wright, Texas, Pulaski, Phelps, and Dent Counties, Missouri* (Chicago: Goodspeed Pub. Co., 1889), 964; John Downing Benedict, *Muskogee and Northeastern Oklahoma* (Chicago: S. J. Clarke, 1922), n.p.

26. Missouri, *Official Manual of the State of Missouri, 1919–1920* (Jefferson City, MO: Office of the Secretary of State, 1920), 39.

27. *Peirce City Weekly Empire,* October 3, 1901, 3.

28. *History of Newton, Lawrence, Barry and McDonald Counties, Missouri,* 924.

29. *Springfield Leader-Democrat,* November 24, 1901, 1.

30. *Springfield Leader-Democrat,* November 26, 1901, 1. Information could not be located for every member of the jury. The names of the jury are as follows: Wiley Pendleton, J. T. Hinkle, A. E. Tubbs, L. J. Fortner, C. F. Porter, G. R. Fowler, James Barber, Robert Knox, Jeff Drake, B. F. Johnson, F. A. Bell, and John Seneker. *Lawrence Chieftain,* November 28, 1901, 1; *State v. Lark,* 1901.

31. *Twelfth Census of the United States, 1900, Population Schedule,* "Lawrence County" (National Archives Microfilm Publication T623, roll 870).

32. Lawrence County Historical Society, *Lawrence County Missouri History* (Mt. Vernon, MO: Lawrence County Historical Society, 1974), 26–27.

33. *Joplin Globe,* March 25, 1906, 1; *History of Holt and Atchison Counties, Missouri* (St. Joseph, MO: National Historical Company, 1882), 177–78; J. A. Sturges, *Illustrated History of McDonald County, Missouri, From the Earliest Settlement To the Present Time* (Pineville, MO: J. A. Sturges, 1897), 283–84.

34. *Lawrence Chieftain,* November 28, 1901, 1.

35. *Springfield Leader-Democrat,* November 25, 1901, 1.

36. *Lawrence Chieftain,* November 28, 1901, 1.

37. *Springfield Leader-Democrat,* November 25, 1901, 3.

38. *Springfield Leader-Democrat,* November 25, 1901, 1.

39. *Springfield Leader-Democrat,* November 25, 1901, 3.

40. *Springfield Leader-Democrat,* November 27, 1901, 1.

41. *Springfield Leader-Democrat,* November 25, 1901, 3.

42. *Springfield Leader-Democrat,* November 26, 1901, 1.

43. *Springfield Leader-Democrat,* November 26, 1901, 1.

44. *Springfield Leader-Democrat,* November 27, 1901, 3.

45. *Stotts City Sunbeam,* November 29, 1901, 2.

46. *Peirce City Weekly Empire,* December 19, 1901, 3.

47. *Pierce City Weekly Empire,* November 26, 1901.

48. Joe Lark's son, Otis "Odie" Lark died in 1913 in Springfield, Missouri, where he lived with his mother and stepfather, but little else can be found regarding the fate of Joseph Lark. An article in the *Springfield Leader-Democrat* on December 7, 1901, announced that Lark and his wife would make their home in Springfield after the Frisco Railroad reportedly gave Lark his job back. Lark, however, does not appear in subsequent city directories. It is possible, though, that Joe Lark lived out his days in Sacramento, California, with his third wife. Death Certificate for Odie Lark, July 3, 1913, File No. 22625, Missouri State Archives.

49. *Springfield Leader-Democrat,* November 27, 1901, 3.

50. *Springfield Leader-Democrat,* November 26, 1901, 1.

51. *Springfield Leader-Democrat,* November 26, 1901, 1.

52. Ayers, *Promise of the New South,* 156–58.

53. *Joplin Daily Globe,* August 23, 1901.

54. *Lawrence Chieftain,* March 30, 1905, 1.

55. Brundage, *Lynching in the New South,* 94–95.

56. *Sarah Godley v. Rodgers,* 1902, Jasper County Circuit Court, Jasper County Records Center, Carthage, Missouri.

57. *Joplin Daily Globe,* February 21, 1903, 8.

58. *Sarah Godley v. Rodgers,* 1902.

59. *Sarah Godley v. Rodgers,* 1902.

60. *Sarah Godley v. Rodgers,* 1902.

61. *Joplin Daily Globe,* February 19, 1903, 8.

62. *Twelfth Census of the United States, 1900, Population Schedule,* "Lawrence County" (National Archives Microfilm Publication T623, roll 870).

63. *Joplin Daily Globe,* February 20, 1903, 8.

64. *Sarah Godley v. Rodgers,* 1902.

65. *Joplin Daily Globe,* February 20, 1903, 8.

66. *Joplin Globe,* December 13, 1930, 1; Sturges, *Illustrated History of McDonald County, Missouri,* 252; Death Certificate for Hugh Dabbs, December 12, 1930, File No. 39804, Missouri State Archives.

67. *Sarah Godley v. Rodgers,* 1902.

68. *Joplin Daily Globe,* February 19, 1903, 8.

69. *Joplin Daily Globe,* February 19, 1903, 8.

70. *Joplin Daily Globe,* February 19, 1903, 8. When the witness stated he heard LeGrande call out, "Help, Mord, help," he may have heard LeGrande say, "Help, Lord, help." It is also possible that the newspaper made an error in the printing process. No one named "Mord" is referenced as a mob participant in any of the surviving newspaper accounts.

71. *Joplin Daily Globe,* February 19, 1903, 8.

72. *Joplin Daily Globe,* February 19, 1903, 8.

73. *Joplin Daily Globe,* February 19, 1903, 8. Notably, in 1884, Sarah Godley had filed for divorce from French Godley, but no judgment was recorded as to whether or not the divorce was granted. Apparently the two must have resolved their differences as they continued to live together as evidenced by the 1900 federal census. *Sarah Godley v. French Godley,* 1884, Lawrence County Circuit Court, Mt. Vernon, Missouri.

74. *Joplin Daily Globe,* February 20, 1903, 8.

75. *Joplin Daily Globe,* February 19, 1903, 8.

76. *Joplin Daily Globe,* February 20, 1903, 8.

77. *Joplin Daily Globe,* February 20, 1903, 8.

78. *Joplin Daily Globe,* February 20, 1903, 8.

79. A. J. D. Stewart, *The History of the Bench and the Bar of Missouri* (St. Louis: Legal Pub. Co., 1898), 587–88.

80. *Joplin Daily Globe,* February 20, 1903, 8.

81. *Joplin Daily Globe,* February 21, 1903, 8.

82. *Sarah Godley v. Rodgers*, 1902. Sapp, originally from Cleveland, Ohio, moved to Joplin where he worked in the mining industry before retiring. *Joplin Globe*, February 25, 1919, 7.

83. *Joplin Daily Globe*, February 25, 1919, 7.

84. The literature on antilynching efforts mentions few cases of African American victims pursuing legal action. Henry and Sarah Godley may have been two of many blacks to sue their assailants, but it remains unknown at this time.

FOUR • JOPLIN: "HAVE MERCY ON MY SOUL"

1. *Joplin Daily News Herald*, April 26, 1903, 7.

2. F. A. North, *The History of Jasper County, Missouri* (Des Moines, IA: Mills & Co., 1883), 393.

3. Dolph Shaner, *The Story of Joplin* (New York: Stratford House, 1948), 30–33.

4. Lawrence O. Christensen and Gary R. Kremer, *A History of Missouri: Volume IV, 1875 to 1919* (Columbia: University of Missouri Press, 1997), 40–41.

5. United States Census Office, *Compendium of the Tenth Census* (Washington, D.C.: Government Printing Office, 1883), 392.

6. Christensen and Kramer, *A History of Missouri*, 92.

7. *1903 Hoye's City Directory of Joplin and Carthage, Missouri* (Kansas City: Hoye Directory Company), 485.

8. *1903 Hoye's City Directory of Joplin and Carthage, Missouri*, 486.

9. *1903 Hoye's City Directory of Joplin and Carthage, Missouri*, 437, 444. Ironically, Newman's was founded in Pierce City, Missouri, but the flagship store was eventually located in Joplin.

10. *1903 Hoye's City Directory of Joplin and Carthage, Missouri*, 437, 438, 461.

11. *1903 Hoye's City Directory of Joplin and Carthage, Missouri*, 438, 440.

12. *1903 Hoye's City Directory of Joplin and Carthage, Missouri*.

13. *Twelfth Census of the United States, 1900*. Washington, D.C.: "Jasper County" (National Archives Microfilm Publication T623, roll 865).

14. Department of Commerce, Thirteenth Census of the United States 1910 Vol. 2 Population 1910 Alabama–Montana (Washington, D.C.: Government Printing Office, 1913). Table I—Composition and Characteristics of the Population for the State and for Counties, 625.

15. Arrell M. Gibson, *Wilderness Bonanza: The Tri-State District of Missouri, Kansas, and Oklahoma* (Norman: University of Oklahoma Press, 1972), 202.

16. *Joplin Daily Globe*, April 3, 1903, 2. This event occurred just days before the lynching of Thomas Gilyard.

17. *Twelfth Census of the United States, 1900*. Washington, D.C.: "Jasper County" (National Archives Microfilm Publication T623, roll 865).

18. Shaner, *The Story of Joplin*, 62–71.

19. Shaner, *The Story of Joplin*, 67; *Joplin Daily Herald*, July 19, 1885, 1.

20. *Joplin Daily Globe*, March 27, 1900, 1.

21. *Joplin Daily Globe*, April 15, 1903, 1. Bullock's store was located at 313 Main Street. Officer Ben May was no stranger to violence. In August 1901, he was nearly

killed when someone struck him in the head with a bottle while attempting to arrest the female proprietor of a saloon. *Joplin Daily News Herald,* August 12, 1901, 2.

22. *Joplin Daily Globe,* April 15, 1903, 1.

23. *Joplin Daily Globe,* April 15, 1903, 1.

24. Shaner, *The Story of Joplin,* 67; *Joplin News Herald,* April 23, 1901, 2.

25. *Joplin Daily Globe,* April 15, 1903, 1.

26. *Joplin Daily Globe,* April 15, 1903, 1.

27. *Joplin Daily News Herald,* April 16, 1903, 3.

28. *Joplin Daily News Herald,* April 16, 1903, 3.

29. *Joplin Daily News Herald,* April 16, 1903, 3.

30. *Joplin Daily Globe,* April 16, 1903, 2.

31. *Joplin Daily Globe,* April 16, 1903, 2.

32. *Joplin Daily Globe,* April 16, 1903, 2.

33. *Joplin Daily News Herald,* April 16, 1903, 1.

34. *Joplin Daily Globe,* April 16, 1903, 1. Very little biographical information can be found regarding Sheriff James T. Owen. Prior to becoming sheriff, Owen worked as a well driller. *Twelfth Census of the United States, 1900, Population Schedule,* "Jasper County" (National Archives Microfilm Publication T623, roll 866). According to one newspaper, local Republicans did not want Owen on the ticket in 1902, but failed to prevent his nomination at the convention. Their fears that he was a weak candidate came true when he failed to stop the lynching. *Joplin Daily Globe,* September 5, 1902, 7. Owen later moved to Texas.

35. *Joplin Daily Globe,* April 16, 1903, 1.

36. *Joplin Daily Globe,* April 16, 1903, 1.

37. *Joplin Daily Globe,* April 16, 1903, 1.

38. *Joplin Daily News Herald,* April 16, 1903, 1.

39. *Joplin Daily Globe,* April 16, 1903, 1.

40. *Joplin Daily Globe,* April 16, 1903, 1.

41. *Joplin Daily News Herald,* April 16, 1903, 1.

42. *Joplin Daily Globe,* April 16, 1903, 1.

43. *Joplin Daily News Herald,* April 16, 1903, 1.

44. *Joplin Daily News Herald,* April 16, 1903, 1.

45. *Joplin Daily Globe,* April 16, 1903, 1.

46. *Joplin Daily News Herald,* April 16, 1903, 1.

47. *Joplin Daily Globe,* April 16, 1903, 1.

48. *Joplin Daily News Herald,* April 16, 1903, 1. Dr. Francis E. Rohan, the son of an Irish immigrant and his Irish-American wife, was raised in St. Louis. He attended Missouri Medical College, which later merged with Washington University's School of Medicine. In 1903, Rohan arrived in Joplin, where he practiced medicine for several years. During World War One he served overseas with the Twenty-seventh Engineers. *Joplin Globe,* July 14, 1936, 3; Walter Stevens, *St. Louis: The Fourth City, 1764–1911* (St. Louis: S. J. Clarke Co., 1909), 504; Pvt. Francis E. Rohan, Co. D, Twenty-seventh Engineers, Service Card, Missouri State Archives.

49. *Joplin Daily Globe,* April 16, 1903, 1.

50. *Joplin Daily Globe,* April 16, 1903, 1.

51. *Joplin Daily Globe,* April 17, 1903, 1.

52. *Joplin Daily Globe,* April 17, 1903, 2. Evett Dumas Nix, a native of Kentucky, was a colorful figure. The son of a Baptist preacher who fought for the Confederacy, Nix worked in the wholesale grocery business before he was appointed U.S. marshal of Oklahoma by President Grover Cleveland in 1893. He resigned his appointment and moved to Joplin where, in 1903, he served as secretary of the Hatcher Mercantile Company. Howard L. Conrad, ed., *Encyclopedia of the History of Missouri,* vol. 5 (New York: Southern Historical Co., 1901), 583–84; Nancy J. Samuelson, *Shoot From the Lip: The Lives, Legends, and Lies of the Three Guardsmen of Oklahoma and U.S. Marshal Nix* (Eastford, CT: Shooting Star Press, 1998); *1903 Hoye's City Directory of Joplin and Carthage, Missouri* (Kansas City: Hoye Directory Company), 299.

53. *Joplin Daily News Herald,* April 16, 1903, 1.

54. *Joplin Daily News Herald,* April 16, 1903, 1.

55. *Joplin Daily News Herald,* April 16, 1903, 1–2.

56. *Joplin Daily Globe,* April 16, 1903, 1.

57. *Joplin Daily Globe,* April 16, 1903, 2.

58. *Joplin Daily Globe,* April 16, 1903, 2.

59. *Joplin Daily Globe,* April 16, 1903, 2.

60. *Joplin Daily News Herald,* April 16, 1903, 2.

61. *Joplin Daily Globe,* April 16, 1903, 1.

62. *Joplin Daily Globe,* April 16, 1903, 2.

63. *Joplin Daily News Herald,* April 20, 1903, 2.

64. *Joplin Daily News Herald,* April 16, 1903, 1.

65. *Joplin Daily News Herald,* April 16, 1903, 2.

66. *Joplin Daily News Herald,* April 16, 1903, 2.

67. *Carthage Evening Press,* April 16, 1903, 6.

68. *Joplin Daily Globe,* April 17, 1903, 3.

69. *Joplin Daily Globe,* April 18, 1903, 1.

70. Department of Commerce, *Thirteenth Census of the United States 1910 Vol. 2 Population 1910 Alabama–Montana* (Washington, D.C.: Government Printing Office, 1913). Table I—Composition and Characteristics of the Population for the State and for Counties, 1122.

71. *Joplin Daily Globe,* April 17, 1903, 1.

72. *Joplin Daily Globe,* April 17, 1903, 1; "Aunt Lou" Barnett was reportedly the oldest employee on the Joplin branch of the Missouri Pacific Railroad. A widow born in Kentucky, her house had eleven rooms, which she shared with her children and grandchildren. As a car cleaner, Barnett was responsible for sweeping, mopping, and scrubbing the interiors of eight coach cars. She was so efficient that each car "was as clean as your parlor and shines like freshly varnished mahogany." *Joplin Daily Globe,* February 22, 1903, 8.

73. *Joplin Daily Globe,* April 17, 1903, 2.

74. *Carthage Evening Press,* April 16, 1903, 6.

75. *Carthage Evening Press,* April 16, 1903, 6.

76. *Carthage Evening Press,* April 16, 1903, 5.

77. *Joplin Daily News Herald,* April 16, 1903, 2.

78. *Twelfth Census of the United States, 1900.* Washington, D.C.: "Jasper County" (National Archives Microfilm Publication T623, roll 865).

79. *1900 Hoye's City Directory of Joplin and Carthage, Missouri* (Kansas City: Hoye Directory Company), 263.

80. *1900 Hoye's City Directory of Joplin and Carthage, Missouri*, 168.

81. *Joplin Daily News Herald*, April 16, 1903, 2. George Wheaton, a native of Henry County, Illinois, was superintendent of the Anderson Mines at Chitwood, just outside of Joplin. Malcolm G. McGregor, *The Biographical Record of Jasper County, Missouri* (Chicago: Lewis Pub. Co., 1901), 246.

82. *Joplin Globe*, January 13, 1935, 2.

83. *Joplin Daily Globe*, April 17, 1903, 2.

84. *Joplin Daily Globe*, April 17, 1903, 2.

85. *Joplin Daily Globe*, April 16, 1903, 1.

86. *Carthage Evening Press*, April 18, 1903, 3.

87. *Joplin Daily Globe*, April 17, 1903, 1.

88. *Carthage Evening Press*, April 18, 1903, 3.

89. *Carthage Evening Press*, April 16, 1903, 8.

90. *Joplin Daily Globe*, April 17, 1903, 1. John W. McAntire was born in Hardin County, Kentucky, prior to the Civil War. Before he became an attorney, he taught school in Scotland County, Missouri. After he was admitted to the bar, he relocated to Joplin where he served one term as Jasper County prosecuting attorney. Howard L. Conrad, ed., *Encyclopedia of the History of Missouri*, vol. 4 (New York: Southern Historical Pub. Co., 1901), 237.

91. Joel T. Livingston, *A History of Jasper County Missouri and Its People*, vol. 2 (New York: Lewis Publishing Co., 1912), 1078–79.

92. Livingston, *A History of Jasper County Missouri*, 696–97.

93. Livingston, *A History of Jasper County Missouri*, 1049. McManamy, orphaned at a young age, grew up in Michigan. In 1876, he arrived in Southwest Missouri to work in the lead and zinc mines. He spent sixteen years in the mines before he was appointed to the Joplin police force.

94. *Joplin Daily News Herald*, April 17, 1903, 1.

95. *Joplin Daily Globe*, April 17, 1903, 1.

96. *Joplin Daily Globe*, April 17, 1903, 1.

97. *Joplin Daily Globe*, April 17, 1903, 2.

98. *Joplin Daily Globe*, April 18, 1903, 1.

99. *Joplin Daily Globe*, April 16, 1903, 3.

100. *Joplin Daily Globe*, April 17, 1903, 4.

101. *Joplin Daily Globe*, April 18, 1903, 3.

102. *Joplin Daily News Herald*, April 19, 1903, 10. Springfield would fall victim to a lynch mob almost three years to the day in 1906.

103. *Carthage Evening Press*, April 18, 1903, 2.

104. *St. Louis Post-Dispatch*, April 17, 1903.

105. *Carthage Evening Press*, April 20, 1903, 5.

106. *Peirce City Democrat*, April 17, 1903, 5.

107. *Peirce City Democrat*, April 24, 1903, 7.

108. *Joplin Daily News Herald*, April 20, 1903, 4.

109. *Joplin Daily News Herald*, April 20, 1903, 4.

110. *Joplin Daily News Herald*, April 21, 1903, 6.

111. *Carthage Evening Press,* April 18, 1903, 6 ; *Twelfth Census of the United States, 1900,* "Jasper County" (Washington, D.C.: National Archives Microfilm Publication T623, roll 865); Pension file, George Abbott, Co. D, 10th U.S. Colored Heavy Artillery, United States Army, NARA Record Group 15: Records of the Department of Veterans Affairs, 1773–2001.

112. *Carthage Evening Press,* April 22, 1903, 4.

113. *Carthage Evening Press,* April 28, 1903, 6.

114. Ayers, *Promise of the New South,* 157.

115. *Joplin Daily Globe,* April 19, 1903, 1.

116. North, *The Story of Joplin,* 393.

117. Ayers, *Promise of the New South,* 157.

118. Brundage, *Lynching in the New South,* 82.

119. Brundage, *Lynching in the New South,* 76–77.

120. *Joplin Daily Globe,* April 17, 1903, 4.

121. *Joplin Globe,* May 13, 1949.

122. Pfeifer, *Rough Justice,* 2–3.

123. Livingston, *A History of Jasper County,* 600–603. In 1908, Assistant Prosecutor David E. Blair, the former law partner of Perl Decker, was elected as the Republican candidate to the Jasper County circuit court.

124. Pfeifer, *Rough Justice,* 4.

125. *Joplin Daily Globe,* April 17, 1903, 1–2.

126. Pfeifer, "The Ritual of Lynching in Missouri," 23.

127. Tolnay and Beck, *Festival of Violence,* 18.

128. Department of the Interior, *Twelfth Census of the United States 1900,* Volume I, Population Part I (Washington, D.C.: Government Printing Office, 1901), Table 23, 625.

129. *Joplin Daily Globe,* April 3, 1903, 2.

130. *Carthage Evening Press,* April 23, 1903, 2. Interestingly, in 1906, a mob threatened to lynch M. Hackney, a resident of Prosperity, a small village outside of Joplin, for almost beating Carrie Buckles to death.

FIVE • JOPLIN: "HURRAH FOR HICKORY BILL"

1. *Carthage Evening Press,* April 20, 1903, 3.

2. The Jasper County, Missouri, Records Center does have the original murder charge against Mitchell, Fields, and Barnes. The trial records, however, are missing. See Box 2189, #3188, for the charges against Fields and Barnes.

3. Redding, a Republican, served with the Forty-third Ohio during the Civil War. He was wounded at the Battle of Corinth, quickly recovered, and accompanied Sherman on his march through Georgia. He was discharged as a major at the end of the war. He served one term as Jasper County prosecuting attorney in 1902, followed by one term as police judge from 1910 to 1912, and finished with one term as Joplin's city attorney from 1914 to 1916 before his death in 1929. *Joplin Globe,* January 9, 1929. Lee Shepherd, Mitchell's attorney, actually marched at the head of Mayor Trigg's volunteer vigilance force. See previous chapter.

4. *Carthage Evening Press,* April 20, 1903, 3. Barnes is also referred to as "D. H. Barnes."

5. *Joplin Daily News Herald,* April 19, 1903, 3.

6. *Joplin Daily Globe,* April 23, 1903, 3.

7. *Carthage Evening Press,* April 27, 1903, 3.

8. Mississippian Andrew F. Donnan's work as chief engineer of the Lexington and Southern Railroad brought him west. In 1877, he arrived in southwest Missouri to assist in laying out the city of Joplin. Something about the area must have appealed to him as he opened up a civil engineering office and remained in Joplin until his death in 1907. *Joplin Daily Globe,* March 26, 1907, 1.

9. *Joplin Daily Globe,* June 3, 1903, 2.

10. *Joplin Daily Globe,* June 4, 1903, 3.

11. *Carthage Evening Press,* June 4, 1903, 5.

12. *Carthage Evening Press,* June 5, 1903, 3.

13. *Joplin Daily Globe,* June 18, 1903, 3. Defense attorney William Newton Andrews grew up in Illinois where he first worked as a printer's devil and journalist. In 1893, he graduated from Illinois Wesleyan University with a law degree. In 1901, Andrews moved to Joplin. By 1905, the Republican Andrews was elected to the first of three terms he served as Jasper County prosecuting attorney. Livingston, *A History of Jasper County Missouri,* 590–91.

14. *Carthage Evening Press,* June 18, 1903, 5.

15. *Carthage Evening Press,* November 20, 1903, 4.

16. *Carthage Evening Press,* November 21, 1903, 5.

17. Death Certificate for Samuel Kirkwood Mitchell, December 28, 1926, File No. 38525, Missouri State Archives.

18. *Joplin Globe,* January 1, 1935, 2; Death Certificate for Bartimeus H. Barnes, January 12, 1935, File No. 1737, Missouri State Archives.

19. William Rufus Jackson, *Missouri Democracy: A History of the Party and Its Representative Members—Past and Present,* vol. 3 (Chicago: S. J. Clarke Publishing Co., 1935), 158–59.

20. Perl Decker Papers, Western Historical Manuscript Collection, Ellis Library, University of Missouri-Columbia.

21. *Joplin Globe,* August 24, 1934, 1.

22. *Carthage Evening Press,* November 21, 1903, 5.

SIX • SPRINGFIELD:
"THE DEVIL WAS JUST AS GOOD A FRIEND TO GOD"

1. George S. Escott, *History and Directory of Springfield and North Springfield* (Springfield, MO: Office of the Patriot-Advertiser, 1878), 114.

2. Escott, *History and Directory of Springfield and North Springfield,* 46–47, 49. The racetrack was later dismantled after its owner, John P. Campbell, joined the Presbyterian Church.

3. Escott, *History and Directory of Springfield and North Springfield,* 47.

4. Escott, *History and Directory of Springfield and North Springfield,* 53.

5. R. I. Holcombe, *History of Greene County, Missouri* (St. Louis: Western Historical Co., 1883), 194.

6. Department of Commerce, *Seventh Census of the United States, 1850, Population Schedule* (Washington, D.C.: Government Printing Office, 1853) Table I—Population by Counties—Ages, Color, and Condition—Aggregates—Continued, 654–55. I compared Greene County's population against the population of the following counties in southwest Missouri: Barry, Jasper, Lawrence, McDonald, Newton, and Taney. Stone and Christian Counties were not yet in existence.

7. Holcombe, *History of Greene County, Missouri*, 210–12.

8. Holcombe, *History of Greene County, Missouri*, 246–47.

9. Local historians have sought for years to verify the burning of two slaves in Carthage, Missouri. The only known account of the burning appears in the *Liberty Tribune* on August 19, 1853, taken from an article that originally appeared in the *Springfield Advertiser*. Two slaves reportedly conspired to lure a Dr. Fisk away from his home, murdered him, and then sexually assaulted the dead man's wife before killing her and her child. They then fled but were quickly apprehended by a white posse. Horrified, local whites chained the slaves to a stake and burned them alive in order to "give a warning to all future transgressors of the kind."

10. Albert D. Richardson, *Beyond the Mississippi: From the Great River to the Great Ocean* (Hartford, CT: American Publishing Co., 1885), 207–8.

11. Holcombe, *History of Greene County, Missouri*, 740.

12. Escott, *History and Directory of Springfield*, 124–25.

13. *Missouri Patriot*, January 4, 1866, 1. A few years later, in 1868, Greene County's temporary superintendent of schools, H. S. Creighton, wrote a scathing letter in which he castigated state officials for taxing citizens to pay for schoolhouses. Worst of all, he thundered, was "your school law [that] provides houses, pay teachers, etc., 'to give them niggers some *larnin,* which is putting them on an equality with us.'" *Report of the Superintendent of Public Schools of the State of Missouri to the Twenty-Fifth General Assembly* (Jefferson City, MO: Ellwood Kirby, 1869), 82.

14. *Report of the Superintendent of Public Schools of the State of Missouri to the Twenty-Fifth General Assembly*, 741.

15. George Ward Nichols, "Wild Bill," *Harper's New Monthly Magazine* 34 (February 1867): 274.

16. Holcombe, *History of Greene County, Missouri*, 768–69.

17. Department of Commerce, *Ninth Census of the United States, 1870, Population Schedule* (Washington, D.C.: Government Printing Office, 1872) Table III—Population of Civil Divisions Less Than Counties, 189.

18. *Ninth Census of the United States, 1880, Population Schedule*, "Greene County, Missouri" (Washington, D.C.: National Archives and Records Administration, Roll: M593 777). J. H. Rector was most likely Julius Rector, a thirty-year-old mulatto schoolteacher born in Missouri, who was living in Springfield with his wife, Margaret, also a schoolteacher.

19. Holcombe, *History of Greene County, Missouri*, 774.

20. *Missouri Weekly Patriot*, August 11, 1870, 3. Among the men who signed the letter were Lewis Tutt, who later served as Springfield's first black police officer; Alfred Adams, who served as coroner; James Stone, who served on the Springfield

City Council; Shadrack Coker, who was Springfield's second black police officer; and two ministers of the gospel.

21. *Springfield Weekly Leader,* April 28, 1870, 3.

22. *Missouri Weekly Patriot,* March 19, 1874, 3.

23. *Missouri Weekly Patriot,* April 16, 1874, 3.

24. *Springfield Leader-Democrat,* January 2, 1902, 2.

25. *Missouri Weekly Patriot,* April 23, 1874, 3.

26. *Missouri Weekly Patriot,* April 23, 1874, 3.

27. Goodspeed Publishing Co., *Pictorial and Genealogical Record of Greene County, Missouri* (Chicago: Goodspeed Brothers, 1893), 289–90. A brief mention of the Tutt-Hickock gunfight can be found in the *Missouri Weekly Patriot* on July 27, 1865, 3.

28. Springfield Metropolitan Bar Association, *100 Years of Service to the Legal Community: 2003 Centennial Directory* (Springfield, MO: n.p., 2003), 20. Callaway's first name is alternately given as "J.A." and "J.P." and "Calloway."

29. Greene County Archives and Records Center, *Black Families of the Ozarks* v. 3-A (Springfield, MO: Greene County Archives & Records Center, Office of the County Clerk), 218–20.

30. Michael K. McGrath, *State Almanac and Official Directory of Missouri for 1878* (St. Louis: John J. Daly & Co., 1879), 36. According to Holcombe's *History of Greene County,* Adams was appointed coroner in 1878 due to Anthony Fisher's resignation. County judges M. J. Rountree and Benjamin Kite voted for Adams while County Judge J. T. Morton voted for Dr. Van Hoose. He was the first African American to hold a county office in Greene County. Holcombe, *History of Greene County, Missouri,* 556. Adams served at least three terms on the Springfield City Council. *Springfield Patriot,* January 31, 1878, 4, and see Appendix of Hoye's 1890–1891, 1892–1893, 1899–1900 Springfield City Directories.

31. *Springfield Republican,* August 16, 1895, 8.

32. *Springfield Republican,* June 20, 1926, 7; *Springfield Republican,* June 27, 1926, 10.

33. *Springfield Republican,* June 27, 1926, 10.

34. *Springfield Express,* October 27, 1882, 3; Michael K. McGrath, *Official Directory of Missouri for 1881* (St. Louis: John J. Daly & Co., 1881), 22.

35. *Springfield Daily Leader,* March 30, 1888, 1; *1888–1889 Hoye's City Directory of Springfield, Missouri* (Kansas City: Hoye Directory Co., 1889), 146.

36. *Springfield Express,* April 6, 1888, 4; *Springfield Leader,* April 4, 1888, 2.

37. *Springfield Daily Republican,* April 4, 1888, 3.

38. *Springfield Daily Republican,* April 7, 1888, 3. Other papers, such as the *Springfield Express,* reported that Berry had a majority of 266 votes.

39. *Springfield Daily Leader,* April 7, 1888, 5.

40. *Springfield Daily Republican,* April 6, 1888, 2.

41. *Springfield Express,* April 13, 1888, 3.

42. *Missouri Patriot,* June 22, 1871, 3.

43. *Missouri Patriot,* June 29, 1871, 3.

44. Fairbanks and Tuck, *Past and Present of Greene County,* 222.

45. *Missouri Patriot,* June 29, 1871, 3.

46. Holcombe, *History of Greene County, Missouri,* 793–95.

47. Escott, *History and Directory of Springfield and North Springfield,* 113.

48. William Kearney Hall, *Springfield, Greene County, Missouri Inhabitants in 1880* (St. Louis: n.p., 1966), 11, 93–94. Hall, a physician and genealogist, produced an annotated version of the census that provides additional information about individuals enumerated in the census that he found in city directories and newspapers.

49. Hall, *Springfield, Greene County, Missouri,* 91. Among those who worked in the railroad shops, John R. Kelley was listed as a mulatto, while Charles Rackliff and George Motley were designated black. White men, such as James McNesby, whose parents were from Ireland, also worked in the railroad shops. Railroad jobs would become highly segregated in years to come.

50. *Springfield, Greene County, Missouri,* 11–13, 41, 117.

51. *Springfield, Greene County, Missouri,* 4, 40–41.

52. *Springfield, Greene County, Missouri,*45.

53. Charles K. Piehl, "The Race of Improvement: Springfield Society, 1865–1881," *Missouri Historical Review* 67, 4 (July 1973): 520.

54. *Springfield Patriot-Advertiser,* March 29, 1883, 3.

55. *Springfield Patriot-Advertiser,* March 29, 1883, 3.

56. *Springfield Patriot-Advertiser,* March 29, 1883, 3.

57. *Springfield Patriot-Advertiser,* April 5, 1883, 2.

58. *Springfield Daily Leader,* August 18, 1888, 4.

59. *Springfield Daily Leader,* August 18, 1888, 4. Officer Palmore was taken to the home of John Patterson, the father of Greene County prosecuting attorney Roscoe C. Patterson who oversaw the prosecution of Doss Galbraith, a member of the lynch mob, in 1906.

60. *Springfield Daily Leader,* August 18, 1888, 3.

61. *Springfield Daily Herald,* August 11, 1888, 8. Only two years earlier, George E. Graham was lynched in Springfield. After Graham, a white man, was found guilty of bigamy and murdering his first wife, a mob of masked men pulled him from the jail and lynched him. For more, see *Springfield Leader,* April 27, 1886, 1–2.

62. *Springfield Daily Republican,* August 5, 1888, 5; *Hoye's 1888–1889 City Directory for Springfield, Missouri* (Kansas City: Hoye Directory Co., 1889), 139. Nannie Lewis is listed as a "domestic" living at 318 W. Brower in Springfield.

63. *Springfield Daily Herald,* August 11, 1888, 8.

64. *Springfield Daily Leader,* August 11, 1888, 2.

65. *Springfield Daily Leader,* August 18, 1888, 4.

66. *Springfield Daily Leader,* August 10, 1888, 3. Bearden was shot by Hollet H. Snow, who served as a law enforcement official for several years.

67. *Springfield Daily Herald,* August 21, 1888, 5.

68. *Knob Noster Gem,* July 28, 1899, 6. Bearden was a tough character. After he was pardoned, he returned to Springfield where he shot and killed Henry Smith in 1914. He died in 1936 at the Greene County Alms House after working as a gardener. Greene County Archives and Records Center, *Black Families of the Ozarks* v. 3-A (Springfield, MO: Greene County Archives & Records Center, Office of the County Clerk, 2005), 174; Death Certificate for Si Bearden, January 10, 1936, File No. 973, Missouri State Archives; Greene County Archives and Records Center, *Index to Superintendent's Register, Greene County, Missouri Alms House* Bulletin No.

12(Springfield, MO: Greene County Archives Bulletin, Office of the County Clerk, 1990), 12.

69. *Springfield Republican,* July 17, 1898, 5.

70. Katherine G. Lederer Ozarks African American History Collection, Special Collections and Archives, Missouri State University. According to his obituary in the *Springfield Republican,* September 25, 1924, James J. Mayes went on to have an illustrious career in the U.S. Army. He later served on General John J. Pershing's staff during World War One, helped General Enoch Crowder draft the Selective Service Draft Act, and served as chief judge advocate general prior to his death.

71. Graham A. Cosmas, *An Army for Empire: The United States Army in the Spanish-American War* (Columbia: University of Missouri Press, 1971), 134.

72. Willard B. Gatewood Jr., *Black Americans and the White Man's Burden, 1898–1903* (Urbana: University of Illinois Press, 1975), 88.

73. Katherine G. Lederer Ozarks African American History Collection, Special Collections and Archives, Missouri State University.

74. *Springfield Republican,* July 9, 1898, 8.

75. *Springfield Republican,* July 17, 1898, 5.

76. *Springfield Republican,* July 8, 1898, 8.

77. *Springfield Leader-Democrat,* July 11, 1898, 5.

78. *Springfield Leader-Democrat,* April 8, 1901, 1.

79. Katherine G. Lederer Ozarks African American History Collection, Special Collections and Archives, Missouri State University.

80. *Springfield Republican,* July 17, 1898, 5.

81. *Springfield Republican,* July 17, 1898, 5.

82. *Springfield Leader-Democrat,* March 3, 1899, 3.

83. *Springfield Leader-Democrat,* March 4, 1899, 1.

84. *Springfield Leader-Democrat,* March 9, 1899, 3.

85. Dean Frank Rea, "A History of the Springfield (Mo.) Leader and Press, 1867–1950" (M.A. thesis, University of Missouri, 1951), 26–30, 86–89. Daniel Curran Kennedy emigrated from Ireland with his parents to Alabama before settling in St. Louis. His legal studies were interrupted when, in 1861, Kennedy enlisted with the Confederate army. He saw action at numerous battles including Pea Ridge, Shiloh, Vicksburg, and Atlanta despite being taken prisoner twice. After the war he settled in Springfield and was admitted to the bar, but found success as the publisher and editor of the *Springfield Leader* until his death in 1903. His son, Robert L. "Bob" Kennedy, assumed editorial control at that time. Bob Kennedy's obituary remarked that, unlike his father, he was "not violently partisan, but took a broad, non-partisan view of things."

SEVEN • SPRINGFIELD: "A SLUMBERING VOLCANO"

1. *Records of the Proceedings of the City Council, Springfield, Missouri, Book 18,* 205; *Springfield Leader-Democrat,* February 6, 1900, 1; Judy Ruestle, *Springfield Smallpox: 1899–1900* (Springfield, MO: Greene County Archives Bulletin No. 5, Office of the County Clerk), 7. The family names that Adams mentions are the names of prominent slave owners in Greene County.

2. *Springfield Leader-Democrat,* February 6, 1900, 1. In his three terms of service on the Springfield City Council, Adams was always designated as a member of the Cemetery Committee, but was denied a seat on any of the other committees, such as the Police, Sanitary, Water, Gas and Electric, and Ordinance committees. See Appendix, Hoye's 1890–1891, 1892–1893, and 1899–1900 Springfield City Directories.

3. *Springfield Leader-Democrat,* August 21, 1901, 4. This view is consistent with the scholarship of Edward Ayers.

4. *Springfield Leader-Democrat,* August 23, 1901, 4.

5. *Springfield Republican,* August 22, 1901, 4.

6. *Springfield Republican,* August 27, 1901, 5.

7. *Springfield Leader-Democrat,* January 1, 1902, 8.

8. *Springfield Republican,* January 2, 1902, 8.

9. *Springfield Leader-Democrat,* January 4, 1902, 4.

10. *Springfield Leader-Democrat,* January 4, 1902, 4.

11. *Springfield Republican,* January 16, 1902, 11.

12. *Springfield Leader-Democrat,* April 15, 1902, 5. It appears the vote was split down Republican and Democratic voting lines on the city council. John R. McNutt, a Democrat who was Springfield's chief of police during the lynchings in 1906, voted against Burns. Voting yes, however, was J. B. Gooch, the uncle of J. Hill Gooch, one of the men charged with the murder of Horace Duncan in 1906.

13. *Springfield Leader-Democrat,* April 4, 1902, 5. The statement "lugging a heavy load of mail" refers to the job of mail carrier. At least two African Americans held this position in Springfield: S. A. G. "Greene" Campbell and William Smith.

14. *Springfield Leader-Democrat,* April 16, 1902, 8.

15. *Springfield Republican,* September 7, 1904, 1. For the criminal charges against Jack McCracken, see Case Number 2441, *State of Missouri v. Jack McCracken,* Greene County Archives Center, Springfield, Missouri.

16. *Springfield Republican,* September 7, 1904, 1. Just three years before, in 1901, Socialist Party member Fred P. Young was threatened with lynching after it was rumored he made "derogatory remarks" about President William McKinley after his assassination. *Springfield Republican,* September 19, 1901, 3.

17. 1905 Grand Jury Report, Greene County Archives and Records Center, Springfield, Missouri.

18. 1905 Grand Jury Report, Greene County Archives and Records Center, Springfield, Missouri. This was the second time Tom Brown was threatened with lynching. The previous year, Greene County sheriff Merwin O. Milliken spirited Brown, an African American accused of killing "Captain" William W. Weir, out of town. Weir, an elderly white amputee, worked as a dishwasher at Springfield's Queen City Restaurant. Brown, intoxicated, stumbled into the restaurant and exchanged words with Weir, then shot him. Sheriff Milliken and a deputy sheriff transported Brown to the Jasper County jail in Carthage for safekeeping as "there was much talk on the streets yesterday and last night against Brown and had he been left in the city it is very probable that an attempt would have been made to lynch him." *Springfield Republican,* October 28, 1903, 1.

19. *Springfield Republican,* September 8, 1904, 4.

20. *Springfield Leader-Democrat,* October 31, 1904, 4. Prior to joining the Springfield police force, he worked as a blacksmith. *1903 Hoye's Springfield City Directory* (Kansas City: Hoye Directory Co.), 70.

21. *1904 Hoye's Springfield City Directory* (Kansas City: Hoye Directory Co.), 425.

22. Mary Clary, "The Easter Offering: A Missouri Lynching, 1906," 5.

23. *Springfield Leader,* December 1, 1904, 1.

24. *Springfield Leader,* December 7, 1904, 1.

25. *Springfield Leader,* July 2, 1908, 1. McCracken's entry in the Register of Inmates records that he was forty-three, stood five feet three inches tall, and weighed one hundred and thirty-eight pounds. McCracken gave his place of birth as Arkansas, identified as a Baptist, and was intemperate in his drinking habits. Although his occupation was listed as laborer, McCracken reported that he had received an education as a youth. Interestingly, when asked if he was supporting anyone, his response was, "Married and parents." Entry for inmate Jack McCracken, aged forty-three years, native of Arkansas; Vol. 5870–7567, 202; Register of Inmates Received, 1836–1931; Missouri State Penitentiary, Record Group 213; Missouri State Archives, Jefferson City.

26. *Springfield Leader,* November 30, 1904, 1.

27. Missouri State Penitentiary Register by Counties, Greene County, 1881–1896 and 1897–1906, Missouri State Archives, Jefferson City, Missouri.

28. Missouri State Penitentiary Register by Counties, Greene County, 1881–1896 and 1897–1906, Missouri State Archives, Jefferson City, Missouri.

29. Bud Cochrane received a ninety-nine-year sentence for killing Frank Coleman, but was later discharged. Prior to the murder of Coleman, he served two separate sentences at the state penitentiary for felonious assault and grand larceny. Missouri State Penitentiary Register by Counties, Greene County, 1897–1906, Missouri State Archives, Jefferson City, Missouri.

30. 1905 Grand Jury Report, Greene County Archives and Record Center, Springfield, Missouri.

31. 1905 Grand Jury Report, Greene County Archives and Record Center, Springfield, Missouri.

32. *Springfield Leader,* December 21, 1905, 1.

33. *Springfield Leader,* December 22, 1905, 1.

34. *Springfield Leader,* December 24, 1905, 1.

35. *Springfield Leader,* December 23, 1905, 1.

36. *Springfield Leader,* December 27, 1905, 3.

37. *Springfield Leader,* December 29, 1905, 1 According to a 1906 Grand Jury Report, on April 4, 1906, Cal Brown testified that Willard Caldwell told him that "he and Elmer were going out on St. Louis Street the night before and Mr. Kinney got to cussing them and made a pocket play and he [Willard] cut down on him."

38. *Springfield Leader,* December 29, 1905, 1.

39. *Springfield Leader,* January 1, 1906, 3.

40. *Springfield Leader,* May 1, 1906, 1.

41. *Springfield Leader,* January 1, 1906, 8. According to his pension record, Obediah P. "O.P." Ruark served in Company K of the Thirty-first Indiana Infantry. He was only 5'6" tall and suffered a gunshot wound in his right hand at Shiloh, Tennessee. Obediah P. Ruark, Thirty-first Indiana Infantry, United States Army, NARA Record Group 15: Records of the Department of Veterans Affairs, 1773–2001.

42. *Springfield Leader,* January 1, 1906, 6.

43. 1906 Grand Jury Report, Greene County Archives and Record Center, Springfield, Missouri.

44. *Springfield Leader,* January 1, 1906, 6.

45. *Springfield Republican,* January 13, 1906, 3.

46. *Springfield Leader,* January 16, 1906, 4.

47. *Springfield Leader,* January 26, 1906, 4.

48. *Springfield Republican,* January 31, 1906, 3. "Bus" Cain is the nickname of George Cain who also used a variety of aliases. In some news accounts, he is referred to as John McGee, while in the 1906 grand jury report he is referred to as George McGee by black witnesses. In the State Training Schools for Boys, Alphabetical Register Number 20, Bus Cain is listed as "George McGee, Number 2034." At the age of eighteen, after he was convicted of grand larceny, McGee was sentenced to two years to the State Training School for Boys at Boonville, Missouri. He entered the facility on March 27, 1903, and was discharged March 25, 1905. State Training Schools for Boys, Alphabetical Register Number 20, "George McGee, Number 2034," 199.

49. *Springfield Republican,* March 28, 1903, 2.

50. *Springfield Republican,* December 24, 1902, 4.

51. *State v. William Allen,* 1900, Lawrence County Circuit Court, Lawrence County Courthouse, Mt. Vernon, Missouri; William Allen, Inmate 2940, Lawrence County, Missouri State Penitentiary Register by Counties, 1897–1906.

52. Interestingly, Allen was sentenced almost at the same time that Thomas Gilyard was lynched in nearby Joplin. Allen was discharged under the Three-Fourths Law on July 13, 1905. *State v. William Allen,* 1903, Greene County Circuit Court, Greene County Archives and Record Center, Springfield, Missouri; William Allen, Inmate 5577, Greene County, Missouri State Penitentiary Register by Counties, 1897–1906; William Allen, Inmate 5577, Dressing Register, 1901–1903, Missouri State Penitentiary, page 689.

53. *Springfield Leader,* January 31, 1906, 1.

54. *Springfield Republican,* February 11, 1906, 1.

55. *Springfield Leader,* March 20, 1906, 5.

56. *Springfield Leader,* March 21, 1906, 1.

57. *Springfield Republican,* February 13, 1906, 2.

58. *Springfield Republican,* February 28, 1906, 8.

59. Williamson, *The Crucible of Race,* 170.

60. *Springfield Republican,* March 1, 1906, 6.

61. *Springfield Leader,* March 31, 1906, 5.

EIGHT · SPRINGFIELD: "THE EASTER OFFERING"

1. Transcription of the 1906 Special Grand Jury Report, Greene County Archives and Record Center, Springfield, Missouri, 24.

2. Transcription of the 1906 Special Grand Jury Report, Greene County Archives and Record Center, Springfield, Missouri, 24; *Springfield Republican,* April 14, 1906, 1.

3. *Springfield Republican,* April 14, 1906, 1.

4. *Springfield Leader,* April 16, 1906, 1.

5. *St. Louis Globe-Democrat,* April 16, 1906, 1.

6. *Springfield Leader*, April 16, 1906, 1 Contemporary newspaper accounts give Edwards's maiden name as "Reeves" and that her father was Bob Reeves of Fair Play, Polk County, Missouri. According to the 1900 federal census for Fair Play, Polk County, Missouri, Mina Edwards was the sixteen-year-old wife of twenty-seven-year-old William Edwards. She was the daughter of Robert J. W. and Mary E. Reeves of Fair Play, Missouri. Robert Reeves, it is worth noting, was born in Mississippi. *Twelfth Census of the United States, 1900, Population Schedule,* "Polk County, Missouri" (Washington, D.C.: National Archives and Records Administration, roll T623–883); Polk County Genealogical Society, *History & Families of Polk County, Missouri* (Paducah, KY: Turner Pub. Co., 2004), 308.

7. *Springfield Republican*, April 14, 1906, 1.

8. *Springfield Leader*, April 14, 1906, 1.

9. *Springfield Leader*, April 16, 1906, 1.

10. Transcription of the 1906 Special Grand Jury Report, Greene County Archives and Record Center, Springfield, Missouri, 35.

11. *Springfield Leader*, April 16, 1906, 1.

12. Transcription of the 1906 Special Grand Jury Report, Greene County Archives and Record Center, Springfield, Missouri, 35.

13. *Springfield Republican*, April 4, 1906, 1.

14. *1903 Hoye's Springfield City Directory* (Kansas City: Hoye Directory Company), 248.

15. *Springfield Leader*, April 4, 1902, 4.

16. *1897 Revised Ordinances, Springfield Missouri* (Springfield: n.p.), 167.

17. *1903 Hoye's Springfield City Directory*, 322.

18. *Springfield Leader*, April 1, 1906, 4.

19. *1903 Hoye's Springfield City Directory*, 501.

20. *Twelfth Census of the United States, 1900, Population Schedule,* "Greene County, Missouri" (Washington, D.C.: National Archives and Records Administration, Roll T623–855).

21. *1904 Hoye's Springfield City Directory* (Kansas City: Hoye Directory Co.), 696.

22. *1903 Hoye's Springfield City Directory,*514; *1904 Hoye's Springfield City Directory*, 661.

23. Fairbanks and Tuck, *Past and Present of Greene County,* 1371–74.

24. *Springfield Leader*, April 1, 1906, 4.

25. *Springfield Leader*, April 2, 1906, 4.

26. *Springfield Republican*, April 15, 1906, 1.

27. Clara Reasoner Barry, *The Pie on the Square* (Springfield, MO: Elkins-Swyers Company, 1946), 29. Prior to the construction of Gottfried Tower, a monument to General Nathaniel Lyon occupied the center of the Springfield square. When it was unveiled in 1882, General William T. Sherman gave the keynote address. By 1885, however, the statute of Lyon was so abused by farmers who threw trash and scraps at it that it was removed to the National Cemetery (27–28).

28. The Goddess of Liberty statue was "Designed by Watts Brothers, Built by Watts Brothers, Put up on the Square by Watts Brothers, Springfield, Missouri." See advertisement, *1903 Hoye's Springfield City Directory*, 5.

29. *St. Louis Globe Dispatch*, April 15, 1906, 1; *Springfield Leader,* April 15, 1906, 1.

30. *Springfield Leader,* April 15, 1906, 1.

31. *Springfield Republican,* April 16, 1906, 1; Katherine Lederer, "And Then They Sang a Sabbath Song," *Springfield Magazine* 2, no. 11, April 1981, 27.

32. Transcription of the 1906 Special Grand Jury Report, Greene County Archives and Record Center, Springfield, Missouri, 7, 23. It is possible that the caller was T. J. Delaney, Springfield's most prominent attorney. Delaney testified that he called Sheriff Horner and warned him that the mob was on its way to the jail.

33. Transcription of the 1906 Special Grand Jury Report, Greene County Archives and Record Center, Springfield, Missouri, 8.

34. Transcription of the 1906 Special Grand Jury Report, Greene County Archives and Record Center, Springfield, Missouri, 6–7.

35. Transcription of the 1906 Special Grand Jury Report, Greene County Archives and Record Center, Springfield, Missouri, 14.

36. *Springfield Republican,* April 15, 1906, 1.

37. Mary Clary, "The Easter Offering: A Missouri Lynching, 1906," 16.

38. *Springfield Republican,* April 15, 1906, 1.

39. *Springfield Republican,* April 15, 1906, 1.

40. John W. Leonard, ed., *The Book of St. Louisians* (St. Louis: St. Louis Republic, 1906), 502; Howard L. Conrad, ed., *Encyclopedia of the History of St. Louis* (New York: Southern Historical Company, 1899), 1947–1948; *Reedy's Mirror* 23, no. 46, December 18, 1914, 194–95.

41. *St. Louis Republic,* April 16, 1906, 1. Sager wrote a brief eyewitness account of the mob's attack on the jail and his efforts to cut off the gas so that the mob would be deprived of light. *Springfield Leader,* April 15, 1906, 1.

42. *Springfield Republican,* April 15, 1906, 1; *Springfield Leader,* April 15, 1906, 1.

43. *St. Louis Republic,* April 16, 1906, 1.

44. *St. Louis Republic,* April 16, 1906, 1.

45. Transcription of the 1906 Special Grand Jury Report, Greene County Archives and Record Center, Springfield, Missouri, 7.

46. *Springfield Leader,* April 15, 1906, 1; April 17, 1906, 5. Sheriff Horner's shotgun was found in a brothel. The proprietor's son, Roy Thompson, was arrested on charges of stealing the shotgun after one of the jail "trusties" reported seeing the young man steal the gun. For more, see *Springfield Leader,* April 18, 1906, 5.

47. *Springfield Leader,* April 15, 1906, 1.

48. *Springfield Republican,* April 15, 1906, 1.

49. *St. Louis Republic,* April 16, 1906, 1.

50. *Springfield Republican,* April 15, 1906, 1.

51. *Springfield Republican,* April 15, 1906, 1.

52. *Springfield Leader,* April 15, 1906, 1; *St. Louis Globe-Democrat,* April 16, 1906, 2.

53. *St. Louis Republic,* April 16, 1906, 1.

54. *St. Louis Republic,* April 16, 1906, 1.

55. *Springfield Republican,* April 15, 1906, 1.

56. *Springfield Republican* April 15, 1906, 1.

57. *St. Louis Republic,* April 16, 1901, 1.

58. *Springfield Leader,* April 15, 1906, 1.

59. *Springfield Leader,* April 15, 1906, 1; *Springfield Republican,* April 15, 1906, 1.

60. *St. Louis Globe-Democrat,* April 16, 1906, 3.

61. *St. Louis Republic,* April 16, 1906, 1.

62. *Springfield Republican,* April 15, 1906, 1.

63. *St. Louis Globe-Democrat,* April 15, 1906, 1 The *Globe-Democrat*'s correspondent, James J. Mayes, was the volunteer U.S. Army captain who resigned from the *Globe-Democrat* to recruit men from Springfield's African American community during the Spanish-American War. He was in charge of Drury College's Corps of Cadets as a commissioned officer in the regular U.S. Army at the time of the lynchings and must have offered to work as a temporary correspondent for his old newspaper. He authored an eyewitness account under his by-line the following day.

64. *St. Louis Globe-Democrat,* April 16, 1906, 1. After his assignment as the head of the Corps of Cadets at Drury ended, Mayes went on to have a successful career in the military. Before his death in 1924, Mayes became assistant judge advocate general of the U.S. Army, served as an aide to General Enoch Crowder, assisted in the development of the Selective Service Draft Act, and worked on the staff of General John J. Pershing during World War One. For more on Mayes, see articles in the *Springfield Republican,* September 25, 1924; *Columbia Daily Tribune,* August 14, 1917; *Springfield Leader,* September 25, 1924.

65. *St. Louis Republic,* April 16, 1906, 1.

66. *Special Grand Jury 1906,* transcription, 19; *Twelfth Census of the United States, 1900, Population Schedule,* "Greene County, Missouri" (Washington, D.C.: National Archives and Records Administration, Roll T623-856).

67. Transcription of the 1906 Special Grand Jury Report, Greene County Archives and Record Center, Springfield, Missouri, 32.

68. *Springfield Leader,* April 15, 1906, 1.

69. *Springfield Republican,* April 16, 1906, 1.

70. *Springfield Leader,* April 15, 1906, 1.

71. *Springfield Republican,* April 15, 1906, 1 ; William Allen, Inmate 5577, Dressing Register, 1901–1903, Missouri State Penitentiary, page 689.

72. *Springfield Leader,* April 16, 1906, 2.

73. *Springfield Leader,* April 16, 1906, 2.

74. Transcription of the 1906 Special Grand Jury Report, Greene County Archives and Record Center, Springfield, Missouri, 19.

75. *Springfield Republican,* April 16, 1906, 1. Decades later, Mary Clary interviewed Walter Langston about the lynchings. Langston, a student at Drury in 1906, claimed that Allen begged him to save him from the crowd. This story, however, does not appear in any other accounts and does not agree with newspaper reports which unanimously depict Allen as stoic in the face of the mob. Clary, "The Easter Offering: A Missouri Lynching, 1906," 14.

76. *Springfield Republican,* April 15, 1906, 1 According to the Special Grand Jury 1906, several witnesses identified the man as J. Hill Gooch, a blacksmith and nephew of former city councilman J. Bone Gooch.

77. Transcription of the 1906 Special Grand Jury Report, Greene County Archives and Record Center, Springfield, Missouri, 16; *1906 Citizens' Directory of Springfield and Greene County, Missouri* (Springfield, MO: Citizens' Directory Company, 1906), 418. According to the testimony of William Forbes, George Queen confessed he helped the mob because "some negroes had pushed his father off the sidewalk."

78. *Springfield Republican,* April 15, 1906, 1.

79. Transcription of the 1906 Special Grand Jury Report, Greene County Archives and Record Center, Springfield, Missouri, 32.

80. *Springfield Republican,* April 15, 1901, 1.

81. Transcription of the 1906 Special Grand Jury Report, Greene County Archives and Record Center, Springfield, Missouri, 14. Fallout from the lynching extended to Monett, where four African Americans hired to work on the new railroad roundhouse were fired upon while asleep in their tent. The men fled without shoes or clothing. Later, however, the men returned and were given shelter and clothing. A reward of one hundred dollars was announced for the arrest and conviction of the guilty parties. See *St. Louis Globe-Democrat,* April 15, 1906, 1.

NINE • SPRINGFIELD:
"THEY CERTAINLY HAD NOT THE BEARING OF DEACONS"

1. Jonathan Fairbanks, Fairbanks Collection, The History Museum for Springfield-Greene County, Missouri, 60.

2. Reuben T. Peak, *Autobiographical Memories of Reuben T. Peak,* unpublished, The History Museum for Springfield-Greene County, Springfield, Missouri. For more on the Peak family, see Fairbanks and Tuck, *Past and Present of Greene County,*1062–64.

3. *Springfield Republican,* April 16, 1906, 1.

4. *Springfield Republican,* April 16, 1906, 1.

5. *Springfield Leader,* April 16, 1906, 2; *Springfield Republican,* April 16, 1906, 1. British author H. G. Wells, in the United States at the time of the lynching, was horrified. He referred to the lynching as a "sort of racial sacrament." Wells sneered that "the edified Sunday-school children hurried from their gospel-teaching to search for souvenirs among the ashes, and competed with great spirit for a fragment of charred skull." Wells observed that the "better element of Springfield society was evidently shocked" when it became known that the three "quite innocent negroes had been used in these instructive pyrotechnics; but the fact remains that a large and numerically important section of the American public does think that fierce and cruel reprisals are a necessary part of the system of relationships between white and colored man." H. G. Wells, *The Future in America: A Search After Realities* (New York: Harper & Bros., 1906), 189.

6. *Springfield Leader,* April 16, 1906, 2 It is also possible that the crowd not only discussed the lynchings, but the appearance of a mysterious light. The light, which had allegedly appeared in Springfield over the last few weeks, was described as a "brilliant giant line of light" that "swooped" over the heads of the crowd and up and down the length of Gottfried Tower. The light enraged the mob who assumed it was a trick played upon them by the police. Several dozen men shot at the light to no avail. It disappeared after it had traveled across the entire mob and was said to be "indescribably weird." See *Springfield Leader,* April 16, 1906, 5.

7. *Springfield Leader,* April 16, 1906, 1.

8. *Springfield Republican,* April 15, 1906, 5.

9. *Springfield Republican,* April 15, 1906, 5. The men who escaped were John Praul, Ed Dupree, Alphonse Grigorious, Harry Smith, William King, Frank Webster, John Williams, Cord Vaughn, Bus Cain, John McMartin, Lee Harris, Ernest Doss, Clarence Mitchell, and Emmet Vaughn.

10. *Springfield Republican,* April 15, 1906, 5; *St. Louis Globe-Democrat,* April 16, 1906, 1. There may be some truth to the dynamite rumor. Katherine Lederer interviewed a member of Springfield's African American community who remembered the night of the lynching. He recalled, "The fellow who had the lime kiln, named Kelso, told his powder monkeys to dynamite all around from Dollison back east where a lot of the colored people lived, and he said, 'If they come down there, just blow 'em all to hell.' That's what he said. So when we found out we felt pretty safe then because we had somebody protecting us." According to the man, the lime kiln's employees were almost all African American, and their employer wanted to ensure their safety. Lederer, "And Then They Sang a Sabbath Song," 35. Katherine Lederer also provided a description of the Westport neighborhood in another article as "a well-populated black neighborhood where most of the families owned their own homes. Narrowly defined, it extended from Central to Phelps and Franklin, bounded on the west by the former Sanford Park (now a city sewer truck depot) and bounded on the east by Broad Street (now Broadway)." See *Springfield! Magazine* 5, no. 5, October 1983, 55.

11. *Springfield Leader,* April 16, 1906, 1.

12. *Springfield Leader,* April 16, 1906, 1.

13. *Springfield Republican,* April 16, 1906, 1.

14. *Springfield Republican,* April 16, 1906, 1.

15. *Springfield Leader,* April 16, 1906, 6.

16. *Springfield Leader,* April 16, 1906, 8.

17. *Report of the Adjutant-General of the State of Missouri for the Year 1905–1906* (Jefferson City, MO: Hugh Stephens Printing Company, 1906), 41.

18. *Springfield Republican,* April 16, 1906, 1.

19. *Springfield Republican,* April 16, 1906, 1; *Report of the Adjutant-General of the State of Missouri for the Year 1905–1906* (Jefferson City, MO: Hugh Stephens Printing Company, 1906), 43–44.

20. *Springfield Republican,* April 16, 1906, 1; *Report of the Adjutant-General of the State of Missouri for the Year 1905–1906* (Jefferson City, MO: Hugh Stephens Printing Company, 1906), 43–44.

21. *Springfield Republican,* April 16, 1906, 1; *Report of the Adjutant-General of the State of Missouri for the Year 1905–1906* (Jefferson City, MO: Hugh Stephens Printing Company, 1906), 43–44.

22. *Report of the Adjutant-General of the State of Missouri for the Year 1905–1906,* 44. The Missouri National Guard began using Krag-Jorgensen rifles on November 30, 1898. Missouri National Guard, *History of the Missouri National Guard* (Jefferson City, n.p., 1934), 85.

23. *Springfield Republican,* April 16, 1906, 1; *Report of the Adjutant-General of the State of Missouri for the Year 1905–1906* (Jefferson City, MO: Hugh Stephens Printing Company, 1906), 44.

24. *Report of the Adjutant-General of the State of Missouri for the Year 1905–1906*, 44.

25. *Springfield Republican*, April 17, 1906, 1.

26. *Report of the Adjutant-General of the State of Missouri for the Year 1905–1906*, 41; *The Adjutants General of Missouri, 1820–1987* (Jefferson City, MO: Missouri Army National Guard, 1987), 36.

27. *Carthage Evening Press*, December 31, 1932, 4.

28. *Springfield Republican*, April 16, 1906, 3.

29. *Springfield Republican*, April 16, 1906, 3.

30. *Springfield Republican*, April 16, 1906, 3.

31. *Springfield Republican*, April 16, 1906, 3.

32. *Springfield Leader*, April 16, 1906, 1.

33. *Springfield Leader*, April 16, 1906, 1.

34. *Springfield Leader*, April 16, 1906, 1.

35. *Springfield Republican*, April 17, 1906, 2.

36. *Springfield Leader*, April 16, 1906, 4.

37. *The Adjutants General of Missouri, 1820–1987* (Jefferson City, MO: Missouri Army National Guard, 1987), 29. DeArmond served as adjutant general until 1909.

38. *Springfield Leader*, April 16, 1906, 1; Sarah Guitar and Floyd C. Shoemaker, eds., *The Messages and Proclamations of the Governors of the State of Missouri* (Columbia, MO: The State Historical Society of Missouri, 1926), 542.

39. *Springfield Leader*, April 16, 1906, 1; *1905 Hoye's Springfield City Directory* (Kansas City: Hoye's Directory Co.), n.p.; *1906 Citizen's Directory for Springfield and Greene County* (Springfield, MO: Citizen's Directory Co.), 103.

40. Greene County Criminal Court Record, Book 14, Greene County Archives and Records Center, Springfield, Missouri, 16, 26, 28.

41. *Springfield Republican*, April 16, 1906, 1; Dan Crane was bonded out by wagon manufacturer H. F. Fellows and A. D. Milligan. Charles Cannefax and Oney Calvey, both Democrats, were bailed out by the following men, most of whom were fellow Democrats: T. E. Cruise, Fred Freeman, G. W. Hackney, C. H. Dalrymple, R. H. Trevathan, Mayor James Blain, F. B. Williams, Luke Calvey, Oscar T. Hamlin, J. J. Nestor, and C. L. Sweet. Greene County Criminal Court Record, Book 14, Greene County Archives and Records Center, Springfield, Missouri, 20–21.

42. Mary Clary, "The Easter Offering: A Missouri Lynching, 1906," 19. The editor of the *Springfield Republican*, E. E .E. "Triple E" McJimsey, a colorful Republican Party figure, called upon Mayor Blain to "give public proof of his sincerity in withdrawing his name from the bond of men" because "public duty is higher than friendship." His appeal was in vain. *Springfield Republican*, April 22, 1906, 12.

43. *Springfield Republican*, April 17, 1906, 2.

44. *Springfield Leader*, April 16, 1906, 1; *Springfield Republican*, April 17, 1906, 1.

45. Lawrence O. Christensen and others, eds., *Dictionary of Missouri Biography* (Columbia: University of Missouri Press), 598.

46. Walter B. Stevens, *Missouri: The Center State, 1821–1915* (Chicago: S. J. Clarke Publishing Company, 1915), 711–12.

47. *Springfield Leader*, April 16, 1906, 1.

48. *Springfield Leader*, April 16, 1906, 1.

49. *Springfield Republican*, April 17, 1906, 1. According to some reports, a small

segment of the troops still wore old blue uniforms. The blue woolen uniforms were phased out in July 1902 when the khaki uniform was adopted. Missouri National Guard, *History of the Missouri National Guard* (Jefferson City, n.p., 1934), 85.

50. *Carthage Evening Press,* December 31, 1932, 4.

51. *Springfield Republican,* April 17, 1906, 1.

52. *Springfield Leader,* April 17, 1906, 2.

53. *Springfield Republican,* April 17, 1906, 1.

54. *Springfield Republican,* April 17, 1906, 1.

55. *Springfield Republican,* April 17, 1906, 1.

56. *Springfield Leader,* April 17, 1906, 1; Springfield *Republican,* April 17, 1906, 1.

57. *Springfield Republican,* April 18, 1906, 1.

58. *Springfield Republican,* April 18, 1906, 1; *1906 Citizens' Directory Company, Springfield and Greene County Directory* (Springfield, MO: Inland Printing & Binding Co., 1906), 72.

59. *Springfield Republican,* April 18, 1906, 1.

60. *St. Louis Republic,* April 18, 1906, 1. Peters and Fielder did not marry. In 1910, Ollie Fielder married Lyman Lane, the son of a Springfield businessman. In 1918, Lyman M. Lane died of pneumonia at the age of twenty-nine. Death Certificate for Lyman M. Lane, October 9, 1918, File No. 32783, Missouri State Archives. The fate of Ollie Fielder Lane remains unknown.

61. *Springfield Leader,* April 17, 1906, 1; *Springfield Republican,* April 18, 1906, 1.

62. *Springfield Republican,* April 18, 1906, 4.

63. *Springfield Leader,* April 17, 1906, 1; *Springfield Republican,* April 18, 1906, 1.

64. *Springfield Leader,* April 17, 1906, 1; Greene County Criminal Court Record, Book 14, Greene County Archives and Records Center, Springfield, Missouri, 20–21.

65. *Springfield Republican,* April 18, 1906, 5; Isaac Stephens does not appear in the 1906 or 1907 Springfield city directories, but Clara Brown appears in the 1907 directory as a laundress. *1907 Citizens' Directory Company, Springfield and Greene County Directory* (Springfield, MO: Inland Printing & Binding Co., 1907), 87.

66. *Springfield Republican,* April 18, 1906, 1.

67. *St. Louis Globe-Democrat,* April 17, 1906, 2; *Kansas City Star,* April 16, 1906, 1.

68. *St. Louis Globe-Democrat,* April 17, 1906, 1.

69. *St. Louis Republic,* April 17, 1906, 1; *St. Louis Globe-Democrat,* April 17, 1906, 3.

70. *St. Louis Republic,* April 17, 1906, 1; *History and Biographical Record of North and West Texas* (Chicago: Lewis Publishing Co., 1906), 217–19.

71. *St. Louis Republic,* April 17, 1906.

72. *St. Louis Republic,* April 17, 1906, 2.

73. *St. Louis Globe-Democrat,* April 17, 1906, 1; *St. Louis Globe-Democrat,* April 17, 1906, 3.

74. *St. Louis Globe-Democrat,* April 17, 1906, 3.

75. *St. Louis Republic,* April 18, 1906, 1.

76. *St. Louis Republic,* April 18, 1906, 1; *St. Louis Globe-Democrat,* April 18, 1906.

77. *St. Louis Republic,* April 18, 1906, 1.

78. *St. Louis Globe-Democrat,* April 17, 1906, 2.

79. *St. Louis Globe-Democrat,* April 17, 1906, 2. Mayes served as a captain of Springfield's African American volunteer regiment during the Spanish-American

War. When he later decided to join the military as a regular commissioned officer, however, he entered at the rank of lieutenant.

80. *St. Louis Globe-Democrat,* April 17, 1906, 2.

81. *Springfield Leader,* April 16, 1906, 2.

82. *Springfield Leader,* April 16, 1906, 6.

83. *Springfield Leader,* April 16, 1906, 5.

84. *Springfield Leader,* April 16, 1906, 5.

85. *Springfield Leader,* April 16, 1906, 5. Samuel W. Bacote, a native of South Carolina born to former slaves, arrived in Kansas City in 1895. He was a graduate of Benedict College and was the first African American graduate of Kansas City University. Charles E. Coulter, *"Take Up the Black Man's Burden": Kansas City's African American Communities, 1865–1939* (Columbia: University of Missouri Press, 2006), 44.

86. *The Independent,* April 21, 1906, v. 15, no. 8 (Kansas City: The Independent), 5. George Creel, a journalist and newspaper publisher, later served as President Woodrow Wilson's chief of propaganda during World War One when he was asked to head the United States Committee on Public Information.

87. *The Independent,* April 21, 1906, v. 15, no. 8 (Kansas City: The Independent), 5.

88. *St. Louis Post-Dispatch,* April 17, 1906, 1.

89. *Springfield Leader,* April 17, 1906, 5.

90. *Springfield Leader,* April 18, 1906, 4.

91. *Springfield Leader,* April 18, 1906, 4.

92. *St. Louis Post-Dispatch,* April 18, 1906, 1.

93. *Springfield Leader,* April 18, 1906, 4.

94. *Springfield Leader,* April 19, 1906, 1.

95. *Springfield Leader,* April 19, 1906, 1.

96. *Springfield Republican,* April 29, 1906, 12.

97. *Springfield Republican,* April 29, 1906, 12.

98. *Springfield Republican,* April 29, 1906, 12.

99. *Springfield Leader,* May 2, 1906, 4.

100. *Springfield Republican,* April 21, 1906, 1.

101. *Springfield Leader,* April 27, 1906, 1.

102. *Springfield Republican,* April 24, 1906, 1.

103. *Springfield Republican,* April 24, 1906, 1.

104. *Springfield Republican,* April 24, 1906, 6; Grant Brown and his wife were not the only interracial couple in Springfield. In the nearby town of Ozark, Missouri, it was reported that citizens there "served notice on Murrell Dillard, a negro, and a white woman, purported to be his wife, both of whom have come here recently as refugees from Springfield, to leave Ozark before sunset tomorrow evening, and if found here after that time, they must abide by the consequences." *Springfield Republican,* April 28, 1906, 3.

105. *Springfield Republican,* April 24, 1906, 1.

106. *Springfield Republican,* April 25, 1906, 8.

107. *Springfield Leader,* April 28, 1906, 2.

108. *Springfield Republican,* April 22, 1906, 6.

109. *Springfield Leader,* April 22, 1906, 1. During a telephone conversation with Cain's nephew, Homer Boyd, Boyd stated that family members told him Cain took

refuge in the basement of a white family's home. The family, reportedly friends with the Cain family, may have been the Gideons. Cain managed to sneak out at "12 o'clock and grabbed a train" at the "corner of Sherman and Pythian streets" and "left for New York." Telephone conversation by the author with Mr. Homer Boyd, Springfield, Missouri, Wednesday, June 24, 2009.

110. *Springfield Republican,* April 26, 1906, 1; *Springfield Republican,* April 24, 1906, 6.

111. *Carthage Evening Press,* April 26, 1906, 8; corporals received fifty cents a day, sergeants sixty cents, first sergeants eighty-three cents, second lieutenants raked in $3.87 a day, first lieutenants $4.17, and captains $5.00. According to the *Press,* camp food primarily consisted of "bacon, potatoes, bread, coffee and syrup," which may have also made the troops ready to return home. *Carthage Evening Press,* April 25, 1906, 8.

112. *Carthage Evening Press,* April 26, 1906, 8.

113. *Springfield Leader,* April 26, 1906, 1.

TEN • SPRINGFIELD: "MURDER IN THE AIR"

1. *Springfield Leader,* April 29, 1906, 1.

2. *1906 Citizens' Directory Company, Springfield and Greene County Directory,* 540; *Springfield Republican,* April 18, 1906, 3; Death Certificate for Charles A. Walterhouse, January 19, 1920, File No. 699, Missouri State Archives.

3. *1906 Citizens' Directory Company, Springfield and Greene County Directory,* 234; *Springfield Republican,* April 18, 1906, 3; Death Certificate for William E. Harlow, December 23, 1922, File No. 34043, Missouri State Archives.

4. *1906 Citizens' Directory Company, Springfield and Greene County Directory,* 159; *Springfield Republican,* April 18, 1906, 3; Death Certificate for Joseph C. Dodson, May 10, 1911, File No. 17536, Missouri State Archives.

5. *Springfield Republican,* April 18, 1906, 3; Death Certificate for Albert B. Appleby, October 26, 1920, File No. 31464, Missouri State Archives.

6. *Springfield Republican,* April 18, 1906, 3; Death Certificate for Charles A. Hubbard, February 13, 1931, File No. 5198, Missouri State Archives; *1906 Citizens' Directory Company, Springfield and Greene County Directory* (Springfield, MO: Inland Printing & Binding Co., 1906), 263. Interestingly, Charles A. Hubbard was the business partner of Richard Henry Trevathan, who was among those who posted bond for Harry Hacker after Hacker was arrested for perjuring himself in front of the grand jury. Walter Williams and Floyd C. Shoemaker, *Missouri, Mother of the West,* rev. ed., vol. 5 (Chicago: American Historical Company, 1930), 193.

7. *Springfield Republican,* April 18, 1906, 3; Death Certificate for August A. Mehl, January 3, 1930, File No. 2347, Missouri State Archives; *1906 Citizens' Directory Company, Springfield and Greene County Directory* (Springfield, MO: Inland Printing & Binding Co., 1906), 350.

8. *Springfield Republican,* April 18, 1906, 3; Death Certificate for William T. Chandler, July 3, 1926, File No. 22187, Missouri State Archives; Death Certificate for Fred H. Marshall, September 4, 1916, File No. 30914, Missouri State Archives.

9. *Springfield Leader,* April 16, 1906, 1.

10. *Springfield Republican,* April 18, 1906, 3.

11. *Springfield Republican,* April 24, 1906, 6.

12. Transcription of the 1906 Special Grand Jury Report, Greene County Archives and Record Center, Springfield, Missouri, 6.

13. Transcription of the 1906 Special Grand Jury Report, Greene County Archives and Record Center, Springfield, Missouri, 8.

14. Transcription of the 1906 Special Grand Jury Report, Greene County Archives and Record Center, Springfield, Missouri, 21.

15. Transcription of the 1906 Special Grand Jury Report, Greene County Archives and Record Center, Springfield, Missouri, 21.

16. Transcription of the 1906 Special Grand Jury Report, Greene County Archives and Record Center, Springfield, Missouri, 23.

17. Transcription of the 1906 Special Grand Jury Report, Greene County Archives and Record Center, Springfield, Missouri, 22.

18. Transcription of the 1906 Special Grand Jury Report, Greene County Archives and Record Center, Springfield, Missouri, 40.

19. Transcription of the 1906 Special Grand Jury Report, Greene County Archives and Record Center, Springfield, Missouri, 25. In her book *White Women, Black Men: Illicit Sex in the Nineteenth-Century South,* the historian Martha Hodes argues that lower-class white women, especially those who defied the rules of patriarchy, "could not count on ideology about female purity to absolve them of illicit sexual activity" (203). Mina Edwards, a domestic servant from a poor farm family who was separated from her husband and out riding late at night with a strange man in the outskirts of Springfield, could only find safety in blaming black men for her assault when it was more than likely her white companion attempted to assault her. Her effort to remain sympathetic failed after Springfield was pilloried by the national media and local whites began to question her class standing and reputation.

20. Transcription of the 1906 Special Grand Jury Report, Greene County Archives and Record Center, Springfield, Missouri, 31.

21. Transcription of the 1906 Special Grand Jury Report, Greene County Archives and Record Center, Springfield, Missouri, 33, 46.

22. *Springfield Republican,* April 28, 1906, 1. According to a submitted family history of the Robert J. W. Reeves family of Polk County, Mina Edwards divorced William Edwards and remarried three more times before her death in 1969. Polk County Genealogical Society, *History & Families of Polk County, Missouri* (Paducah, KY: Turner Pub. Co., 2004), 308.

23. Transcription of the 1906 Special Grand Jury Report, Greene County Archives and Record Center, Springfield, Missouri, 14.

24. Transcription of the 1906 Special Grand Jury Report, Greene County Archives and Record Center, Springfield, Missouri, 19.

25. Transcription of the 1906 Special Grand Jury Report, Greene County Archives and Record Center, Springfield, Missouri, 32.

26. Transcription of the 1906 Special Grand Jury Report, Greene County Archives and Record Center, Springfield, Missouri.

27. Transcription of the 1906 Special Grand Jury Report, Greene County Archives and Record Center, Springfield, Missouri, 34.

28. *Springfield Leader,* May 24, 1906, 6.

29. *Springfield Leader,* May 24, 1906, 6.

30. *Springfield Leader,* May 24, 1906, 6.

31. *Springfield Republican,* May 24, 1906, 1. Seventeen men, in addition to Gooch and Galbraith, were identified as members of the lynch mob: Marshall Keesee, Ed H. Williams, Ike Thompson, Charles Cooper, Charles Potter, Dick Weddle, Oat Hall, Fred Stracke, Pea Ridge Newton, Ed Brumfield, George Queen, William "Tobe" Wimberly, Charles Comfort, John Gussom, Claude Egbert, Harry Hacker, and Guy Massey. *Springfield Republican,* December 25, 1909, 1.

32. *Springfield Republican,* May 24, 1906, 1; Greene County Criminal Court Record, Book 14, Greene County Archives and Records Center, Springfield, Missouri, 16, 68.

33. *Springfield Leader,* May 24, 1906, 1.

34. Will Allen, Horace Duncan, and Fred Coker, Coroner's Inquest, 1906, Greene County Archives and Records Center, Springfield, Missouri.

35. *Springfield Leader,* June 6, 1906, 1; *State v. Galbraith,* 1906, Greene County Archives and Records Center, Springfield, Missouri; *1906 Citizens' Directory Company, Springfield and Greene County Directory,* 108, 168, 326.

36. *Springfield Republican,* August 9, 1906, 1.

37. *Springfield Leader,* June 6, 1906, 1; *Springfield Republican,* June 6, 1906, 1. Newspaper accounts reported differing ages for Galbraith and Gooch, but I believe the ages I have listed are correct after consulting their death certificates. Death Certificate for Doss D. Galbraith, May 31, 1914, File No. 19106, Missouri State Archives; Death Certificate for John Hill Gooch, March 30, 1950, File No. 8291, Missouri State Archives.

38. *Springfield Leader,* June 6, 1906, 1; *Springfield Republican,* June 6, 1906, 1; *1906 Citizens' Directory Company, Springfield and Greene County Directory,*92, 214, 230, 482.

39. *State v. Galbraith,* 1906, Greene County Archives and Records Center, Springfield, Missouri; *Springfield Republican,* June 6, 1906, 1; *Springfield Republican,* June 8, 1906, 1. According to the article in the *Republican,* Galbraith worked as a special policeman under Springfield chief of police Brice C. Howell six years prior to the lynching. *1906 Citizens' Directory Company, Springfield and Greene County Directory* (Springfield, MO: Inland Printing & Binding Co., 1906), 37, 192, 262, 326, 469, 544.

40. *Springfield Republican,* June 8, 1906, 1; *1906 Citizens' Directory Company, Springfield and Greene County Directory* (Springfield, MO: Inland Printing & Binding Co., 1906), p. 523, 536.

41. *Springfield Republican,* June 10, 1906, 1, 3; *Springfield Leader,* June 10, 1906, 1.

42. *Springfield Leader,* June 10, 1906, 1.

43. *Springfield Republican,* June 10, 1906, 1. The expression "Kilkenny cat fight" refers to an Irish tale in which two cats fight so fiercely with each other that only their tails remain.

44. *Springfield Republican,* June 10, 1906, 1.

45. *Springfield Republican,* July 4, 1906, 5.

46. *Springfield Republican,* July 17, 1906, 1.

47. Walter B. Stevens, *Missouri, The Center State,* vol. 3 (Chicago: S. J. Clarke Publishing Co., 1915), 133–34.

48. *Springfield Leader and Press,* May 31, 1941, 10.

49. Walter Williams and Floyd C. Shoemaker, *Missouri, Mother of the West,* vol. 3 (Chicago: American Historical Society, 1930), 308–9.

50. William Rufus Jackson, *Missouri Democracy: A History of the Party and Its Representative Members, Past and Present,* vol. 2 (Chicago: S. J. Clarke Publishing Co., 1935), 142.

51. Fairbanks and Tuck, *Past and Present of Greene County,* 1383–84.

52. *Springfield Sunday News and Leader,* December 16, 1928, B4.

53. *Springfield Republican,* July 27, 1906, 1.

54. *Springfield Republican,* August 2, 1906, 1.

55. *Springfield Republican,* August 4, 1906, 1.

56. *Resources of Missouri: Photo and Biographical Sketches of Her State Officers and the Thirty-Eighth General Assembly* (St. Louis: J. H. McCracken, n.d.), 26; *Official State Manual of the State of Missouri 1911–1912* (Jefferson City, MO: Hugh Stephens Printing Co., 1912), 68.

57. *Springfield Republican,* August 8, 1906, 1.

58. *Springfield Leader,* August 2, 1906, 3.

59. *Springfield Leader,* August 2, 1906, 3.

60. *Springfield Leader,* July 22, 1906, 1; August 8, 1906, 1.

61. *Springfield Leader,* August 8, 1906, 1–2.

62. *Springfield Republican,* August 9, 1906, 1.

63. *Springfield Republican,* August 9, 1906, 1.

64. *Springfield Republican,* August 9, 1906, 10.

65. *Springfield Republican,* August 10, 1906, 1.

66. *Springfield Republican,* August 10, 1906, 1.

67. *Springfield Republican,* August 11, 1906, 5.

68. *Springfield Republican,* August 12, 1906, 1.

69. *Springfield Leader,* August 13, 1906, 1; *Springfield Leader,* August 17, 1906, 1; *1905 Hoye's Springfield City Directory,* 453. In the city directory, Simon B. Phifer is listed as the proprietor of Phifer's Real Estate Exchange.

70. *Springfield Leader,* August 14, 1906, 1.

71. *Springfield Leader,* August 17, 1906, 1.

72. *Springfield Leader,* August 14, 1906, 1.

73. *Springfield Leader,* August 17, 1906, 1; *St. Louis Republic,* August 25, 1906, 1.

74. *Springfield Leader,* August 17, 1906, 1.

75. *Springfield Leader,* August 20, 1906, 1–2; *Springfield Republican,* August 21, 1906, 1.

76. *Springfield Republican,* August 21, 1906, 1.

77. *Springfield Leader,* August 20, 1906, 1–2.

78. *Springfield Leader,* August 20, 1906, 1–2.

79. *Springfield Republican,* August 22, 1906, 1; *Springfield Leader,* August 21, 1906, 1.

80. *St. Louis Post-Dispatch,* August 21, 1906, 2.

81. *Springfield Republican,* August 22, 1906, 1.

82. *Springfield Republican,* August 22, 1906, 1; *Springfield Leader,* August 21, 1906, 1.

83. *Springfield Leader,* August 21, 1906, 6.

84. *Springfield Republican,* August 22, 1906, 1.

85. *Springfield Republican,* August 22, 1906, 1.

86. *Springfield Leader,* August 21, 1906, 8.

87. *St. Louis Republic,* August 21, 1906, 2.

88. *Springfield Leader,* August 21, 1906, 1.

89. *Springfield Leader,* August 22, 1906, 1.

90. Greene County Criminal Court Record, Book 10, Greene County Archives and Records Center, Springfield, Missouri, 213–14. Galbraith had been found guilty of disturbing the peace just four years earlier.

91. *Springfield Leader,* August 22, 1906, 1; *Springfield Republican,* August 23, 1906, 1.

92. *Springfield Leader,* August 22, 1906, 1–2.

93. *Springfield Leader,* August 22, 1906, 1–2.

94. *Springfield Republican,* August 22, 1906, 1.

95. *Springfield Republican,* August 23, 1906, 1.

96. *St. Louis Republic,* August 24, 1906, 1.

97. *St. Louis Republic,* August 24, 1906, 2.

98. *Springfield Leader,* August 23, 1906, 1.

99. *Springfield Leader,* August 23, 1906, 1.

100. *Springfield Leader,* August 23, 1906, 2.

101. *Springfield Leader,* August 23, 1906, 2.

102. *Springfield Leader,* August 23, 1906, 2.

103. *St. Louis Republic,* August 24, 1906, 1.

104. *Springfield Leader,* August 23, 1906, 2.

105. *Springfield Leader,* August 23, 1906, 2.

106. *Springfield Leader,* August 23, 1906, 2.

107. *Springfield Leader,* August 23, 1906, 2.

108. *Springfield Leader,* August 23, 1906, 2.

109. *Springfield Leader,* April 24, 1906, 2.

110. *St. Louis Republic,* August 24, 1906, 1.

111. *St. Louis Republic,* August 24, 1906, 1.

112. *Springfield Republican,* August 24, 1906, 3.

113. *Springfield Leader,* April 24, 1906, 2.

114. *Springfield Republican,* August 24, 1906, 3.

115. *Springfield Republican,* August 24, 1906, 3; *Springfield Leader,* April 24, 1906, 2.

116. *Springfield Leader,* April 24, 1906, 2.

117. *Springfield Leader,* April 24, 1906, 2; *Springfield Republican,* August 24, 1906, 3.

118. *Springfield Republican,* August 24, 1906, 3.

119. *St. Louis Post-Dispatch,* August 25, 1906, 1.

120. *Springfield Republican,* August 25, 1906, 1.

121. *Springfield Republican,* August 25, 1906, 1.

122. *St. Louis Post-Dispatch,* August 25, 1906, 1.

123. *St. Louis Post-Dispatch,* August 25, 1906, 2.

124. *St. Louis Post-Dispatch,* August 25, 1906, 2.

125. *St. Louis Globe-Democrat,* August 25, 1906, 8. An article in the *Springfield*

Leader confirms that as of September 1906 blacks were barred from Springfield saloons. The *Leader* mused, "Just what effect the excluding of all negroes from Springfield saloons would have is hard to say. It may result in the running of one or two saloons for the patronage, or it may bring about an opening of the illegal negro dives that flourished here some time ago." *Springfield Leader,* September 5, 1906, 2.

126. *St. Louis Post-Dispatch,* August 26, 1906, 2.

127. *St. Louis Post-Dispatch,* August 26, 1906, 2.

128. While researching her master's thesis in 1969, Mary Newland Clary was alerted to the existence of "two bronze discs commemorating the lynching." According to Clary, one of the discs was "dug up near the site of the Mayfield black-smith shop where Hill Gooch was employed." One of the discs is in the possession of Drury University in Springfield and refers to the lynching of Duncan, Coker, and Allen as an "Easter Offering." Clary, "The Easter Offering: A Missouri Lynching, 1906," 29.

129. Clary, "The Easter Offering: A Missouri Lynching, 1906," 29.

130. Scholar Amy Louise Wood points out that "mobs at mass spectacle lynch-ings" were often "dominated by skilled laborers, and white-collar workers—members of the rising middle class." Although these newly minted members of the middle class were not wealthy, "they were not under direct economic threat from black men, nor were they dependent on black labor." These men, often employed as managers, salesmen, and mechanics, had a sense of "moral propriety and self-discipline, as well as a sense of authority over their households, came to define their social worth and assure their social ascent. These traits, after all, distinguished them from poor whites and, most of all, from African Americans." Amy Louise Wood, *Lynching and Spectacle: Witnessing Racial Violence in America, 1890–1940* (Chapel Hill: University of North Carolina Press, 2009), 7.

131. *Springfield Leader,* August 17, 1906, 2.

132. *Springfield Leader,* August 18, 1906, 1.

133. *Springfield Leader,* September 23, 1906, 3.

134. *Springfield Leader,* November 3, 1906, 3.

135. *Springfield Leader,* November 1, 1906, 1.

136. *Springfield Leader,* November 4, 1906, 1.

137. *Springfield Republican,* November 8, 1906, 1.

138. *Springfield Republican,* November 7, 1906, 1. The only Republican who lost was former Springfield mayor Josiah E. Mellette, who challenged Democratic incumbent Frank M. McDavid. Mellette won Greene and Dade Counties, but McDavid successfully carried the remaining counties. *Springfield Republican,* November 7, 1906, 1.

139. *Springfield Republican,* October 19, 1912, 1; Death Certificate for Willard Caldwell, October 18, 1912, File No. 32676, Missouri State Archives; Death Certificate for Elmer Hancock, August 19, 1923, File No. 23942, Missouri State Archives.

140. *Springfield Republican,* August 25, 1907, 1.

141. *Springfield Republican,* December 25, 1909, 1; The names of the indicted men were kept secret at the time, but once the charges were dropped, their names became public knowledge: Marshall Keesee, Ed H. Williams, Ike Thompson, Charles Cooper, Charles Potter, Dick Weddle, Oat Hall, Fred Stracke, Pea Ridge Newton, Ed Brumfield, George Queen, William "Tobe" Wimberly, Charles Comfort, Claude Egbert, John Gussom, and Guy Massey.

142. Clary, "The Easter Offering: A Missouri Lynching, 1906," 42; Death Certificate for Doss Galbraith, May 31, 1914, File No. 19106, Missouri State Archives.

143. Death Certificate for John H. Gooch, March 30, 1950, File No. 8291, Missouri State Archives; Death Certificate for Harry M. Hacker, August 13, 1926, File No. 27519, Missouri State Archives.

144. Death Certificate for Charles Cannefax, February 27, 1947, File No. 2176, Missouri State Archives.

145. *Springfield Leader-Democrat,* July 31, 1935, 20.

146. Coroner's Jury Report for Oat Hall, Coroner's Index, Book 2, February 2, 1910, Greene County Archives.

147. *Springfield Republican,* May 24, 1911, 1.

148. *Springfield Republican,* May 29, 1918, 8; Death Certificate for Everett V. Horner, May 28, 1918, File No. 16748, Missouri State Archives.

149. *1932 Souvenir Review of the Department of Police, City of Springfield* (Springfield, MO: Allied Printing, 1932), 6, 8; Death Certificate for Henry C. Waddle, February 22, 1933, File No. 5469, Missouri State Archives.

150. *1932 Souvenir Review of the Department of Police, City of Springfield* (Springfield, MO: Allied Printing, 1932), 10; Death Certificate for William M. Bishop, November 30, 1939, File No. 39646, Missouri State Archives.

151. Fred T. Corum and Hazel E. Bakewell, *The Sparkling Fountain* (Springfield, MO: Corum & Associates, 1989), 125–26.

152. *Springfield Leader and Press,* August 31, 1941, 13.

153. *Springfield Sunday News and Leader,* December 16, 1928, B4.

154. *Springfield Leader,* November 28, 1910, 1.

155. *Springfield Leader-Democrat,* August 15, 1942, 8.

156. *Springfield Leader and Press,* May 31, 1941, 10.

157. *Springfield Leader and Press,* October 23, 1954, 8; Lawrence Christensen, et al., *The Dictionary of Missouri Biography* (Columbia: University of Missouri Press, 1999), 598–99.

158. *Springfield Republican,* July 2, 1906, 1.

159. Jack McCracken, Commutation File 877, Missouri State Archives, Jefferson City.

160. Jack McCracken, Commutation File 877, Missouri State Archives, Jefferson City.

161. Katherine Lederer, "Where Are We Going, Mr. Harper?" *Ozarks Watch,* 11, no. 3 & 4 (1998): 27.

162. *Springfield Daily Leader,* September 16, 1908, 8; *Springfield Republican,* August 4, 1908, 8; *J. R. Brake v. Nancy M. Brake,* Greene County Circuit Court, Case File 42121, September 17, 1908, Book 96, 476.

163. Thomas E. Baker, "Human Rights in Missouri: The Legislative, Judicial, and Administrative Development of Black Liberties" (Ph.D. dissertation, University of Missouri, 1975), 179–80.

164. Katherine Lederer, "Where Are We Going, Mr. Harper?", 27. Dr. Katherine Lederer, professor of English at Southwest Missouri State University, discovered that Clarence, the child of Anna Brake and Jack McCracken, still lived in Springfield. He was adopted by Moses and Louise Harper, an African American couple, and knew very little about his parentage.

165. *Springfield Leader,* October 17, 1930, 30.

166. *New York Times,* December 28, 1919, 1–5; B0147, Admission Registers for Prisoners to be Executed, 1891–1946, Number 70822, Frank Kelley, Sing Sing Prison, New York State Archives, Albany, New York, 269.

167. *New York Times,* December 28, 1919, 1, 5.

168. *New York Times,* December 28, 1919, 1, 5.

169. *New York Times,* January 1, 1920, 11.

170. *New York Times,* December 29, 1919, 6.

171. *New York Times,* January 6, 1920, 12.

172. *New York Times,* January 7, 1920, 4.

173. *New York Times,* January 9, 1920, 34.

174. *New York Times,* January 10, 1920, 8.

175. *New York Times,* August 27, 1920, 4; Daniel Allen Hearn, *Legal Executions in New York State* (Jefferson, NC: McFarland & Co., 1997), 151–52; B1244. Log of Actions Relating to Inmates Scheduled for Execution, 1915–1967, Number 70822, Frank Kelley, Sing Sing Prison, New York State Archives, Albany, New York; B0147. Admission registers for prisoners to be executed, 1891–1946, Number 70822, Frank Kelley, Sing Sing Prison, New York State Archives, Albany, New York, 269. Interestingly, Bus Cain lied up until his death. He listed his birthplace as Los Angeles, California, and his mother and siblings as residents of Los Angeles. His mother and siblings, however, were living in Springfield, Missouri, at the time of his execution according to Springfield city directories and census information.

176. *Springfield Republican,* September 3, 1920, 6; *Springfield Republican,* September 4, 1920, 9; *Springfield Leader,* September 2, 1920, 1. Frank Kelley's death certificate verifies that his body was shipped from Sing Sing to Springfield, Missouri, for burial on August 30, 1920. New York Department of Health, Death Certificate for Frank Kelley, August 26, 1920.

177. *Springfield Leader,* October 27, 1906, 1.

178. *Springfield Republican,* October 28, 1906, 1–2.

179. *Springfield Daily News,* February 26, 1932, 10. The "Old Timer" column recalled that "Bud Anderson was a power in politics in his day. In a ward fight he beat one of the most prominent Republican lawyers in the city which caused the lawyer to say he would not have had it to happen for $5. This incident gave Bud so much prominence that he became a newspaper feature and he complained that the Democratic press had about succeeded in destroying his influence."

180. *Springfield Daily News,* February 26, 1932, 10.

181. *Springfield Daily News,* February 26, 1932, 10.

182. *Springfield Republican,* March 11, 1907, 1.

183. *Springfield Republican,* March 12, 1907, 1.

ELEVEN • HARRISON: "THEIR VOICES FILLED THE AIR"

1. Ralph R. Rea, *Boone County and Its People* (Van Buren, AR: Press-Argus, 1955), 95–96.

2. Goodspeed Publishing Co, *A Reminiscent History of the Ozark Region* (Chicago: Goodspeed Bros., 1894), 331–32.

3. Rea, *Boone County and Its People,* 95–96.

4. Rea, *Boone County and Its People,* 97.

5. Rea, *Boone County and Its People,* 99–100.

6. Robert R. Mackey, *The Uncivil War: Irregular Warfare in the Upper South, 1861–1865* (Norman: University of Oklahoma Press, 2004), 62.

7. Rea, *Boone County and Its People,* 99–100.

8. Rea, *Boone County and Its People,* 100–101.

9. Rea, *Boone County and Its People,* 83–84.

10. *A Reminiscent History of the Ozark Region,* 118, 123.

11. Rea, *Boone County and Its People,* 83.

12. Rea, *Boone County and Its People,* 85–86. Moses Hopper, the father of Gillum and James Hopper, was killed by bushwhackers during the war for his Unionist sympathies. Both Gillum and James signed up for service with the Union army, although their brother Archibald reportedly served with the Confederate army. See *A Reminiscent History of the Ozark Region,* 511–12.

13. *A Reminiscent History of the Ozark Region,* 118, 123.

14. *A Reminiscent History of the Ozark Region,* 118.

15. Ralph R. Rea, "Sidelights on Boone County History," *Arkansas Historical Quarterly* 13, no. 1 (Spring 1954): 69. The term "navies" refer to the Colt navy revolvers that many of the men carried.

16. Thomas A. DeBlack, *With Fire and Sword: Arkansas, 1861–1874* (Fayetteville: University of Arkansas Press, 2003), 228.

17. Gordon D. Morgan, *Black Hillbillies of the Arkansas Ozarks* (Fayetteville: University of Arkansas Department of Sociology, 1973), 24, 61–62.

18. Rea, "Sidelights on Boone County History," 119–20.

19. Jesse Lewis Russell, *Behind These Ozarks Hills* (New York: Hobson Book Press, 1947), 36.

20. Rea, "Sidelights on Boone County History," 121.

21. *Harrison Times,* September 12, 1885, 4.

22. Clyde R. Newman, *One Hundred Years: A History of the Methodist Church in Harrison, Arkansas* (Harrison, AR: Times Publishing Co., 1973), 31.

23. Russell, *Behind These Ozarks Hills,* 34.

24. Brooks Blevins, *Hillfolks: A History of Arkansas Ozarkers and Their Image* (Chapel Hill: University of North Carolina Press, 2002), 74.

25. Russell, *Behind These Ozarks Hills,* 37. The railroad later became the Missouri and North Arkansas (MNA) Railroad.

26. Russell, *Behind These Ozarks Hills,* 33–34.

27. *Berryville Star Progress,* November 30, 1950, 3.

28. Robert G. Winn, *Railroads of Northwest Arkansas* (Fayetteville, AR: Washington County Historical Society, 1986), 83.

29. James R. Fair Jr., *The North Arkansas Line: The Story of the Missouri and North Arkansas Railroad* (Berkeley, CA: Howell-North Books, 1969), 38.

30. Rea, "Sidelights on Boone County History," 139.

31. Timothy P. Donovan and Willard B. Gatewood Jr., *The Governors of Arkansas: Essays in Political Biography* (Fayetteville: University of Arkansas Press, 1981), 114.

32. Ayers, *Promise of the New South,* 412.

33. Donovan and Gatewood, *The Governors of Arkansas,* 118.

34. Raymond Arsenault, *The Wild Ass of the Ozarks: Jeff Davis and the Social Bases of Southern Politics* (Knoxville: University of Tennessee Press, 1988), 211–13.

35. Froelich and Zimmerman, "Total Eclipse," 147. Froelich and Zimmerman state, "For most of the cases heard by this grand jury, complete notes of the witnesses' testimony exist in the recorded minutes . . . In the matter of Harrison's mob violence, the record consists of a note handwritten by the grand jury foreman, Max Dampf of Searcy County."

36. *Marshall Mountain Wave,* October 14, 1905, 1; *Springfield Leader,* October 9, 1905, 5. The article, which was reprinted from the *Harrison Times,* refers to "last Saturday," which seems to indicate that Richards was killed on September 30, 1905, the same day that Dan broke into Dr. Johnson's home.

37. *Arkansas Gazette,* October 6, 1905, 1. This article most likely appeared in the *Harrison Daily Times.*

38. Loren Watkins, "Some History of Boone County, Arkansas," *Boone County Historian* 7, no. 1 (1984): 282.

39. Watkins, "Some History of Boone County, Arkansas," 282.

40. Rea, *Boone County and Its People,* 141–42.

41. *Marshall Mountain Wave,* October 14, 1905, 1.

42. *Arkansas Gazette,* October 6, 1905, 1.

43. Froelich and Zimmerman, "Total Eclipse," 145.

44. Fay Hempstead, *Historical Review of Arkansas,* vol. 1 (Chicago: Lewis Publishing Co., 1911), 463. Rogers died in his sleep at Little Rock on April 17, 1911, while "holding court for Judge Trieber."

45. Hempstead, *Historical Review of Arkansas,* vol. 3, 1298–99.

46. Froelich and Zimmerman, "Total Eclipse," 147–48.

47. Rea, *Boone County and Its People,* 141.

48. Roger B. Logan Jr., *History of Boone County, Arkansas* (Paducah, KY: Turner Publishing Co., 1998), 49.

49. *Springfield Republican,* January 19, 1909, 1. The article most likely was reprinted from the *Harrison Times.*

50. *Arkansas Gazette,* January 29, 1909, 1; January 19, 1909, 1.

51. *Springfield Republican,* January 19, 1909, 1.

52. *Springfield Republican,* January 19, 1909, 1.

53. *Twelfth Census of the United States, 1900, Population Schedule,* "Marion County, Arkansas" (Washington, D.C.: National Archives and Records Administration, Roll T623–67).

54. *Springfield Republican,* January 19, 1909, 1.

55. *Twelfth Census of the United States, 1900, Population Schedule,* "Boone County, Arkansas" (Washington, D.C.: National Archives and Records Administration, Roll T623–51); *Harrison Daily Times,* February 28, 1941, 1. The obituary remarked that she still resided on the original Lovett homestead, but no mention was made of Charley Stinnett or the events of 1909. Lovett was buried in Maplewood Cemetery.

56. *Springfield Republican,* January 19, 1909, 2.

57. *Arkansas Gazette,* January 22, 1909, 1.

58. *Arkansas Gazette,* January 23, 1909, 1.

59. *Arkansas Gazette,* January 29, 1909, 1.

60. *Arkansas Gazette,* January 29, 1909, 1. Just a few years later, in 1911, Dick

Fancher died in Eureka Springs, Arkansas. He was buried in the Eureka Springs Colored Cemetery in a lot purchased by Colonel J. Polk Fancher, the son of his former owner, James Fancher. Dick Fancher was hailed as an "honest, good darkey, respected by all who knew him." *North Arkansas Star,* May 5, 1911, n.p.

61. *Arkansas Gazette,* March 25, 1909, 1.

62. *Arkansas Gazette,* March 25, 1909, 1.

63. *Arkansas Gazette,* March 23, 1909, 1.

64. *Springfield Republican,* March 25, 1909, 1.

65. *Arkansas Gazette,* March 25, 1909, 1.

66. *Springfield Republican,* March 25, 1909, 1. The article originally ran in the *Harrison Times* on March 24, 1909.

67. *Thirteenth Census of the United States, 1910, Population Schedule,* "Muskogee County, Oklahoma" (Washington, D.C.: National Archives and Records Administration, Roll T624–1264).

68. Death Certificate for Lettie Stinnett, May 3, 1937, File No. 20366, Missouri State Archives.

69. Death Certificate for Tom Stinnett, April 23, 1942, File No. 14654, Missouri State Archives.

70. Brooks R. Blevins, "The Strike and the Still: Anti-Radical Violence and the Ku Klux Klan in the Ozarks,"*Arkansas Historical Quarterly* 52 (Winter 1993): 409. For more on the Harrison strike, see Orville Thrasher Gooden, *The Missouri and North Arkansas Railroad Strike, Studies in History, Economics, and Public Law* (New York: Columbia University Press, 1926); J. K. Farris, *The Harrison Riot, or The Reign of the Mob on the Missouri and North Arkansas Railroad* (Wynne, AR: 1924); Walter F. Bradley, *An Industrial War: History of the Missouri and North Arkansas Railroad Strike and a Study of the Tremendous Issues Involved: An Unprecedented Result of a Common Occurrence in American Industry and its Aftermath* (Harrison, AR: Bradley & Russell, 1923).

71. Blevins, "The Strike and the Still," 412.

72. Blevins, "The Strike and the Still," 425.

73. Russell, *Behind These Ozark Hills,* 34.

74. Morgan, *Black Hillbillies of the Arkansas Ozarks,* 64.

75. Morgan, *Black Hillbillies of the Arkansas Ozarks,* 63–66. The sociologist Gordon D. Morgan asserts, "The changing economic base of Arkansas as a whole and the failure of large scale industry, whether farming or manufacturing, to be established in the northern counties, are probably as responsible for the development of 'gray towns' as any overt action on the part of white people to deny black people the right to live and work in these towns."

76. Rea, *Boone County and Its People,* 143–44; Morgan, *Black Hillbillies of the Arkansas Ozarks,* 62.

TWELVE · CONCLUSION

1. *The Ozarks Mountaineer,* June 1952, v. 1, no. 3, p. 4.

2. *The Ozarks Mountaineer,* August 1952 v. 1, no. 4, p. 4.

3. *The Ozarks Mountaineer,* August 1952 v. 1, no. 4, p. 4.

4. *The Ozarks Mountaineer,* August 1952 v. 1, no. 4, p. 4.

5. *The Ozarks Mountaineer,* August 1952 v. 1, no. 4, p. 4.

6. *Springfield Daily News,* November 22, 1932, 6.

7. Charles Morrow Wilson, *The Bodacious Ozarks: True Tales of the Backhills* (New York: Hastings House, 1959), 10.

8. Department of Commerce, *Thirteenth Census of the United States 1910 Vol. 2 Population 1910 Alabama–Montana* (Washington, D.C.: Government Printing Office, 1913). Table I—Composition and Characteristics of the Population for the State and for Counties, 1109.

9. Department of Commerce, *Fourteenth Census of the United States Vol. 3 Population 1920* (Washington, D.C.: Government Printing Office, 1922), 555.

10. Department of Commerce, *Fifteenth Census of the United States 1930, Population Vol. 3, Part I, Alabama–Missouri* (Washington, D.C.: Government Printing Office, 1932), 1332.

11. Department of Commerce, *Thirteenth Census of the United States 1910 Vol. 2 Population 1910 Alabama–Montana* (Washington, D.C.: Government Printing Office, 1913). Table I—Composition and Characteristics of the Population for the State and for Counties, 1110.

12. Department of Commerce, *Fourteenth Census of the United States Vol. 3 Population 1920* (Washington, D.C.: Government Printing Office, 1922), 556.

13. Department of Commerce, *Fifteenth Census of the United States 1930, Population Vol. 3, Part I, Alabama–Missouri* (Washington, D.C.: Government Printing Office, 1932), 1332.

14. Department of the Interior, *Twelfth Census of the United States 1900, Volume I, Population Part I* (Washington, D.C.: Government Printing Office, 1901), Table 19, pg 546.

15. Department of Commerce, *Fourteenth Census of the United States Vol. 3 Population 1920* (Washington, D.C.: Government Printing Office, 1922), 551–58.

16. Department of Commerce, *Fourteenth Census of the United States Vol. 3 Population 1920* (Washington, D.C.: Government Printing Office, 1922), 551–58.

17. *St. Louis Post-Dispatch,* August 25, 1901, 1.

18. Loewen, *Sundown Towns,* 92–93.

19. Brundage, *Lynching in the New South,* 1.

20. Christensen and Kremer, *A History of Missouri,* 179–80.

21. Hodes, *White Women, Black Men,* 6.

22. Brundage, *Lynching in the New South,* 60.

23. Brooks Blevins, "Revisting Race Relations in an Upland South Community," in *History and Hope in the Heart of Dixie* (Tuscaloosa: The University of Alabama Press, 2002), 5. Ozarks scholar Blevins offers insight into why at least one community in the southern Ozarks did not experience racial unrest.

24. Charles Neider, ed., *The Complete Essays of Mark Twain* (Garden City, NY: Doubleday, 1963), 673. The essay was entitled, "The United State of Lyncherdom."

BIBLIOGRAPHY

PRIMARY SOURCES

Archival Collections

1897 Revised Ordinances, Springfield, Missouri. Springfield: n.p.

B0147, Admission Registers for Prisoners to be Executed, 1891–1946, Number 70822, Frank Kelley, Sing Sing Prison, New York State Archives, Albany, New York.

B1244, Log of Actions Relating to Inmates Scheduled for Execution, 1915–1967, Number 70822, Frank Kelley, Sing Sing Prison, New York State Archives, Albany, New York.

Coroner's Inquest for Will Allen, Horace Duncan, and Fred Coker, 1906, Greene County Archives and Records Center, Springfield, Missouri.

Death Certificate for William Abbott, July 9, 1916, File No. 27024, Missouri State Archives.

Death Certificate for Albert B. Appleby, October 26, 1920, File No. 31464, Missouri State Archives.

Death Certificate for Bartimeus H. Barnes, January 12, 1935, File No. 1737, Missouri State Archives.

Death Certificate for Si Bearden, January 10, 1936, File No. 973, Missouri State Archives.

Death Certificate for William M. Bishop, November 30, 1939, File No. 39646, Missouri State Archives.

Death Certificate for Willard Caldwell, October 18, 1912, File No. 32676, Missouri State Archives.

Death Certificate for Charles Cannefax, February 27, 1947, File No. 2176, Missouri State Archives.

Death Certificate for William T. Chandler, July 3, 1926, File No. 22187, Missouri State Archives.

Death Certificate for Joseph C. Dodson, May 10, 1911, File No. 17536, Missouri State Archives.

Death Certificate for Doss D. Galbraith, May 31, 1914, File No. 19106, Missouri State Archives.

Death Certificate for John Hill Gooch, March 30, 1950, File No. 8291, Missouri State Archives.

Death Certificate for Harry M. Hacker, August 13, 1926, File No. 27519, Missouri State Archives.

Death Certificate for Elmer Hancock, August 19, 1923, File No. 23942, Missouri State Archives.

Death Certificate for William E. Harlow, December 23, 1922, File No. 34043, Missouri State Archives.

Death Certificate for Beedie Hampton, June 8, 1950, File No. 20232, Missouri State Archives.

Death Certificate for Everett V. Horner, May 28, 1918, File No. 16748, Missouri State Archives.

Death Certificate for Charles A. Hubbard, February 13, 1931, File No. 5198, Missouri State Archives.

Death Certificate for Odie Lark, July 3, 1913, File No. 22625, Missouri State Archives.

Death Certificate for Fred H. Marshall, September 4, 1916, File No. 30914, Missouri State Archives.

Death Certificate for August A. Mehl, January 3, 1930, File No. 2347, Missouri State Archives.

Death Certificate for Samuel Kirkwood Mitchell, December 28, 1926, File No. 38525, Missouri State Archives.

Death Certificate for Lettie Stinnett, May 3, 1937, File No. 20366, Missouri State Archives.

Death Certificate for Tom Stinnett, April 23, 1942, File No. 14654, Missouri State Archives.

Death Certificate for Mary Thomas, December 13, 1910, File No. 38993, Missouri State Archives.

Death Certificate for Henry C. Waddle, February 22, 1933, File No. 5469, Missouri State Archives.

Death Certificate for Charles A. Walterhouse, January 19, 1920, File No. 699, Missouri State Archives.

Death Certificate for Sarah Woods, January 3, 1920, File No. 951, Missouri State Archives.

Jack McCracken, Commutation File 877, Missouri State Archives, Jefferson City.

Jonathan Fairbanks Diary, Fairbanks Collection, The History Museum for Springfield- Greene County, Missouri.

Marriage Record for Nathaniel Woods and Sarah Godley, Jackson County, Missouri.

Missouri State Archives. *Missouri State Penitentiary, Dressing Register, Volume R, 1891–1893.*

Missouri State Archives. *Missouri State Penitentiary, Record of Inmates, Volume R, 1891–1893.*

Missouri State Archives. Entry for inmate Jack McCracken, aged 43 years, native of

Arkansas; Vol. 5870–7567, p. 202; *Register of Inmates Received, 1836–1931;* Missouri State Penitentiary, Record Group 213.

Missouri State Archives. State Training Schools for Boys, Alphabetical Register Number 20, "George McGee, Number 2034."

Missouri State Archives. Pvt. Francis E. Rohan, Co. D, Twenty-Seventh Engineers, Service Card.

Records of the Proceedings of the City Council, Springfield, Missouri, Book 18.

Reuben T. Peak, *Autobiographical Memories of Reuben T. Peak,* unpublished, The History Museum for Springfield-Greene County, Springfield, Missouri.

Perl Decker Papers, Western Historical Manuscript Collection, Ellis Library, University of Missouri-Columbia.

Katherine G. Lederer Ozarks African American History Collection, Special Collections and Archives, Missouri State University.

State Reports

Missouri. *State Almanac and Official Directory of Missouri for 1878.* St. Louis: John J. Daly & Co., 1879.

Missouri. *Official Directory of Missouri for 1881.* St. Louis: John J. Daly & Co., 1881.

Missouri. *Official Manual of the State of Missouri for the Years 1891–92.* Jefferson City: Tribune Printing Co., 1891.

Missouri. *Official Manual of the State of Missouri for the Years 1895–96.* Jefferson City: Tribune Printing Co., 1895.

Missouri. *Official Manual of the State of Missouri for the Years 1897–98.* Jefferson City: Tribune Printing Co., 1897.

Missouri. *Official Manual of the State of Missouri for the Years 1901–1902.* Jefferson City: Tribune Printing Co., 1901.

Missouri. *Official State Manual of the State of Missouri 1911–1912.* Jefferson City, MO: Hugh Stephens Printing Co., 1912.

Missouri. *Official Manual of the State of Missouri, 1919–1920.* Jefferson City, MO: Office of the Secretary of State, 1920.

Missouri. *Report of the Adjutant-General of the State of Missouri for the Year 1901.* Jefferson City: Tribune Printing Co., 1902.

Missouri. *Report of the Adjutant-General of the State of Missouri for the Year 1905–1906.* Jefferson City, MO: Hugh Stephens Printing Company, 1906.

Missouri. *Report of the Superintendent of Public Schools of the State of Missouri to the Twenty-Fifth General Assembly.* Jefferson City, MO: Ellwood Kirby, 1869.

Missouri National Guard. *History of the Missouri National Guard.* Jefferson City, n.p., 1934.

———. *The Adjutants General of Missouri, 1820–1987.* Jefferson City, MO: Missouri Army National Guard, 1987.

Court Records

1905 Grand Jury Report, Greene County Archives and Records Center, Springfield, Missouri.

1906 Grand Jury Report, Greene County Archives and Record Center, Springfield, Missouri.

America Godley v. Rodgers, 1902, Jasper County Circuit Court, Jasper County Records Center, Carthage, Missouri.

"Record of Bills of Cost on Information 1898–1901," Lawrence County Historical Society, Mt. Vernon, Missouri.

J. R. Brake v. Nancy M. Brake, Greene County Circuit Court, Case File 42121, September 17, 1908, Book 96.

Coroner's Jury Report for Oat Hall, Coroner's Index, Book 2, February 2, 1910, Greene County Archives.

Greene County Criminal Court Record, Book 10, Greene County Archives and Records Center, Springfield, Missouri.

Greene County Criminal Court Record, Book 14, Greene County Archives and Records Center, Springfield, Missouri.

Henry Godley v. The City of Pittsburg, 1903, Crawford County District Court, Crawford County Courthouse, Girard, Kansas.

Sarah Godley v. Rodgers, 1902, Jasper County Circuit Court, Jasper County Records Center, Carthage, Missouri.

Beedie Hampton v. Rodgers, 1902, Jasper County Circuit Court, Jasper County Records Center, Carthage, Missouri.

State ex rel. Snyder v. Aldermen of Pierce City, 3 S.W. 849 (1887).

State v. Lark, 1901, Lawrence County Circuit Court, Lawrence County Courthouse, Mt. Vernon, Missouri.

State v. Galbraith, 1906, Greene County Archives and Records Center, Springfield, Missouri.

Transcription of the 1906 Special Grand Jury Report, Greene County Archives and Record Center, Springfield, Missouri.

Census

Ninth Census of the United States, 1880, Population Schedule, "Greene County, Missouri." Washington, D.C.: National Archives and Records Administration, Roll M593 777.

Tenth Census of the United States, 1880, Population Schedule, "Lawrence County, Missouri." Washington, D.C.: National Archives and Records Administration, Roll T9–698.

Tenth Census of the United States, 1880, Population Schedule, "St. Louis County, Missouri." Washington, D.C.: National Archives and Records Administration, Roll T9–727.

Twelfth Census of the United States, 1900, Population Schedule, "Marion County, Arkansas." Washington, D.C.: National Archives and Records Administration, Roll T623–67.

Twelfth Census of the United States, 1900, Population Schedule, "Greene County, Missouri." Washington, D.C.: National Archives and Records Administration, Roll T623–856.

Twelfth Census of the United States, 1900, Population Schedule, "Jasper County." National Archives Microfilm Publication T623, roll 865.

Twelfth Census of the United States, 1900, Population Schedule, "Lawrence County" National Archives Microfilm Publication T623, roll 870.

Thirteenth Census of the United States, 1910, Population Schedule, "Muskogee County, Oklahoma." Washington, D.C.: National Archives and Records Administration, Roll T624–1264.

Thirteenth Census of the United States, 1910, Population Schedule, "Lawrence County." National Archives Microfilm Publication T624, roll 795.

Fourteenth Census of the United States, 1920, Population Schedule, "Lawrence County." National Archives Microfilm Publication T625, roll 932.

Department of the Census. *Negro Population 1790—1915.* Washington, D.C.: Government Printing Office, 1918.

Department of Commerce. *Seventh Census of the United States, 1850, Population Schedule.* Washington, D.C.: Government Printing Office, 1853. Table I—Population by Counties—Ages, Color, and Condition—Aggregates—Continued.

Department of Commerce. *Ninth Census of the United States, 1870, Population Schedule.* Washington, D.C.: Government Printing Office, 1872. Table III—Population of Civil Divisions Less Than Counties.

Department of Commerce. *Thirteenth Census of the United States 1910 Vol. 2 Population 1910 Alabama—Montana.* Washington, D.C.: Government Printing Office, 1913. Table I—Composition and Characteristics of the Population for the State and for Counties.

Department of Commerce. *Fourteenth Census of the United States Vol. 3 Population 1920.* Washington, D.C.: Government Printing Office, 1922.

Department of Commerce. *Fifteenth Census of the United States 1930, Population Vol. 3, Part I, Alabama–Missouri.* Washington, D.C.: Government Printing Office, 1932.

Department of the Interior. *Twelfth Census of the United States 1900,* Volume I, Population Part I. Washington, D.C.: Government Printing Office, 1901, Table 23, pg 625.

Pension file, John Farnsworth, Fourth Regiment U.S. Colored Volunteer Heavy Artillery, United States Army, NARA Record Group 15: Records of the Department of Veterans Affairs, 1773–2001.

Pension file, Alexander Kelly, 115th Regiment U.S. Colored Volunteer Infantry, United States Army, NARA Record Group 15: Records of the Department of Veterans Affairs, 1773–2001.

Pension file, George Page, Thirteenth Regiment U.S. Colored Volunteer Heavy
    Artillery, United States Army, NARA Record Group 15: Records of the
    Department of Veterans Affairs, 1773–2001.

Pension file, Washington Robison, 109th U.S. Colored Volunteer Infantry, United
    States Army, NARA Record Group 15: Records of the Department of Veterans
    Affairs, 1773–2001.

Pension file, Obediah P. Ruark, Thirty-first Indiana Infantry, United States Army,
    NARA Record Group 15: Records of the Department of Veterans Affairs,
    1773–2001.

Pension file, John Scott, 108th U.S. Colored Volunteer Infantry, United States Army,
    NARA Record Group 15: Records of the Department of Veterans Affairs,
    1773–2001.

United States Census Office. *Compendium of the Tenth Census.* Washington, D.C.:
    Government Printing Office, 1883., 392.

Directories

Appendix, Hoye's 1890–1891, 1892–1893, and 1899–1900 Springfield City Directories.

1888–1889 Hoye's City Directory of Springfield, Missouri. Kansas City: Hoye
    Directory Co., 1889.

1900 Hoye's City Directory of Joplin and Carthage, Missouri. Kansas City: Hoye
    Directory Company.

1903 Hoye's City Directory of Joplin and Carthage, Missouri. Kansas City: Hoye
    Directory Company.

1903 Hoye's Springfield City Directory. Kansas City: Hoye Directory Company.

1904 Hoye's Springfield City Directory. Kansas City: Hoye Directory Company.

1905 Hoye's Springfield City Directory. Springfield, MO: Hoye's Directory Company.

1906 Citizens' Directory Company, Springfield and Greene County Directory.
    Springfield, MO: Inland Printing & Binding Co., 1906.

Newspapers

Arkansas Democrat, 1905, 1909

Arkansas Gazette, 1905, 1909

Berryville Star Progress, 1950

Carthage Evening Press, 1901–1903, 1906

Cassville Republican, July 1894, October 1901

Chicago Tribune, August 1901

Fayetteville Democrat Weekly, August 1901

Harrison Times, 1885

Joplin Daily Globe, August 1901, September 1902, April 1903, March 1907

Joplin Daily News Herald, May 1900, April 1903

Joplin Globe, January 1929, August 1934, May 1949

Kansas City Star, 1906

Knob Noster Gem, July 28, 1899

Lawrence County Chieftain, August–September 1894, July 1899, November 1901

Lawrence Chieftain, March 1905, September 1929

Marshall Mountain Wave, 1905

Missouri Patriot, January 1866, June 1871

Missouri Weekly Patriot (Springfield), June 1868, August 1870, April 1874

Mt. Vernon Fountain and Journal, September 1889, September 1891

Monett Times, August–September 1901, January 1951

Neosho Miner and Mechanic, April 1887, August 1901

Neosho Times, October 1871, July 1894

New York Times, 1919, 1920

North Arkansas Star, 1909

Peirce City Democrat, April 1903

Peirce City Weekly Empire, 1877–1902

Pierce City Leader-Journal, 1917, 1923, 1925, 1934

Pittsburg Daily Headlight, 1901–1903

The Southwest Journal, 1912–1916

St. Louis Globe-Democrat, October 1887, 1906

St. Louis Post-Dispatch, 1887–1903, 1906

St. Louis Republic, 1906

Springfield Express, October 1882, April 1888

Springfield Daily Herald, August 1888

Springfield Daily Leader, March 1888, August 1888, July 1898

Springfield Daily News, 1932

Springfield Leader-Democrat, 1900, 1901, 1902, 1903, 1935, 1942

Springfield Leader, 1904, 1905, 1906, 1908

Springfield Leader and Press, 1941

Springfield Patriot-Advertiser, March 1883

Springfield Republican, April 1888, August 1888, August 1895, July 1898, April 1906, December 1909, September 1924, June 1926

Springfield Sunday News and Leader, 1928.

Springfield Weekly Leader, April 1870

Stotts City Sunbeam, August–November 1901

SECONDARY SOURCES

Books

1932 *Souvenir Review of the Department of Police, City of Springfield.* Springfield, MO: Allied Printing, 1932.

Arsenault, Raymond. *The Wild Ass of the Ozarks: Jeff Davis and the Social Bases of Southern Politics.* Knoxville: University of Tennessee Press, 1988.

Ayers, Edward L. *The Promise of the New South: Life after Reconstruction.* New York: Oxford University Press, 1992.

Benedict, John Downing. *Muskogee and Northeastern Oklahoma.* Chicago: S. J. Clarke, 1922.

Blevins, Brooks. *Hillfolks: A History of Arkansas Ozarkers and Their Image.* Chapel Hill: University of North Carolina Press, 2002.

Brown, Miriam Keast. *The Story of Pierce City, Missouri, 1870–1970.* Cassville, MO: Litho Printers, 1970.

Brundage, W. Fitzhugh. *Lynching in the New South Georgia and Virginia, 1880–1930,* Chicago: University of Illinois Press, 1993.

Capeci, Dominic J. *The Lynching of Cleo Wright.* Lexington: University Press of Kentucky, 1998.

Christensen, Lawrence et al. *The Dictionary of Missouri Biography.* Columbia: University of Missouri Press, 1999.

Christensen, Lawrence O., and Gary R. Kremer. *A History of Missouri: Volume IV, 1875 to 1919.* Columbia: University of Missouri Press, 1997.

Compton, Lem. *1880 Federal Census: Lawrence County, Missouri.* Mt. Vernon, MO: Lawrence County Historical Society.

Conard, Howard L., ed. *Encyclopedia of the History of Missouri,* vol. 4. New York: Southern Historical Pub. Co., 1901.

———. *Encyclopedia of the History of Missouri,* vol. 5. New York: Southern Historical Pub. Co., 1901.

———. *Encyclopedia of the History of St. Louis.* New York: The Southern Historical Pub. Co., 1899.

Corum, Fred T., and Hazel E. Bakewell. *The Sparkling Fountain.* Springfield, MO: Corum & Associates, 1989.

Cosmas, Graham A. *An Army for Empire: The United States Army in the Spanish-American War.* Columbia: University of Missouri Press, 1971.

Coulter, Charles E. *"Take Up the Black Man's Burden": Kansas City's African American Communities, 1865–1939.* Columbia: University of Missouri Press, 2006.

DeBlack, Thomas A. *With Fire and Sword: Arkansas, 1861–1874.* Fayetteville: University of Arkansas Press, 2003.

Donovan, Timothy P., and Willard B. Gatewood Jr. *The Governors of Arkansas: Essays in Political Biography.* Fayetteville: University of Arkansas Press, 1981.

Easley, Barbara P. *Obituaries of Benton County, Arkansas: Volume One 1884–1898.* Edited by Barbara P. Easley and Verla P. McAnelly. Bowie, MD: Heritage Books, 1994.

Escott, George S. *History and Directory of Springfield and North Springfield.* Springfield, MO: Office of the Patriot-Advertiser, 1878.

Fairbanks, Jonathan, and Clyde Edwin Tuck. *Past and Present of Greene County, Missouri.* Indianapolis: A. W. Bowen, 1915.

Gatewood, Willard B., Jr. *Black Americans and the White Man's Burden, 1898–1903.* Urbana: University of Illinois Press, 1975.

Gibson, Arrell M. *Wilderness Bonanza: The Tri-State District of Missouri, Kansas, and Oklahoma.* Norman: University of Oklahoma, 1972.

Gilmore, Robert K. *Ozark Baptizings, Hangings, and Other Diversions: Theatrical Folkways of Rural Missouri, 1885–1910.* Norman: University of Oklahoma Press, 1984.

Gerlach, Russell L. *Immigrants in the Ozarks: A Study in Ethnic Geography.* Columbia: University of Missouri Press, 1976.

Goodspeed Publishing Co. *Pictorial and Genealogical Record of Greene County, Missouri.* Chicago: Goodspeed Publishing Co., 1893.

———. *History of Laclede, Camden, Dallas, Webster, Wright, Texas, Pulaski, Phelps, and Dent Counties, Missouri.* Chicago: Goodspeed Publishing Co., 1889.

———. *History of Newton, Lawrence, Barry and McDonald Counties, Missouri,* Chicago: Goodspeed Publishing Co., 1888.

———. *A Reminiscent History of the Ozark Region.* Chicago: Goodspeed Bros., 1894.

Greene County Archives and Records Center. *Index to Superintendent's Register, Greene County, Missouri Alms House,* Bulletin No. 12, Springfield, MO: Greene County Archives Bulletin, Office of the County Clerk.

———. *Black Families of the Ozarks,* vol. 3-A. Springfield, MO: Greene County Archives & Records Center, Office of the County Clerk.

Greene, Lorenzo J., Gary R. Kremer, and Antonio F. Holland. *Missouri's Black Heritage,* revised edition. Columbia: University of Missouri Press, 1993.

Hall, William Kearney. *Springfield, Greene County, Missouri Inhabitants in 1880.* St. Louis: n.p., 1966.

Hearn, Daniel Allen. *Legal Executions in New York State.* Jefferson, NC: McFarland & Co., 1997.

Hempstead, Fay. *Historical Review of Arkansas,* vol. 1. Chicago: Lewis Publishing Co., 1911.

History of Holt and Atchison Counties, Missouri. St. Joseph, MO: National Historical Company, 1882.

Hodes, Martha. *White Women, Black Men: Illicit Sex in the Nineteenth-Century South.* New Haven, CT: Yale University Press, 1997.

Holcombe, R. I. *History of Greene County, Missouri.* St. Louis: Western Historical Co., 1883.

Interstate Historical Society. *History of Lawrence County, Missouri.* Springfield, MO: Interstate Historical Society, 1917.

Jackson, William Rufus. *Missouri Democracy: A History of the Party and Its Representative Members—Past and Present,* vol. 2 & 3. Chicago: S. J. Clarke Publishing Co., 1935.

Jaspin, Elliot. *Buried in the Bitter Waters: The Hidden History of Racial Cleansing in America.* New York: Basic Books, 2007.

Kessyar, Alexander. *The Right To Vote: The Contested History of Democracy in the United States.* USA: Basic Books, 2000.

Lederer, Katherine. *Many Thousand Gone: Springfield's Lost Black History.* S.l: s.n., 1986.

Leonard, John W., ed. *The Book of St. Louisians.* St. Louis: St. Louis Republic, 1906.

Lewis Publishing Company. *History and Biographical Record of North and West Texas.* Chicago: Lewis Publishing Co., 1906.

Livingston, Joel T. *A History of Jasper County Missouri and Its People,* vol. 2. New York: Lewis Publishing Co., 1912.

Loewen, James W. *Sundown Towns: A Hidden Dimension of American Racism.* New York: Touchstone, 2006.

Logan, Roger B., Jr. *History of Boone County, Arkansas.* Paducah, KY: Turner Publishing Co., 1998.

McGregor, Malcolm G. *The Biographical Record of Jasper County, Missouri.* Chicago: Lewis Pub. Co., 1901.

Mackey, Robert R. *The Uncivil War: Irregular Warfare in the Upper South, 1861–1865.* Norman: University of Oklahoma Press, 2004.

Morgan, Gordon D. *Black Hillbillies of the Arkansas Ozarks.* Fayetteville: University of Arkansas Department of Sociology, 1973.

Neider, Charles, ed. *The Complete Essays of Mark Twain.* Garden City, NY: Doubleday, 1963.

Newman, Clyde R. *One Hundred Years: A History of the Methodist Church in Harrison, Arkansas.* Harrison, AR: Times Publishing Co., 1973.

North, F. A. *The History of Jasper County, Missouri.* Des Moines, IA: Mills & Co., 1883.

Pfeifer, Michael J. *Rough Justice: Lynching and American Society, 1874–1947.* Chicago: University of Illinois Press, 2006.

Polk County Genealogical Society, *History & Families of Polk County, Missouri.* Paducah, KY: Turner Pub. Co., 2004.

Rafferty, Milton D. *Historical Atlas of Missouri.* Norman: University of Oklahoma Press, 1982.

———. *The Ozarks: Land and Life, 2nd* ed., Fayetteville: University of Arkansas Press, 2001.

Rea, Ralph R. *Boone County and Its People.* Van Buren, AR: Press-Argus, 1955.

Reasoner, Clara Barry. *The Pie on the Square.* Springfield, MO: Elkins-Swyers

Company, 1946.

Resources of Missouri: Photo and Biographical Sketches of Her State Officers and the Thirty-Eighth General Assembly. St. Louis: J. H. McCracken, n.d.

Richardson, Albert D. *Beyond the Mississippi: From the Great River to the Great Ocean.* Hartford, CT: American Publishing Co., 1885.

Ruestle, Judy. *Springfield Smallpox: 1899–1900.* Springfield, MO: Greene County Archives Bulletin No. 5, Office of the County Clerk.

Russell, Jesse Lewis. *Behind These Ozarks Hills.* New York: Hobson Book Press, 1947.

Samuelson, Nancy J. *Shoot from the Lip: The Lives, Legends, and Lies of the Three Guardsmen of Oklahoma and U.S. Marshal Nix.* Eastford, CT: Shooting Star Press, 1998.

Shaner, Dolph. *The Story of Joplin.* New York: Stratford House, 1948.

Shawnee County, Kansas, World War One Honor Roll. Topeka Genealogical Society, Topeka, Kansas.

Spencer, Thomas, ed. *The Other Missouri History: Populists, Prostitutes, and Regular Folk.* Columbia: University of Missouri Press, 2004.

Springfield Metropolitan Bar Association. *100 Years of Service to the Legal Community: 2003 Centennial Directory.* Springfield, MO: n.p., 2003.

Stevens, Walter B. *Missouri, The Center State,* vol. 3. Chicago: S. J. Clarke Publishing Co., 1915.

———. *St. Louis: The Fourth City, 1764–1911.* St. Louis: S. J. Clarke Publishing Co., 1909.

Stewart, A. J. D. *The History of the Bench and the Bar of Missouri.* St. Louis: Legal Pub. Co., 1898.

Sturges, J. A. *Illustrated History of McDonald County, Missouri, From the Earliest Settlement To the Present Time.* Pineville, MO: J. A. Sturges, 1897.

Taft, William H. *Missouri Newspapers: When and Where, 1801–1963.* Columbia, MO: State Historical Society of Missouri, 1964.

Tolnay, Stewart E., and E. M. Beck. *A Festival of Violence: An Analysis of Southern Lynchings, 1882–1930.* Chicago: University of Illinois Press, 1995.

Tuskegee Institute. *Lynchings by States and Race 1882–1959.* Tuskegee, AL: Tuskegee Institute Department of Records and Research, 1959.

Wells, H. G. *The Future in America: A Search After Realities.* New York: Harper & Bros., 1906.

Williams, Walter, and Floyd C. Shoemaker. *Missouri, Mother of the West,* rev. ed., vol. 3. Chicago: American Historical Company, 1930.

———. *Missouri, Mother of the West,* rev. ed., vol. 5. Chicago: American Historical Company, 1930.

Williamson, Joel. *The Crucible of Race: Black-White Relations in the American South Since Emancipation.* New York: Oxford University Press, 1984.

Wilson, Charles Morrow. *The Bodacious Ozarks: True Tales of the Backhills.* New York: Hastings House, 1959.

Winn, Robert G. *Railroads of Northwest Arkansas.* Fayetteville, AR: Washington County Historical Society, 1986.

Woodward, C. Vann. *Origins of the New South, 1877–1913,* rev. ed. Baton Rouge: Louisiana State University Press, 1971.

Book Chapters

Blevins, Brooks. "Revisting Race Relations in an Upland South Community." In *History and Hope in the Heart of Dixie.* Tuscaloosa: The University of Alabama Press, 2002.

Articles

Blevins, Brooks R. "The Strike and the Still: Anti-Radical Violence and the Ku Klux Klan in the Ozarks." *Arkansas Historical Quarterly* 52 (Winter 1993).

Froelich, Jacqueline, and David Zimmerman. "Total Eclipse: The Destruction of the African-American Community of Harrison, Arkansas, in 1905 and 1909." *Arkansas Historical Quarterly* 58 (Summer 1999).

Linzee, E. H. "Registration and Drawing For Opening of Kiowa and Comanche Country, 1901." *Chronicles of Oklahoma* 25, no. 3.

Morrow, Lynn. "Where Did All the Money Go? War and the Economics of Vigilantism in Southern Missouri." *White River Valley Historical Quarterly* 34, no. 2 (Fall 1994).

Mieswinkel, Fred, ed. "The Strawberry Letters." *Lawrence County Historical Society Bulletin,* January. Mount Vernon, MO: Lawrence County Historical Society, 1986.

Navarro, Jason. "Under Penalty of Death: Pierce City's Night of Racial Terror." *Missouri Historical Review* 100, no. 2 (2006).

Parrington, Burton L., and Penny L. Harter. "The Easter and Tug-of-War Lynchings and the Early Twentieth-Century Black Exodus from Southwest Missouri." *Visions and Revisions: Ethnohistoric Perspectives on Southern Cultures,* ed. George Sabo. Athens: University of Georgia Press, 1987.

Pfeifer, Michael J. "The Ritual of Lynching: Extralegal Justice in Missouri, 1890–1942." *Gateway Heritage* 13, no. 3 (Winter 1993).

Renner, G. K. "Strawberry Culture in Southwest Missouri." *Missouri Historical Review* 1 (October 1969).

Woods, Randall B. "C. H. J. Taylor and the Movement for Black Political Independence, 1882–1896." *Journal of Negro History* 67, no. 2 (1982).

Theses and Dissertations

Baker, Thomas E. "Human Rights in Missouri: The Legislative, Judicial, and Administrative Development of Black Liberties." Ph.D. dissertation, University of Missouri, 1975, 179–80.

Clary, Mary N. "The Easter Offering: A Missouri Lynching, 1906." M.A. thesis, Southwest Missouri State University, 1970.

Rea, Dean Frank. "A History of the Springfield (Mo.) Leader and Press, 1867–1950." M.A. thesis, University of Missouri, 1951.

Stith, Matthew M. "At The Heart of Total War: Guerrillas, Civilians, and the Union Response in Jasper County, Missouri, 1861–1865." M.A. thesis, University of Arkansas, 2004.

Periodicals

"The Lynching Horror." *Nation,* vol. 73, August 29, 1901.

The Independent, April 21, 1906, v. 15, no. 8, Kansas City: The Independent.

Lederer, Katherine. "And Then They Sang a Sabbath Song." *Springfield Magazine,* v. 2, n. 11, April 1981.

Lederer, Katherine. *Springfield! Magazine* v. 5, no. 5, October 1983.

Lederer, Katherine. "Where Are We Going, Mr. Harper?" *Ozarks Watch*11, no. 3 & 4 (1998.

Nichols, George Ward. "Wild Bill." *Harper's New Monthly Magazine* 34, February 1867.

The Ozarks Mountaineer, June 1952, v. 1, no. 3.

The Ozarks Mountaineer, August 1952 v. 1, no. 4.

Rea, Ralph R. "Sidelights on Boone County History." *Arkansas Historical Quarterly* 13, no. 1 (Spring 1954).

Reedy's Mirror v. 23, no. 46.

Watkins, Loren. "Some History of Boone County, Arkansas." *Boone County Historian* 7, no. 1 (1984).

Phone Conversations

Telephone conversation by the author with Mr. Homer Boyd, Springfield, Missouri, Wednesday, June 24, 2009.

INDEX

KIMBERLY HARPER is an Ozark native who lives in Missouri. She received her master's in history from the University of Arkansas.